The Cinema's Third Machine

# The Cinema's Third Machine
## Writing on Film in Germany
# 1907
# 1933

## Sabine Hake

University of Nebraska Press, Lincoln and London: 1993

Library of Congress Cataloging-in-Publication Data   Hake, Sabine, 1956-   The cinema's

third machine: writing on film in Germany, 1907-1933 / Sabine Hake.   p.   cm. – (Mod-

ern German culture and literature)   Includes bibliographical references (p. ) and index.

ISBN 0-8032-2365-X (cl)   1. Film criticism – Germany.   1. Title.   11. Series.   PN1995.H215

1993   791.43′015′09430904—dc20                          92-33085   CIP

The publication of this book was assisted by a grant from the Andrew W. Mellon Foundation

For Michael Pestel

# Contents

## Acknowledgments

I would like to thank the following individuals who have been very helpful at various stages of the project: David Bathrick, Günter Hake, Maud Lavin, Stephen Levine, Clark Muenzer, Patrice Petro, Wayne Rothschild, Azade Seyhan, Katie Trumpener, Elizabeth Wylie-Ernst. I also wish to thank the J. Paul Getty Foundation and the Andrew W. Mellon Foundation for research scholarships that were essential to the completion of the project.

Parts of chapter 11 have been published previously as "Girls and Crisis: The Other Side of Diversion" in *New German Critique* 40 (Winter 1987): 147–64.

# Introduction

Discourse about the cinema is . . . its third machine: after the one that manufactures the films, and the one that consumes them, the one that *vaunts* them, that valorises the product — CHRISTIAN METZ, *The Imaginary Signifier*

Every time a new cultural practice emerges, the established systems of thought are put into question, and, for a short moment, critical paradigms are open to reexamination and renegotiation. In such a situation, critics have the chance to explore new avenues of thought and address issues that otherwise have no place in the everyday business of writing. They can explore issues relevant to culture and society at large, or they can seek insights into established cultural practices, including their own participation in those practices. They can use the confrontation with the New and the Other to strengthen their positions in the public sphere — for instance by appropriating or altering characteristics of the New — or they can turn a medium's Otherness into a means through which to affect more radical changes in the critical paradigms.

Early German writings on film assumed precisely such a metadiscursive function: they were at once about film and about its effect on critical discourse; they simultaneously addressed questions of representation and interpretation; and they dealt with both the institutionalization of cinema and the institution of criticism. The emergent discourses defined their function in relation to cinema, which had occasioned their appearance on the scene of writing, and the bourgeois public sphere, of which they either were, or tried to become, a part.

One of the first goals of early critics was to assign a name to and thereby identify what was alternately perceived as a new technology, a new industry, and a new form of mass entertainment. By receiving a name, the new medium would take its proper place among the arts and sciences, and the writers and critics would be the ones in charge of attributing and distributing meanings. During the last four years of the Wilhelmine Empire a surprising number of names were in circulation, among which *Kino* (cinema) emerged as the perfect compromise between the cinema's technological basis — cinematography — and the particular conditions of mass reception. However, in the years after World War I, the concentration on film production, distribution, and exhibition made necessary a greater emphasis on the product in critical as well as linguistic terms. The rise of the so-called classical German cinema was accompanied by a growing preference for *Film* (film) as the term commonly used to describe the individual film and its artistic or commercial value.[1] These changes in name — and the accompanying shift in emphasis from the social experience of cinema to film as a work of art, and from the conditions of reception to the properties of the industrial product — are indicative of far-reaching changes in critical discourse.

The German cinema until 1933 seems well suited for such a historical-critical approach, since it was the focus of very diverse social, political, and cultural questions at a historical juncture that was itself characterized by conflict and radical change. Just as the Wilhelmine Empire and the Weimar Republic set the stage on which film/cinema was represented through the means of critical discourse, the writings on film/cinema defined the field of contention in which a complicated process of doubling took place: the introduction of social and political concerns into the various practices associated with the new medium, and the reduplication of these concerns in writings about cinema and film.

Calling for a museum of film history, Béla Balázs once argued: "With film we have an opportunity that is unique and exceptional in cultural history. We are eye witnesses to the emergence and the rapid growth of a new art form. We are in a position to document first-hand where and how something emerged for the first time" (1984, 2:284). The same can be said of the process of discourse formation during a time when the boundaries between film criticism and theory were still fluid and in a society where writing about film meant writing about mass culture and class society, questions of national and sexual identity, and the experience of modernity. Early German film criticism fulfilled a double function. It promoted and evaluated films, and it used their narratives to discuss problems relevant to culture and society at large. On a more conceptual level, emerging film theory did the same: theorists analyzed the mechanisms by which film was constituted as a cultural and artistic practice and, on the basis of its formal characteristics, tried to articulate the relationship between narrative, representation, and visual pleasure.

The present study explores that double function in the context of Wilhelmine and Weimar cinema, from the first articles written in 1907 to the repression of all critical discourse in 1933. Within this historical framework, writing about film made possible the cinema's integration into middle-class culture, but it also shows how criticism's parameters were changed in turn. Criticism was a weapon in the struggle for cultural dominance, it was a product of modern consumer culture, it was a form of political and intellectual resistance. While these writings laid the foundation for a theory of film, they also contributed to the formulation of new social and cultural theories. They participated equally in the conceptualization of visual pleasure and of other modern forms of entertainment. Questions of spectatorship marked the beginning and end of these debates, and the relationship between the cinema and the masses played a central part in them. Through a critical rereading of the critical texts, spectatorship is reinstated at the center in a process of discourse formation that, once removed from the historical circumstances, easily falls prey to the universal claims of film aesthetics.

The division of this book into two parts—writings on cinema in Wilhelmine Germany and on film in Weimar Germany—underscores the highly politicized nature of criticism, with the collapse of the monarchy, the founding of the republic, and the rise of fascism as the major dividing points. The introduction of sound in 1927 brought less rupture than is frequently suggested by the expression "silent film theories." While it made necessary a reassessment of formal means in the context of the sound film, its more immediate impact on critics was a growing concern with the process of economic concentration and what was perceived as betrayal of the cinema's original mission as a democratic, international art for the masses. Writing on the cinema from its first appearance at the margins of society to its integration into middle-class culture inevitably draws attention to the importance of criticism as a productive force in the development of cultural products and practices. As a focal point for problems in modern mass society, the discourses on film functioned simultaneously as symptom and cause for the crisis of bourgeois culture, and they contributed to the negotiation of social and political differences by alternately providing an instrument and a projection screen. This process was influenced by two factors that in many ways distinguished the critical reception of film in Germany: first, an unyielding belief in the power of criticism and, implicitly, in the bourgeois public sphere as a place for the free exchange of ideas; and, second, the seemingly irreconcilable opposition between high culture and mass culture.

Following in the tradition of Enlightenment thought, early-twentieth-century criticism was regarded as essential to the constitution of the public sphere, and to the transformation of audiences into a public in the traditional sense. As a place of public assembly and the site of re-presentation, the cinema gave new meaning to the Classical notion of the theater as a political stage, a place for the acting out of political conflicts and the formulation of new ideas. The cinema and its discourses were seen as a means to facilitate communication and to provide a sense of identity; therein lay its emancipatory potential. However, the conditions under which critics could explore these possibilities had changed considerably since the eighteenth century. The classical bourgeois public sphere, as it has been defined by Jürgen Habermas and others, formed a link between the private sphere and the institutions of power; it found a privileged means of expression in literary journals and reviews (Habermas 1972). The critics acted as representatives of the public, expressing their ideas and engaging in discussions relevant to society at large. Although access to the public sphere was regulated, it continued to be based on egalitarian principles. The commercialization of the publishing industry in the late nineteenth century and the different socioeconomic pressures associated with late capitalism shattered this dream and turned the autonomous critic into a servant of the consciousness industry. It was precisely for these reasons that writing on film proved so appealing to many critics: its industrial mode of production and its openly commercial orientation gave them a chance to redefine the notion of the public sphere. Standing at the intersection of modern mass society and modern technologies, the emerging cinema *was* the quintessential modern public sphere.

The intense reactions to the cinema showed Wilhelmine Germany to be a society that made overly sharp distinctions between high and low culture. Imperial Germany's belated industrialization and urbanization, as well as its rigid class structure, not only contributed to the politicizing of cinema, but also accounted for the overdetermined responses to its products and its audiences. In this regard, the cinema came to be ostracized from two sides. It was associated with the rising working class and the demand for forms of entertainment appropriate to their working and living conditions. At the same time, it was linked to states of psychological and social regression that many thought antithetical to the exigencies of modern society. While the cinema inspired visions of democratic internationalism, its association with the fear of losing all boundaries was much more pronounced because it was founded in social experience. As a result, the question of cinema became inextricably linked to questions of identity. Critics responded to these challenges by making the cinema the basis for a new folklore or a proletarian public sphere, or they tried to eliminate the tension between the masses and the nation by calling for a strong national cinema. In all cases the critical reference points were of a social and cultural nature, even when such influences were denied in the attempt to replace politics with aesthetics.

✳ ✳ ✳

Just as the cinema took on different characteristics, depending on the perspective from which it was viewed in the formative years, writing the history of early German film theory and criticism has focused on different questions at different times. These assessments have taken place within, and at the intersection of, various disciplines such as German literature, communication studies, and film studies; as a consequence, they have helped to expand and redefine their respective disciplinary boundaries. Four major areas of inquiry can be identified: the study of Weimar cinema as a national cinema with specific characteristics and a specific problematic; the literary debates on the cinema and their implications for a redefinition of literature and the literary sphere; working-class culture and attendant questions about mass culture, cultural hegemony, and the existence of a proletarian public sphere; and the search for critical traditions in prefascist Germany that might serve as a model for more interdisciplinary approaches to modern mass culture and modernity.

In the United States the study of early German film theory has been closely linked to the study of Weimar cinema and the more theoretical questions it raises about film and ideology, cinema and urbanization, and film and spectatorship. The connections are especially obvious in the work of Siegfried Kracauer, whose psychological study *From Caligari to Hitler* (1947) has had a great influence on the critical reception of this national cinema. In conjunction with a growing interest in the media-theoretical writings of Bertolt Brecht and Walter Benjamin and out of the desire to reassess the often problematic relationship of critical theory to mass culture, the journal *New German Critique* has translated some of Kracauer's earlier essays and devoted special issues to Weimar film theory and mass culture.[2]

At the same time, Weimar cinema has played an increasingly important role in film study discussions of spectatorship, both in psychoanalytic and historical terms. A good example is the work of Thomas Elsaesser, who has written extensively about structures of identification in Weimar cinema that defy identification with a specific class or gender position. It was out of a desire to challenge both the notion of early cinema as a proletarian public sphere and the association of Weimar cinema with male anxiety that feminist critics like Miriam Hansen, Heide Schlüpmann, and Patrice Petro introduced the perspective of female spectators, and of female spectatorship, into the debates (cf. Hansen 1983; Petro 1987 and 1989; Schlüpmann 1990b and 1990c).[3] In so doing, they established a link between the problems of modernity and femininity and confirmed the importance of combining close textual analysis and critical historiography. Most recently, Bruce Murray has presented a historical study, *Film and the German Left in the Weimar Republic* (1990), that continues to explore some of the concerns of earlier German scholarship on the topic within a more general framework, including a survey of leftist film criticism. Though often arguing from different perspectives, most British and American scholars working on Weimar cinema — studies on the Wilhelmine period are bound to follow soon — treat it as a national cinema particularly suited to stage more productive encounters between film studies and cultural studies, as well as more in-depth studies on the relationship between film history and film theory. While Weimar film theory has, with the exception of Kracauer, played a marginal role in the scholarly writings on Weimar cinema and its history, the readings of certain key films have enabled scholars to challenge basic theoretical assumptions about cinema in a way that is often lacking in the study of national cinemas.

For the most part, literary and political concerns have dominated German scholarship on early German film theory. Beginning in the early seventies, and as part of a wider attempt to redefine literature in relation to mass culture, literary scholars turned to silent film as the paradigmatic site of this difficult relationship. During the same time, the Weimar cinema experienced a reevaluation within the context of leftist historiography and discussions about a proletarian public sphere. After the influential 1976 exhibition *Hätte ich das Kino! Der Schriftsteller und der Stummfilm,* a number of anthologies were published that contained previously unavailable or unknown texts. Anton Kaes's *Kino-Debatte* (1978) presented texts from the literary debate on the cinema and included a lengthy introduction confirming the centrality of cinema to the experience of modernity (see also Prawer 1979). Making similar arguments for the case of working-class culture, a group of scholars from the German Democratic Republic, under Gertraude Kühn, published an annotated two-volume anthology, *Film und revolutionäre Arbeiterbewegung in Deutschland 1918–1932* (1975), that documented the educational and propagandistic role of leftist film criticism. Around the same time, the growing interest in critical theory led to the rediscovery of the early writings of Siegfried Kracauer and the publication of his early essays and reviews under the editorship of Karsten Witte. More recent anthologies such as Fritz Güttinger's extensively annotated *Kein Tag ohne Kino* (1984), and its companion volume, *Der Stummfilm im Zitat der Zeit* (1984), emphasize the yet unwritten reception history of early German cinema and pay special attention to the writer as spectator (cf. Diederichs 1985c).

As is to be expected, literary concerns have left their mark on the kinds of questions, the methods of inquiry, and the underlying assumptions that characterize much scholarship in this area, beginning with a clear preference for the postwar years and for poetological issues. Similarly, the emphasis on the relationship between film and the Weimar left has shifted the focus of inquiry to the last years of the republic and often limited the investigations to questions of mass manipulation and propaganda.

Five critical monographs published in the last ten years have tried to open up new perspectives. Informed by an ideology-critical approach, Heinz-B. Heller's *Literarische Intelligenz und Film* (1984) is perhaps most thorough in outlining the process of discourse formation, although his study, too, focuses on the representatives of the literary sphere and excludes the film-critical writings of Béla Balázs, Siegfried Kracauer, and Rudolf Arnheim (Diederichs 1985b, Hummel 1986; Pankau 1989). Helmut H. Diederichs's *Anfänge deutscher Filmkritik* (1986) offers a very detailed study of the beginnings of film criticism, particularly in the journal *Bild und Film*, but relies on sociological categories that tend to neglect the ideological function of criticism (cf. Heller 1984, 6n9). While Thorsten Lorenz's *Wissen ist Macht* (1988) theorizes aspects of early German film theory in the context of psychoanalytic and poststructuralist thought, Peter Wuss, in *Kunstwert des Films und Massencharakter des Mediums* (1990), discusses early German film theory within an international context and with special attention to the opposition of art and commodity as a constituting element of narrative film. Heide Schlüpmann's feminist analysis of Wilhelmine cinema in *Die*

*Unheimlichkeit des Blicks* (1990) represents perhaps the most convincing example of how to bring together the close textual readings of specific films and genres and the critical writings of cinema reformers and literary writers for the more far-reaching project of a historicizing of film theory.

On the basis of previous scholarship, and in order to contribute to this historicizing of film theory, *The Cinema's Third Machine* was written to achieve three goals: to make accessible to English-speaking readers an important period in the formation of critical discourses on film; to develop an interdisciplinary approach that combines political, economic, pedagogical, literary, aesthetic, and theoretical perspectives; and to expand the notion of critical discourse beyond the traditional distinctions between "serious" and "journalistic" writing, and those between critical and fictional writing. It is in these points that the present study distinguishes itself from all previous ones and offers the first comprehensive account of early German film theory and criticism in all its complexity and diversity.

With few exceptions (Lukács, Kracauer, Arnheim, Richter), none of the texts under discussion is presently available in English translation. With the exception of a few specialized accounts (e.g., Kaes on the literary debates, Hansen on early cinema, Murray about leftist film activism), little is known about the discursive field in which these texts have to be placed. And with the exception of writings devoted to the three canonized theoreticians (e.g., Schlüpmann and Petro on Kracauer, Koch on Balázs and Arnheim), few in-depth studies have explored the contribution of early critical writings to the historiography of early cinema. It is for these reasons that *The Cinema's Third Machine* considers as many primary texts and as many critics as possible. While some texts are discussed at greater length because they express typical concerns, the emphasis clearly lies on preserving the multitude of voices, including their different tones and qualities, that made writing about film a field of contention. Even at the risk of presenting too much primary material, this study is intended to reproduce the heterogeneity of discourse to which various academic disciplines laid claim, and to restore the process of discourse formation on the level of historical analysis. Consequently, the different perspectives on cinema — as a social space, an industry, an art form — are not contained within their respective disciplines but are brought together to preserve the kind of interrelatedness that gives emerging discourses their intensity and complexity.

This study even enlists journalistic and fictional texts in the reconstruction of a discursive formation characterized by, to a large degree, imaginary relations. Interdisciplinarity, therefore, comes to mean not only the inclusion of literary, pedagogic, and political concerns, but also of various modes of discourse, whether they be critical or affirmative, celebratory or instrumental.

The accomplishment of these goals necessarily results in other omissions and limitations. Considerations of space have made it impossible to add a comparative perspective, for instance by introducing the French debates on film and theater or by identifying similar reformist ideas in the writings of American critics.[4] The desire to make available as many texts as possible has left little room for tracing specific key concepts back to their origins in idealist philosophy or for identifying similar discursive configurations in the debate on national literature in the nineteenth century. The emphasis on historical documentation and, closely related, the desire to pay equal attention to the major forces in the discursive construction of film, independent of their critical currency, also prevented a more direct engagement with previous scholarship on the subject; abbreviated material in endnotes partially compensates for this shortcoming.

Finally, the historical framework excluded from the outset any comparisons between the earlier and the later work of Balázs, Kracauer, and Arnheim. These choices were made based on the recognition that only a historical account of the early writings on film in Germany provides the basis for more theoretical inquiries, including those into the relationship between early German film history and film theory. If this study initiates such a process, it will have fulfilled its purpose.

# Part 1

Writing on Cinema in Wilhelmine Germany
1907–1918

# Chapter 1
Early Beginnings in the Trade Press

From the beginning, film criticism was defined within an institutional framework that represented economic rather than aesthetic concerns. A short overview of early German cinema will help to illuminate this relationship and place writing in a historical context, beginning with the cinema's point of inception. On the first day of November 1895, the brothers Skladanowsky introduced the so-called Bioscop at the first public screening of a motion picture in the Wintergarten, a popular vaudeville theater in Berlin. Their nine short film strips were shown at the end of the program and included variety acts with jugglers, acrobats, dancers, and a boxing kangaroo. The last scene showed Max and Emil Skladanowsky as they took a bow, already assuming artistic responsibility for the screened films.

A poster announced the event as "The Bioscop! The most amusing and most interesting invention of modern times. . . . Photographs presented through the original invention of Messrs. Skladanowsky." Another flier promised "the naturalistic reproduction of life . . . through the lightning projection of innumerable photographs in front of large audiences" (Zglinicki 1956, 245). Thus film exhibition and writing about film originated more or less in the same historical moment.

The Skladanowskys' success was repeated in many other German cities, always accompanied by enthusiastic announcements in the daily press. Nine days after their premiere, the first motion picture show in Düsseldorf inspired the following note: "It is, after all, such a rare and nice pleasure to view these various street scenes and other settings, which are reproduced so naturally that one almost believes in a miracle. The opportunity to study the apparatus is also worth mentioning" (Schäfer 1982, 11). With this rather innocent observation, the parameters of writing on the cinema were firmly in place. Over the following years, the film producer and the film critic would both pursue a double strategy. By emphasizing the technical side of the cinematic apparatus, each treated the technology of cinema as an attraction in its own right. The one did so by displaying the projector, or by experimenting with special effects; the other resorted to vivid imagery and detailed descriptions. Just as the early films emulated the exhibition practices of the variety show, so did the early reviews try to strengthen the cinema's ties with consumer culture. The transformation of cinematography into, quite literally, an object of desire and admiration eliminated the classical distinction between art and commodity, and allowed its products to be both.

From the presentation of an attraction on the screen to the duplication of its effects in language, from the exhibition of the apparatus to speculations about future technological developments, the discourse of cinema was formulated at the intersection of cultural, technical, and economical practices. It constituted itself, and was constituted, within a field of oppositions defined by the film and and the review, disregarding the audience and reception as the third side in a triangular configuration. This vacillation between art and technology distinguished the emerging film criticism from other kinds of criticism (e.g., literary criticism, theater criticism, music criticism), all of which were predicated on the notion of authorship and the uniqueness of the creative process. At the same time, the cinema's affinities with consumer culture, which found expression in the effusive tone with which both advertised their products, underscored the medium's foundation on the laws of commodity production. That is why the early cinema and its spectacles stood closer to the new department store than to the autonomous work of art and the disinterested enjoyment demanded by the latter.

Film historians have emphasized that film exhibition preceded film production as an economic undertaking (Bächlin 1975, 19–54; Spiker 1975, 9–33). During the period of the traveling cinemas (*Wanderkinos*), the cinematic apparatus continued to be an attraction in its own right. Projectionists regularly mentioned their projectors by name—Edison's Vitagraph or Lumière's Kinematograph—and praised their respective qualities. Roughly until 1906, and in isolated cases until 1915, exhibitors would travel from town to town and present their theater of living photographs. The programs included nature scenes and humorous sketches, and a surprisingly large number of actualities and local newsreels; these were often characterized by an astonishing realism. As a rule, film exhibitors came from the fairground milieu of traveling artists and showmen. They produced their own films, and began only slowly to form a network with other exhibitors. Admission prices were based on the length of a film or program. Since the films were owned by the exhibitors, they were shown as long as audiences wanted to see them.

Drawn by the visual attractions and popular themes, and seduced by the low admission prices, the majority of the audience came from the lower classes. A relatively large number of children attended the shows on a regular basis. The situation changed as economic expansion and increased prices became unavoidable. Without the institutional framework needed for specialization and rationalization, the itinerant motion-picture business had only limited possibilities. Faced with growing economic competition, the film producers and exhibitors decided to improve their products artistically as well as technologically.

Beginning in 1905, small entrepreneurs began to convert storefronts, beer pubs, and coffeehouses into what soon became known as the *Kientopp* (movies). These primitive facilities often contained no more than a few wooden benches, a projector, and a canvas suspended at the end of the room. The first permanent movie theaters in Germany opened in 1904 in Mannheim and 1906 in Düsseldorf; by 1910, there were 456 around the country. In the larger cities, screenings took place continuously from eleven in the morning to ten o'clock at night. The programs lasted approximately fifteen minutes and were accompanied by piano or mechanical orchestrion and, not infrequently, by the explanations of a commentator.

Leaving behind the fairground and the variety show, the cinema eventually developed cultural ambitions. The shift from one- to two-reelers was a first step in this direction; so were various attempts to improve the quality of cameras, projectors, and film stock. Soon it became obvious that a new mass diversion was staking its claim, and that a new public sphere was being formed in the process. Attempts to improve film exhibition resulted in longer programs, fewer daily screenings, larger auditoriums, and higher admission prices. The conditions of production changed considerably with the emergence of film distributors in 1906. Previously, the local proprietor had taken requests from the regular clients and selected his program accordingly. With the expansion of the distribution system and with the higher economic risks involved, new strategies had to be found for securing a film's commercial success. Advertising and criticism offered themselves as the most effective methods of achieving this goal.

Originally dismissed as a technological curiosity and considered unworthy of critical scrutiny, the new medium began to attract the attention of those who had a professional interest in mass entertainment. The earliest articles on film appeared in show business trade journals. As early as 1896, *Der Komet*, published in Pirmasens under the editorship of Wilhelm Neumann, included regular columns on film that offered information and advice on practical questions, especially concerning film exhibition; after 1906, its first critical reviews appeared (Diederichs 1985a). Since most contributors and readers were actively involved in the film business, the articles had a strong practical orientation.

To satisfy the growing need for a more specialized journal, a number of critics associated with *Der Artist* started one of the first journals devoted entirely to film, *Der Kinematograph* (1907–1935).[1] Published in Düsseldorf, with an edition of 5,000 to 7,000 copies, the weekly introduced itself as the "the journal for all projection arts," the first of its kind that "as a medium for everybody, offers its service to everybody" (6 Jan. 1907). A later editorial confirmed that "everybody interested in the promotion of cinematography should fully welcome and support the publication of the first professional journal that plans to improve communication between, and offer assistance to, everyone involved" (1 June 1907).

Under the editorial leadership of Emil Perlmann, *Der Kinematograph* (Cinematography) accommodated the interests of film stock manufacturers, printing laboratories, optical firms, outside investors, theater owners, film distributors, and the general public. Reports about the latest technological innovations and notes from professional organizations stood side by side with synopses of new films, which were identified by the film company's name and often included comments on their technical quality, and advertisements for everything from pornographic films and new projectors to offers of employment for musical accompanists and film editors. The journal also provided valuable information on city ordinances, building codes, fire regulations, censorship laws, and other matters of relevance to film distributors and exhibitors; typical columns in the journal included "Technical Information and New Patents," "The Voice of Practice," "Americana," and such service-oriented rubrics as "Mail Box" and "Tips by Readers."[2]

A 1907 adaptation of Schiller's *Die Räuber* (The Robbers) had inspired a lengthy description, complete with photographs from the film, but the first critical articles in *Der Kinematograph* were devoted to specific genres, notably the immensely popular "nature scenes," which inspired effusive statements about the beauty of nature. The critic Gustav Melcher asserted: "Criticism is as powerless against cinematographic presentations as philosophy is about life. . . . The kind of thorough criticism that is the rule in an educated Germany is completely out of the question" (*Der Kinematograph,* 12 Feb. 1909).

Claiming that audiences had lost interest in chases and romances, a growing number of articles discussed film's relationship to the other arts, and authors wrote favorably about the French-inspired *Kunstfilm* (art film), which promised the highest standards of photographic and dramatic quality. Underscoring the cinema's cultural mission, the critic Paul Lenz-Levy coined the term "images without words" (*Der Kinematograph,* 8 June 1910), a coy reference to literature's "words without images." The higher ambitions of *Der Kinematograph* were already evident in the journal's title design, which in the course of one year changed from an old-fashioned nineteenth-century city silhouette, with a glorified representation of the cinematic apparatus (i.e., the projector) in the center, to a floral ornament, to a stylized *Jugendstil* pattern and a decidedly modern typography. Similar changes in title design can be observed in other early trade journals.

The success of *Der Kinematograph* inspired similar publishing ventures, among them the *Erste Internationale Film-Zeitung* (1908–20, First international film newspaper), edited by Willi Böcker, the *Lichtbild-Bühne* (literally Light-image-stage), which was introduced in 1908 by Arthur Mellini and by 1911 sold 2,500 copies a week, and the reformist *Bild und Film* (1912–15, Image and film), edited by Lorenz Pieper. By 1913, twelve trade journals on the cinema were published on a regular basis throughout Germany (Sattig 1937).[3] They had various formats, but they rarely exceeded sixteen pages in length. A growing number of journals catered to the special needs of particular branches of an enterprise growing from a cottage industry into a powerful part of the consciousness industry. As clearinghouses for members of the same branch (e.g., theater owners, optical firms), these special-interest journals provided information on how to deal with legislators, banks, and social pressure groups such as religious groups or teachers' organizations. These journals included the Düsseldorf-based *Der Lichtbild-theaterbesitzer* (1909–11, The motion picture theater owner), the Berlin-based *Das lebende Bild* (1909–14, The living image), which appealed to exhibitors, distributors, and actors, and *Film und Lichtbild* (1912–14, Film and slide), published in Stuttgart, which dedicated itself to "scientific and technical cinematography and projection."

While the specialized journals contributed to the ongoing process of professionalization, the big trade journals established the critical paradigm in which the economic consolidation and social recognition of cinema were to be achieved. Calling itself the "trade journal for the film industry," *Lichtbild-Bühne* soon assumed a leadership role, initiating discussions between different branches of the industry and reaching out to politicians, legislators, and social pressure groups. The first essays on aesthetic questions appeared in response to the growing public interest in the cinema — in other words, as a part of public relations. Soon a concerted effort was made to overcome existing prejudices — many bourgeois critics found the cinema offensive on moral and artistic grounds — and to portray the cinema as a respectable form of entertainment that could be equally appealing to the lower and the middle classes.

The critics in the early trade journals subscribed to the same kind of positivist, pseudoscientific writing style, with occasional metaphysical overtones, that had characterized the discourse on early photography. The reviewers of the *Lichtbild-Bühne,* for instance, applied it equally to films, the theater as an architectural space, and the projector, praising time and again its various technical features. Paul Lenz-Levy's reviews, appropriately called *Kinokritik* (cinema criticism), often described in great detail the interior design of a new movie theater only to end with lengthy descriptions of a particular projection system, or the highlights of a musical side program.

By paying attention to all aspects of the cinematic apparatus, Lenz-Levy made its practices accessible to critical scrutiny but also invited proposals for improvement; he wrote from the perspective of a producer, and not a passive recipient, of cinematic effects. His attention to detail, of course, was both necessary and appropriate, given the professional interests of most readers. The almost emotional tone in some articles, however, must be seen as a residue of the nineteenth century, which had celebrated technical inventions as heroic deeds and turned machines into wondrous toys deserving praise in their own right. Although technical questions remained important, these paeans to technology began to sound increasingly old-fashioned and inappropriate. As new technologies were introduced, the naive belief in the liberating qualities of the machine gave way to a growing awareness about the oppressive aspects of mechanization. Still more significantly, the fetishization of the apparatus stood in the way of a kind of criticism that could transform film into an object of contemplation and aesthetic appreciation.

Focusing on the film itself allowed the critics to restore the kind of unity that had been destroyed by specialization. Consequently, the production-oriented criticism practiced by Lenz-Levy and others was no longer desirable. While the trade journals continued to provide technical information and economic prognoses, their reviewers explored more theoretical approaches. The function of the new reviews was precisely to suppress all knowledge of the machine, to obliterate the traces of its existence, and to introduce in its place a discourse of illusionism that duplicated the cinema's main purpose, entertainment, on the level of critical discourse. In writing about the cinema, these reviews suggested, the means of production had to be effaced if the cinema was to become a middle-class diversion, and if film was to aspire to the status of art. Therefore, the projector had to disappear, literally and figuratively speaking, into a soundproof box. Once the economic, technological, and artistic aspects were separated and channeled into specialized discourses, the cinema—now reconstituted as popular entertainment—no longer challenged traditional oppositions between art and technology. This respectability, however, came at the price of a knowledge that had existed in the early years of cinema, a knowledge of the infinite complexity of its economic, social, and cultural determinations.

Since the large trade journals tried to accommodate very different interests, a style of critical writing had to be found that could be appreciated by all readers and that could serve as a kind of public discourse on film. The language of advertisement was very influential in this regard, providing the rhetorical means for the appealing mixture of fact and fiction that would soon become the trademark of promotional writing and, to a lesser degree, of film reviews as well. The following 1911 advertisement for a two-hour film program already contains all the main characteristics of the early film review: "'In a Barrel across Niagara Falls!' Thrilling, highly-interesting sensations. / 'The Thief in the Closet.' Great comedy! Great comedy! / 'The Dark Spot!' Great sensational drama in three acts! A touching life story!" (Warstat 1982, 267). This film advertisement not only classifies films according to traditional genres (comedy, drama) but also mentions the intended emotional effects ("touching," "thrilling," "sensational"). Its mixture of story fragments, bold images, and value judgments simulates the rapid succession of filmic images and their fragmented, condensed nature. The sensationalist style relies as much on the opposition of instant gratification and permanent deferral as the films themselves. It was through such affinities that the hyperbolic language of advertisement taught film reviewers the most effective ways of capturing the reader's attention. In a less obvious way, the reviewers also found inspiration in film posters. Their short, captivating slogans set an example for the exaggerated tone with which a review might praise or dismiss a particular film; their graphic style, and the limitation to a few characteristic images, would then be translated into writing by means of linguistic formulas and clichés (see Tannenbaum 1987, 61–71).

With the growing emphasis on promotion and advertisement, the conditions of exhibition had to be improved in order not to betray the promises made in the advertisements. As an extension of the cinematic illusion, new movie theaters distinguished themselves from their predecessors through pretentious names like Roxy, Royal, or Palace and an architecture and design that imitated "legitimate" theater. Chairs and benches were replaced by firmly installed rows of seats, the projector was confined to a fireproof box, and building codes were enforced. The new cinemas could be found on the main boulevards and thoroughfares, in proximity to other public places such as the railway station and the department store. Theater owners were required to obtain a licence for publicly showing films, a fact that further contributed to economic concentration and introduced the element of control.

Central to this transformation process was the introduction of city ordinances on public safety, special admission policies for children and adolescents, and censorship. Censorship laws first appeared around 1910 in the form of a preventive censorship (*Präventivzensur*) under the supervision of local police. Films had to be presented twenty-four hours prior to a screening, but the standards of evaluation were less than unified. Censorship practices varied greatly between cities and rural areas, and between liberal and conservative states. For the most part, decisions were based on audience response, that is, on the emotional impact rather than the content of a particular film. Confronted with such lack of direction, conservative teachers' organizations made the fight for stricter censorship laws a priority in their national education programs.

In addition to the normative effects of censorship, the levying of a local entertainment tax (*Lustbarkeitssteuer*) after 1913 contributed significantly to the institutionalization of cinema and placed the cinema firmly among the public diversions, rather than the arts. While new laws helped to curb moral excesses, they obviously bore witness to the cinema's growing influence on the local economy and sociopolitical structure; before World War

I, up to 60 percent of city revenues were generated through local entertainment tax.

\* \* \*

The moral and economic development of the medium attracted the growing interest of the bourgeois press. Around 1909–10, the cinema became the subject of intense discussions in the leading journals, from the popular family magazine *Die Gartenlaube* to prestigious reviews like *Velhagen & Klasings* or *Der Kunstwart,* from politically oriented journals like Karl Kraus's *Die Fackel* to Friedrich Naumann's *Die Hilfe*. No matter whether the tone was dismissive or celebratory, the sheer amount of writing on the cinema raised the level of public awareness, especially among middle-class readers. The cultural journals opened their pages to critical essays and polemical debates, while the daily newspapers and popular magazines took a more pragmatic approach: they began to publish film reviews. These reviews informed readers about the latest releases, advised them in their choice of films, and established standards of evaluation. Closest perhaps to the promotional hype of the trade press, their critical style differed equally from the reformist zeal of the teachers and the feuilletonism of the literary critics. The primary function of these reviews was information and advertisement. As they replicated the fiction effect of film in everyday life, reading about films became a preliminary exercise for the audience's inevitable return to the cinema.

By 1910, only a few newspapers had published film reviews on a regular basis. There was the occasional short article, badly written and devoid of any real understanding for the new medium. Some provincial newspapers refused to publish film reviews on principle, because they wanted to preserve the cinema's "primitive" nature. Such attitudes were undermined by the emergence of the feature-length film, the product of several parallel developments in the area of film production. Once the introduction of Agfa film stock assured independence from French firms, a number of production companies were founded in Germany, among them the Deutsche Bioscop, Eiko-Film, Projektions-AG Union (PAGU), and Messters Projektion GmbH. Most of them were located in Berlin, with production facilities in Tempelhof and, later, Babelsberg. Producers like Paul Davidson of PAGU and the inventor and entrepreneur Oskar Messter played crucial roles in the transition from the old show business to a new industry with an increasingly specialized work force and growing demands on its products.

The star system forged a bond between films and audiences that the individual companies needed in their struggle for economic survival. The star's name guaranteed the profits that were necessary to justify higher investments, and the film publicists and reviewers functioned as mediators in this process. The first actors promoted as stars included Alfred Basser-mann, Paul Wegener, Henny Porten, and the unforgettable Asta Nielsen, whose film *Afgrunen* (1912, The abyss) was the first to be distributed nation-wide.[4] After the much-discussed screen appearance of Alfred Bassermann, an accomplished character actor on the stage, in Paul Lindau's *Der Andere* (1913, The other), many well-known stage actors turned to screen acting, making it a reputable profession. At the same time the cinema produced its own stars who, like Asta Nielsen, rejected theatrical acting styles for a more natural approach. Often these stars became the objects of great admiration and inspired the most addictive form of film viewing.

Through the technical expertise of cinematographers like Oskar Mess-ter, Guido Seeber, and Karl Freund, films developed a visual language of their own; the imaginative set designs by Rochus Gliese, Hermann Warm, and Paul Leni introduced new approaches to cinematic mise-en-scène. Film directors played an increasingly important role and were often associ-ated with particular genres. Ernst Lubitsch and Max Mack became famous for comedies, Joe May for detective films, and Franz Hofer for melo-dramas; evidence of their new status was the regular appearance of their names above the film title on the theater marquee and in advertisements. Some studios also developed a reputation for specific genres; the Stuart-Webbs Film Co., for instance, was known for detective films.

Scenario writing developed in marked distance to literary traditions. Through the contribution of famous scenarists like Hanns Heinz Ewers and Carl Mayer, films began to explore their inherent visual and narrative possibilities. The fantastic film, with its references to the Romantic tradi-tion and its skillful use of special effects, embodied perfectly this new mix-ture of technology and imagination. It should therefore not surprise that it was a fantastic film, *Der Student von Prag* (1913, The student of Prague), with Paul Wegener in the title role, which invited the educated classes to overcome their prejudices (Heller 1984, 80–98). Because of these passion-ate calls for the *Autorenfilm*, the new medium could no longer be ignored; the critical success of the French *film d'art* proved that the infusion of high culture into the cinema was not only feasible, but also highly profitable (cf. Zaddach 1929). Under the motto "Films of Famous Authors Are the Future of Cinema!" production companies secured the film rights to the dramatic works of Gerhart Hauptmann, Hermann Sudermann, and Arthur Schnitzler, to name only a few. The name of the author was invoked to establish a connection between films and other cultural practices, and through its repeated mention the notions of creativity and self-expression entered into the discourses on film.

Most significantly, the formal characteristics of the films began to change, initiating the transition from an earlier "cinema of attractions" (Gunning, 1986) to a narrative cinema characterized by different spatio-temporal relationships and a different approach to the profilmic event (i.e., everything that happens in front of the camera). Newsreels from such companies as Pathé, Gaumont and Messter continued to be popular, since they showed images from exotic countries and news about great political figures and events. But the multireel film brought with it a whole range of new techniques related to camerawork, mise-en-scène, framing, and editing. While the early films emphasized the spectacular, exhibitionist qualities of cinema, thus betraying its origins in the variety revue and the magic show, the new films strove for narrative continuity, verisimilitude, and psychological motivation.

Between 1910 and 1913, the longer narrative film emerged as the predominant form and relegated all non-narrative forms to the margins, with the exception of the newsreel. The almost documentary realism of many early films was rejected in favor of the imaginary relations that constituted the cinema as a middle-class diversion with clearly defined narratives and figures of identification. The popularity of the melodrama reflected this development in the way that social experiences were reduced to psychological processes, rendering the protagonists powerless and without the possibility of personal change. The new historical films linked the bourgeois individual to the spectacle of the commodity and, in so doing, displaced the conditions of modern consumer culture into the splendor of historical settings. Not surprisingly, it was as early as 1916 that critic Hans Rost mourned the disappearance of the old peepshows: "[In the old days] there was no haste, no sensational hits, no rushing and buzzing and flickering like that in the modern movies, nothing disjointed. Changes did not take place from one second to the next. Nothing symbolizes the change in times better than a comparison between the peepshop [*Guckkasten*] and the movies [*Kino*]. The romance of the peepshow is gone. The nerve-racking thrill of the movies rules today's quest for images" (Rost 1916–17, 381).

Reacting to these changes, the representatives of the trade press started a heated debate about the responsibilities of the film critic. According to Arthur Mellini, the editor of *Lichtbild-Bühne,* the relationship between the film industry and the daily press had, for the most part, been governed by the fact that newspapers relied on film advertisement as a source of revenue. Speaking for himself and his colleagues, he openly admitted: "We literally bought the sympathy of the press" (*Lichtbild-Bühne,* 4 Mar. 1911). The prospect of lucrative advertisements was indeed a strong incentive for newspaper publishers and editors to revise an initial hostility toward the cinema, which was based on middle-class prejudices and bourgeois tastes. Because a commercial product was involved, reviewers were often dismissed as agents of the studios, without the personal independence and integrity to make sound critical judgments. In light of the growing trend toward quality and value, they had to improve their reputations and introduce standards of professional ethics that justified their role as arbiters of taste. It was not until 1923 that the *Reichsverband der deutschen Presse,* the professional organization for journalists, publicized specific guidelines for film critics. Only the strictest regulations, it would be argued then, prevented corruption; hence their ruling that "whoever works in publishing as a film critic or film journalist is not allowed to entertain any professional ties to film producers or exhibitors" (Heller 1987, 120).

The fact that such statements were necessary attests to the great difficulty in defining the cinema's position between art and industry. The accusations of corruptibility and the defenses of commercialism were symptomatic of a more fundamental problem, and not its solution. Yet the fact that such declarations were made at all draws attention to a complicated entanglement with bourgeois culture that found expression in the critics' persistent belief in their intellectual autonomy, even when they worked for the public relations departments of the film studios.

With the emergence of the feature-length film, reviews appeared more regularly in the daily newspapers; they changed their format and "advanced" from the local to the cultural pages. From then on, it was the responsibility of the theater critic, rather than the city reporter, to review the films playing at local theaters. Modeled on drama criticism, the earliest film reviews displayed many of drama's aesthetic preferences, such as the strong emphasis on acting and mise-en-scène. As a rule, they included information about the genre and story line, a few remarks about the actors, and a brief assessment of the film's artistic quality and entertainment value.

Studios and actors were regularly mentioned, whereas scenarists and directors received the mark of authorship much later, and often only in the more prestigious productions.

A growing interest in aesthetic questions was reflected in a survey among critics and journalists organized in 1912 by the trade journal *Erste Internationale Film-Zeitung*. Responding to the question "Should film drama be criticized?" Walter Turszinsky wrote: "I believe that a critique that judges the cinematic products not with pretentious gushing, but on the basis of serious artistic considerations could be of greatest use to the cause of cinema, and its separation from the slag of bad taste in particular" (quoted by Heller 1990, 27).

The critics' plan to influence film scenarists and directors and to educate audiences was based on an ideal definition of criticism, rather than its reality. Limitations of space, as well as the time constraints under which most reviewers had to work, prevented longer contributions from the outset and gave rise to a style of writing that was more impressionistic than thorough and that relied heavily on critical commonplaces. Few reviewers were known by name, and large national newspapers such as the *Frankfurter Zeitung* or the *Berliner Börsen-Courier* did not publish regular film reviews until the early twenties.

The critical reception of *Quo Vadis?* (1913), a film based on the popular Henryk Sienkiewicz novel, changed this situation and introduced the film critic as a personality with distinct style and temperament. Kurt Pinthus's "Quo vadis-Kino?" was one of the first ambitious reviews published in a German newspaper, the *Leipziger Tageblatt,* though not the first, as the author would later claim (cf. Diederichs 1983). The ironic tone of the opening lines reveals how much attitudes had changed already: "As I spread Keiler jam on a breakfast roll, I open an envelope that contains an invitation printed on the finest handmade paper. Its content: 'Königspavillon-Theater, Promenaden Street No. 8. Sir, you are respectfully asked to attend a premiere on Thursday, April 24th, 1913, 8 P.M.' . . . I learn from the program that the 'most respectable film drama of all times, *Quo Vadis?,* will be screened, introduced by a few short musical numbers and a prologue. The invitation suggests evening dress. Rising victoriously from working-class neighborhoods and small gloomy halls, the movies pretend to have become socially acceptable — at last" (Kaes 1987, 72).

Pinthus's mild contempt for the cinema suggested that all attempts to imitate the theater were doomed to failure. This did not prevent him from describing, in great detail, the film's highlights, the gladiator fights, and the spectacular fire of Rome. On the contrary—the celebration of cinema as a primitive spectacle, as a feast for the eyes, only underscored its distance from the theater. By relying on such oppositions, Pinthus confirmed existing prejudices but, at the same time, prepared the ground for compromise. The reader who identified with the author's ironic attitude could enjoy the cinema without losing his self-respect as an educated individual. Therefore the half-serious indignation about the cinema's false artistic aspirations validated the cinema as a cultural experience in which acceptance of the inevitable was an integral part.

Compared to the prevalent attitudes, Karl Bleibtreu's contributions to the Swiss journal *Die Ähre* (1913–14) represented somewhat of an exception. Under the heading "Filmkritik," Bleibtreu reported on a weekly basis from the cinemas in Zurich (Güttinger 1984b, 205–16). His reviews neither exhibited the mixture of snobbery and disdain that characterized the writings of many literary critics nor did they use specific films as a pretense to elaborate on other problems. Instead, they were written from the perspective of the spectator. Time and again, Bleibtreu defended the cinema against detractors. "Since the representatives of the cinema make a desperate attempt to dismiss the cinema as unartistic," he wrote, "they must tolerate a knowledgeable Thebanian who speaks up and attacks such obvious humbug" (Güttinger 1984a, 208). In practice, this meant discussing film's unique features: the experimentation with movement, the nuances of the human face, the spectacular settings, the beautiful female stars—everything but narrative. Bleibtreu repeatedly dismissed a film's story, only to praise the actors; but unlike Pinthus, he did not perceive the lack of psychological motivation as a shortcoming. While Bleibtreu was one of the first to take the cinema's mass appeal seriously, he also recognized its masterpieces; about *The Student of Prague,* for instance, he wrote: "a real cinema poem—as we like them to be" (Güttinger 1984a, 272).

The breakthrough for the German film industry came with World War I. Isolated from the international market, German companies had a chance to divide up the domestic market among themselves; finally, the French dominance could be broken. Before the war, less than 12 percent of all films had been of German origin. Apart from their technical sophistication, French, American, and Danish films distinguished themselves through better actors and a distinct visual style. But with the discovery of film as a means of political propaganda, the German cinema found a new purpose in promoting German culture and strengthening German nationalism.[5] During the war years, the cinemas provided the main diversion for the populace. The greater amount of discretionary income among those working in the war industries, the organization of patriotic film-days, and the need for escapist entertainment contributed to the growth of the industry. Between 1914 and 1919, almost 700 new theaters opened and attendance increased considerably.

The military, which first used cinematography in ballistic studies, recognized the propagandistic value of film after seeing the anti-German films produced by the French and British. From then on, Emperor Wilhelm, who had a personal interest in film, appeared regularly in newsreels of military parades, victory celebrations, and maneuvers with his beloved Royal Navy.

In addition to organizing screenings at the front, many film companies produced war films (see Bub 1938). These patriotic dramas and comedies strengthened the bond between the soldiers at the front and their families back home. The first German newsreels, the Eiko-Woche and the Messter-Woche, were produced by commercial companies. Initially less than successful, these newsreels soon adopted a more narrative style, replacing monotonous long shots with dynamic editing and including comic episodes. One of their functions was to disperse rumors about the horrors of the war and to highlight the soldiers' discipline and morale.

The various attempts to transform the war into a cinematic spectacle and to use film for propagandistic purposes were brought together in the foundation of two organizations closely associated with the military-industrial complex. The Deulig (Deutsche Lichtbild Gesellschaft) was formed in 1916 by Ludwig Klitsch as a promotional tool for German heavy industries in the Balkans; its primary goal was to support their expansionist tendencies. In 1917, the German High Command under General Ludendorff founded the propaganda unit Bufa (Bild- und Film Amt, or photo and film office) with the explicit goal of supporting the war effort. Messter later recapitulated the lesson of the war, noting: "We have underestimated the political influence exerted by film for mass suggestion. . . . Modern warfare not only involves economic, military, and financial weapons, but also journalistic ones" (Wippermann 1972, 274).

As a result, General Ludendorff wanted to strengthen the German film industry by forging an even stronger bond between government and private capital. The 1917 foundation of Ufa (Universum Film-AG) brought together the Reich, represented by Emil Georg von Stauss, large corporations like AEG, Hapag-Lloyd, and Robert Bosch, and the Dresdener Bank. With a starting capital of more than 30 million Reichsmarks, Ufa was able to acquire such large companies as Nordisk, Messter-Film, and PAGU; only the Emelka Company in Munich survived as a southern counterweight to the Ufa dominance in Berlin. After the war, the shares owned by the Reich were bought by the Deutsche Bank, and Ludendorff's project of nationalistic propaganda through mass entertainment came to an end.

The foundation of Ufa led to a restructuring of the industry that affected all areas of production, distribution, and exhibition, and that increased political influence on the film industry, especially after the collapse of the Wilhelmine Empire. Alfred Hugenberg, the director of the Krupp munitions organization and a representative of the Rhine-Ruhr industrial complex, began to play an important role in aligning industrial and national interests; so did Ludwig Klitsch, who, as director of the Scherl publishing conglomerate, participated actively in the reorganization of Ufa during the years following the war. The most noticeable sign of these changes was the confirmation of Berlin as the center of the German film industry. The Reich capital offered production facilities, print laboratories, banks and financing houses, and, most significantly, a large pool of skilled and unskilled labor: set and costume designers from the big theaters, actors who needed additional income, writers with literary ambitions, critics from the large publishing houses, and a growing number of unemployed persons who could be used as extras in Ufa's prestigious historical films.

\* \* \*

With the foundation of Ufa in 1917, the film industry consolidated its economic and political power and established more firmly the rules of self-presentation. Writing on film in the trade press and the daily newspaper was, from then on, defined by two opposing forces, the readers' need for information and the hyperbole of promotion. The growing emphasis on film as the art of the masses required a more convincing balance between economic and artistic issues, with the industrial product now promoted as a work of art. The reviewers tried to create a larger audience for the cinema, either by emulating established forms like the drama review or by appealing directly to the members of the middle class. While the majority preferred a congenial tone, trying to convince rather than to slander readers, some showed disdain for those individuals who still rejected the cinema.

One of the earliest popular film books, *Der Allotria Kientopp* (1914, The tomfoolery movies), provided a positive identity for film audiences by poking fun at the cultural elite. Written in a very filmic style — hence the subtitle, "The Funniest Comedies Filmed [i.e., written] by Felix Schloemp" — the book comprises a hilarious dialogue between a certain Cosima from Bayreuth, a 16-year-old movie addict from Berlin, and Professor Schwartenwälzer, who at one moment delivers a passionate speech against the cinema. Obviously these caricatures were aimed against the cinema reformers who challenged the industry on economic and political grounds. Mocking their inflated rhetoric, Eugen Jacobson, in his treatise *Flimmeritis* (1918, Moviemania), elevated film addiction to a rather pleasant illness: "Moviemania is a modern scourge that even attacks citizens who are otherwise relatively harmless and reasonable, and it results in wild pandemonium and extremely dangerous insanity" (Jacobson 1918, 5). Published by the *Illustrierte Film Woche,* the booklet presented the facts about filmmaking, film stars, and audiences with the confidence of the economically successful. The imitation of dour reformist phrases only underscored the fact that the cinema represented the voice of pleasure and instant gratification, thus already claiming a leadership role in modern consumer culture.

Taking a slightly different approach, Friedrich Porges's *Fünfzig Meter Kinoweisheit* (1919, Fifty meters of cinema wisdom) treated the new medium with an attitude usually reserved for the older, more established arts, but did so in a tone that combined the frivolity of its products with the seriousness of its producers. The notion of wisdom in association with cinema evoked traditions that, in their absence, had to be projected into the future as another proof of its inevitable rise to power. At the same time, the announcement of a "studio report" by a man with experience — Porges was a film critic in Vienna and wrote scenarios for the Austrian film company Sascha-Film — promised information that could be useful for the serious film fan as well as for the aspiring film author; the detailed comments about filmmaking and the inclusion of film scenarios suggests such diverse usages.

In this mixture of instruction, promotion, and critical analysis available to the reader, one must locate the origins of film aesthetics. As early as 1913, Kurt Ullmann published a short treatise, *Wege zu einer neuen Filmkunst* (1913, Ways toward a new art of film), in which he combined concrete suggestions on scenario writing with theoretical pronouncements about film. Guided by an unyielding belief in film as art, Ullmann appealed to filmmakers as well as critics to close the gap between the cinema's present practices and its future possibilities, and to focus exclusively on artistic means: "It is important not to hide the crisis of film behind wordy paper façades, but to further develop film's characteristic techniques: not a revolution, but an evolution from the inside!" (Ullmann 1913, 9).

Like many of his contemporaries, Ullmann envisioned a cinema of sensations, actions, and adventures. To illustrate his theoretical claims about appropriate story material and strengthen his case against the film drama, he included two story treatments, "The Three North Pole Explorers" and "The Aviator's Dreams." Instead of living up to their promises, however, the stories distinguish themselves only through their exotic locales, and his list of filmic means simply declares present limitations to be aesthetic qualities; hence lengthy comments on the graphic quality of monochrome film, the flatness of the image, and the absence of language.

Ullmann's approach may have been influenced by cinema's technical possibilities at the time, but it also repeated widespread prejudices about popular culture as primitive and conveyed historically formed preferences, such as the staging conventions of the *tableaux vivants* (Heller 1984, 61). While it is evident from the practical section of the book that Ullmann had little knowledge of filmmaking, it is precisely his attempt to translate historical conditions into formal categories and turn social functions into aesthetic values that reveals the normative power of writing—it imposes standards on the cinema that originate in the bourgeois perception of popular culture.

The consolidation of the film industry brought with it more and more publications about the cinema as a profession; these included instructional textbooks, how-to manuals, and practical guides. A number of small publishing companies took advantage of the expansionist tendencies by publishing job guides. For the most part, these books provided an overview of the new industry, gave detailed job descriptions (e.g., director, scenarist, set designer), described the various phases of film production, and gave step-by-step advice on "how to make it" in the film world. Others offered crash courses on becoming a successful film scenarist. Peter Paul's *Das Filmbuch* (1914, The film book) gave detailed advice on how to find ideas for good film scenarios; Wilhelm Adler's *Wie schreibe ich einen Film?* (1917, How do I write a film?) even answered such specific questions as "Why do film factories reject manuscripts?" Years later, a relatively short-lived series titled "Das Drehbuch" (The film scenario) would even publish scenarios—for instance, Carl Mayer's celebrated scenario for *Sylvester* (1924)—in order to advance scenario writing as a new literary genre and facilitate critical exchange among scenarists.

Presenting the film business as a field with unlimited possibilities, the less respectable works on scenario writing promised instant success to the aspiring film author, who supposedly only had to know the right formulas to make a fortune. Here the film business was depicted as if it existed outside the social order, a product of the imagination like the films themselves. Written by men who were actively involved in film production, these books treated the new medium as a profession and a craft; their professionalism had a positive influence on public attitudes. The pervasive feeling of accomplishment spilled over into more critical discourses, with the result that practical information about film production often gave rise to the celebration of cinema as a new collective art, and that detailed suggestions about theater design culminated in tributes to its democratic internationalism.

Therein lies the contribution of the technical discourse on cinematography, a contribution that is often forgotten since it originates from a position behind the illusion, a place where art is unmasked as techniques and meaning demeaned by considerations of money. Just as the film reviewer created an audience for the cinema, the authors of instructional manuals established the parameters of scenario writing, acting, and directing. In this regard, they practiced film criticism from the side of production.

The implications of what amounted to an ongoing reassessment of the artistic process through the discourses of criticism and instruction can be studied in the large number of books devoted to film acting. Many were published by trade journals which, because of their close ties to the industry, had a vested interest in preparing nonprofessionals and stage actors for the specific requirements of film acting. Published by the *Lichtbild-Bühne,* Richard Ott's first volume to *Der Weg zum Film* (1918, The road to film) discussed all aspects of film acting, from the different uses of makeup to the growing popularity of natural acting styles. Leo Beck's *Wie werde ich Filmschauspieler?* (1919, How do I become a film actor?) gave detailed advice on how to build a portfolio with photographs and references and how to approach film producers. Oskar Diehl's guideline for *Mimik im Film* (1922, Acting in film) even suggested face and body exercises through which aspiring actors could learn how to produce emotional effects without having to rely on makeup and costume.

Many instructional manuals on film acting welcomed the shift from the face as the site of true character to the body as the manifestation of modern consciousness. In their discussion of acting methods, the body became an instrument for creating the most subtle gestures and expressions. The requirements of role-playing were subsumed under the laws of physiognomy, while the actors' screen presence was to endow the role with the kind of authenticity necessary for proper spectator involvement. Through the discourse on acting, the autonomous individual was reconstituted outside of language, namely as the modern body. By establishing the parameters of the relationship between body and soul and by providing a catalogue of expressions, the manuals on film acting thus brought forth the subject in the cinema.

Because of the central role played by actors in a discourse on film authorship, it is not surprising that some were actively involved in the fight for better films. Paul Wegener's 1916 lecture "New Cinema Goals" (Güttinger 1984, 341–50) marked the first time that an actor spoke out in favor of the cinema and what he described as a new technology of the fantastic. Wegener, who played the title roles in *The Student of Prague* (1913, 1920) and the *Golem* films (1914, 1917, 1920) and who would go on to write, direct, or appear in fairy tale films like *Rübezahls Hochzeit* (1916, Rübezahl's wedding) and *Der Rattenfänger* (1918, The Pied Piper), criticized the established arts for preventing the cinema from developing its visual potential. He demanded: "The real poet of film must be the camera. The possibility of a continuous change of position for the spectator, the many tricks like split screen, mirror effects, and so forth — in short, the technique of film — must determine the choice of the content" (Güttinger 1984a, 348).

Portraying film as an imaginary world accountable only to the laws of "pure kinetics" and "optical lyrics," Wegener saw the fantastic and its challenge to everyday perception as the most promising area of application for film. His approach introduced a radically new perspective into the discourse on film authorship, as he replaced the creative individual before and behind the camera with the cinematic apparatus, the instrument of perceptual liberation. However, Wegener's examples of a visionary cinema also limited these possibilities to more traditional images so that the "optical vision," "this great symphonic fantasy," turned out to be nothing more than a kind of animated Böcklin painting, complete with ocean-sprayed Nereids and Tritons — evidence that awareness of the camera's power did not always go hand-in-hand with the search for new subject matter.

Cinematographers, film producers, and film directors were among the first to discuss artistic and technical problems, using the opportunity to confirm their professional identity and improve their public image. Cameramen and set designers wrote about the practical aspects of filmmaking, and theater owners gave detailed advice on how to set up screening facilities, whereas producers often took the opportunity to emphasize the importance of the film industry for the national economy. *Die Lichtbild-Bühne* and *Der Kinematograph* provided a forum where directors could speak about problems of film production while also addressing artistic issues, including questions of film authorship.

Famous directors like Ernst Lubitsch, Joe May, Max Mack, and Richard Oswald were well prepared to fill the need for figures of mastery in an industry often associated with fickleness and disorder. Some directors were as well-known as actors—some of them, like Lubitsch and Mack, had previous acting experience—but they also exuded the seriousness of the writer or artist. Profiting from the widespread assumption that organizational control presupposed artistic control, Max Mack, who also published a professional guide for film actors in 1919, characterized the task of the director as one of preventing disagreements and furthering collaboration, "a collaboration for the higher glory of the film under the guidance of the director, who has the full overview and is solely responsible for everything" (1920, 13).

Discussing problems of authorial control, Richard Oswald described his relationship to actors as one of forceful conviction, and, to give an example of his artistic responsibility, spoke repeatedly of the need for qualified film criticism. The direct appeal to the film critics was made to confirm the director as the creative individual toward whom the former should direct their critical comments (Oswald 1920). While Oswald argued in favor of greater directorial control, Ernst Lubitsch called for more good film scenarios and complained that "what is missing is film poetry (*Filmdichtung*)" (1920, 1,146). Unlike Julius Sternheim, who in the same issue of *Das Tage-Buch* had made a distinction between the average film author (*Filmautor*) and the creative film poet (*Filmdichter*), Lubitsch had in mind a kind of writing in images that distinguished itself sharply from literary film scripts (*Film-Manuskript*); hence also the linguistic distinction between poetry and script.

In the more popular film journals, many directors also spoke about their collaboration with famous film stars; Lubitsch, for instance, engaged in a public debate with Asta Nielsen about their problems during the shooting of *Rausch* (1920, Intoxication). Such controversies became more frequent as the film world became an object of public curiosity and its members figures of public admiration. The personality cult around the film star and the star director contributed indirectly to the formulation of aesthetic categories and standards of evaluation. No matter how sensationalist or lurid at times, interest in the person promoted belief in the unity of life and work that brought with it from the literary and theatrical spheres a whole set of ideas about artistic genius and creativity. Furthermore, no matter to what degree the stars were transformed into images ready for public consumption, their presence provided a culminating point for various discourses on appearance. Even as the process of commodification extended to those workers with greatest public exposure in the film industry, the glorification of the creative individual cast a veil of originality and authenticity over the conditions of production, thus shrouding the industrial product in the discourses of art.

The tension between the discourses of art and production were most evident in specialized writings by film directors, such as Ewald André Dupont's *Wie ein Film geschrieben wird* (1919, How to write a film). This very instructive book not only provided information on various shot sizes, the basic rules of continuity editing, the composition of a scene, and the direction of actors; for illustrative purposes, it also contained excerpts from Dupont's scenario for the Oswald film *Es werde Licht!* (1917, Let there be light!) and his own *Ferdinand Lassalle* (1918). Dupont used this professional framework to proclaim the complete identity of film author and film director. Calling for greater distance from literature, he argued that "the best film scenarists are to be found among the film directors themselves. In other words, the best film directors are also the best authors" (1919a, 14).[6]

Nonetheless, experience did not prevent some directors and scenarists from reiterating the myths that were created elsewhere to negate film's industrial foundation. Especially when addressing a larger audience, film professionals tended to describe the cinema in purely philosophical terms. *Die zappelnde Leinwand* (1916, The lively screen), an early anthology edited by Mack with contributions by, among others, Dupont and Rudolf Kurtz, was supposed to give background information about the film industry, but all too often resorted to the most hackneyed clichés about the cinema and its inherent spirituality. One of the contributors, Hans Brennert, first praised film as a "stockmarket of imagination," alluding to its capitalist roots, and then introduced into his analysis of modern society the most charming little fairies and elves. "After all, just as the devil in the old folk tales bought souls for the secret of *black* magic, the film-devil of the art of *light* robs his apprentices of their *imagination,* an imagination that brings forth billions of small, square-shaped celluloid images" (Mack 1916, 10). A "new race of poets," who were called film-footage poets (*Kinometerdichter*) because of their modern approach to writing, was called upon to investigate film's vast possibilities: "These people have brought about a new revolution, the revolution of the imagination. Finally, after two thousand years of dramatic art, and its presentations of the most subtle psychological processes, it is now possible to show the external world to the spectator" (1916, 20). Obviously, even expertise failed to protect critics from the temptations of make-believe. Only the encroachment of cinematic consciousness on theory itself could have made possible this narrativizing of modern film production as a fairy tale.

Urban Gad's *Der Film. Seine Mittel — seine Ziele* (1921, Film: Its means — its aims) must be regarded as one of the most extensive contributions by a film professional (cf. Wuss 1990, 77–83). Gad's book was praised by a contemporary as "a very profound theoretical treatise, which makes the first attempt to present a kind of film dramaturgy and to describe the artistic means and goals of cinematography" (Friedell 1923–24, 156). The famous Danish director put together a comprehensive volume discussing all phases of preproduction, production, and postproduction, including scenario writing, set design, lighting, on-location shooting, acting, directing, editing, film printing, and advertising. Through this close attention to technical detail, Gad hoped to arrive at a theory of film based on its characteristic techniques. He clearly stated his goal in the introduction: "It will be demonstrated how plain technical things, through cinematic representation, can be put to the service of spirituality, so that art may arise from this collaborative effort of spirit and technology" (1921, 5). Like most film directors, Gad discounted direct references to the other arts: "Film, in brief, is narration in images — a combination of two art forms, and thus cannot be compared to any previous art form, nor be judged by the rules valid for them" (1921, 279).

In addition to his emphasis on technical perfection, Gad showed great awareness of the social significance of cinema. Repeatedly, he underscored its importance as a means of mass education and entertainment. However, as a product of its time, *Der Film* also displayed the same preference for the rhetoric of spiritual redemption that characterized some of the other writ-

ings of the day. Betraying his attention to detail with the following grandiose vision, Gad ended his extensive study on a hopeful note: "All human
beings — these amorphous, naive masses — should recognize themselves in
film like in a mirror, but a mirror hanging high, forcing the gaze upward.
The cinema should provide a platform where social concerns can be discussed in clear, simple, gripping images; at the same time, it should be a
place where people can find freedom from sorrows, and relief from pressure, simply by watching scenes that speak to them as individuals" (1921,
281).

This mixture of pragmatism and techno-romanticism was rather typical
of works that tried at once to emphasize the professionalism of the film
industry and to create a mythology for its product. The success of the
project can be measured by the ease with which technical innovation and
profitability were made part of the new scenarios of spiritual redemption.
Film directors and scenarists had little difficulty in combining these very
disparate elements under the heading of a future film art.

# Chapter 2
## The Cinema Reform Movement

A s the first public debate on the cinema, the *Kinoreformbewegung* (cinema reform movement) played a crucial role in defining the place of cinema in relation to the institutions of dominant culture, and to the educational system in particular. Its representatives were the first to analyze the social and sociopsychological function of the cinema and to determine its contribution to the building of a strong nation. They believed the cinema could be transformed into an instrument of social mediation and national renewal through information, education, legislation, and a wide range of noncommercial media initiatives. For only a healthy national cinema, the reformers asserted, could stop the gradual disintegration of the public sphere and reunite the various groups in society under the unifying force of German nationalism.

"Sanctimonious folks and hypocrites, morality sleuths in male and female guise went to war against the cinema" (Kullmann 1935, 42). This is how one theater owner described the cinema reformers in 1921, when their influence on public debates was already greatly diminished and their proposals superseded by the realities of cinema. Compared to the commercial film industry, the reformist endeavors in film exhibition and media education had little impact; and measured against the writings of the literary authors, their critical insights were often marred by exaggerations and misconceptions. Because of their strong prejudices against the narrative film and their unyielding belief in film as an educational tool, the reformers stood at the margins of a film culture primarily concerned with entertainment. However, the contribution of the cinema reformers should not be underestimated; their pedagogical concepts continue to influence today's approaches to media education.

Reformers were first called to action by what they perceived as the lack of effective censorship laws, the scandalous conditions of film exhibition, and the devastating impact of "movie addiction" on the nation's youth. Around 1910, they began to write articles, pamphlets, and instructional booklets, publish journals and monograph series, organize meetings and conferences, introduce bills on the regional and national level, and form educational associations. Ostracizing the cinema for its destructive qualities, while at the same time fascinated by its mass appeal, the reformers concentrated their efforts in three distinct but closely related areas: public morality, social harmony, and national education. Early reform publications emphasized the need for censorship laws, boards of review, exhibition licences, and admission policies. Initiatives for a better cinema extended to all levels of local and state politics, and involved film production as well as distribution. The greatest advances came with the founding of communal theaters and the screening of educational films in schools (Warstat and Bergmann 1913; Schulze 1977).

With strongholds in the Ruhr region, Thuringia, and the Baltic harbor cities, the reform movement proved most successful in industrialized centers with a large working-class population. The nation's capital, whose rich film culture inspired many literary essays on the cinema, played no significant role in the movement, neither as a national headquarters nor as a testing ground for reformist projects. In sharp contrast to the intellectuals, the reformers aligned themselves openly with the existing power structures. Many supported the national conservative parties, although the movement was much less unified than is often assumed (Heller 1984, 99–108). For instance, the reactionary Karl Brunner, with his diatribes against the trashy film, had little in common with the more liberal Hermann Häfker, who advocated a realist cinema; Erwin Ackerknecht and Adolf Sellmann were primarily interested in pedagogical issues, while Konrad Lange focused on aesthetic questions.

All of them pursued the cause of cinema reform with the confidence of professional ideologues. Education, not aesthetics, was their primary concern. The majority belonged to the educated middle class; teachers, pastors, and civil servants occupied the leading positions. Their institutional affiliations instilled in them the ambition to stop disruptive tendencies and uphold traditional values, while their political convictions gave them the confidence to take on this enormous task. For them, writing about cinema served a very concrete purpose: it made them part of a struggle—not *against* the cinema as such, but rather *for* a cinema conducive to the ideas of nationalism.

The reformers responded to the outbreak of World War I by continuing their projects on the national level. Their more radical demands, including calls for a nationalization of the film industry, disappeared, and pedagogical initiatives became part of a larger investigation into the propagandistic uses of cinematography. The theories developed in the subordination of cinema to the goals of nationalism, only confirm to what degree the discourse of cinema was implicated in the political processes that led to the war and brought about the downfall of the Wilhelmine Empire. The reformist example shows why early German film criticism cannot be separated from the question of national identity.

Not surprisingly, many of the reformist writings are characterized by an argumentative style that is driven by political concerns and their underlying contradictions. A fundamental ambivalence toward the cinema remains, as the reformers move back and forth between their fear of social change and their hope for a national revival. Thus the cinema appears alternately as the future of German nationalism, a tool of capitalist internationalism, a hotbed of political dissent, an incarnation of primitive eroticism, and an accessory to the process of social disintegration. The texts simultaneously express and suppress social conflicts by transforming them into conflicting ideas; as a result, the experience of class difference disappears into the scenarios of German nationalism, with France playing the role of Other. Vacillating between repulsion and fascination, the reformers regularly deny any personal appreciation of films, yet they write highly subjective reports "from the movies." As Hermann Halter insists: "I have personally studied these programs in all sorts of cinemas, but only for my research, and I say, expressly, research, not pleasure" (1921, 19).

These contradictions pervade reformist writings about cinema, through exaggeration and repetition, through analogies and oppositions, and through the frequent use of metaphor. This excess in language bears witness to a complicated negotiation process within bourgeois culture. And it is here, in language and in the reformist fixation on that which was threatened most by the emergence of cinema — the rigid class structure and the sharp divisions between high and low culture — where the failure of the discourse of integration becomes glaringly evident. Apart from providing the tools through which to approach and ultimately take possession of the new medium, the reformist discourse thus functioned like a distorting mirror for the experience of modernity.

The chosen images attest to a pervasive sense of crisis. Horror visions abound, ranging from bizarre concoctions like "film hooch" (Noack), "drop of poison" (Conradt), and "scourge-bacteria images" (Halter) to a rather common expression like "shame slough of German pseudo-art" (Finger). Watching a film, these descriptions suggest, can be as dangerous as alcoholism, drug addiction, or infectious diseases. Other writers resorted to military metaphors to explain the cinema's triumphant rise to power. Here verbs like *flickering, flashing,* and *flaring* suggest a situation in which the viewing subject is under fire. Popular phrases like "the ray aimed at the spectator" or "the bombardment of the senses" suggest affinities between visual pleasure and the war experience.

While comparisons to the military emphasize the cinema's aggressive qualities, water metaphors treat its destructive and constructive potential. Perceiving the rapid growth of the film industry as a catastrophe, Brunner spoke of the devastating powers of this high flood, "if censorship does not erect a protecting wall" (1913, 24).[1] Samuleit, however, expressed doubts about the effectiveness of censorship laws, asking: "Will this protective dam be high enough?" (1914, 13). Having "survived" the early years of cinema, Walter Bloem declared in 1921 that "wisdom and morality demand that we become the frontmost waves of this stream, and at least try to direct it toward nobler goals, since we can no longer stop it" (1921, 245). On a more positive note, Erwin Ackerknecht called for immediate actions that would "turn the increasingly marshy areas of public life into fertile cultivated land" (1918, 12). Some reformers speculated about harnessing the energies that had been set free by the cinema, very much like an engineer would use water power as a source of energy. Arguing in this vein, Richard Muckermann compared the cinema to "a naturally growing mountain spring that, already after a few hundred meters, could operate several water mills" (1925, 5). Otto Steinbrinck, on the other hand, praised the calming effect of water and compared the cinema to the North Sea spas frequented by middle-class tourists for recreational purposes (1925, 92).

Other reformers introduced the notion of lineage to endow the cinema with a past, present, and future. In most variations on this theme, the cinema was cast as the son. While the "bad" cinema inspired female imagery and scenarios of male seduction, the "good" cinema was invariably described as young, male, and very much in need of educating. In the more optimistic scenarios, the cinema appeared as "the son of an honorable father, cinematography, who has fallen in with bad company" (Noack 1913, 4), "the prince from the fairyland [who] has become a prodigal son" (Pieper 1912, 4), or "the big, ingenious child who forms his figures in clay—good ones as well as bad ones—and throws them away with careless indifference" (Gad 1921, 273). Cinema reform, if one wanted to interpret these comparisons, had to be understood as something akin to going to reform school.[2]

Confronted with a new medium and a largely undefined field of critical discourse, the cinema reformers began by reevaluating the old critical categories, introducing new methods of interpretation, and establishing firm standards of evaluation. They combined, in a rather eclectic fashion, ideas from Social Darwinism, mass psychology, and cultural pessimism and integrated them into the larger context of what was called *Bildung* (education), an educational and political concept that had played a central role in the public debates on German national and cultural identity since the nineteenth century. Wilhelm von Humboldt's ideal of humanism and the social-reformist proposals of Johann Pestalozzi, to name two important advocates of *Bildung,* provided the backdrop against which the reformers developed their model of the cinema as an educational institution. They were determined to raise the masses to a higher level and reunite them with the goals of the nation as culture nation (*Kulturnation*); their effusive descriptions of a future German cinema betray these political motivations.

In presenting their arguments, the reformist writers often relied on configurations of the self and the Other, as is made evident by emotionally charged oppositions like culture (*Kultur*) versus civilization (*Zivilization*), community (*Gemeinschaft*) versus society (*Gesellschaft*), tradition versus progress, crafts versus mechanization, and so forth. A standard element in the cultural debates, *Kultur* was invoked to distinguish the contribution of German artists from the degenerative effects of (French) *Zivilisation*. Convincing in their suggestive inaccuracy, these oppositions allowed the reformers to deal simultaneously with the decline of the bourgeois public sphere and with the threat of a proletarian revolution. Like the nineteenth-century critics who used the concept of national literature to create a cultural identity for the various German states, the cinema reformers focused on one particular aspect of modern culture—the cinema—and turned it into a vehicle for strengthening national identity. Unlike the nineteenth-century critics, however, they were confronted with a medium that resisted traditional definitions of art and, furthermore, a social structure that required new definitions of nation and class. In writing about the cinema, the reformist critics tried to identify these conflicting forces and integrate them in the larger vision of a cinema for the masses and the nation.

Through their critical writings and publishing ventures, the cinema reformers laid the foundation of media pedagogy (Kommer 1979, 13–86). The Lichtbilderei in Mönchen-Gladbach, an organization for the educational use of visual media, contributed significantly to this project. With equally close ties to the Catholic church and the film industry, the Lichtbilderei tried to find a compromise between its educational mission and the requirements of the marketplace. It published the first noncommercial film journal, *Bild und Film,* as well as an ambitious monograph series titled *Lichtbühnen-Bibliothek.* Founded in 1912 and edited by Lorenz Pieper, *Bild und Film* appeared on a monthly basis until 1915; the journal contained no advertisements (Diederichs 1986a, 84–163). Regular contributors included the prolific Hermann Häfker, the art critic Willi Warstat, the reformist activists Adolf Sellmann and Albert Hellwig, and one of the first woman film critics, Malwine Rennert (Schlüpmann 1986 and 1990c, 242–43).

As a public forum for those actively involved in the cinema reform movement, *Bild und Film* focused on the possibilities of cinema as an educational tool. Initially, the journal's critics argued that the masses had to be elevated to the level of high culture and its specific modes of appreciation. This attitude accounts for the many dismissive remarks about audiences and their lack of sophistication. Caught between their plan to educate the lower classes and their resistance to working-class culture, some critics took a slightly paternalistic attitude, referring (like Pieper) to the audience as "this big child."

As a way of making contact with the masses, *Bild und Film* critics decided to pay more attention to the film drama. Their interest in film reviews remained limited, as Alexander Elsner noted: "The only thing that can be expected of cinema criticism today is to boycott the products of certain companies and pave the way for the films of other factories" (1912–13, 262). But the growing number of film reviews in *Bild und Film* — the first was of Urban Gad's *Der Totentanz* (1914, The dance of death) — indicates that the reformist critics were at least willing to consider the needs of audiences and to engage in discussions with the proponents of the film drama. They also continued to insist, however, that films should explore the beauty of movement and the visible world; hence their interest in the so-called cultural film (*Kulturfilm*) with its educational, scientific, geographical, or cultural themes. The emotional appeal of fiction, they argued, could even be used for educational purposes and help to promote filmic realism.

Despite these programmatic comments, the actual reviews in *Bild und*

*Film* took a rather traditional approach modeled on literary criticism. Much of the discussion focused on problems of mise-en-scène, whereas filmic techniques such as editing and camerawork were more or less ignored. The strong emphasis on actors placed the human being at the center of the filmic narrative and, at times, inspired disturbing comments on national physiognomies and body types.

In addition to *Bild und Film*, the Lichtbilderei published the eight-volume monograph series *Lichtbühnen-Bibliothek,* with an additional film bibliography by Gustav Budjuhn. For this series, Hermann Häfker wrote three monographs, *Kino und Kunst* (1913, Cinema and art), *Kino und Erd-kunde* (1914, Cinema and geography), and *Der Kino und die Gebildeten* (1915, The Cinema and the educated), each of which examined the possibilities of film under one particular aspect. For Häfker, whose name is most closely linked to the reformist debate on filmic realism, the camera had to "present a black-and-white image of real events with documentary authenticity" (1913, 13); in other words, it was the primary source of realism in the cinema (Schlüpmann 1990c, 262–67). From the first day of shooting to the first public screening, Häfker insisted, everything had to be subordinated to the goals of what he described with the neologism *Kinetographie,* in opposition to the film drama (*Kinodrama*).[3] As he described it, *Kinetographie* offered the best possibilities for studying nature and the beauty of movement, for overcoming space and time, and for understanding the world's secret rhythm (Diederichs 1990). Its products also were of immeasurable value for later generations, namely as "documents of the present and the past" (1913, 23).

Häfker's definition excluded all so-called staged scenes as inappropriate material for filmic representation. The rejection of the film drama opened up entirely new applications, for instance in geography, to quote Häfker's favorite example. As a contribution to the systematic study of other nations and cultures, he argued, geographical films could demonstrate the German need for colonies and the importance of foreign trade. Arguing in accordance with his nationalist convictions, Häfker concluded: "Cinematography can help promote a healthy *international* attitude, precisely by demonstrating where the strength and uniqueness of the *fatherland* lies—and where we need *not* search for it" (1914, 51).

\* \* \*

The discourse of cinema reform originated, to a large degree, in debates on censorship. Censorship laws, which were first introduced on the local level

and which were concerned primarily with film exhibition, offered an effective means of control. While the constitution protected freedom of
speech in literature and, to a lesser degree, in the theater, the cinema was
counted among the public diversions for the masses; hence its different
form of taxation (*Lustbarkeitssteuer*). The reformers, however, were not
only interested in prohibition, or direct results; they also used the question
of censorship to address other, more fundamental issues. Censorship as a
critical category created the dividing line between the self and the Other,
the trivial and the profound, the productive and the destructive. In that
function, it provided both a means of categorization and a strategy of
critical evaluation.

Common to all positions on censorship was the conviction that the
cinema, this "enemy of morality," to employ a common epithet, represented a threat to the nation, and could only be fought through the joint
efforts of legislators, police, and social pressure groups. Walther Conradt's
desperate outcry "When will the Hercules arrive who can clean out this
Augean stable?" (1910, 26) and Paul Samuleit's statement "Without the
brutal intervention of the state, the hydra of modern cinematography
cannot be fought" (Samuleit and Born 1914, 47) bear witness to an atmosphere of fanaticism and hysteria. In the prewar years, discussions focused
on the conditions of mass reception rather than on specific films or film
genres. Karl Brunner, who was editor of the antismut journal *Hochwacht*
and actively involved in drafting the cinema bill in Baden, wrote: "I do not
believe that cinematography, just because it is relatively new, still suffers
from developmental shortcomings that will disappear automatically in the
near future. On the contrary, I believe that it is in the very nature of
cinematic representation — at least with today's commercial orientation —
that cinematography cannot be improved" (1913, 26).

The problem, according to Brunner, could only be attacked from the
side of reception, and not production. He claimed the most objectionable
films did not appeal to a sophisticated audience but had a devastating effect
on the lower classes — people, he said, with dubious morals standards and
bad taste. Hence the need for an effective rating system. Arguing along
similar lines, Ackerknecht demanded: "Since the degree of involvement
and the effect on public morality are not counterbalanced by any aesthetic
constraints — especially not on this primitive level of emotional film viewing — it is doubly important that it [the film drama] does not appeal to the
lowest instincts such as brutality, cruelty, envy, and greed" (1918, 84).[4]

Without the restraining effect of clear aesthetic standards, the reformers posited, the moving images posed a threat to the public order. That is why the state had to intervene. Consequently, Häfker demanded that the question of censorship be handed over to the police, the military, and selected members of the public who possessed that mysterious quality known as "good taste." They were supposed to establish a standard of morality. Frequently the threshold referred to the percepts of Robert Gaupp and Konrad Lange — a "general shame level" based on the sensibility of women and children (Gaupp and Lange 1912, 33).

Under the motto "Ruin to the trashy film, support for the good film, that be the solution!" Albert Hellwig went so far as to propose a censorship law based on the emotional impact of films (*Wirkungszensur*), and not their content (Hellwig 1911, 139). Behind all these proposals stood the hope that the transgressive qualities of the cinematic experience could be controlled through an ethics of representation. The suspicion, nevertheless, remained that even the most effective laws might fail in influencing the psychological processes set into motion by the narrative film.

Not surprisingly, many reformers questioned the effectiveness of strict censorship laws. They believed that bans and restrictions had to be complemented by preventive measures if the project of cinema reform was to have any success, and if they themselves were to play any part in a cinema based on the needs of the nation, and not the masses. Sellmann warned: "The institutions [the board of censors and the police] are quite capable of preventing the worst, but can never create something good" (1912, 14). The problem was no longer one of enforcing standards of taste and morality *post factum*, but of changing the conditions of exhibition and production. Prevention, rather than prohibition, became the new goal.

To be sure, most reformers did not oppose popular entertainment on principle; they simply wanted to direct the emotional impulses of the masses toward what they considered more "worthwhile" causes. Acker-knecht conceded a need for visual stimuli that could no longer be dismissed as an aberration. Instead, he said, it had to be regarded as a biological necessity, "a natural, instinctive counterreaction to the exaggerated emphasis on intellectual skills in a growing number of professions" (1918, 62). That is where the communal cinemas assumed their role as centers of media education. A supporter of community-owned cinemas, Sellmann envisioned a kind of free education for all: "In modern cultural life, the individual not only has to learn more; knowledge also has to be communicated to the broad masses and to all social classes. Here cinematography is an excellent means of democratizing knowledge" (1914, 16).[5]

The proposal to give the less privileged better access to cultural and educational events was modeled on similar attempts in the theater (e.g., the *Volksbühne* organizations). Yet when applied to a mass medium like film, these ideas lost most much of their critical impetus. Ernst Schultze asked Germany to "utilize as much as possible this wonderful product of technology for our culture, because it has the potential of becoming a powerful tool of national education" (1911, 8). His demand revealed an instrumental approach that completely negated the emancipatory potential inherent in all art. The main goal for Schultze was social reconciliation through education. As the tensions between city and country, crafts and industry, bourgeoisie and proletariat grew, the cinema in his view had important tasks to fulfill as the great mediator and the unifying force holding together the nation.

Much of the reformist discourse was devoted to the problem of the *Schundfilm* (trashy film) which was frequently equated with the film drama and sometimes with narrative film in general. The *Schundfilm* favored specific stories and themes (romance, melodrama) but its reformist definition also included questions of reception. While paying little attention to specific films, the majority of reformers rejected the trashy film or film drama as a perversion of the cinema's inherent possibilities. Since it was too late to eliminate the genre altogether, censorship had to prevent its worst excesses. In descriptions, references to trashy or pulp literature abounded, for instance in Konrad Lange's definition of the trashy film as "the worthy child of a father of ill-repute, namely the backstage or trashy novel [*Kolportageroman*]" (1918, 36).[6] As typical products of modern mass culture, Lange argued, the trashy novel and the trashy film appealed through their simplistic stories, stereotypical characters, sharp distinctions between good and evil, and a fatalistic view of society that rendered the individual powerless. Because of the special conditions of mass reception, the trashy film had to be considered the more dangerous of the two, responsible not only for the nation's infiltration by foreign elements, but also for its destruction from within. Paul Samuleit feared for the German soul: "In the internationalist cinema drama [*Kinodrama*], the wildest passions of all nations come together for a gruesome rendezvous" (Samuleit and Born 1914, 24). Erich Schlaikjer exclaimed: "As the darkness of imminent destruction descends on our country, our films have become so disgustingly obscene that they cannot even be sold in otherwise sufficiently insensitive foreign countries" (1920, 234). Lange concluded: "Ceterum censeo, drama cinematographicum esse delendam" (1920, 94). The allusion is to Cato the Elder's dictum on Carthage, the enemy city. It means: "Incidentally, I am of the opinion that the cinematographical drama must be destroyed."

Hidden behind the exaggerated political rhetoric, the reformers' arguments against the film drama also involved aesthetic concerns, including the prevention of "cross-fertilization" with traditional art forms. Thus Lydia Eger declared that the adaptation of classical dramas jeopardized cinematography's true mission: "Drama wants to depict ideas and bring them to the spectator's critical attention. In order to achieve this, it needs language, gesture, and movement. It uses the senses to activate the spectator's mind and produces emotions through the representation of psychological processes. However, drama needs an active mind. . . . Precisely that mental involvement is missing from the cinema drama [*Kinodrama*], because it lacks language" (1920, 11). Eger concludes that dramatic forms should be reserved for the stage, and that each art form should explore its own specific qualities: "Cinematography and cinema have a right to exist and to grow as long as they remain within the areas defined by their nature" (1920, 15).

Focusing on possible transgressions, many reformers blamed the film drama for the crisis of cinema. Reducing drama to the spoken word, and extending the equation of language and narrative to fiction in general, Sellmann spoke for many when he concluded that "the cinema can only improve if these film dramas disappear" (1912, 31). Such statements did not mean that the reformers refused categorically to include story elements in educational films. But by focusing on the excesses, they could use the controversy over the film drama for a more far-reaching critique of society. With cause and effect now reversed, social problems were reduced to problems of representation and the cinema was saved for another form of public entertainment, one that provided education instead of diversion, and filmic realism instead of cheap illusionism. Again it was Lange who expressed the prevailing sentiment by proclaiming: "I am still a friend of the cinema and an enemy of the cinema drama [*Kinodrama*]" (1920, 5).

Since comparisons between genres added little to the understanding of mass reception, some reformers began to examine in more detail the structures of identification in the film drama. The most convincing attempt was made by Konrad Lange who, in *Das Kino in Gegenwart und Zukunft*

(1920, The cinema in the present and the future), moved beyond the usual sensationalism to analyze the formal characteristics shared by all films. Unlike most reformers, who concentrated on questions of content, Lange proposed a structural analysis. All film genres, he argues in *Das Kino,* employ a dualistic system of representation based on class difference. While scenes depicting revolutionary uprisings can always be eliminated by the censors, a film's narrative structure remains indestructible. As Lange explains, many films take advantage of the existence of social differences by building their stories around antagonistic positions: "When analyzing and comparing a great number of films with erotic, criminal, and sensationalist subject matter, one makes the strange observation that the story usually takes place in two diametrically opposed social groups. Poor and rich, main house and back house, castle and hut — that is how one could schematically describe these oppositions" (1920, 46). The film drama, Lange continues, uses these social stereotypes to implicate the spectators in its emotional constellations. Above all, it satisfies their curiosity about the life-styles of the wealthy and makes them forget their misery by portraying the upper classes in a negative light. Lange rejects this dualistic structure on aesthetic and political grounds, since identification can all too easily lead to dissatisfaction, perhaps even open revolt. "One should not assume that the people in the audience respond coldly or without passion to such stories. The images are much too impressive, too much like reality. One often hears remarks like 'I could kill him' when a rich man does something scandalous" (1920, 50).

Other examples suggest that, between the subversive power of fantasy and its co-optation by dominant practices, misinterpretations are always possible. Exposed to films with rich protagonists and luxurious settings, the workers might suddenly demand the same. Halter's warning, "What you see, you desire; what you perceive, you do yourself" (1921, 22), referred precisely to such moments when fiction and reality became indistinguishable, and when compensation suddenly turned into a revolutionary program. Their fear of social unrest also explains why many reformers accused the film drama of exaggeration and falsification. "Even the grimmest class hatred finds new fuel in the depiction of contrasts not existent in reality. Must one be surprised for one moment that the working class . . . develops an even greater desire to strike it rich and to live it up like those luckier ones on the screen?" (Halter 1921, 13). Lange had earlier wondered why "laziness and labor-strike fever run rampant among those who have always made up the majority of the cinema audience?" (1920, 46). His question found an answer in the cultural practices themselves. They created their own images of destruction, albeit only imaginary ones.

The most compelling argument against the film drama — and, accordingly, the most useful tool in the fight for stricter censorship laws — focused on the conditions of mass reception. Many reformers realized that the frequently reported experience of a loss of reality had little to do with an unrealistic story or a stereotypical character. The darkness in the auditorium, which allowed spectators to fall into a dreamlike state, helped to blur the boundaries between subject and object, fiction and reality. In the film drama, Sellmann argued, identification reached pathological dimensions. "Sometimes the films contain such adventurous romances and such wild fantasies that the movie regulars begin to lose their calm, clear sense of reality and construct out of these elements a false and imaginary image of the world. . . . When they leave this movie-dream world, with its sensuous salon atmosphere, and return to their dull workshop and their factory hall, dissatisfaction and resentment invariably fill their souls" (1912, 27).

Analyzing these psychological mechanisms, Albert Hellwig identified the longing for strong identification figures as the psychological root of the trashy film. The attorney claimed that the emotional response to the film drama had its origins in the "real" world, where changing work conditions and urban life-styles made it increasingly difficult to maintain a position of critical detachment. According to Hellwig, this was particularly true for workers, women, and adolescents, all of whom were highly susceptible to outside influences. Consequently, the film drama had to be seen as a relative category, a process rather than a product. Its emotional impact was, above all, determined by the conditions of reception, the composition of the audience, and the accompanying advertising campaigns and newspaper reviews. Taking a position that departed radically from formal analyses of the genre, Hellwig concluded: "It is the bad taste of the audience that ultimately makes the trashy film" (1911, 33).

\* \* \*

In spite of their disagreements, Lange, Sellmann, and Hellwig agreed on one point: the cinema, as the personification of international capitalism and mass society, stood in the service of distinctly un-German forces and had to be fought with all means. Such was the scenario: the masses in the streets and cinemas were formless, spontaneous, and uncontrollable. The nation, on the other hand, stood firm, symbolizing order and discipline. Between the nation and the masses, it was argued, stood the cinema, the *agent provocateur* of class struggle. The ideologically overdetermined distinction between nation (*Volk*) and masses (*Masse*) provided an instrument with which to separate social groups according to class, race, and nationality. The specter of "the masses" legitimated these strategies of exclusion, projection, and, very often, bourgeois self-affirmation.

Committed to the project of national renewal, the reformers thus used the nation-masses opposition to implicate the cinema in the class struggle. Control of the cinema, no matter whether through legal or educational measures, meant control over the masses. As a result, the cinema became the battlefield where the nation encountered the internal and external enemy—the rising working class and other nations. The nation-masses opposition assumed greatest significance during the war years, when the cinema and its discourses were enlisted in the struggle of national survival. Reservations about the cinema during the prewar years had resulted in its characterization as "the rape of the nation's soul" (Troll 1919, 55), but the need for effective propaganda tools quickly gave rise to a new configuration, with World War I now referred to as "father of the German film" (Bub 1938, 120).[7] Respective changes in the reformist positions on the cinema must be seen in relation to their primary commitment to the nation; this is even evident in the way the reformers introduced religious concerns into the debates and made use of the terminology of anticapitalism.

With their attemtps to transform the cinema into a tool of German nationalism, the churches stood at the front line. Not only were a large number of reformers associated with Catholic organizations; the church also had a considerable interest in forms of sociability not entirely dissimilar to its own. From enraptured spectators, ushers spraying scented disinfectants, and screens glowing like relics to attributes like "temple of vision" or "holy halls of images," descriptions of the cinematic experience underscored the similarity to liturgical rituals. Initiatives for a Christian cinema were strongest during the prewar years and experienced a short revival in its aftermath. Jakob Overmans of the Jesuits spoke for many when he justified the close links between church and state and described their cooperation in the fight against the cinema as a first step toward change. "It is obvious that mass attendance of the cinema, where young and old live through all vices with feverish tension and glaring blatancy, paralyzes, indeed destroys those precious energies that are urgently needed for the reconstruction of Germany" (1920, 3).

Concentrating their efforts on questions of morality, Lutheran reformers were especially active in developing stricter moral guidelines for the cinema. Taking the Ten Commandments as his point of reference, pastor Walther Conradt, in *Kirche und Kinematograph* (1910, Church and cinematography) randomly selected 250 films (predominantly of French origin) and found 97 murders, 51 adulteries, 19 seductions, 22 kidnappings, 45 suicides, 176 robberies, 25 prostitutes, 35 drunkards, and so forth. Fortunately, the German nation had not yet surrendered to these alien influences — a fact that, according to Conradt, only proved its moral superiority. "But with every meter of film projecting murder and adultery and theft and deception on the silver screen, with every new drop of poison injected into our nation's body, my hope grows: it has to get really bad in order to become good" (1910, 72). The wounds of the nation's body needed to be cauterized, and all alien elements eradicated; then the antidote of a cinema based on Christian principles could be injected with greatest success.

Going even further in their concern with national identity, some reformers blamed capitalism for the decline of German culture. With its "unGerman" emphasis on external appearance and its crude mixture of art and profit, the cinema supposedly promoted a kind of international materialism and destroyed all indigenous traditions in the process. As early as 1912, Lange complained about the popularity of foreign films. "The German nation permits such [foreign] elements to determine her aesthetic needs. From them, she receives her culture" (Gaupp and Lange 1912, 32). In 1915 his complaint was taken up by Häfker, who, in *Der Kino und die Gebildeten*, praised the war as the great purifier that had finally put an end to this foreign invasion. The time had arrived for the cinema reformers to rid the nation of these parasitic, destructive influences once and for all. As Häfker admitted openly: "The real damages that we fight in the case of cinematography are actually not of a cinematographic nature. Instead, they have to do with ideological aberrations and the crisis of the will: results of the deep 'corruption' of our times that only found a very favorable breeding ground in cinematography, from then on spreading like the plague" (1915, 27). Statements like these sometimes contained visions of racial superiority, as was the case in Willy Finger's definition of a future nationalistic cinema: "As we free our people from the bondage of low instincts, we show them the way to the resurrection of the German race. This, after all, is the wish of all good Germans, who reverently make their pilgrimage to the Holy Grail of pure humanity" (1918, 44).

Rabid anticapitalist polemics against the cinema, and against profit-hungry film producers in particular, often accompanied the fight for stricter censorship laws and in some cases the call for a nationalization of the film industry. Given the reformers' political orientation, however, the discussion of cinema and capitalism produced little more than nostalgic longings for a preindustrial society. Since the capitalist system was more often than not associated with other nations, its rejection gave rise to nationalist dreams of expansion and empowerment, and inspired a critique of capitalism that was antifeudal rather than anticapitalist. According to Karl Brunner, foreign film companies, "who are very interested in our decline" (1913, 5), were largely responsible for the cancerous growth of the most sickening cultural phenomena. Films with "a touch of French *esprit,* English humor, American brutality and — German soul" (Brunner 1913, 10) contaminated the innocent spectator with alien ideas. Materialism slowly invaded all areas of German culture, destroying everything meaningful with its hyperbole, superficiality, and inherent barbarism; hence Brunner's warning: "We must not forget, cinematography works in the service of big capital" (1913, 12). In a similar vein, Häfker called for the nationalization of the film industry and the centralization of national film censorship. He obviously knew the enemy. "It is the unbridled private interest of big capitalist corporations that, like a parasite, weighs heavily on our culture" (1915, 71).

Many reformers dreamed of a cinema that would put an end both to the excesses of capitalist film production and the aggressive demands of the rising working class. Theirs was a national film culture committed simultaneously to the ideas of nationalism, anticapitalism, and imperialism. While attitudes varied considerably concerning the film drama and the reasons for its popular appeal, all reformers wanted to use the new medium for educating the masses and strengthening the nation.

# Chapter 3

Theorizing the Cinema, the Masses, and the Nation

**A**community for little more than two hours, a coincidental gathering of strangers, a hotbed of social dissent, a convenient setting for erotic transgressions—the cinema audience of the prewar years was associated with a variety of states. For the middleclass intruder, their otherness evoked images of blissful regression, as well as the specter of class struggle. Descriptions of "the masses" were filled with references to social chaos and destruction, and often contained shocking images of moral and cultural decline. Behind the middle-class fear of social delimitation stood a powerful longing to cast off the fetters of bourgeois individualism, to become one with the crowd and partake in its illicit pleasures. No matter which elements dominated, "the masses" provided the magic concept through which the cinematic experience could be captured and contained. Revealing very little about German society at the time, the masses as a discursive category made it possible to substitute emotionally charged statements for a precise analysis of class, and to designate the cinema as that place where the scenarios of fear and dissent could be acted out. With social conflicts reduced to psychological effects, even the distinctions of gender and class disappeared in the unifying realm of "the masses." As a term without boundaries, "the masses" provided the discursive space into which these distinctions could be inscribed anew—but as rhetorical figures rather than social categories; hence the peculiar mixture of detailed observation and free association that characterizes many of the early reports from the movie theater. These imaginary configurations proved much more influential than the fact that the audience actually lacked the uniformity and the collective strength of masses in the historical sense (e.g., as the revolutionary masses, the working class, the urban crowd).

While the fascination with mass reception was strongest among artists and intellectuals, even a stalwart Social Democrat like Franz Förster was capable of noting that, in the cinema, "the psyche of the masses expresses itself through pure mass rhythm" (1914, 486). Whether in the context of reformist articles on media education or leftist analyses of working-class culture, the cinema and its audience were almost always characterized as the personification of negative forces in the society. What is even more, spectatorship continued to be described in these undifferentiated terms after the first systematic audience studies by Emilie Altenloh, Franz Schönhuber, and others were published. Even the more scientific studies on the cinema and the masses moved in these grey zones of fear and fascination, and the discursive function of "the masses" can be analyzed in a variety of contexts: in the first sociological studies, in the association of the cinema and the feminine, in the work of conservative and leftist critics, and in the often highly suggestive descriptions of film audiences by writers like Alfred Döblin and Carlo Mierendorff.

In theorizing the masses, authors relied heavily on an eclectic mixture of philosophical, psychological, and political concepts. Their preoccupation with the collective experience originated in ideas formulated most poignantly by Friedrich Nietzsche, who lamented the disappearance of the individual and predicted the emergence of a new barbarism. Literary critics saw his worst predictions confirmed in the willingness with which the masses surrendered to the phantasmagoria of the cinema. Their cultural pessimism sprang from the same feeling of doom that gave rise to Oswald Spengler's monumental essay, *Der Untergang des Abendlandes* (1918; *The Decline of the West*, 1918). Germany's fascination with the masses and mass phenomena also reveals the influence of Gustave LeBon's *Psychologie des foules* (1895; *The Crowd*, 1897). In his influential study, LeBon defined the modern age as one dominated by the masses. "We see, then, that the disappearance of the conscious personality, the predominance of the unconscious personality, the turning by means of suggestion and contagion of feelings and ideas in an identical direction, the tendency to immediately transform the suggested ideas into acts; these, we see, are the principal characteristics of the individual forming part of a crowd. He is no longer himself, but rather, has become an automaton who has ceased to be guided by his will" (1897, 12). Especially in the reformist debate on the cinema, LeBon's ideas found fertile ground, explaining spectatorship while also confirming anxieties about social change.

The fact that mass psychology played such a central role in the early discourses on cinema must be interpreted as a sign of their highly politicized nature. The invocation of the masses was both rhetorical and symptomatic; its function was both to confirm social differences and to lament their dissolution (Guttmann 1919, 7). Conservative and progressive writers took as their point of departure the conditions in society and projected them into the darkened auditorium, thus reproducing the real within the parameters of the cinematic experience. This process cannot be fully understood without that which was salvaged, namely the dream of a strong, united Germany. The theater producer Erich Oesterheld noted: "The masses are thought's natural enemy. They are satisfied with the surface of events, with the logical stringing together of images without mind and soul, just like superficial people are content with a person's external appearance instead of his whole personality. In other words, they are the born movie consumers and, like a stream, pull down the nation's better elements with them" (Kaes 1978, 99). With all critical distance gone and the distinctions between subject and object erased, many feared, more devastating consequences were inevitable. The most pressing concern, then, was to liberate the cinema from the sickly embrace of the masses and to claim it for that higher spirituality represented by the nation.

In contrast to mass psychology and its generalizations, the first sociological studies on audiences introduced an empirical perspective. Modern sociologists — Max Weber, Alfred Weber, Ferdinand Tönnies, Georg Simmel, and Werner Sombart come to mind — provided the critical categories for a more systematic approach and established the basis for an appreciative investigation of the cinema and its audience. A number of field studies began to gather data about the social composition, attendance pattern, and aesthetic preference of film audiences. The earliest of these studies was Emilie Altenloh's *Zur Soziologie des Kino* (1914, Sociology of cinema), written as a dissertation under the sociologist Alfred Weber; it was one of the first film dissertations, and the first written by a woman. The critical reception of her study in the trade journals was hurt by the fact that she sympathized with the reformers; in an earlier article in *Bild und Film*, for instance, Altenloh had explained the cinema's victory over the theater with the typical reformist oppositions of art and entertainment (Altenloh 1912–13). Not surprisingly, Emil Perlmann responded in *Der Kinematograph*: "While the tendency is not exactly pro-cinema, one must admit that the author used the available material without prejudice" (*Der Kinematograph*, 25 Mar. 1914).

*Zur Soziologie des Kino* combines empirical and theoretical interests and can be described as the first theory of spectatorship in the cinema. The author, who carried out her questionnaire in Mannheim, begins by placing the cinema within a historical context and challenging the widespread notion of the cinema as mere working-class entertainment. As evidenced by the trend toward higher admission prices, "the cinema has already stopped being exclusively the theater of the little man" (1914, 9). Speculating about the reasons for its growing popularity, Altenloh notes that "both the cinema and its audience are typical products of our time, which is characterized by constant activities and nervous agitation. Locked into their jobs during the daytime, people cannot even shake off this haste when they want to relax. Passing by a movie theater, they enter it to seek diversion and distraction for a short time, already worried about how to fill the next hours" (1914, 56). This description illustrates Altenloh's method perfectly. She moves beyond the external factors — the low ticket prices, the continuous admission — and places the cinema at the center of the experience of modernity. Nervousness, boredom, and an inexhaustible need for new stimuli are its main characteristics.

Taking the changes in cultural attitudes and modes of perception as her point of departure, Altenloh categorizes the various groups that make up the cinema audience. Based on categories that include sex, age, marital status, profession, religious denomination, and political affiliation, she describes the typical moviegoer as a young single male, a factory worker with little money but strong recreational needs. Rather than using her results to confirm the social divisions within society, Altenloh focuses on the inner disposition, an attitude toward life that is not limited to one particular class. Her research suggests that a growing number of film regulars can be found among those who do not fit easily into the traditional class structure. These include low-skilled workers, secretaries and salesgirls, the unemployed, social outcasts, artists and intellectuals — in short, all those whose lives have been deeply affected by the process of modernization. Unmarried couples attend the shows more frequently than married ones, she points out, and it is usually the woman who selects the films for an evening out with her boyfriend or husband. At the same time, young male employees visit the cinemas more regularly than their female colleagues, who often have family obligations. Adolescents are a noticeable presence in the theaters, so are mothers with small children. Conversely, men and women in more traditional professions, people with strong religious or political convictions, and those involved in community work or social movements show little interest in the cinema.

Women audiences receive special attention in Altenloh's study, as can be seen in graphic descriptions of the exhausted working-class woman, the ambitious shopgirl, the vain urban flapper, and the pampered bourgeois wife (Hansen 1983, 176–79; Petro 1989, 18–20; Schlüpmann 1990c, 238–42). In addressing gender issues, Altenloh distinguished herself from contemporaries who, more often than not, disapproved of the presence of women in the cinema. Yet even Altenloh was not entirely free of the prejudices of her time and class. This is particularly evident in the portrayal of working-class women, of whom she writes that "it is boredom rather than real interest that drives them to the cinema. While the men are at the election meetings, the women go to the neighborhood theater, and they pick up their men after the show" (1914, 78). These women, she continues, go to the cinema to compensate for what is denied to them in reality, and soon habit turns into addiction. Altenloh makes no distinction here between the boredom that comes from overstimulation and the kind of mental and physical exhaustion that seeks temporary release in apathy. According to her questionnaire, female employees, including the many women working in private households, suffer from a similar lack of motivation. In fact, the pervasive sense of boredom seems to increase with social status. Even upper-middle-class women use the cinema as a stimulating "fashion journal" that helps them make it through the day.

Altenloh's reading suggests a fundamental difference between men and women, as well as a specifically female disposition toward fantasy. "They [women] form a much more homogeneous group than the men, because their interests are limited to two areas: the theater and the cinema. . . . During the screening, they live in another world, in a world of luxury and consumption; they forget about the monotony of everyday life" (1914, 78). Factors like age, marital status, social standing, or even individual character traits were considered less important than the overwhelming need for diversion. Women, Altenloh suggests, are not only responsible for planning cultural activities, they also play an increasingly important role as the quintessential modern consumers. Through their buying decisions—and here she could have only middle-class women in mind—the filmic experience is extended into everyday life, be it through consumer articles, fashion and beauty products, or interior design. Women, for Altenloh, embody the progressive as well as regressive aspects of mass culture; thus she concludes:

"The female sex, which supposedly responds to every impression with pure emotions, must be considered especially receptive to cinematographic representation. On the other hand, highly intellectual people find it almost difficult to imagine themselves in the fragmented and often arbitrarily connected scenes" (1914, 91).

While Altenloh was certainly right in defining female spectatorship through the conditions that constitute female experience, her emphasis on sexual difference distracts from the social conditions that divide women. The more general remarks about women always mean bourgeois women, as is made evident by her discussion of consumption and leisure time. Their association not only excludes working-class women but also naturalizes the relationship between women and consumerism. Rather disappointing in this context is her disregard for women's intellectual abilities and the assumptions about their inherently passive, receptive nature.

Altenloh introduces the notion of scopophilia (*Schaulust*, the pleasure of looking) in order to account for these changes in cultural consumption and to shift her center of inquiry from the artistic product to the conditions of reception. The new term allows her to present the cinema as part of a long tradition of popular culture venues (e.g., fairground, panorama, magic show) that privilege visual over narrative considerations. At the same time, the notion of visual pleasure forges a link between the cinema and other ephemeral phenomena of urban life. Scopophilia, as Altenloh uses the term, describes a permanently shifting desire. Taking the place of direct contact, it attaches itself to parades, traffic accidents, shop windows, and popular festivals, and finds a center, a moment of rest, only in a state of diffusion. Here the cinemas, centrally located in the big cities and close to the new office buildings and department stores, offer relief from boredom and loneliness, as they facilitate a return to early childhood pleasures and quasi-archaic forms of communality. The individual disappears in the cinema's imaginary spaces and is transformed into the modern city dweller, the man (or woman) of the masses. Altenloh's analysis of visual pleasure shows how the cinema supported the process of industrialization, but from the side of recreation. With the stimulating sequence of fleeting images exercising audiences in the new modes of sensory perception, she can rightly conclude that "the cinema belongs above all to modern man, those who drift along and live according to the laws of the moment" (1914, 95).

Altenloh was not the only sociologist to carry out audience studies. Other reformers, too, revised their hostile attitude toward the cinema and began to study people's living and working conditions. Focusing on a relatively small group, Franz X. Schönhuber interviewed high school students from Leipzig and published his results in a pedagogical series under the title *Das Kinoproblem im Lichte von Schülerantworten* (1918, The cinema problem in light of student responses). Interested in the circumstances and frequency of movie attendance among high school students, he designed his questionnaire to shed light on the psychological impact of films on the nation's young. In his summary, Schönhuber mentions physiological side effects — the students repeatedly speak of sleepiness, inflamed eyes, and headaches — but his conclusions leave no doubt about their real interests, which include the longing for suspense, strong visual stimuli, and new experiences (Schönhuber 1918, 34–38).

Other writers, like Lydia Eger in her study on *Kinoreform und Gemeinden* (1920, Cinema reform and the communities), were particularly intrigued by the social composition of the audience. Instead of a homogeneous working-class audience, Eger found a very mixed group of skilled workers, lowly clerks, craftsmen, and bohemians, none of whom easily fit in the traditional class structure. She describes them as individuals "who live above the minimum of existence, but do not share the quest for knowledge prevalent among the more intellectual workers. Consequently, they see the weekly movie program as part of their *standard of living* [sic], and they attend every new Friday night show as casually as other groups in society attend the opening nights at the opera" (1920, 9).

\* \* \*

These sociological studies notwithstanding, the comments on cinema audiences relied heavily on mass-psychological categories, and often included comparisons to pathological phenomena. Many reformers were deeply worried about the degree to which the cinema exerted control over the public and private spheres. Three areas of concern stand out: the assault on the physical and moral health of the working class, the destruction of the family, and the hidden threat to the nation.

From the very beginning, the cinema had been blamed for its detrimental effect on the viewers' health, especially their eyes and nerves. Only a small number of reformers actually believed that films caused physiological problems such as blindness, pneumonia, madness, and venereal disease. The neurologist Robert Gaupp, however, had few doubts about the unhealthy side effects. "From the point of view of public health, nothing is left to us but to demand that the state remove the poison that undermines the health of our growing youth" (Gaupp and Lange 1912, 12). The majority of reformers focused primarily on unhealthy conditions in the auditorium, complaining about the foul air, the passive sitting, the flickering of the images, the unpleasant music, and, most of all, the dubious company. Whether these descriptions were accurate or not — the studies by Altenloh and Eger cast some doubt on these horror scenarios — the recurring appeals to issues of public health do draw attention to their rhetorical function. For these references functioned primarily as a metaphor for the state of the nation. Accordingly, the assumption of a physically weakened audience only served to underscore the destructive side of cinema and gave expression to the more frightening idea of a nation ailing in body and soul.

Noting similarities between cinema attendance and addictive behavior, many reformers turned to the repulsive details of social pathology. One initial "fix" of visual pleasure, Hermann Halter argued, was enough for the viewer to become addicted to this cunning tool of Satan. "In a few minutes — I emphasize, a few minutes — such 'scourge-bacteria images' can implant a deadly sting in a young man's innocent heart, paralyzing him for life, if not actually inducing decay and putrefaction" (1921, 31). Others compared the viewing experience to the intoxicating effect of cheap liquor. For Victor Noack, a movie regular was like an alcoholic. "The analogies between the movies [*Kientopp*] and the pub become evident in many ways. Films descended upon the nation — the *entire* nation! — like a spell. . . . Watching the obligatory film hit playing at his favorite 'pub,' a movie addict [*Kientoppschleicher*] falls into a mental stupor, very much like the alcoholic [*Destillenbruder*] receiving his desperately needed dose of ether" (Noack 1913, 8). Carrying these comparisons to their absurd conclusion, some reformers toyed with the idea of using the cinema as an accomplice in the fight against alcoholism. An inexpensive alternative to the ubiquitous pubs and beer halls, they argued, the theaters were not only more hygienic but also less harmful to their customers' emotional well-being. One critic raved: "Trashy films reduce the crime rate. Without them, the living conditions of the urban proletariat would be unbearable. What remains is liquor. Or the will to life will have to find criminal outlets" (Greve et al. 1976, 28). Grouped together with booze and petty crime, the cinema found itself in a select group of vices.

Given these associations, the cinema was perceived as a threat to the emotional and intellectual well-being of the nation's youth. It had already created a situation that forced the teacher Sellmann to ask polemically. "Are we producing a generation of movie-children who will be superficial, lazy, fussy, and too spoiled to work?" (1912, 4).[1] Precisely this horror-vision of a child surrendering to an illogical succession of images fueled the campaigns for a cinema guided by educational concerns. Children, according to Walther Conradt, a Lutheran pastor, responded intuitively to the cinema's cheap sensations, because they lacked critical detachment. Skeptical about the success of national education programs, many reformers reported gender-specific differences. Hellwig, who was actively involved with teachers' organizations in Hamburg, examined several genres under this aspect and found significant differences between the brutalizing effect of crime stories on boys and the eroticizing effect of sentimental love stories on girls (1911, 60). Lange proposed different rules of admission for boys and girls. Referring to the importance of population growth, he admonished. "One day, our boys must become strong and resilient men, and our girls healthy and fertile women" (1918, 18).

With children supposedly falling victim to the cinema's dubious offerings, the impact on families and communities was bound to be devastating. As Conradt noted: "The movie theater becomes the place where the inner soul makes its deep fall. This carries over to the outside, into real life, and causes many conflicts among male and female adolescents or among family members" (1910, 37, 39). The cinema was also held responsible for people's financial problems. Noack pointed out that some working-class parents spent their last pfennigs on its cheap diversions, and passed on their addiction to the children like a hereditary disease. "The expenses for the movies [*Kientopp*] have become a major item in the average lower- and middle-class budget, to the detriment of more basic needs. People have their favorite theater that changes its program twice a week, usually on Wednesdays and Saturdays. On those evenings the movie addict [*Kientoppschleicher*] is unable to stay at home. He has to see the new program, the new hits, must see them *immediately*. . . . Just as father and mother yearn for the 'spell of passion,' so do their children yearn for it as well" (1913, 9). Such waste of financial and human resources had to be stopped, Noack concluded, especially in light of what he envisioned as the devastating consequences for the national economy.

As was to be expected, the reformers' attitude toward women in the audience was one of moral indignation. They repeatedly offered descriptions of old whores and young mothers with their babies, or the "sixteen-year-old girl who, sitting next to her date in the darkness of a dubious movie theater, inhales the sensuous content of a pornographic film [and] is as good as ready for use" (Moreck 1926, 212). The presence of "unchaperoned" women in a predominantly male audience became an important topic in reformist writings. Their appearance in the public sphere represented such a challenge to traditional notions of femininity that conservatives like Noack felt compelled to declare. "One should prefer to see those mothers at home at the family table, among their children" (1913, 9). Their presence confirmed widespread anxieties about the changing social and economic status of women; the early women's movements and their fight for equal rights only reinforced such anxieties. The image of women seeing, rather than being seen, contributed to the impression that the cinema had a liberating effect on women.

Unlike Altenloh, however, most reformers were more concerned with rhetorical effects than sociological accuracy; their goal was to reverse the process of women's emancipation, not to explain it. The result was a conflation of the spectacle of women at the cinema and the spectacle of cinema. By associating the cinema with the feminine, the reformist authors responded to something real — the dramatic changes in the definition of gender roles — but used that reality to construct an idea, both of cinema and of women. The problem of female spectatorship was translated into various scenarios of seduction, and the experience of real women was suppressed in the process.

At times, the cinema was depicted as a cruel seductress who exercised her powers over a weak, emasculated audience. The aggressive assault on the senses inspired comparisons to castration. At other times, the audience was cast in the feminine role, either as the cinema's helpless victim or its unwilling accomplice. Here, spectators came to represent the nation that had fallen prey, been raped and sucked dry by a vampirelike creature, the cinema. As Max Prels noted. "Film fever has attacked thousands. . . . With the polyp-arms of its incalculable, long celluloid strips, it embraces the crowd, it takes its images from their imagination, it targets the people" (1922, 8).

The theorizing of the masses along the lines of gender was, of course, predicated upon women's exclusion from power. At the same time, these references to the feminine were not simply manifestations of a historical reality but rather the product of a long literary and iconographic tradition, in other words, a chimera in itself. A comparison between the writings of

Altenloh and, say, Conradt or Noack would show how woman as historical subject and the feminine as a discursive figure are by no means identical. Since the late nineteenth century, images of the feminine — in literature as well as in the visual arts — had been put into circulation to represent the liberating and threatening aspects of modern society. Examples include female allegorical representations of the steam engine or the revolutionary masses in nineteenth-century graphic art, the figure of the femme fatale in turn-of-the-century literature, and the many castrating females in Symbolist and *Jugendstil* painting. Discourses about the cinema and its audience continued this tradition, expressing the same ambivalences and using the same rhetorical strategies. As a representation superimposed on the conflicts in society, the cinema as feminine enabled the reformers to transform reality into the fictions of cinema. In representing excess and exaltation, sexuality actually worked in the service of repression, with the sexual imagery supporting reformist ideas about family planning and sex education. Like the specter of "the masses," who at any given moment could take control of the streets, these scenarios of unrestrained sexuality must be regarded as an ideological construct. The explicit language only provided the rhetorical means for justifying the exclusion of women from the public sphere.

✳ ✳ ✳

While film historians have frequently described the early cinema as an authentic proletarian public sphere, they have paid little attention to the similarities between leftist and conservative discourse on mass reception. In the early writings on cinema, critics from both sides of the political spectrum resorted to the same anticapitalist and nationalist slogans (Korte 1980, 60–64). Conveying an almost hysterical fear of social disintegration, many critics showed open contempt for the masses and their "primitive" forms of entertainment. Most conservative reformers would have sympathized with the socialist teacher from Hamburg who complained about the adversities of field research. "For months I have been wandering through all the movies [*Kientöppe*] known to me. . . . And for months I have watched how our cherished working-class youth sucks in the dramas playing on the screen, their faces glowing with expectation. For months, I say! Not even the strongest man can take that for long" (quoted by Kinter 1985, 110). Most political activists dismissed film-viewing as a purely emotional experience without any intellectual requirements; hence their unwillingness to treat film as an art form, hence their eagerness to test its propagandistic possibilities. Instead of exploring the power of narrative, both groups subordinated the question of cinema to the requirements of party politics. Only the political scenarios differed in which film was to assume its new functions. The discussion so far has focused on the national-conservative parties, many of whom were involved in reformist projects. But leftist groups, including the Social Democrats and the Communists, also perceived the cinema as an obstacle to class consciousness, and their rigid theoretical position prevented the development of more sophisticated approaches.

Until 1906, the socialist press published very few articles on cultural topics, because culture was considered a phenomenon of the superstructure, a reflection of economic conditions. This theoretical position, together with a rather traditional approach to cultural products, explains their initial contempt for the cinema and its audience. With the distinction between high and popular culture firmly in place, the main goal of socialist cultural politics was to develop a workers' education program based on humanistic ideals. As the socialist leader Wilhelm Liebknecht once noted. "The proletariat has been excluded from the temple of knowledge; now it must acquire this education through its own sheer effort" (quoted by Kinter 1985, 74). His statement more or less summarized the cultural politics of the Social Democratic party (SPD) during the Wilhelmine years. Their opposition to mass culture was part of a more extensive critique of decadent phenomena in literature and the arts that first exploded in a controversy over Naturalism at the 1896 Party Convention.

When the reformers claimed the cinema for a national educational program, most socialist critics still insisted on treating culture and politics as two autonomous spheres. New cultural practices, they argued, could only develop in a postrevolutionary age. The Muses, according to Franz Mehring, had to remain silent in the wake of imminent social change. "The less it seems likely that a new art will emerge from the proletarian class struggle, the more certain is it that the victory of the proletariat will bring about a worldwide transformation in support of the arts, toward an art form that will be better, greater, and more splendid than anything ever seen by human eyes" (1961, II:226). Mehring, whose writings on socialist culture had a great influence on later discussions on a revolutionary cinema, dismissed Naturalism as a sign of decadence, but he praised the classics, and the historical dramas of Friedrich Schiller in particular, as high points of German culture. At times, these aesthetic choices gave rise to rather bizarre controversies. When the Lessingtheater in Hamburg, named after the famous German dramatist Gotthold Lessing, opened its doors in 1913, for instance, the Social Democratic press reacted with outrage. Scandalized by the use of Lessing's name for such a dubious establishment, they demanded immediate action. "One should rap these guys' fingers until they lose all interest in desecrating our great classics" (quoted by Kinter 1985, 132).

The question of entertainment played a central role in early leftist writings on the cinema, for it brought to the fore the problematic relationship between the spheres of production and reproduction and the distinction between high culture and popular culture. Socialist critics were always willing to take into account the workers' lack of formal education when commenting on their recreational activities and their need for escapist diversions. Since the late nineteenth century, numerous organizations had been founded to accommodate the workers' need for cultural practices relevant to their working and living conditions. Working-class culture, in subsequent years, meant evening schools, soccer and bicycle clubs, and lay song and theater groups, to name only a few examples.[2] These forms of mass organization no longer relied on the notion of compensation but instead derived their significance from the recognition of class difference and the existence of two cultures. However, many critics continued to promote ideas that had been challenged by the cultural practices themselves; the reality of social change failed to bring forth a similar change in the critical paradigms.

Instead of questioning the usefulness of notions like mass manipulation or surrogate satisfaction, many Social Democratic teachers' organizations even joined the cinema reformers in their relentless fight against the trashy film. They, too, called for stricter censorship laws. "The youngsters get improperly excited; they are kept from educating their minds and souls and become overly receptive to quite indecent kinds of entertainment. That is not good for the mental and physical development of our youth; even in regard to the latter, the movies have long-lasting effects, especially on the eyes and the nerves" (quoted in Kinter 1985, 115). And like his conservative colleagues, a contributor to the Social Democrat party organ, *Vorwärts*, discovered connections between madness, crime, and cinema addiction. "The majority of films, like trashy novels, arouse unhealthy and dangerous sensations in adolescents, who have a rich fantasy life; indeed, some films give them detailed instructions for committing criminal acts" (quoted in Kinter 1985, 159).

Not surprisingly, many socialist critics believed that these problems could only be resolved through radical changes in the film industry itself; all other strategies had to be considered counterproductive (Heller 1984, 137–41; Diederichs 1986a, 86–87). In 1914, the Social Democratic weekly, *Die Neue Zeit,* published a series of articles that dealt with the influence of cinema on working-class audiences. Some contributors resorted to idealist categories in order to reject the cinema's artistic claims; others demanded that the working-class organizations come to terms with mass culture and start using films for educational purposes. The majority of critics simply refused to address the question of entertainment, and postponed the consideration of alternatives to a distant future. As Samuel Drucker noted. "Only the transformation of the conditions of production can seize the evil of the trashy film by its roots, because it destroys its basis. Offering the proletarian a spiritual center in socialism, we hope to separate him from the trashy film. It robs the dispossessed of their last pfennigs at a time when the proletarian movement has not yet become broad and strong enough as a social force" (1914, 868; cf. Murray 1990, 16–18). Young proletarians were advised to stay away from the cinema and join the party's cultural organizations. Political activism, it was believed, provided sufficient protection against the temptations of the cinema. It is arguments like these — found even in later debates about a proletarian cinema — that put into question the notion of early cinema as a proletarian public sphere, as they dismantle the alleged proletarian identity of the audience from the perspective of class consciousness.[3]

\* \* \*

The representatives of the literary sphere shared many viewpoints with the cinema reformers and the socialist critics when it came to describing audiences (Güttinger 1984b, 9–22). In their "reports from the movies," a mixture of amusing observations, personal confessions, and thoughtful comments, they played with various styles including hyperbole and irony. Yet behind their literary ambitions lurked a deep-seated fear of the masses that was just as revealing as the reformist polemics against trash and smut. Often, the texts read as if their authors had entered, at danger to their health, a terra incognita, like an anthropologist entering the jungles of Africa to study its primitive tribes. In the service of truth, these cultural explorers deliberately visited the most disreputable places in order to study the new primitives, the inhabitants of the modern metropolis. While their descriptions wavered between open voyeurism and a regressive longing for community, their discourse remained firmly within a system of oppositions that prevented any actual encounters, either in the physical or the discursive sense.

As the site of real and imagined scenes of transgression, the cinema was thus transformed into a microcosmic aspect of society — a new democratic art or a new barbarism, depending on the author's political convictions. In describing these processes reformers and writers often resorted to the same imagery. Both groups formulated the question of mass reception in relation to the working class, thereby acknowledging its political significance. The sudden interest in social issues seemed rather unusual for writers whose primary concerns had, so far, been to protect the rights of the creative individual. In fact, some gave the impression that their own "primitive" needs, rather than a sense of social responsibility, had lured them into the movie theaters. As the essayist Frank Thiess explained: "Film exists only for the masses, and the emotions stirred by it are mass emotions. That is why individuals of higher intellectual and artistic standing only go to the movies when they want to feel part of a collective and be one with the masses" (1925, 118). Where the reformers wanted to educate and where the leftist activists wanted to agitate, the writers either tried to redefine the function of literature vis-à-vis the new mass media or they withdrew into the ivory tower of *l'art pour l'art*.

The majority of literary critics accepted what they perceived as cinema's sensationalist, escapist nature. With little to no interest in educating the nation through films, they looked for another way of analyzing the cinema's sociopsychological function while denying its social origins. The position taken by the dramatist and screenwriter Berthold Viertel was fairly typical in this regard, and it demonstrates to what degree even a position in favor of the masses could hide fear of their actual power. A firm believer in the cinema's future, Viertel argued: "Even if the cinema produced and increased antisocial instincts in a few isolated cases, it does have a clear social hygienic function: it confines such drives to the imagination, and neutralizes emotional tensions which, otherwise, would have disturbing and destructive effects" (Kaes 1978, 70).[4] By defining the cathartic function in terms of social hygiene, Viertel fails to see escapist entertainment as a function of specific conditions; instead he uses the present practices to reintroduce the old distinctions between art and entertainment. A more hidden elitism returns when Viertel declares that "to rob people of the amusing but vulgar cinema and to want to force dry edification upon them is pedagogical insanity and evidence of an underdeveloped sense of reality" (Kaes 1978, 71). His typical conclusion implies that art should remain the privilege of a chosen few. Obviously, the new-old class system of cultural practices, even when proposed in the name of tolerance or pragmatism, continued to justify the continuous exclusion of the lower classes from what was considered worthwhile by the representatives of bourgeois culture. The defense of cinema's vulgarity, then, indirectly confirmed the superiority of literature and the other arts.

Alfred Döblin's famous short essay "Das Theater der kleinen Leute" (1909, The theater of the little man) illustrates to what degree the cinema intensified the problem of class difference (Döblin 1910).[5] It does so by imitating the cinema's shifting perspectives, its emphasis on montage, and its privileging of the visual sense. The writer-physician turns the audience into a mirror through which he, the bourgeois outsider, can protect himself from the dangers of mass reception while at the same time surrendering to its thrills. "The little man, the little woman, know of no literature, no development, no direction," Döblin states emphatically, and explains: "In the evenings, they stroll through the streets, stop for a chat under the railroad bridges, watch a fallen horse. They want to be touched, titillated, shocked, and then burst out into laughter. The strongest fares are available to them. These are torture chambers, sea animals, perhaps even participation in revolutions" (Kaes 1978, 37). Through the confrontation of "they" and "I," the educated intruder confirms his own existence, and that of bourgeois culture as well.

At the same time, Döblin pokes fun at the cultural snobbery of the educated middle class and the unrealistic proposals for cinema reform. His mocking style enables him to move back and forth between these two positions and inspires the following thoughts on cinema and alcoholism: "The movies [*Kientopp*] are an excellent weapon against alcoholism, the sharpest competition for the pubs [*Sechserdestillen*]. Just wait and see whether or not the cases of liver cirrhosis and of children born with epilepsy will decline over the next ten years. One shouldn't deprive the people and the young of trashy literature and movies. They need this very bloody diet more than the indigestible gruel of folk literature and the watery brews of morality. But the better-educated will leave the premises, most of all happy that the movies are silent" (Kaes 1978, 38).

More than a decade after Döblin's polemical essay, the writer and political activist Carlo Mierendorff conjured up very similar images of mass reception (Wolfradt 1920–21). In the manifesto "Hätte ich das Kino!" (1920, If I had the cinema!), Mierendorff nearly elevates the cinema to a means of survival for the nameless urban masses, "those with a vocabulary of sixty words" (Güttinger 1984a, 385), those who have found new hope in this "jargon of the world." Under the motto "Ten thousand films against capitalism," he focuses on what most writers addressed only in passing, and what most reformers fought with almost hysterical calls for state control: the cinema as a political force in its own right. The cinema for Mierendorff represented the only place left where the masses encountered themselves. It allowed them to be part of a classless audience, and thus to experience the conditions under which a new society could emerge. An understanding of this powerful dynamic and the underlying utopian potential was a prerequisite of all future political activism; hence his conclusion. "We must try to reach the masses, if all attempts of changing reality are not doomed to fail. We must have the cinema" (Güttinger 1984a, 386).

Written in a transitional period, "Hätte ich das Kino!" combines the exclamatory style of Expressionism with the self-justified wrath of those unmasking bourgeois hypocrisy. By violating the taboo and naming the unnameable, Mierendorff's act of literary transgression allows for the unintentional representation of his anxieties (Heller 1984, 119–36). With him as a guide, the reader enters a nightmarish world of bad smells, crowded bodies, and unrestrained eroticism. "The film plays. Now he grabs the woman up there. Down there every woman feels grabbed, grabs every man. Fever rises, sighs. An umbrella falls. Someone bends over and reaches under skirts. Flesh dances close to flesh. Darkly the room dances on our necks. Through the thick air projectiles clatter, greenish: room, edge of the wood, gentlemen. Who can still escape? The white light flares up. Blackness scurries. . . . Body odors impregnate the senses. Many already lean forward, wavering in their sleep. Head resting on meager chest. Embraces. Whispers. Applause. Hello. Protest. Staring. Dirty jokes. Smirking. Lights flare up, the spell is broken; relieved, silent, redeemed, they look around: construction workers, mailmen, top hats, sailors, stokers, receptionists, head scarves, soldiers, miners, prostitutes, coaches, dandies, apprentices, waitresses, tailors, sergeants, straw hats, gentlemen in cut, balloon caps, poets, husbands, intellectuals. It already seems that man has to go to the cinema in order to exist" (Güttinger 1984a, 386–7).

Mierendorff's closing image of people from all classes and all nations streaming to the silver screen recalls images of pilgrimage, and of salvation. "People arrive from machine halls and department stores, out of cellars and tenement houses, from country houses, east of the big cities, out of subways, trams, out of foundries, factories, offices. An endless trail into the cinemas of the big cities and provincial towns" (Güttinger 1984a, 396). These images of salvation are juxtaposed with scenes of a primitive, archaic quality, suggesting an almost animistic view of cinema. Here Mierendorff speaks of life-giving and life-taking qualities ("It is here that [the social outcast] receives life"), the hypnotic powers of the screen ("a squarish shimmering eye performing magic"), the devouring power of the lobbies ("with their greedy jaws wide open"), and the almost vampirelike existence ("They [the cinemas] live for everybody, they live from everybody") (Güttinger 1984a, 386).

Yet behind the ecstatic vision of a new world community created through film, the same fear of the masses surfaces again. Behind the intended shock effect, the same biases emerge that the author set out to unmask in others. Obsessively, Mierendorff seeks the terrifying sight of an audience under the influence, but only in order to exorcize it in the name of a classless society based on class prejudice. Leaving its meaning open to speculation, his account concludes with a provocative statement: "He who has the cinema will rule the world" (Güttinger 1984a, 396).

# Chapter 4
## The Literary Debates on the Cinema

For many writers and literary critics in Wilhelmine Germany, writing about the cinema took the form of a very personal undertaking. It was involved, biased, often highly subjective, and had all the characteristics of public debate. Writing about the cinema provided a way of confronting the artistic challenges of the new medium, but it also forced the writers to address questions about their own social responsibilities, about the relationship between literature and the other arts, and about the future of mass culture and its standardized products.[1]

In contrast to the cinema reformers, the guardians of high culture — as they preferred to see themselves — cultivated this personal perspective, for they saw the expression of strong opinions as their privilege and obligation. Contemporaneous with similar developments in the trade press and the reform movement, the first literary articles on the cinema appeared in literary journals around 1907. The debates were most lively between 1909 and 1912, assumed a more subdued tone after the outbreak of World War I, and continued throughout the twenties, albeit with less intensity (Lichtwitz 1986; Heller 1982b).

Three areas of concern can be identified: the cinema's artistic ambitions, its industrial mode of production, and the specific conditions of mass reception. While the controversies often revolved around categories like "eternal truth," "human values," or "good taste," they invariably led back to those aspects of cinema that most personally challenged the writers as autonomous subjects, in their definitions of the creative process, and in their belief in the redeeming qualities of literature.[2] For the most part, however, the writers had little interest in producing a coherent body of texts, even less a theory of cinema. They participated in the controversy for a limited time, an impassioned outburst, a sudden flash of inspiration.

Most contributions remained essayistic: short, fragmentary, spontaneous — an expression also of the modernity of the subject matter.

Some writers were carried away with enthusiasm; others felt the need to be both aggressive and defensive. The degree to which feelings of ambivalence prevailed can be seen in the apologetic tone with which many commented on their involvement, as if fearing the consequences of their own insights. Disclaimers, references to moral duty, and the retreat to a position of ironic detachment were obviously considered necessary in order not to succumb to, or be devoured by, the subject of inquiry. For this reason, the literary debate on the cinema also bears witness to a concerted effort by the representatives of bourgeois culture to come to terms with that which represented the embodiment of Otherness, the cinema. Their writings mark a crucial moment in the history of modern mass culture, but do so with little awareness of the wider implications of this controversy. Precisely this lack of purpose, which must not be confused with their obvious ability to formulate more immediate aims, sheds light on the very process of discourse formation. Vacillating between journalistic and literary traditions, between calls for action and the celebration of pure expression, the texts are as much the product of conflicting positions within literature as they represent the attempt to define the cinema within the paradigms of literature.

Following a short analysis of the literary representation of cinema, this chapter will discuss these literary writings and analyze their contribution to the changes in the public sphere and in the definitions of culture. Special attention will be paid to the intersection of cinema and Expressionist literature. Poetological concerns, including comparisons to literature and the theater, will be presented as an attempt to understand the cinema's difference, and the return to other traditions like folklore or pantomime will be related to the urgent need for new cultural practices and new critical concepts.

The significance of the literary debate on the cinema can be measured by the critical gestures with which the contributors defined their positions, as well as by the emotional atmosphere in which the discussions took place. For it is, above all, in exaggerated rhetoric that their analytical function becomes evident — that is, to provide the writers with a critical framework and a discursive object for coming to terms with modernity. Stylistically, the texts cover a broad range from sober reportage to subjectivist stream-of-consciousness, often combining fictitious and factual elements to the point of indistinguishability. In many the writer has tried to duplicate the mixture of forms and styles, and the alternating viewpoints and shifting distances, found in the cinema. In a way, writing becomes the unclaimed territory where the language of the Other can be spoken, where literary culture can be salvaged. Using cinema as a marker of difference also explains why the "low" quality of the films posed a smaller problem than one would expect from individuals known for their discriminating taste. Speculating about the new medium's future was clearly more important than coming to terms with its present limitations.

Thus films are rarely mentioned. The opposite holds true for audiences. The indifference to aesthetic questions, which might be interpreted as resistance to the claims of a new art form, is more than compensated for by an almost exaggerated attention to the conditions of reception. The act of "going to the movies" — in other words, the cinema-as-event — inspired hymnal praises, amusing vignettes, voyeuristic confessions, and gruesome incantations of a coming Armageddon. Accounts of these excursions into foreign territory were often relegated to the privacy of a diary or personal letter. When made available to the public, the descriptions tended to be less than accurate. Impressions, often presented in a sensationalist style, took the place of observation, and social analysis gave way to polemics.

These documents of cultural encounters are meaningful primarily in relation to what remains the primary reference point even in its absence: literature. To be sure, literature in this constellation is a field of contention itself. A writer's attitude toward the cinema often crossed the lines of party politics and literary movements. The Expressionists counted among them "film enemies" (Franz Pfemfert, Carl Einstein) as well as "film friends" (Kurt Pinthus, Yvan Goll, Else Lasker-Schüler); those who were highly critical of the cinema included socialists as well as conservatives. Even the film-drama controversy, which focused on formal concerns, failed to unite the representatives of high culture. The fear of marginalization influenced their work just as much as the desire to utilize film for literature. By studying what was most removed from the literary sphere, the writers hoped to gain new insights into mass culture and, in so doing, to redefine the role of literature in these changing configurations. And by writing about what seemed so very different from the reading experience, they tried to grasp the dynamics of modern pleasures and desires. The confrontation with the cinema's audience — and, of course, with their own reactions — therefore gave rise to the proliferating fictions of cinema, and the following examples will show some of the recurring motifs.

In 1908, Peter Altenberg, one of Vienna's promising young authors, exclaimed, "I herewith excommunicate everyone who, with 'the best of intentions' or because of commercial interests, opposes the cinema at this very time" (Güttinger 1984a, 63). In the same year, Karl Kraus used his satirical skills to make a very different statement: "A world willing to accept its end if it were not denied a cinematographic representation thereof cannot be afraid of the Unknowable" (*Die Fackel* 1908:261–62; cf. Lensing 1982). It was against the backdrop of such contemptuous, hostile attitudes that the panegyrics of cinema must be read. Under the Latin motto "Nulla dies sine Kinema!" Karl Bleibtreu confessed: "I thank my Creator that I was there to experience the cinema" (Güttinger 1984a, 277). The Swiss poet Carl Spitteler publicized his conversion to the cinema with similar enthusiasm: "There are, after all, values other than literary ones: those worth living for, those worth following. Victory of good over evil, generous forgiveness, moist eyes that sparkle with gratitude and love: desperately searching for the same in real life. No, the movies are not immoral; on the contrary: they are ultra-moralistic, pedantically moralistic" (Güttinger 1984a, 338).

Female poets, who were usually found among the "art-minded *Kintopisten*" (Lapp 1912, 356), to quote a detractor, regarded the cinema as their spiritual home. Else Lasker-Schüler wrote: "If my heart were healthy, I would first jump out of the window; then I would go to the movies and never come out again" (1912–13, 18). Similarly, Claire Goll wrote in 1922: "In the movies / On five continents simultaneously / Is my homeland" (1973, 13). In the short-lived genre of "cinema poetry," old-fashioned dithyrambic verse existed side by side with the most daring lyrical experiments; the disrupted syntax, nominal style, and exclamatory fervor of Expressionist poetry proved most convincing in simulating the experience of cinema.[3]

Poets often showed a greater interest than novelists or dramatists, whose work was directly threatened by the new competitor. Challenging literary as well as filmic conventions, Yvan Goll greeted the dream world of cinema with effusive words: "Here, at the movies, you are beyond the earth. The good and bad of life are, after all, only reflections—just like the screen's black and white. Nothing is. Everything is!" (1917, 688). At the same time, an unknown writer by the name of Fritz Müller resorted to the most conventional rhyme schemata in order to sketch a brighter, reformist future for the cinema. Following scenes from the bleak present—"Before the screen sits and stares / Day for day the somber mass / And they bring to the movies / All the longing of their class"—the last stanza culminates in a desperate plea to film scenarists and directors: "Please, help the people at the movies / And, above all, try to put / Soul into your work — / Then the movies will be good" (1912–13, 13). Other writers retold the most lurid film plots in verse form, implying a natural affinity between lyric poetry and film. A telling commentary on the cinema's addictive nature, many poems ended with the fearfully anticipated moment when the show was over. The sudden confrontation with the outside world was, at least in these early years, often associated with feelings of guilt: "Then, at night, in the leach of tears / One lies down flicker-tired / With eyes inflamed / And curses the movies" (quoted by Güttinger, 1984b, 28).

Taking a more systematic approach, several newspapers used the questionnaire form to document the attitudes prevalent among members of the cultural establishment. In 1912, the liberal *Frankfurter Zeitung* published the survey "About the Merits and Demerits of the Movies." Among the respondents, confidence in the cinema's quick demise prevailed, though the possibility of more far-reaching effects could not be excluded. In a manner that was fairly typical, the politician and *homme des lettres* Walter Rathenau dismissed the cinema as a mere fad bound to end up in Africa, for "art has nothing to do with pleasure" (Kaes 1978, 66).[4]

Illustrating his argument with examples from sensationalist films, Alfons Paquet called upon physicians and psychiatrists to spearhead the fight for stricter censorship laws. There were, of course, other voices. Wilhelm Schäfer, the author of popular novels and plays, drew attention to the "cinema instinct" (*Kinoinstinkt*), which he defined as a kind of modern disposition that brought everything, from the *Gesamtkunstwerk* to trashy literature, under its equalizing influence. Many intellectuals, Schäfer argued, were so preoccupied with eternal values, yet so indifferent to, and contemptuous of, popular culture, that they failed to grasp its enormous significance. Since the people's need for distraction could only increase in the face of such elitist attitudes, Germany's intellectual elite was partly to blame for the cinema's crudeness and sensationalism. Thus Schäfer concluded: "Our culture relies so little on eyes, ears, and emotions that the most inane barbarism triumphs at the first opportunity" (Kaes 1978, 69).

A year later, in 1913, a similar questionnaire was carried out by the trade paper of the publishing industry, the *Börsenblatt des deutschen Buchhandels*. Here the positions wavered between open resistance and fatalistic surrender to the "complete chaos of cinematography's present existence" (Kaes 1978, 92), to quote the publisher Paul Cassirer. The majority of re-

spondents argued in favor of a sharper distinction between film and literature, thereby opting for the most convenient method of denial and exclusion. In their view, the cinema stood at the forefront of a wave of illiteracy
that had befallen modern civilization, and that demanded to be stopped.
Confronted with the growing popularity of literary adaptations, the writer
Michael Georg Conrad, representing the book world, declared with horror: "Silent movie-scopophilia, applied to narrative events, has something
stupefying about it. A real movie-gaper is lost to the book!" (Kaes 1978, 91).
Such dismissive statements did not merely express elitist tastes or preferences. Above all, the strong rhetoric was a defensive reaction to the economic competition between the film and publishing industries, which was
bound to increase as the cinema developed bourgeois ambitions.

\* \* \*

For many, the cinema conjured up visions of decline that were captured by
the Expressionist critic Franz Pfemfert in a rather grim picture: "The torch-
carriers of culture rush to the top. But, down there, the people listen to the
clicking of the cinematograph" (Kaes 1978, 62). But the much-discussed
crisis of literature actually predated the cinema, and had much more to do
with the dramatic changes in book publishing and the literary profession
since the late nineteenth century (Berman 1983). The commercialization of
book culture—through trashy novels, newspaper serials, and the illustrated press—had radically changed the symbolic function of the book,
turning it from a prized possession into an object of daily use. Reading as a
cultural activity was no longer associated with social privilege but took
various forms, including that of reading for instant gratification. Faced
with the transformation of book publishing into a mass market, the writers
experienced a loss of social and economic status; this explains their often
vitriolic attacks on the film industry. Rather than confronting the situation,
many contented themselves with slandering the new profession of scenario
writing. They complained about the fact that filmmaking, at least in their
view, required neither skill nor talent. The avid moviegoer Max Brod translated his frustration into an imaginary film scene about "a poet in a lonely
chamber, who is getting desperately angry about the difficulties of intensive
but reserved modes of representation" (Kaes 1978, 41). The prospect of
becoming mere suppliers for the culture industry seemed especially terrifying for German writers, since they worked in a society that had always
celebrated literature as the center of cultural identity.

Apart from being blamed for problems in the literary profession, the cinema was held responsible for the decline of the traditional reading public. Alfred Polgar's ironic advice, "I tell you, go to the movies if you want to know what paralysis means!" (1917, 401), or Ulrich Rauscher's laconic statement "The movies use the total passivity [of the spectator], and are therefore invincible" (Güttinger 1984a, 138) summed up the two attitudes available to the cultural pessimist: open contempt and fatalistic surrender. Both critics would have argued as follows: While literature requires active involvement, the cinema invited passivity. While literature challenges everyday perceptions, the cinema exploits them without shame. While literature demands a certain distance from everyday life, the cinema embraces the ephemeral as its foremost principle of organization. The relationship between film and literature was, in fact, much more complex, since the articles on cinema were also written for people who were equally interested in new literary works and the latest film releases. Writing about cinema recruited film audiences among members of the middle class as well as new readers among those who already went to the cinema on a regular basis. This reciprocal relationship was rarely acknowledged in the eulogies to the traditional reader of literature; it would have drawn attention to the material conditions under which these comments were made.

Especially during the prewar years, the debate on the cinema was closely associated with the Expressionist movement (Vietta and Kamper 1983, 123–32; Vietta 1975; Zmegac 1970). It was this highly visible group of critics, essayists, poets, and dramatists who made the most engaged and engaging contributions to the debates and often used them to elaborate on poetological problems. Phenomenological, vitalist, and cultural-pessimist ideas spawned important impulses and showed the direction for further investigations; Nietzsche's critique of modernity was an omnipresent point of reference. The Expressionists found in the cinema many of the features that, for them, also characterized literary modernity. The new medium already seemed to practice, in its fleeting images, what the writers tried to introduce into literature as a radically different poetic. Expressionist literature as well as the so-called Expressionist film (a term whose shortcomings will be discussed later) dealt extensively with the instability of personal and social identities. They often painted a somber, fatalistic atmosphere and exhibited a pronounced tendency toward stylization; recurring themes included the big city, social unrest, family strife, madness, and crime. Jacob van Hoddis and Alfred Lichtenstein explored the possibilities of montage and other filmic techniques in their lyric poetry, creating a style alternately referred to as "three-second style," "telegram style," or "cinema style" (*Kinostil*). Its main characteristics include seemingly objective, cameralike perspectives, paratactic constructions and sentence fragments, the free play of associations and discontinuities, and a strong emphasis on looking and synaesthetic perception.

The term *Kinoismus,* later coined by Georg Kaiser as an alternative to Expressionism, reformulated this intense involvement with the cinema as an aesthetic and sensory experience. In the Expressionist drama, references to film were used to produce a distancing effect and to comment on the crisis of subjectivity and representation; this is made evident by Ernst Toller's *Die Wandlung* (1919, The transformation) and Yvan Goll's *Methusalem* (1922). In Expressionist prose, the camera often served as a choice metaphor for alienation; at other times, it became a vehicle for explicit social criticism. Introducing a collection of essays with a text titled "Prologue at the Movies," René Schickele thus compared his narrator to a cameraman who "merely" records the events unfolding before him: "Casually, I lean on the apparatus, / The digit finger on the light crank" (1913, 11). And Carl Einstein's *Bebuquin* (1912) presented the first film star in a novel, the affected Fredegonde Perlenblick, whose chauffeur roams the rainy streets with a flashing "Kintopp" [sic] sign on the roof, "a racing cinema" (1980, 1:90).

For the most part, however, the cinema's influence on Expressionist literature and drama was less significant than is commonly assumed. At best, the cinema offered a poetological model based on the more fleeting relationships of looking; at worst, it served as a fashionable device. There was little engagement with its technical aspects because of the Expressionists' almost exclusive concern with the crisis of the individual. More often than not, they simply adjusted the cinema to their own visions of modernity, rather than using it as the model of a new literary paradigm. The encounter of Expressionism and cinema produced, above all, a literary interpretation of cinema. Such judgments do not in the least diminish its significance. Representations of cinema, including its misrepresentations, are just as much a material force as the films themselves. In this case, the inconsistencies confirm to what degree the relationship to the cinema was founded on, and sustained by, ambivalence. Vacillating between a self-satisfied individualism and violent antibourgeois polemics, between a nostalgic longing for the past and the uncritical celebration of everything new, the Expressionists used writing to take conceptual possession of the cinema and to reproduce its qualities within the confines of, and according to, the laws of literature. As a discursive and fictional construct, the cinema was now in a position to accommodate conflicting desires. Those yearning for a world community "discovered" a place from where a new kind of mass sociability could arise. Those who feared social unrest "found" sufficient proof of the innate barbarism of mass culture. Yet both groups, the "film friends" and the "film enemies," always returned to what they feared most: the decline of literary culture and their marginalization in the bourgeois public sphere.

While the Expressionists may have been the most verbal participants, other voices could be heard as well. Yvan Goll, for instance, introduced the viewpoint of those members of the literary avant-garde with a more international orientation, including Dada, Surrealism, and Futurism. Among the writers of the prewar generation, Goll was one of the few who praised the cinema for its liberating influence on bourgeois culture and society (Goll 1920). Influenced by Futurist poems and early slapstick comedy, he celebrated movement as the essence of modernism: "A new element, like radon or ozone, invades all the other arts: movement. All genres — poetry, painting, sculpture, dance — are affected by it, experience it. For one moment, all the crafts stand dead and silent. . . . The laws of statics are knocked over. Space, time — overpowered. The foremost goals of art, synthesis and the play of oppositions, become possible and are made possible though the means of technology alone. We have film" (Kaes 1978, 141–43).

As Goll saw it, technology had destroyed the old distinctions between classes, genres, and art forms and laid the foundation for a nonliterary, purely visual cinema subject only to the laws of movement. Goll welcomed this technological revolution and praised its effects — the suspension of time and space, the liberation of the imagination — in the great synthesis of modernity (Zmegac 1970, 248–50). His techno-romanticism, and his equation of industrialization and urbanization with democratization, distinguished Goll from the majority of German writers, whose contempt for things technical often disguised a deep-seated fear of technology. While his metaphysics of movement and speed neglected the socioeconomic conditions that in reality restricted its expression, it had a liberating effect on the imagination — as a playing of possibilities that could, sometime in the future, create the need for social change.

Just as productive exchanges between film and literature remained the exception, so did real defections from "serious" literature to scenario writing. The "low" quality of most films and existing prejudices against the cinema limited the number of contemporary works of literature adapted to the screen.[5] More appropriate story material was usually found in folk tales, pulp novels, light comedies, and popularized versions of the classics; this situation did not change significantly with the introduction of the so-called *Autorenfilm* (author film) in 1913–14. Thus only a small number of writers showed actual interest in the cinema. Whereas some minor literati would later make a career in scenario writing, the film projects of such critically acclaimed authors as Hugo von Hofmannsthal, Arthur Schnitzler, Gerhart Hauptmann, Georg Kaiser, and Carl Zuckmayer often were doomed from the outset, a further "proof" of the incompatibility of literature and film.

By contrast, well-known film scenarists like Hanns Heinz Ewers, who wrote *The Student of Prague* (1913, 1926) and *Alraune* (1919, 1927), or Carl Mayer, whose name is associated with such Expressionist classics as *The Cabinet of Dr. Caligari* (1920), *Nosferatu* (1922), and *The Last Laugh* (1924), had come to the cinema without prior affiliations (Kortländer 1982; Keiner 1987). As early as 1907, Ewers provocatively referred to the cinema as an integral part of everyday life. The "*circenses* of the twentieth century" (Güttinger 1984a, 12), he argued, offered instant gratification, were more hygienic than all the noisy, filthy pubs, and possessed many yet-unexplored educational values.[6] His observation that there are "people who never go to the movies. There are also people who never take a bath" (Güttinger 1984a, 20) already bears witness to the growing confidence of those associated with the film business. For Ewers, it was a confidence that also extended to the cinema as an art form: "I want to prove that good art is possible even in the cinema, even *without* the word. People may call me a rogue if I cannot keep my promise" (Kaes 1978, 103). The gesture was aimed at literary critics like Karl Kraus who once used the phrase "auf den Film gehen," a word play on "auf den Strich gehen" (to prostitute oneself), to characterize film scenarists (Kraus 1914, 19).

Among these largely programmatic statements, *Das Kinobuch* (1913, The cinema book) remains an exception, for it tries to put some of the claims into practice. This unique literary experiment conveys the enthusiasm of the contributing authors, but also reveals their prejudices and misconceptions (Re 1983; Heller 1984, 67–79; Wuss 1990, 42–46). Following a suggestion by Kurt Pinthus, several young Expressionists, including Walter Hasenclever, Else Lasker-Schüler, Max Brod, Anton Rubiner, and Arnold Höllriegel, each contributed a film scenario to the anthology. In the intro-

duction, Pinthus sharply rejected the elitist attitudes of German intellectuals and expressed his longing for a cinema true to its own means of
expression: "This is why we younger poets and writers, we who believe
that enhancing life (perhaps art appreciation as well) means to be moved
deeply, to be thrown into the vertigo of the human and the metaphysical;
this is why we must not fight the cinema (even though it is the enemy of
high art). It gives us pleasure through the movement of the masses. It
thrills us through things that never happened. It expands the horizons. It
touches the hearts" (1983, 24).

Guided by such high hopes, the authors of *Das Kinobuch* invented stories of abundance, beauty, and great love: of working-class uprisings and
human tragedies in a mining town; of the idealism of first youth and the
passions of greed; of little secretaries and oriental despots; of a locomotive
gone wild and of Ulysses, the great hero, waiting to be adapted to the
screen. All scenarios were written with the explicit purpose of exploring
alternatives to the film drama and its enduring preference for dramatic
stories and staged settings. Fast-paced actions and fantastic effects predominate, and make superfluous any considerations of probability. While
the human protagonists are reduced to stock characters, objects take over as
the new heros of cinema through the emphasis on animation and trick
photography. The creative imagination is no longer bound to the subject as
the primary reference point but, instead, is free to attach itself to the moving images. The writers in *Das Kinobuch* strongly believed in the uniqueness of cinema and what they considered its main qualities, the visual and
dynamic quality and the mass appeal.

As the individual contributions reveal, such validation of the trivial and
the sensationalist was not always unproblematic (Zmegac 1970, 243–45).
The emphasis on movement and action reflects the sensibilities of the modern individual, but the recurring use of clichés and stereotypes also confines
the cinema to the world of cheap diversions and insures its continuous
exclusion from high culture. The superficial engagement with inherent
qualities disguises a more ambivalent relationship to mass culture that
comes to the fore in the preference for the fantastic, a genre traditionally
used to express conflict through the means of displacement and defamiliar-
ization. Not surprisingly, several reviewers objected to the anthology's mixture of techno-romanticism and bourgeois elitism. Herbert Tannenbaum
called *Das Kinobuch* "an experiment that certainly doesn't hurt, but certainly doesn't help either" (1987, 51), and Arnold Höllriegel spoke of "a

defeat with battle music and with all flags flying" (1913, 1,028–29; cf. Behne 1914 and Elsner 1914). As if anticipating such reactions, Pinthus warned: "Perhaps this world of unreality (made real by the movies) reflects more of our earthly world than we would want to believe. Thus it is not really important whether these film scenarios ever reach the silver screen, or whether they live on as they began: as movies of the soul" (1983, 28).

Writing about the cinema ultimately strengthened the cause of literature and enabled its representatives to influence the struggle for cultural hegemony in their favor. They turned to the genres they knew best — the essay, the polemic piece, and persiflage — to come to terms with the cinema, the changes that it had already brought about and that were to be expected. As a somewhat reluctant muse, the new medium actually raised literary productivity and provided an opportunity for self-reflection. The blurring of the boundaries between literature and journalism had already begun before the emergence of that "worthy" enemy of literature, the cinema, which now forced the writers to confront reality, including the dramatic changes in literary production. Through writing, the cinema came to be identified with a mass culture held together by the unifying forces of the image and the imagination. And through writing, the cinema was associated with the yet-unknown powers of a consumerist culture that replaced social experience with spectatorial relations. Thus it seems rather ironic that writing about the cinema would contribute to the affirmation of literature, "modernizing" its means of production but also safeguarding its privileges against the claims of the new mass media. What, from the side of the writers, was often portrayed as a problem of cultural crisis then concerned, above all, the changing role of literature in modern culture, including its economic and social implications. This situation could only be resolved through a long-overdue reassessment of literature. The cinema was both the obstacle and the instrument in this process.

\* \* \*

The initial question in the poetological discussions was whether or not film could be regarded as an art form at all, and if not, whether it could ever reach this status. Yvan Goll's declaration, "The basis of all future arts is the cinema" ( Kaes 1978, 137), and Carl Hauptmann's dismissive "This chicory never will become coffee" (Güttinger 1984a, 370) represent the two extreme positions. While the underlying assumptions were never examined in detail, the discussion as such created and defined the subject of inquiry in the process of identifying its qualities. In a way, raising the question meant already answering it. By introducing the possibility of film as the seventh art, the writers established the very conditions under which the process could take place.

These debates were possible in the first place because the representatives of the literary sphere shared a number of basic beliefs about the cinema. In contrast to the reformers, who rejected the film drama in favor of documentary films, the writers realized very quickly that the cinema's mass appeal lay in its ability to tell stories and offer cheap entertainment. Conversant with fictional genres like the novel and the drama, most writers paid little attention to what the reformers considered the inherent realism of cinema. Few would have agreed with the Naturalist critic Julius Hart, who repeatedly praised the cinema's great potential as a means of documentation: "Cinematography is an apparatus that can be aimed at the external world, the material phenomena, nature, and living things . . . but not at our inner emotional and intellectual world, at psychological states and processes. . . . And one should give art what is due to art and cinematography what is cinematography's due" (Güttinger 1984a, 296). The ability to record reality as it unfolds before the camera, according to Hart, excluded the cinema from the creative arts, but found expression in an almost natural relationship between the cinematic and the real.

Less concerned about social implications, and perhaps less interested in the technical side of the new medium, the majority of writers limited their discussions to narrative film and problems of representation. Their preference for literary models of analysis also explains the marginal role played by the visual arts, including architecture. Surprisingly few contributions dealt with the relationship between film and painting, in spite of the masterfully composed frames, the dramatic lighting, and the rich iconographic references that gave many early films a painterly, rather than theatrical, look. For the same reasons, only a small number of literary articles exhibited the moralistic zeal that made the reformist discourse so unpalatable to their contemporaries. While there was sharp disagreement about the cinema's artistic values, most writers recognized that moralistic appeals or stricter censorship laws would be useless in the fight against the cinema. Their ambition was to participate actively in the cultural process rather than to define culture based on prohibitions. Moritz Heimann, editor for the prestigious publishing house S. Fischer Verlag, noted: "He who wants to wipe out this plague with antiseptics will find himself in increasingly smaller company" (Kaes 1978, 77). Speaking out against the hypocritical philosophers who "dress up their basic, dreary need for distraction with profundities" and the inarticulate masses "who stubbornly and silently rush to the silent images," Heimann spoke in favor of compromise and moderation. Like the phonograph, he stated, the cinema had become an indispensable part of everyday life. "Since the cinematograph cannot be removed from this world . . . we must learn to tame it. First let us try to ascertain what good it can achieve; then, *how* it can achieve this good. This is not the task of one individual, but of all those concerned with, and working together for, the common good" (80). Heimann's proposal to eliminate the worst excesses and to explore alternatives to the drama expresses the prevailing sentiment among literary writers and critics.

The discussion about film as an art form reveals the strong influence of the comparison between poetry and sculpture in Lessing's *Laocoön* and Schiller's writings on theater as the site of aesthetic and political education. Paradoxically, the cinema, as the quintessential mixed medium, enabled—indeed, often compelled—writers to resort to aesthetic categories that were structured around essential differences. Continuing in the tradition of German Classicism, they focused on the relationship between the cinema and the other arts, and tried to define its inherent qualities against the backdrop of traditional forms and genres. Based on their perception of the theater as a mirror of society and as a facilitator of social change, writers perceived the cinema's mass appeal within the framework established by the classics, especially Lessing and Schiller. However, their writings influenced the debate on the cinema primarily through its inclusion in the canon of humanist education, rather than through explicit references or extended rereadings. What counted was the gesture with which the writers laid claim to uncharted territory; what they wanted was a taxonomy, not a theory of cinema. Their reliance on intellectual traditions that, for many, still represented the emancipatory potential in bourgeois culture helped to integrate the cinema into an established system of interpretation and, in so doing, to diffuse its challenges.

From the perspective of bourgeois culture, successful classification inevitably meant co-optation. Thus the confrontation with the cinema reactivated, perhaps for the last time, the apparatus of normative poetics. Only the old concepts, it seemed, could protect the traditional arts from the new mass medium, only the autonomous work of art could domesticate the cinema's Otherness. The fetishizing of the work at the expense of the process and the emphasis on formal rather than social criteria were means to this end. The underlying goal was to subject the cinema to the old categories of evaluation and, in an act of critical appropriation, to assert the superiority of literary culture. As a means of systematization, normative poetics promised order through rigid definitions, peaceful coexistence through generic integration, and preservation of the status quo through the denial of historical change. It provided the critical tools through which the experience of modernity could be obliterated and its profound impact on culture and society be denied, if only on the level of critical discourse. By containing the difference of cinema within obsolete categories of distinction, the writers distracted attention from the oppositions existing in society, including those of gender and class. And by insisting on a hierarchical order, they preserved the distinction between high and low culture. However, the attempt to transfer the concepts from one paradigm (high culture) to another (mass culture) was doomed to fail and, in failing, revealed the shortcomings of the existing models of interpretation. The poetological classification of cinema only served to underscore the enormity of its provocation.

As a rule, comparisons provided an effective method of dealing with the cinema in conceptual rather than purely impressionistic terms. Usually the critic's choice of the "other" art, the indicator of difference, reflected his own artistic preferences. The act of comparing certain highlighted characteristics at the expense of others resulted in definitions that were often diametrically opposed. With literature, theater, painting, or pantomime as the point of reference, the cinema assumed a wide range of identities; the choice of a particular literary genre added further variations.

To quote a few examples, the supporters of the theater opposed comparisons between theater and cinema, and Georg Troll asserted: "The cinema of today is based on a number of errors. The most obvious one has to do with the cinema's intention to depict events and things that can be shown more effectively and realistically on the stage" (1919, 176). The enemies of the film drama shared this conviction with the proponents of a cinema true to its own means of expression. Thus Pinthus argued that film and drama were fundamentally different. "The representation of human fate through language is the essence of the drama. Yet the essence of the film scenario resides in an entertaining milieu, represented through a graphic story and visualized through movement and gesture" (1983, 20). Not the drama, Pinthus concluded, but the novel provided the most appropriate model for narrative film, since both relied on shifting narrative positions and strong character identification. Alexander von Gleichen-Rußwurm likened the cinema to old picture books and praised its epic possibilities. "To tell—aptly, artistically, impressively, enchantingly—that is what we shall demand from the cinema [*Lichtspiel*]. Telling Images!" (1917, 51).

Conversely, the advocates of prose fiction rallied against the scandalous practice of bringing novels to the screen; they spoke, like Max Bruns and Paul Scheerbart, of "barbarism," or, like the poet Richard Dehmel, of "prostitution." (Kaes 1978, 83–93). Completing the three basic literary genres, Oskar Kanehl dismissed proposals to use poetry in film as totally misguided, but he conceded: "That must not mean that the cinema would be completely incapable of creating something lyrical, such as atmospheric pictures and lyrical scenes; it only means that it has no place for the lyric as an art form" (Kaes 1978, 50). In Kanehl's view—and he, in a way, completes the circle of comparisons—the cinema stood closest to the theater, and would only flourish as a dramatic art.

The implications of the controversy were spelled out most clearly in relation to the drama. As the literary genre most similar to film, the drama (and its institutional framework, the theater) became the leading "antagonist" in the struggle for definitions. Initially, most writers rejected the idea of creative encounters between the drama and "the poor drama's poor cousin" (Kahn 1923–24, 502). Their opposition to what was, appropriately, called the film drama was based on two arguments, its foundation on technology and its lack of dialogue. The cinema's conditions of reproduction, the writers argued, made impossible the development of artistic qualities. In the words of the theater critic Julius Bab: "These representations—naturalistic in the word's most negative connotation—allow human beings to sink to the lowest level of their most brutal instincts. . . . Because of this ineptitude and humiliating physical vulgarity, the particular features of a film screening can never be reproduced in a real theater" (1912, 312; see also Bab 1920). Naturalistic in this context refers to the ability of the cinematic apparatus to render visible physical reality and initiate a momentous shift from the anthropocentric order of the stage to the objective viewpoint of the camera.

The anxiety concerning the disappearance of the individual as the center of meaning stood behind the most serious argument against the film drama, the absence of language. The Expressionist playwright Paul Kornfeld asserted: "Tragic man is metaphysical, and, because of this metaphysical condition, can never be portrayed outside of language. Anyway: it is a mistake to look for parallels between film drama and drama; film is epic" (Kaes 1978, 131). Without language, Kornfeld concluded, the film drama was limited to sensationalist stories and lurid effects. Behind this appeal to metaphysics stood the knowledge of another kind of physicality, in which the body would begin to speak, and in which the image would take over the function of the word. For many writers this new order was synonymous with the death of the individual as eternalized on the bourgeois stage.

One of the most prominent contributors to the film-drama controversy was the literary theorist and philosopher Georg Lukács (Thal 1985, 53–89; Wuss 1990, 47–53). In a short essay entitled "Gedanken zu einer Ästhetik des Kino" (1913, "Thoughts on an Aesthetic for the Cinema," 1981), Lukács tried to shed light on the relationship between film and drama by examining their different concepts of time and space, as well as their equally different relationship to the problem of absence and presence. As he points out, the theater not only places the individual at the center, but actually uses the experience of absolute presence to confirm its artistic superiority. Since complete presence can be achieved only on the stage, Lukács argues, the cinema has come to represent its opposite — insurmountable absence. "The lack of this 'presence' is the key characteristic of the 'cinema.' It is not because films are imperfect, not because their characters can presently only move but not speak. It is precisely because they are not people, but the movements and actions of people. This is not a lack of the 'cinema'; it is its limitation, its *principium stilisationis*" (1981, 3).[7]

The experience of absence, according to Lukács, influences all formal aspects of cinema and structures all of its relationships. As human beings and objects become subject to the same cinematic gaze, the anthropocentric order can no longer be upheld; therein lies the cinema's innovative power. It introduces a radically different order of time and space, one seemingly unaffected by the laws of causality: " 'Everything is possible,' that is the philosophy of the 'cinema.' Because its technology is able to express the absolute (even if empirical) reality of any given moment in precisely that moment, 'possibility' is no longer an oppositional category of 'reality.' Each category is the equivalent of the other; they assume a single identity. 'Everything is true and real, everything is equally true and equally real.' That is the lesson of the 'cinema's' sequence of images" (1981, 3).

On the basis of this definition, Lukács encourages film scenarists to study the fantastic in literature and painting and calls for more stories in the style of Edgar Allan Poe, Jules-Amédée Barbey-d'Aurevilly, E. T. A. Hoffmann, and Achim von Arnim. The ability of the fantastic to challenge existing modes of perception — the knowing and not-knowing — and the ability of cinema to alter the visible world through special effects establish the parameters in which Lukács develops his poetics of the cinema. Technology and the fantastic thus bring forth a cinematic reality that is neither real nor illusionary, but that exists in between (Levin 1987, 37–43). For Lukács, as for Paul Wegener, the fantastic offers a valid alternative to the film drama and its theatrical conventions. Once the cinema takes over some of the theater's social functions, "the theater will once again be forced to fulfill its true mission: to serve the great tragedy and the great comedy. And amusement . . . may find a more appropriate environment at the 'cinema' " (Lukács 1981, 4).

The main purpose of this division of labor is, of course, to confirm the old distinction between high and low culture and to revive the theater with the help of modern mass media. While Lukács's analysis of absence as a constituting element of filmic representation must be regarded as one of the most compelling contributions to the often pedantic film-drama controversy, his subsequent translation of these qualities into filmic techniques limits the new medium to the paradigm of technology and entertainment, as expressed in the equation of cinema and the fantastic. For this reason, Lukács's reflections on the cinema remain double-edged, providing both a clarification of important categories — for instance, in his analysis of the difference between cinematic and dramatic representation — and a confirmation of the marginality of cinema through its association with a classical marginal genre, the fantastic.

The art historian Herbert Tannenbaum — regarded by some critics as the first German film theoretician (Diederichs 1987, 7–30) — developed similar ideas in his monograph *Kino und Theater* (1912, Cinema and theater). Like Lukács, he predicted that "the cinema will bring about the rebirth, not the decline, of our theaters" (1912, 8). But unlike Lukács, he approached the conditions of reception from a sociological perspective. Tannenbaum, who wrote his 1913 dissertation on cinematography and copyright, was especially interested in the possibility of cultural diversity within the context of social harmony. He insisted that the interactions between cinema and theater were to the advantage of both. Given the popular failure of the theater, the cinema had to provide the masses with adequate forms of entertainment. But once the lowly pleasures were taken care of, the theater could devote itself entirely to its cultural mission. Proposals like these recall reformist arguments about cinema and its purifying effect on the established arts. While Tannenbaum's articles for *Bild und Film* showed his familiarity with the rhetoric of cultural renewal, his approach to the film drama proved his strong commitment to aesthetic questions. Instead of lamenting its hybrid character, he developed a catalogue of criteria that took into account film's precarious position between theater and pantomime.

A successful film drama, in Tannenbaum's view, consisted of a few well-defined characters and a compact, action-oriented story; it possessed clarity of presentation and sufficient internal motivation; and the screening had to be accompanied by the appropriate music. But its realization depended on the degree to which the film expressed the vision of its individual director. Tannenbaum's definition of film authorship, which needs to be distinguished from the literary *Autorenfilm,* emphasized the need for organization and control. "Wherever films are shot and produced, one person must assume total artistic control over the staging and recording" (1912, 28). The cinema would only become the modern *Gesamtkunstwerk* when the composition of a particular shot was decided by the film director and not the cameraman, who for Tannenbaum personified the technical side of filmmaking. To lay the ground for these processes was the responsibility of the critics; that is why he felt the cinema "urgently needs the attention and contribution of all those who see themselves as the intellectual leaders of our nation" (1912, 36).

While most critics, including Lukács and Tannenbaum, focused on questions of representation and authorship, there was a growing interest among some writers to define the relationship between cinema and theater from an institutional perspective. After all, calls for sharper distinctions between film and drama were only partially caused by the low quality of most films. An assertion by Karl Bleibtreu — "With all that hate poured out over the film drama, one can suspect that it is here that we find the true power and significance of film" (Güttinger 1984a, 218–19) — is very telling in this regard, since it points to the reactive nature of a controversy that used aesthetic categories to cover a more basic problem, the growing competition for audiences. Statements like Bleibtreu's, then, acknowledged the apprehension with which a subsidized public institution such as the theater — from prestige institutions like the Deutsche Theater in Berlin to the countless smaller city theaters all over Germany — reacted to the success of the cinema, a purely commercial enterprise. When the acclaimed stage actor Albert Bassermann appeared in *The Other,* the Deutsche Bühnenverein, the actors' professional organization, issued a statement prohibiting its members to work for the film industry (this decision was later reversed). Many dramatists and theater critics rallied against the cinema because they feared the loss of their livelihood. Not surprisingly, their loyalty to the theater only grew as the cinema and similar mass diversions showed bourgeois aspirations. The cinema, they argued, had already taken away from the theater its most devoted supporters, mutilated the great masterpieces, and corrupted many theater actors, set designers, and directors who had signed contracts with the big film studios. If the cinema were to become like the theater, the nation's cultural downfall would be inevitable, and the fight against mass culture forever lost.

However, the proliferation of motion-picture theaters more or less forced the advocates of the theater to reevaluate the traditional forms of entertainment. The result was an increased awareness of the cinema as a public sphere and a greater attention to the stabilizing influence of cinema in a divided society. From reformist writers like Konrad Lange to theoreticians like George Lukács, critics repeatedly invoked the cinema to defend the theater's indifference to popular tastes. As in the separation process between pure and impure metals, the cinema was to be the slag from which the traditional arts could rise again — without the burden of entertainment. Thus the Expressionist poet Alfred Lichtenstein wrote: "The more people rush to the cinemas, the sooner some of them will become weary of the swindle. Of the hundred thousand that populate the cinemas, a few hundred will return to the theater in a given year. . . . But the theater, which, thanks to the cinemas, is freed of all constraining weights and detrimental influences, will have to return to the sacred art of acting" (Kaes 1978, 82).[8]

These wish-scenarios of renewal and purification were quite common. They reveal the overdetermined character of the debate on theater and cinema, and bring into play the various defense strategies against the mass audience. The dramatist Friedrich Freksa proposed a classification system that recalls Tannenbaum's distinction between theaters for sophisticated individuals and theaters for the masses, but also carried further its political implications. Hoping to define, for all time, the boundaries between art and entertainment, Freksa demanded an exact reduplication of the social hierarchies within the cultural practices. His plan called for a few intimate theaters for the connoisseurs, several large festival halls for the staging of monumental plays and spectacles, and a large number of movie theaters for the uneducated masses and their daily needs. There is no doubt that the sudden interest in the cultural needs of the masses was motivated by self-interest; it inspired, among others, a growing number of proposals for what essentially amounted to the "gentrification" of the cinema.[9]

More often than not, the comparative mode produced a critical impasse in relation to poetological and social concerns. Drawing attention to this problem, Rudolf Leonhard noted succinctly: "The paradox of film is perhaps most accurately described by the following: it is a literary genre that belongs to the visual arts" (Güttinger 1984a, 405; cf. Leonhard in Zehder 1923, 101–14). No matter whether critics welcomed or opposed the idea of film as the seventh art, the act of comparison alone set up a field of forces and introduced a system of equivalences based on comparability and, hence, compatibility. Literature was confirmed as the standard against which everything had to be measured; the confrontation between the old and the new turned into an exercise of power at the end of which bourgeois culture incorporated the Other into its systems of thought. The very assumption of comparability (i.e., belief in comparison as a critical method) was already a product of the conditions under which the cinema would eventually take its place on the margins of bourgeois culture. While the writers flirted with the Otherness of cinema, they rejected the possibility of a shift in the critical paradigm. Instead, they developed increasingly complicated models of cultural diversification. Comparability brought with it a sense of entitlement on the basis of which all later strategies of appropriation would be both necessary and legitimate. By confronting this paradox with elaborate systems of classification, the writers annihilated the real power of cinema. The rhetoric of unity triumphed again, infusing everything with its visions of sameness and permanence. With the cinematic subsumed under the literary, the cinema could be claimed for bourgeois culture, though the details of this process remained subject to controversy.

\* \* \*

While comparisons to the drama remained the most common method of assessing film's formal characteristics, the other arts provided models for a new way of writing about the cinema. Looking for inspiration, the representatives of the literary sphere turned to popular diversions that were radically different from bourgeois culture (Koebner 1977, 12–18). Fascinated by the cinema's muteness, although in truth the films always had musical accompaniment, many writers likened its use of gestures to the art of pantomime (Kaes 1987, 23–28). In so doing, they were able to leave behind the dramatic paradigm without having to deny the cinema's obvious similarities to the stage. Films needed no longer be blamed for failing to depict dramatic situations — the most frequent criticism — and could be appreciated for the expressiveness of the bodies displayed on the screen. Performance emerged as the central category of evaluation in these new discursive configurations, but it was a notion of performance that, instead of suggesting role-playing, focused on the human body in its physical characteristics. Walter Turszinsky captured its difference to stage acting in the concept of a "precision of gesture" (1910, 989). When Max Bruns claimed that "pantomime is the closest relative of the film drama" (Kaes 1987, 66), he referred precisely to their shared dependency on the actor as the source of all meanings. Paul Ernst argued in a similar manner: "An event or a sequence of events is recreated by actors with the means of pantomime; thus the film drama stands closest to pantomime" (Güttinger 1984a, 57).

As these examples indicate, the emancipation from the stage drama brought with it a blurring of the distinctions between reality and representation; the cinema appeared often as little more than filmed pantomime. Neither Bruns nor Ernst mentioned filmic techniques like framing or editing and, because they did not, demoted the camera to a mere recording device. In its place, the body became the true medium of cinema, endowing its images with the kind of authenticity that was no longer available through, and in, language. It is therefore not surprising that the term "film pantomime" could refer alternately to such filmed stage pantomimes as Max Reinhardt's *Die Insel der Seligen* (1913, Isle of the blessed) and *Sumurun* (1920), brought to the screen by Ernst Lubitsch, and the mute, dancelike quality attributed to filmic representation as such. A few writers mentioned the absence of the real body, including Julius Bab, who described the film drama as a "bodiless pantomime" (1912, 312). Accordingly, he placed the film pantomime somewhere between the shadow plays known from the magic show and the more physical spectacle of modern pantomime and dance.

The frequent references to pantomime would have been unthinkable without the modern dance movement. By rejecting classical choreography, dancers and choreographers like Mary Wigman and Rudolf Laban contributed significantly to a growing interest in the expressive potential of the human body. With their calls for a return to primitive ritual, folklore, and myth, they hoped to liberate the archaic language of the body and reclaim its spiritual qualities. Jo Haïri Peterkirsten, a practitioner of eurythmics, even published a short philosophical treatise, *Volks-Filme* (1918, People's films), in which she explored the similarities between pantomime, spirituality, and cinema, guided by the insight that "today's moviegoers are our true soul searchers — clandestine searchers for answers" (1918, n.pag.). As victims of modern civilization, Peterkirsten argues, the masses turn to the cinema with starved senses and an insatiable need for spiritual community, thereby expressing "an intuitive will to life." They find relief under the conditions of mass reception, in what is defined by the author as the "collectivization of expression and experience."

The cinema, in Peterkirsten's view, reunites what language has separated: "After all, only film is able to compress into a few hours not just one human life in all its wealth — its harmonies as well as disharmonies — but many human lives; not only for the period of one decade, but for many decades, indeed centuries; and not just in one country, but around the entire globe" (1918, n.pag.). Because of its collective nature, the author concludes, the cinema has to be regarded as a legitimate successor of the great mystery plays and the religious rituals of earlier times. This retrogressive longing for human community, of course, only points to actual divisions in society, and the denial of the cinema's industrial basis must be considered symptomatic of a more fundamental resistance to technological progress. Through the silent spectacle of pantomime, the original unity of meanings is magically restored, and, through the concomitant shift to visual perception, the crisis of culture suddenly appears as a necessary phase in the emergence of a new spiritual body culture.

To be sure, the speculations on film pantomime stood in direct relation to the marginal role of pantomime among the performing arts. Lacking the institutional framework of the theater and its eloquent critics, pantomime seemed particularly appealing to writers with a philosophical agenda but without much interest in social issues. To those concerned about the widening gap between classes and nations, the film pantomime embodied the principles of mediation on the level of both artistic production and reception. Film pantomime not only took its inspiration from the universal language of the body, it was the quintessential mixed medium, with dance, theater, and music as the most important influences. As the first silent art, its proponents argued, pantomime had actually prepared the ground for the cinema and should therefore serve as the model for all future developments. Playing with these connotations, Willy Rath placed the cinema in the popular tradition of the fairy tale, the grotesque, and the magic show. In *Kino und Bühne* (1913, Cinema and stage), he defined film as "the mechanic-graphic reproduction of a pantomime" (1913b, 42) and asserted that "the peculiar appeal of pantomime lies in the fact that it flirts with the other arts without surrendering to any one entirely" (1913b, 43).

The reason behind such categorizing was, again, the protection of the bourgeois theater and its cultural mission. Sharply distinguished from the theater's purity of form and content, the cinema represented the perfect *mixtum compositum;* here arts and crafts, there high drama; here visual pleasure, there critical thought; here mechanical reproduction, there artistic creation. Cultural diversification was necessary—everyone agreed on that—but not at the price of total equality between the cinema and the theater. That is why Rath, who openly sympathized with the cinema reformers and called the backwardness of the German film industry "a proof of its higher culture," concluded: "The cinemas must be demobbed, the stage must become more popular so that a fruitful balance can be achieved for both, individually and as a whole" (1913b, 52). Film pantomime was a means to this end, and its products were welcomed accordingly—a point that was commented upon in a critical review by Malwine Rennert (1913–14).

Giving the cinema a premodernist identity allowed writers to assess its social and cultural functions while ignoring its actual challenges to bourgeois culture. Searching for literary genres that, like the cinema, had strong roots in popular culture, a number of writers discovered folk culture and what they considered as its last remaining manifestations, the ballad and the fairy tale. As the perfect hybrid form, the critic Ulrich Rauscher proclaimed in 1913, the example of the ballad made the cinema's liberation from the theater complete. "What is suitable for ballads is also suitable for films! The ballad's tempo, its apparent incoherence—which, in due time, will prove itself to belong to a higher, more consistent order of things—its casual innuendos, its constant back and forth: all of that can be found in film, too . . . It will be the task of the poets to bring these colorful, joyful, and inspired ballads to the silver screen so that those starving in body and spirit may find fulfillment" (Güttinger 1984a, 147, 149). In a similar vein, the novelist Fedor von Zobeltitz described film as the modern successor of the fairy tale. "On the stages of cinematography, our entire world of sagas and fairy tales could experience a lively revival; and our old folk books, with their lyrical power, could reclaim their influence over the nation" (1911, 1,102).

The concept of film folklore—to be understood here as a popular tradition and a communal experience—introduced formal standards while taking into account the cinema as a public sphere; therein lay its advantage over formalistic comparisons to the drama. At the same time, the imaginary return to the preindustrial community associated with folklore made possible the repression of the cinema's proletarian aspects; mass culture could be theorized outside of working-class culture. Unlike the film-drama controversy, which relied on a single standard of evaluation for both genres, the notion of film folklore recognized and accepted essential differences. Whether the cinema was glorified or ostracized in the process, its essentially antimodern quality allowed the writers to embrace difference and, moreover, to designate a space for the experience of difference. Now the transgressions between cinema and the other arts could be contained. In order for the process to take place, critical attention had to turn away from social reality and focus exclusively on imaginary relations in the cinema. The implications of this aestheticizing of the unreal can be seen in the frequent references to the fantastic, the perfect combination of folklore and technology. The creation of the fantastic through special effects (e.g., superimposition, stop motion) was only possible in the cinema, critics argued, and therefore confirmed its uniqueness. While it encouraged more film-specific stories, the fantastic restricted the cinematic imagination to uncanny effects. Thus the undercurrents of protest against reason and rationality were contained by generic requirements.

The comparisons to folklore emphasized the collective experience of cinema, and appealed to a tradition without authors, but with universally valid characters and themes. Here authors deliberately evoked another tradition in German literature, the fascination with folklore as the authentic voice of the people, the self-expression of an indigenous culture as transmitted through folksongs and folktales. Reaching back to Herder's writings on epic and nation, and finding its foremost expression in the fairy tale collection of the Brothers Grimm, the interest in folklore originated in the nineteenth-century critique of mechanization and in widespread fears about the disappearance of all regional characteristics. Against an elitist book culture and against an internationalist film industry, the notion of film folklore promised at once reconciliation between the classes and re-affirmation of Germany's cultural heritage. In the process, the critical focus shifted from the obsession with form to the conditions of reception, or, to be more precise, both categories reached identity. Entertainment and education were no longer perceived as conflicting categories, but as working toward the same goal. Depending on the larger context in which film folklore was defined, this either meant the gradual institutionalization of cultural practices for the masses, or the nostalgic quest for forms of cultural expression that could only be retrieved as authentic ones in the form of a modern reappropriation.

One way of integrating the notion of folklore into a modern trajectory was to propose a stage model of artistic development in which film occupied the lowest level, the level of folklore. Doing precisely that, the film critic and scenarist Willy Haas maintained that each art form started out as a craft. "We should not be afraid to boldly claim: film is in the stage of the folksong" (Güttinger 1984a, 455). The lack of individual authorship, he argued, proved that the cinema was still in the mechanical, "precosmic" stage of aesthetic development.

As the writings of Haas, Rath, and others prove, the return to folklore was crucial for analyzing the conditions of mass reception from a cultural and historical perspective. It drew attention to the cinema's precarious position between escapism and utopian promise and problematized its function as a repository for the aborted dreams of modernity. Likewise, mass reception could finally be linked to the experience of an all-encompassing unity, involving body and soul, individual and society. The retrogressive thrust behind such arguments cannot be ignored, of course, for it was only after rejecting the modernity of cinema that critics were able to sketch such positive scenarios of cinema. Only after the working class, as a critical category, was eliminated from the search for definitions did the "good" masses find entry into critical discourse. Not surprisingly, the vision of cinema as the folklore of the urban masses held a particular attraction for conservative writers. As a remembrance of things past, film folklore was supposed to compensate for the shortcomings of capitalism. It had to close the gap between traditional forms of representation and the reality of modern existence. The association with folklore made possible the denial of cinema's technological and industrial foundation. Promising preindustrial bliss, film folklore reversed the experience of modernity. Under these conditions, its proponents were able to accommodate social groups previously

ignored by bourgeois culture. With demands for public recognition si-
lenced through the reverence paid to an older popular tradition, the cinema
had found its "proper" place, namely, in the world of folklore and arts and
crafts. Whether or not it had been intended, the liberation of cinema from
the confining framework of the drama came at the price of its trivialization.

Once the cinema had been separated, at least theoretically, from the
other arts, its future could be defined in relation to social rather than
aesthetic concerns. In the context of cinema reform, this would have
required a clarification of the relationship between the cinema and the
state, including the institutions of higher education. However, in the
context of the literary debates, these issues surfaced only occasionally in
discussions about visual pleasure, popular culture, and mass society. Pinthus was one of the few critics who commented at length on the educational possibilities of film, but he meant literary rather than political education when he argued: "I am convinced that the thick layer of hatred,
stupidity, numbness, and melancholia that virtually suffocates mankind
could be lifted and mitigated with the help of film" (Zehder 1923, 129). To
mitigate, of course, meant to reach the masses through their emotions, to
satisfy their longing for happiness, and to compensate for the experience of
social injustice by emphasizing eternal values and the beauty of art. The
means to achieve this goal, he believed, could be found in the language of
gesture that gave the cinema immediate access to the unconscious. Guiding
the masses toward a higher consciousness, then, was to be regarded as the
cinema's ultimate goal.

By validating difference, the notion of folklore afforded writers the
opportunity to see the cinema from afar. It relegated the cinema to a place
outside bourgeois culture, a place so removed from the other arts that the
question of boundaries did not even arise. With comparability no longer a
problem, this new folklore for the masses provided an outlet for the dreams
of another, more human world. At the same time, the cinema's actual
difference from folklore provided a safeguard against the call for direct
political action often associated with such dreams. The cinema, therefore,
came to represent the power of subversion and the pleasures of compensation. The "yes" of social acceptance could be spoken, once the danger of
"real" Otherness (i.e., of class consciousness) had been banned through the
transformation of cinema into a metaphysical entity, no matter whether it
was called film pantomime or film folklore. Short of any external points of
reference — these ideas were never applied to actual films — most of the

poetological definitions remained untested. They amounted to little more than exercises in terminology or nostalgic musings about popular culture, wavering between patronizing warnings and false euphoria. Ultimately, the discrepancy between the modernity of cinema and the backwardness of its discourses produced its own critical impasse.

# Chapter 5
## On Visual Pleasure and Spectatorship

"It is my opinion that the cinema and its representations really have nothing at all in common with literature, and that it maintains only tenuous connections to the visual arts," wrote the novelist Georg Hermann in 1913 (Kaes 1978, 91). His remark draws attention to the inherent limitations of the comparative approach. As has been argued in the previous chapter, comparisons between film and drama presupposed a notion of historical continuity that could no longer be maintained in the face of modern mass culture and its obsession with the eternally new. Likewise, comparisons between genres were, more often than not, based on a system of equivalences that, no matter whether it produced variations of the same or resulted in oppositional pairs, nullified the very possibility of radical change. The difficulty in defining the cinema in relation to the other arts must, therefore, be seen as an effect of discursive struggles, and not a critical shortcoming. Above all, it reveals the pressures under which the old categories of interpretation were forced to account for the new mass medium. A similar problem haunted the descriptions of audiences, whether they were based on essayistic or sociological approaches. Chapter 3 has shown how the notion of the masses failed to subsume the heterogeneity of the audiences under a unifying concept and how the scenarios of mass reception transformed the cinema into a place of frightening Otherness, a place where the old social and critical distinctions no longer existed. This chapter will try to describe another configuration, the relationship between cinema, urbanism, and visual pleasure, whose theoretical concepts were developed in direct confrontation with these phenomena.

Consequently, it seems logical to turn from the spectacle of the masses to the experience of visual pleasure, and to explore in what ways early theories of spectatorship tried to bridge the gap between new cultural practices and the discourses attending to them. The growing attention to questions of spectatorship, no matter how unsystematic and speculative at times, opened up a new perspective in the literary debates on the cinema. Reacting to the constraints imposed by genre distinctions, and weary of prescriptive slogans in the style of "what should be done," some writers began to approach the cinema from the side of visual pleasure rather than through the rhetoric of cultural decline. Instead of focusing exclusively on the filmic text, they described the cinematic experience as an ongoing production involving films, audiences, public places, and modes of perception; hence their frequent references to technological innovations, advances in industrial production and scientific management, and trends in modern architecture and urban planning. These disparate cultural practices seemed to accommodate best the rampant eclecticism of their very subject of inquiry. The experience of mass culture provided the point of departure for the formulation of new concepts and ideas, and the cinema offered the model on the basis of which a new critical discourse could emerge.

Many critics pointed out that the new medium, in fact, already practiced what its detractors still tried to conceptualize. Here the notion of experience became a pivotal category in their search for a new paradigm. The cinema, it was argued, reproduced the experience of modern mass society within its own parameters, thus turning a social experience into an aesthetic one. At the same time, the experience of visual pleasure afforded audiences the opportunity to exercise those perceptual and intellectual faculties that were necessary to their survival in the spaces of modernity. Unlike the cinema reformers, the representatives of the literary sphere had little interest in turning visual pleasure into a pedagogical asset or a political weapon. Instead, they used it as a heuristic device to map the field of modern diversions in which they would have to find their place as artists and intellectuals. Even when they analyzed the sociopsychological aspects of spectatorship, they focused on the individual and his relationship to the outside world. Therefore, writing about visual pleasure always meant writing about the bourgeois subject in crisis.

By making the cinema part of the urban landscape, and by analyzing its mass appeal in terms of experience, the writers relied on ideas that first appeared in sociological studies on the effects of mechanization and urbanization. As early as 1904, the social philosopher Friedrich Naumann had described how modern technology invaded all aspects of everyday life and how it changed people's living conditions as well as their experience of reality. In "Die Kunst im Zeitalter der Maschine" (1904, Art in the machine age), Naumann commented on the changed attitude toward time: "But we perceive this old concept [of time] as complicated and heavy. We want to arrest the instantly appearing, the quickly disappearing, we want to fully experience the smallest segments of our hurried existence! To phrase it differently, we do not want the 'thing in itself' but the appearance, the mood. It is only there that we can find profundity and superficiality at the same time" (1964, 198).

Arguing along similar lines, the sociologist Georg Simmel showed in "Die Großstädte und das Geistesleben" (1903, The metropolis and mental life) how the urban experience affected people's intellectual and emotional life (Frisby 1986, 38–108). Simmel used ephemeral phenomena to present his argument, thus accounting for the fragmentation and the arbitrariness that characterized modern existence. The essay's critical thrust — theorizing aspects of modernity without falling back onto traditional notions of subject and object, surface and depth — becomes evident in Simmel's discussion of nervousness as the quintessential modern disease. "The psychological basis, from where the type of the urban individual is created, is the increase of nervousness that originates from the swift and continuous shift of external and internal stimuli. Man is a being dependent on differentiation, that is, his consciousness is stimulated through the difference of the momentary impression against the preceding one; remaining impressions, the slightest differences between them, conventional regularity of the passing and their oppositions require less consciousness, as it were, than the rapid telescoping of changing images, pronounced differences within what is grasped at a single glance, the unexpectedness of violent stimuli" (1971, 325).

Simmel's writings on urbanism and modern culture were published just as the cinema made its appearance as the quintessential modern medium; they also provided the matrix on which the cinema would assume one of its most important discursive functions — to become, like the big city, a metaphor of modernity. Not surprisingly, it was through the notion of visual pleasure that *Lebensphilosophie* (vitalism) and phenomenology left their mark on the literary debates on the cinema. The attention to perception shed new light on the process of spectatorship, but it also allowed the writers to elevate visual pleasure to a new kind of consciousness. The subjectivity of the individual, threatened by the visual spectacle of mass reception, was reconstituted in the moment of lived experience, while any references to social reality could be made to disappear in the perceptions of the real. Simmel's work, in particular, bears witness to this tension between critical re-presentation and simulation. His essays on money, fashion, or cocquetry — they are collected in *Die Philosophie des Geldes* (1900, The philosophy of money) and *Philosophische Kultur* (1911, Philosophical culture) — portray modernity as an eternal present that, at its most extreme, makes all hopes for historical change superfluous.

The relationship between cinema and urbanism was first thematized from a negative perspective. While the French Dadaists celebrated the modern metropolis, and while the Italian Futurists turned the machine into a source of artistic inspiration, German writers rarely described the big city with excitement or enthusiasm (Kaes 1987, 10–15). The Expressionist *Großstadtlyrik* (big city poetry), with its bleak descriptions of crowded streets and squalid bars, revealed a strong anti-urban sentiment among German artists and intellectuals. For the same reason, the literary references to the process of industrialization emphasized its dehumanizing rather than its liberating effects. The most diverse phenomena — mechanization, rationalization, urbanism, consumerism, tourism, Americanism, and so forth — were evoked to describe that which, according to the logic of degeneration, was destroyed in the process. For instance, the dramatist Paul Ernst blamed the machine for the decline of German culture. "In our times, human labor is increasingly being replaced by the machine. Today people are about to realize that the results . . . are questionable, even when it comes to the most simple tools; whenever we want to have an emotional relationship to the object, mechanization seems crude and vulgar. In the cinema, the attempt is made to produce art, this most noble of all human activities, with the help of a machine. That this attempt must fail is more than evident; that it is made at all remains one of the worst signs of the barbarism in our times" (Güttinger 1984a, 73).

Many writers shared these antitechnological sentiments and used the cinema in the literary campaign against a dehumanizing technology and a hostile urban environment. Franz Pfemfert, editor of the influential Expressionist journal *Die Aktion,* captured the feelings in his repeated references to Edison as the personification of technological progress. "'Edison' is the formula that characterizes our times. 'Edison' — the mating of genius and triviality. . . . 'Edison' is the battle cry of an epoch that is about to murder culture" (Kaes 1978, 60, 61). And he closed with a telling account of modern religiosity. "Nick Carter, the cinema, and Berlin tenement houses, this profane trinity belongs together. . . . A bad novel can mislead the reader's imagination. The cinema destroys the imagination. The cinema is the people's most dangerous educator" (62). Such remarks could be dismissed as cultural pessimism or be described as typical lamentations by the apologists of bourgeois culture. However, the feelings expressed in them reveal to what degree the cinema was perceived as an integral part of modern mass culture, and in what ways the discourse of cinema always included the discourse of mass culture and modernity. In this regard, conservative critics were often more receptive to the cinema's transgressive qualities than its proponents, who frequently resorted to antiquated definitions of art.

A number of writers studied the cinema's mass appeal in relation to the real and imaginary spaces of the city and the phenomenon of urbanism. Ferdinand Hardekopf was one of the few Berlin Expressionists who, as early as 1910, welcomed the instant gratification it provided; the use of the French term *cinéma* only underscored his distance from Expressionist dogma. The Swiss-born author coined the expression *cinéma-Phantasien* to show its reliance on visual images and fast action, just as he spoke of *cinéma-Menschen* to explain the medium's preference for clearly defined, one-dimensional types. He also pointed to the vacillation between dramatic and comic elements in the films themselves, in order to establish a connection between the conditions of industrial labor and forms of mass diversion. It was precisely this correspondence between the requirements of the workplace and "the alternating current" of emotions in the cinema that, in Hardekopf's view, made the cinema so appealing to the masses, and that prompted his warning to fellow intellectuals not to "underestimate the potential of these auditoriums. Here a new form of publicity stakes out its terrain" (Güttinger 1984a, 46). In 1912, Hans Kienzl expressed similar thoughts when he maintained: "The psychology behind the triumph of cinematography is big-city psychology . . . because the soul of the big city, this constantly rushed soul, staggering back and forth between cursory impressions that are as unique as they are unfathomable, embodies the soul of cinematography" (1911–12, 219).

These propositions, presented in the form of a warning or an empirical fact, were based on an analysis of modernity in which one specific aspect came to represent the whole, and where causes and effects were often treated as interchangeable. By essentializing the cinema along these lines, the writers could disregard its institutional aspects and reduce the question of spectatorship to one of different sensibilities, a psychology of modern perception, that "short distance from impulse to reflex" (Lewin 1912, 314), as one detractor described the viewing experience.

At the same time, the notion of modernity as a unifying force allowed writers to draw attention to the actual standardization behind the appearance of diversity and fragmentation. The interrelatedness of cultural practices, with the cinema at their center, confirmed this point. Joseph August Lux, for instance, drew attention to the affinities between cinema and the illustrated press and situated both in a historical continuum. "Instead of being the cause, it [the cinema] only reinforces those phenomena through which the new *Zeitgeist* expresses itself. The cinema only continues with success what our glossy journals have begun so splendidly" (Kaes 1978, 94).

Common to all assessments were the foci of perception, lived experience, and visual pleasure as critical categories that made the cinema synonymous with the modern. These offered an alternative to the subject-object dichotomy, according to which the anonymous crowds, the fleeting impressions, the countless diversions, and the mixture of boredom, overstimulation, and loneliness appeared invariably as deviation, deprivation, deficiency. And the contributions recognized the degree to which the cinema as a discursive model was able to accommodate these states in between; hence the emphasis on psychology rather than aesthetics, hence the shift from the filmic text to the conditions of reception, hence the close attention to the ephemeral and the quotidian, and hence the growing awareness of cinema as the site of pleasure and desire.

Not surprisingly, writers often spoke of hunger when describing people's almost elementary need for visual stimulation. The famous playwright Gerhart Hauptmann compared the cinema to a physiological necessity ruled by lack and abundance. "The need for cinema creations is so enormous that one can actually count this mental food among the basic foods, like bread and potatoes" (Kaes 1978, 159). Providing instant gratification, a visit to the cinema was like drinking a glass of beer or eating a snack, argued the Austrian novelist Karl Hans Strobl. "Above all, the cinema is a fast food restaurant of scopophilia. It affords the opportunity to satisfy one's recreational needs during the daytime, or for a short period of fifteen minutes" (Güttinger 1984a, 52). From this perspective of culture consumption, the cinema and spectatorship appeared as an integral part of consumer culture, characterized by its active and passive components.

Other writers tried to find explanations for what, in the larger context of mass consumption, gave rise to the new aesthetics of deprivation and compensation. As Friedrich Freksa, the novelist, noted: "Almost never before has a period suffered so much from visual hunger as ours. The telegraph, newspapers, and traffic connections have brought the world closer together. But from all sides, strange sensations attack the working man while he is tied to his seat, sensations which he can no longer connect to any real concepts. This has to do with our impoverished, abstract language" (Güttinger 1984a, 98). The split between the thing and the word that, in the view of many writers, had caused the crisis of language, could be magically overcome in the moment that the image took the position of the absent object. As the beauty of the visible replaced bloodless abstraction, the fullness of meaning was restored to a world in which everything seemed at once distant and close, wanting and overabundant. Describing this peculiar imbalance, Willy Rath noted. "Consciously or secretly, passionately or patiently, a need for fulfillment controls every healthy soul, a longing to leave behind the limitations of the individual. One could also say a *horror vacui,* a shuddering in the face of inner emptiness, in the face of mortal life's ineptitude, and its invincible loneliness. Let us simply call this drive the hunger for life" (1913b, 14). This *horror vacui* was nothing but an indication of a crisis of the subject that could no longer be resolved through well-meaning appeals to cultural tradition; the rewards of inwardness had already been supplanted by the hunger for life. That is why the cinema became the spiritual home of the mass individual.

The theorizing of cinema in terms of modern experience also challenged existing notions of culture, and the distinction between high and popular culture in particular. No longer willing to apologize for the cinema's "lowly" origins, some authors saw its distance from bourgeois conventions as the actual prerequisite for its mass appeal and the main reason for its enormous success. Standing outside of dominant discourse, they argued, the cinema offered release from the pressures of everyday life and its norms and conventions. Walter Hasenclever's definition of cinema as an "increased enjoyment of life" and an "enrichment of the imagination" referred, precisely, to its resistance to traditional definitions. "The hostility toward the cinema [*Kintopp*] rests on a misunderstanding: it is not an art in the sense of the theater, not a sterile form of spirituality; it is by no means an idea. . . . The cinema will always have something American, something brilliant, something kitschy about it. That explains its popularity; as such it is good" (Güttinger 1984a, 283). The author of the quintessential Expressionist drama, *Der Sohn* (1914, The son), found in the cinema a concern for human happiness that gave it moral and social significance. Kitsch, in Hasenclever's words, satisfied the legitimate need for happiness that the modern stage could only satisfy, in its absence, through formal innovation. Carrying these ideas one step further, the influential architecture critic Adolf Behne questioned the legitimacy of book culture altogether. Inspired by the American model, he exclaimed: "American civilization is based on the heart and the soul of the masses. Therefore, we call it kitsch. But with this kitsch, Americans only protect themselves against our inhumanity. For the European only one relationship is conceivable between art and the masses: that of hatred" (Kaes 1978, 161). Rejecting this kind of cultural elitism, Behne concluded: "Film is the simple, logical, and legitimate continuation of the book — Edison, the new Gutenberg. . . . Aristocratic book poetry [*Buch-Dichtung*] is being challenged by democratic film poetry [*Film-Dichtung*] — an art from below" (Kaes 1978, 162, 163).

By making the cinema an integral part of modern life, the writers not only overcame the limitations of traditional aesthetics, they also developed a new set of aesthetic categories. Just as they discovered affinities between the urban experience and the cinema's different mode of perception, they were able to find traces of this experience in the formal qualities of film. According to the essayist Egon Friedell, film's disregard for spatio-temporal conventions was most evident in the fragmented appearance, the constantly changing scenes, and the preference for exotic locations. Films, he argued, tried to simulate the experience of modernity through techniques like framing, editing, camera movement, mise-en-scène, and so forth. They created a second-hand reality, a simulacrum as it were, that found perfect expression in the lifelike quality of films and the artificial, filmlike appearance of modern cities like Berlin. By transforming a sociopsychological experience into an aesthetic pleasure, films showed the modern spirit in all its ambiguities. "They are brief, rapid, as if coded, and they don't stop at anything. They have something concise, precise, militaristic to them. This fits perfectly into our era, which is an era of extracts. . . . The cinema has something sketchy, abrupt, uncompleted, fragmented about it. In light of modern taste, a great artistic advantage" (Kaes 1978, 43, 44). Inserted into this new critical framework, the cinema did not simply become synonymous with modernity; it was actually perceived as accelerating the process of modernization, since it advanced the kind of consciousness that was about to transform all aspects of social and individual existence.

\* \* \*

The growing interest in visual pleasure and the frequent references to dreams and eroticism call to mind the work of Sigmund Freud, whose publication of *The Interpretation of Dreams* (1906), "On Narcissism: An Introduction" (1914), and "Instincts and their Vicissitudes" (1915) was contemporaneous with the debate on the cinema and addressed similar issues within the framework of psychoanalysis. Freud's writings on dreams identify the main characteristics of the dream work, including its strong visual orientation, the primacy of symbols, and the dream's incoherent appearance. The function of the dream, Freud argues, is to satisfy repressed desires. He might have said the same about the cinema. While there are few explicit references to Freud's theory of dreams in the writings on cinema, its influence on Hugo von Hofmannsthal is undeniable. It is also noticeable in many later writings wherein the description of film as dream, and of the spectator as dreamer, became a critical commonplace.

Freud's writings on voyeurism and on what he calls *Schaulust* (scopophilia or scoptophilia, or the scopic drive) had an even stronger influence on the theorizing of spectatorship than the theory of the dream. According to Freud, visual pleasure is closely linked to the oppositional nature of all drives, including voyeurism and exhibitionism. Scopophilia refers to a narcissistic formation related to the infantile organization of desire; it means the enjoyment of one's own body. Freud distinguishes the following stages and layers: "a) scoptophilia as an activity directed towards an extraneous object; b) abandonment of the object and a turning of the scoptophilic instinct toward part of the subject's own persona; therewith a transformation to passivity and the setting of a new aim — that of being looked at; c) the institution of a new subject to whom one displays oneself in order to be looked at" (Freud, 14:116). In a less clinical sense, but certainly with the same sexual connotations, the notion of visual pleasure played an important role in the cinema's emancipation from literary models of explanation and the development of a more pervasive/perverse theory of pleasure. If writings on visual pleasure frequently repeated arguments first made about the cinema and and the big city, they also introduced a sexual dimension missing from accounts that focused only on the disinterested pleasures of perception without recognizing its close ties to the eroticism of the cinematic gaze.

Walter Serner, a short-time member of the Zurich Dada, was one of the first to draw attention to the sexual foundation of visual pleasure (Schlüpmann 1990c, 296–307). In 1913, he wrote: "Day after day, the rise of civilization deprives people of what neither the attractions of the stage nor the dull sensations of the circus, the variety, and the cabaret are able to deliver; now something archaic has been given back to the people: the pleasure of looking. . . . That is why the cinemas triumph without effort; they are exclusively devoted to the eyes and their desire" (Güttinger 1984a, 190, 191). Serner defines visual pleasure, and feasts of the cinema that demand complete receptivity from the spectator, as "not just the harmless kind, which is only inspired by movement or color, or both, but one that is a terrifying lust, and as powerful as the deepest desire — one that makes the blood rush and pound until that unfathomable, powerful lust rushes through the flesh, that which is common to all desire" (Güttinger 1984a, 189).

Comparing the cinema to similar scenarios of visual pleasure in history such as the Trojan War, the Fire of Rome, medieval tournaments, and the executions on the guillotines of the French Revolution, Serner draws a connection between its psychosexual and political implications. These references to a long tradition of public spectacle and visual pleasure are most convincing in regard to the archaic, infantile, and polymorphously perverse aspects of desire. For the duration of the screening, the spectator — and the bourgeois intruder, who is invariably male — indulges in the illegitimate pleasures of passivity and complete receptivity, and regresses to a state in which more primary needs govern his aesthetic choices and where even kitsch can be elevated to the level of truth. Filled with the memory of such experiences, some writers expressed the desire to renounce their bourgeois identities and surrender entirely to the cinema's acoustic and visual stimuli. The frequently reported confusion about a film's story only confirmed the deliberate nature of their capitulation to "raw" emotionality; it was often nothing but a flirtation with what they perceived as primitive intelligence.

Not every writer believed that visual pleasure was predicated on one's willingness to submit passively to the images on the screen. Alfred Baeumler, in an essay on cinema audiences, claimed the opposite. While he criticized film's lurid sensationalism, he insisted on the importance of active participation. "One must pay attention in order to follow the silent innuendos and hints, and to comprehend the quickly passing scenes. Film activates, the spectator must collaborate, otherwise everything is lost to him. That is why the audience in the cinema experiences a peculiar, intellectual tension that everybody senses almost physically as soon as they enter the auditorium. The same atmosphere, only infinitely stronger, rules the concert hall or the theater" (Güttinger 1984a, 107). Arguing along similar lines, Victor Klemperer distinguished varying forms of participation in order to separate the primitive lower classes — "those teeming masses" — from the educated classes. "After all, while the naive spectator . . . perceives the moving image as reality, searching for its soul, the more sophisticated spectator knows at every given moment that he is not dealing with real things, but only with their shadow images" (Güttinger 1984a, 83–84). Alfred Polgar commented on such problems with his famous sense of irony: "The sublime world of cinematography leads only to embarrassment because of the many pretty girls who populate the silver screen and smile into the audience. There is no sense in smiling back. And there is no sense in waiting for these young ladies behind the screen when the show is over. . . . Here the spectator really regrets the missing third dimension" (Güttinger 1984a, 60–61).

In most accounts of spectatorship, the experience of visual pleasure was associated with the excesses of others. Critical insight only seemed possible from a position of secure distance. Like the image of the masses, the description of visual pleasure gave rise to sexual metaphors through which the instability experienced in looking — this oscillation between control and surrender — could be represented along the lines of gender, though not necessarily the gender of the actual spectator.[1]

Visual pleasure was most often perceived as becoming feminine in the act of looking; in that association with the feminine, the cinema further revealed its foundation on sexuality, or rather, on the existing discourses of sexuality. The majority of male writers described the cinematic experience as threatening and victimizing, in other words: as feminizing. Although the calls for redemption through visual pleasure originated in an analysis of sexual repression, looking was still perceived as a passive activity. And since passivity was associated with the feminine and with the masses, the presence of the audience was required in order for the writers to maintain power and control.

By addressing the question of cinema from the side of spectatorship, writing about visual pleasure reintroduced the problem of subjectivity into the debate. The notion of visual pleasure, despite its association with excess and self-deliverance, confirmed the male spectator as the center of meaning production and the master over time and space, taking into account his desire to surrender control to an outside source, if only temporarily. Notwithstanding memories of oceanic bliss and self-abandon, the preservation of identity remained the foremost concern. Insofar as the spectator was still able to continue a narrative with himself at the center, the world was intact; even if this narrative was called confusion. Because of this concern with control, the writers blurred the boundaries between fact and fiction in their description of nights at the movies, but only to bring the reader under the influence of their own perceptions — a strategy not dissimilar to the cinema's own play with the real and the imagined.

Within these parameters, writing about visual pleasure represented one way of coming to terms with the cinema's phenomenal success and of redefining the social function of the writer, as either a participant in, or a critic of, cultural change. It was an attempt to understand and, at the same time, to repress. Describing others through these carefully constructed oppositions sometimes resulted in the smug confirmation of the critic's own intellectual superiority. At times it took on a fraternizing tone, but it was always a process of negotiation.

\* \* \*

Visual pleasure was frequently compared to dreaming, that peculiar emotional state between sleeping and waking. This comparison allowed the writers to resolve the crisis of language through conscious withdrawal into the cinema and its imaginary spaces and states. Only spectatorial relations, they seemed to suggest, were free of the violence that had been inflicted upon language, and, in turn, inflicted by language on the world. Reacting to the nightmare of a modern Tower of Babel, the writers conjured up utopian visions of redemption through sheer specularity. Subsequently, the various modes of looking — staring, observing, watching, gazing, and so forth — were elevated to dignified social activities through which alienated modern man could overcome his personal and social isolation and find a new identity in the dark, warm interior of the cinema. Even the cinema's simple stories and artistic limitations suddenly appeared more authentic than the works of literature which, as was claimed, only masked an irrepressible emptiness. Arguing in this vein, the Swiss writer Isabella Kaiser confessed an almost childlike love for the cinema, "this living dream of the day" (Güttinger 1984a, 365).

Hugo von Hofmannsthal, the Austrian dramatist, was the first to discuss the affinities between cinema and dream in greater detail (Faber, 1979; Furthman-Durden 1986). Hofmannsthal's interest in this "box of charming junk" (Güttinger 1984a, 448) evolved out of his literary interests in the fantastic and the uncanny. Apart from the vast possibilities of altering visual reality, it was the silence in the cinema — or, to be more precise, the absence of language — that brought him to study its relationship to pantomime, the true language of the body.[2]

In "Der Ersatz für die Träume" (1921, The substitute for dreams) Hofmannsthal analyzes the cinema's dream economy and tries to define its sociopsychological function, yet with problematic results. Placed at the center of a group of three essays, his text makes a celebratory gesture toward cinema, but only to confirm the power of language. Under these conditions Hofmannsthal seems more than willing to present film as the universal language that transcends all boundaries of class and national culture. To support his claims, he points to the deep crisis of meaning that, while affecting all aspects of life, has a most devastating impact on the urban masses. "Countless hundred thousands escape to the dark hall with the moving images. That these images are silent adds to their attraction; they are as silent as dreams. And deep inside, without knowing it, these people fear language, because in language they fear the tools of society" (Güttinger 1984a, 447). Hence their almost instinctive resistance to the rhetoric of self-improvement which, as Hofmannsthal points out, only confirms those traditions that caused the crisis in the first place.

The appeal of cinema, according to Hofmannsthal, resides in its ability to compensate for a life devoid of meaning. Through its effective use of close-ups, time and space, and the eloquent muteness of its images, he argues, the cinema succeeds more than any other medium in stimulating the senses. By providing instant satisfaction, and by acknowledging the collective basis of visual spectacle, the cinema responds to needs that have been neglected for too long. But films not only imitate the structure of dreams, Hofmannsthal argues; in modern mass society, they also assume the compensatory functions associated with the dream. As the "substitute for dreams," only the cinema will save the urban masses from alienation and despair. "It seems to me that the atmosphere in the cinema alone provides an atmosphere where the human beings of our times — those who form the masses — establish a wholly unmediated, wholly spontaneous relationship to an enormous, even though strangely mutilated, spiritual legacy. Life to life! And the crowded, half-darkened auditorium with the flickering images seems to me, I cannot express it otherwise, almost venerable, a place of refuge where souls flock together in their somber fight for identity: from a digit to a vision" (Güttinger 1984a, 449).

The cinema, in Hofmannsthal's reading, is a reminder of the ineradicable lust for life. The realization of this vital potential, he is quick to add, requires that the cinema, including its specific means of representation, be sharply distinguished from the immateriality of the dream. The spectator must maintain his own identity and, in fact, is only able to do so because of the mechanical basis of cinematography. In the cinema "the dreamer knows he is awake; he can fully commit himself; with every fiber, including the most hidden folds, he gazes at this flickering wheel of life—eternally turning" (Güttinger 1984a, 449). As a result, the imaginary transgressions made possible by the cinema pose no serious danger, neither to the identity of the individual, nor to the order of society. Maintaining the precarious balance between reality and its simulation, the cinema provides a space where repressed desires can be satisfied without demanding their satisfaction elsewhere.

Hofmannsthal's "Substitute" essay exhibits a tendency among writers to combine, and often confuse, the critique of modern living conditions with a deep longing for human community. Consequently, his expression of solidarity with the lower classes remains half-hearted and is more literary than political, as he limits social analysis to quaint descriptions of working-class misery. The many references to degrading jobs, bleak row houses, and the monotony of daily life, for instance, cannot hide the distance between the observed and the observer; social injustice appears primarily as an aesthetic problem. While Hofmannsthal, though not immune to the rhetoric of compensation, abstains from overly moralistic judgments, he, too, must disassociate himself from social reality in order to fit the cinema into his reflections on the crisis of language. In the process, the masses' legitimate demand for beauty and truth becomes shrouded in mystery, a welcomed subject for bourgeois fantasies.

Given the interest in spectatorial relations, the notion of the dream also prompted more far-reaching investigations into the libidinal economy of cinema. The degree to which the dreamlike quality of spectatorship depended on the accompanying music was mentioned by several authors. In "Die Melodie im Kino," (1914, The melody in the cinema), the philosopher Ernst Bloch commented on this phenomenon in detail (Güttinger 1984a, 158–75). Music in the cinema, Bloch argues, functions like a carpet. Since all other senses except the visual are eliminated, the ear assumes the crucial task of anchoring all impressions within a network of meanings. "As visitors to the cinema, we rely exclusively on the eye. Originally, however, the sense of touch gives the strongest impression of reality. Confronted with the filmic image, we must relinquish everything that lends full verisimilitude to the perception of things, be that pressure, warmth, smell, sound, and actual presence. Skin, smell, hearing, all other senses are eliminated, while the eye rules tantamount. . . . Now, however, the ear fulfills its peculiar task. It stands in for all the other senses" (Güttinger 1984a, 315).

Apart from the references to music, the comparisons between the cinema and the dream inspired references to traveling, which shares with the cinema (and with the dream) similar formal and perceptual features, including the presence of fleeting images. Like mass tourism, the early cinema opened up the world as a perceptual space. As two closely related forms of pseudoexperience, both used visual pleasure to transform the foreign into the exotic, and thereby contained the threat of real difference within their respective scenarios of detached participation.

The ideal film, the Austrian novelist Theodor Heinrich Mayer argued, resembled railroad travel. With all distracting sounds muffled and replaced by a monotonous, lulling rhythm, images pass by in rapid succession, without giving the spectator a chance to grasp their precise meaning. "Let us take a sequence shot from a train in motion. To visualize its effects, one has to place oneself in an imaginary compartment, looking out through its window. . . . Thus we take something non-existing to be existing, in order to create an illusion of life about something that we actually saw but which, as we know, doesn't exist. . . . We really see the image as such, but we see 'life' only as movement. . . . Real and unreal things are joined together in a mysterious phenomenon for which there exists no appropriate name, but which is closest to that very quiet dreaming with open eyes" (Güttinger 1984a, 121).

The affinities between film and the dream produced valuable insights into the nature of spectatorship, but, without a theoretical framework, conclusions were often marred by the elements of cultural pessimism that inspired them in the first place. The belief in a new human community forming at the margins of literary culture often originated a problematic mixture of irrationalism, mysticism, and new hedonism. With descriptions of the cinematic experience modeled on the memory of prenatal, intrauterine bliss, phantasies of omnipotence and instant satisfaction abounded.

The same atmosphere of despair that had given birth to the film-as-dream metaphors now seemed to justify the eternal unattainability of the desires represented by them.

Though initially a source of inspiration, comparisons to the dream and the daydream all too easily prevented the subversive potential of the cinema from being realized in cultural practices. Similarly, attention to questions of spectatorship often came at a high price. For only by neglecting the film's industrial basis were the writers able to accept its mass appeal. Only by taking the fictional effect as their point of departure could they embrace mass reception as an experience almost equivalent to life. Though aware of the work involved in producing this impression of reality, the writers concentrated on questions of reception, rather than on those of production. As a result, the technological and economical aspects of mass reception were subsumed under a psychopathology of the cinema, with the "image" and the "look" as the main points of anchorage. Between the conception of the scenario and the moment of viewing, nothing seemed to interfere with the splendor of the cinematic illusion. With the myth of the masses, an "unconscious" was created inside critical discourse that allowed the writers to at once express and repress the modernity of cinema and its redemptive qualities. Through the myth of visual pleasure, a projection screen was set up as well as a place for forgetting. Thus the crisis of bourgeois individualism brought forth the chimera of the masses.

# Part 2
Writing on Film in the Weimar Republic
1918–1933

# Chapter 6
## The Rise of Film Criticism

anguage is a good indicator of change, and it was indeed through the terminological shift from *Kino* to *Film* that the new approaches to the medium first entered public consciousness. Once the cinema ceased to be a place of public disturbance, film's transformation into a respectable mass diversion was achieved, and its elevation to a work of art seemed within reach. "One should not say 'film' and mean 'cinema,'" Hermann Tobers wrote in 1925, and he appealed to his readers: "Let the cinema have the entertainment film, the sensations, the sentimental love story . . . but do support the rise of film culture" (1925–26, III).

While the term *Kino*, like its predecessors *Kientopp* and *Kinematograph*, still acknowledged the technological foundations of cinema, the term *Film* claimed independence from all external influences, and thus legitimated the critic's exclusive attention to the individual film and its particular artistic qualities. Both terms referred to the same phenomenon, but they never reached complete identity; a residue of nonidentity, of difference, always remained. Whereas *Kino* emphasized the side of reception, including the framework of exhibition and the diverse cultural practices associated with the cinema as an experience and event, *Film* referred primarily to the finished product, in its function either as a commodity or a work of art. *Film* drew attention to the filmic text, whereas *Kino* put a stronger emphasis on the social setting.

Etymologically, *Kino* represented the earlier term; as the abbreviation of two other expressions, *Kinematographie* (or *Kinematograph*) and *Kientopp*, it still bore witness to the medium's origins in technological innovation and popular culture.[1] It was only after 1918–19 that *Film* would be used more frequently, making possible the cinema's gradual integration into middle-class culture. The replacement of *Kino* by *Film* brought with it a number of changes in the critical paradigm, including a shift from visual pleasure to art appreciation, from the "infamous" masses to the sophisticated city-dweller, and from the production of social relationships to the inherent characteristics of the new medium.[2]

With the growing preference for *Film* also came a stronger interest in forms, styles, and genres—a process by which the threatening aspects of *Kino,* including its real and imagined ties to the working class, could be disregarded and denied. What was gained in terms of a more rigorous analysis of individual films and a more systematic study of filmic representation brought with it a rather schematic view of spectatorship, in comparison to the extensive prewar writings on visual pleasure. Through the fetishization of the filmic object, the utopian dream of cinema as a democratic art was replaced by the categories of value and quality—until the late twenties, when the concept of film as a political weapon would again give meaning to the term "mass medium."

It will be the purpose of this chapter to provide a brief overview of film in the Weimar Republic and to examine the relationship between film production and film criticism, with a special emphasis on trade magazines and daily newspapers.[3] The heated debates on the task of the film critic and the highly self-reflexive nature of film criticism will be used to identify the larger issues at stake, the cinema's gradual integration into middle-class culture and the various attempts by writers to affirm the centrality of critical discourse in the process of cultural innovation and social change. Writing about film and film criticism always included a testing of the boundaries of social consensus and freedom of expression, and it always reached beyond the new medium to discuss problems of legitimation in the changing public sphere; the exemplary reviews of Herbert Ihering, Willy Haas, Hans Siemsen, and Kurt Tucholsky bear witness to this process.

Most importantly, the linguistic shift from *Kino* to *Film* sanctioned the transformation of the film business from a small cottage industry into a large industrial complex that included production facilities, motion picture theater chains, publishing ventures, and a large pool of skilled and unskilled labor. The process of concentration culminated in the foundation of Ufa in 1917 and established the conditions under which longer narrative films with high production values could be produced. As a result, film criticism could no longer limit itself to general reflections about cinema; it had to perform more specific tasks. In their reviews, articles, and books, film journalists thus tried to create a new audience for a new product and set out to determine the future parameters of culture consumption.

In order for this process to take place, laws had to be introduced on the national level that regulated the distribution and exhibition of films in a more effective way. Censorship decisions had previously been under the jurisdiction of local or federal agencies — a system that was time-consuming for everybody involved and allowed for great regional differences. When film censorship was briefly abandoned in 1918, so-called sex education films (*Aufklärungsfilme*) flooded the market. The introduction of the national film law (*Reichs-Lichtspielgesetz*) in 1920 put an end to such "excesses" by denying film the freedom of speech constitutionally guaranteed to the other arts. Moreover, the rather vague formulations of the *Lichtspielgesetz* made it an effective instrument for political censorship.

The first years of the Weimar Republic saw a great increase in the number of smaller film companies who profited from the devaluation of the Reichsmark and the lack of competition in the export business. Due to galloping inflation and the high unemployment rate, the studios were able to export their films at competitive prices, while foreign companies found it increasingly difficult to distribute their films in Germany. The recognition that film could be a profitable investment led to a growing involvement of banks and the availability of enormous sums of money for large prestige films. The giant film corporation Ufa, in the meantime, continued its expansionist tendencies and acquired the Decla-Bioscop studio in 1922.

The so-called German art film — or to use a rather problematic term, the Expressionist film — must be seen as a product of these economic processes. Far from being the norm, these films, perhaps no more than forty of them, were made with an explicit goal: to create a quality product and attract middle-class audiences to the cinema. The success of *Das Kabinett des Dr. Caligari* (1920, The Cabinet of Dr. Caligari) paved the way for films characterized by highly stylized sets, dramatic lighting, and fantastic stories; examples include *Der Golem* (1920, The Golem), *Die Straße* (1924, The Street), *Das Wachsfigurenkabinett* (1924, Waxworks), and *Variété* (1925, Variety). Whether working in an expressionistic or more realistic mode, such directors as Fritz Lang, E. A. Dupont, Robert Wiene, F. W. Murnau, G. W. Pabst, Paul Leni, and Lupu Pick had a discernable, personal style that marked their films as works of a particular artist with a creative vision. Together with set designers like Robert Herlth, Kurt Richter, Erich Kettelhut, and Hermann Warm and cinematographers including Guido Seeber, Karl Freund, and Eugen Schüfftan, these filmmakers were largely responsible for the emergence of an art cinema that used the most advanced technology for expanding the filmic imagination. Their names, and their association with the discourse of authorship, promised the kind of quality that middle-class audiences had come to expect from the theater and other established arts. The participation of famous stage actors like Emil Jannings, Alfred Abel, or Rudolf Klein-Rogge contributed to film's newly gained respectability, as did the cults surrounding female stars like Pola Negri, Henny Porten, and Asta Nielsen.

Ending the inflation-induced hyperactivity of the postwar years, the Dawes plan and the subsequent introduction of the so-called Rentenmark in 1924 led to a growing influx of American investment capital. Since the German film industry was threatened by the new competition, protective laws were passed to restrict foreign imports. American companies reacted by producing so-called quota or contingency films (*Kontingenzfilme*), which were inexpensive, low-quality films produced in Germany to assure a continuous American presence on the German market. Losing millions on monumental films like *The Nibelungs* and *Metropolis* and failing to establish a stronger presence on foreign markets, Ufa experienced growing financial difficulties and, in 1925, entered into an agreement concerning distribution rights with Metro-Goldwyn-Mayer and Paramount, known as the Parufamet agreement. Other film companies signed similar contracts, including Terra-Film with Universal and Phoebus with MGM, but while the Americans increased their market share, only very few German films were ever distributed in the United States. By 1925, 40 percent of the films shown in German theaters were of American origin.

Following in the footsteps of Lubitsch, Jannings, and Negri, a growing number of film artists received lucrative offers and moved to Hollywood. American films continued to be popular with German audiences, who liked them for their simple stories, fast-paced action, explicitly physical humor, and glamorous stars. In order to remain competitive, Ufa, Emelka, Terra, and others began to pursue a double strategy. On the one hand, they continued in the art film tradition by introducing new genres like the so-called street film (*Straßenfilm*) or the "cross-section" film (*Querschnittsfilm*) and by cultivating new avenues of filmic expression such as Pabst's realism or Lang's mass choreography. On the other hand, they utilized some of the formulas of genre cinema in their own approach to character and story development. Such trends were exemplified by Lang's Mabuse films and early film musicals like *Die Drei von der Tankstelle* (1930, The three from the gas station). Sentimental comedies and rustic comedies often proved very successful with audiences, while critics rejected them because of their belief in the inevitable failure of German entertainment.

The introduction of the the sound film led to further concentration in the German film industry. Tobis and Klangfilm secured the majority of sound patents and sold licenses to Ufa, whose *Melodie des Herzens* (1929, Melody of the heart) was the first German sound film. A ruthless patent war with American companies followed. While the costs of converting film and projection facilities to sound were enormous, the new language barriers brought relative economic stability for those film companies that survived the stock market crash of 1929. In the meantime, Alfred Hugenberg, the director of Krupp, continued to expand his media empire, acquiring, among other interests, the publishing house August Scherl, the Telegraphen-Union, a news agency, and the Deulig, a film company specializing in newsreels. A prominent member of the DNVP (German National People's Party), Hugenberg got increasingly involved in right-wing politics and, as a first step toward aligning Ufa with the goals of German nationalism, bought out the American interests. The films then produced by Ufa reflected these developments, avoiding formal experiments and promoting nationalistic subject matter. At the same time, pacifist films like Pabst's *Westfront 1918* (1930) or Lewis Milstone's *All Quiet on the Western Front* (1930) experienced censorship problems and were often boycotted by right-wing groups. Faced with these political and economic difficulties, the major studios were ready to turn to the state for support and protection. In 1933, their representatives thus welcomed a restructuring of the film industry in accordance with National Socialist film politics.

This brief overview shows to what degree film criticism in the Weimar Republic contributed to, and was affected by, the intrusion of economic and political concerns into all aspects of cultural life. Even in its absence, politics influenced the way films were discussed in the print media, whether by emphasizing their universal appeal, or by insisting on the fundamentally apolitical nature of mass entertainment. During the last years of the republic, critical writings on film conveyed a sense of urgency and fearful anticipation missing from previous debates. Yet they still exhibited an unusual openness for intellectual exchange and controversy.[4]

Economic expansion and concentration, the institutionalizing of cinema as an integral part of modern life, and the instrumentalization of film for political purposes — these then were the conditions under which film criticism was practiced in the trade press, the popular magazines, and the literary journals. The first years after the war saw a dramatic increase in the number of film-related publications. In 1919 alone, seventeen new journals appeared; the vast majority were based in Berlin, which emerged as the center of film publishing and the film industry. Fritz Olimsky, in one of the first historical studies on the subject, referred to these years as a "boom in film publishing that, in retrospect, we can only describe as grotesque. The result was an invasion of dilettantes and often rather dubious characters — conditions that certainly did not improve the bad reputation of the film industry. The galloping inflation brought total collapse, since most of these superfluous film journals could only have flourished in unusual times like these" (1931, 30). Many ceased publication after a few months, unable to attract a larger readership and to provide the desired mixture of entertainment and information. Some had peculiar titles, like *Die Film-Hölle* (1920–23, The film hell), a satirical magazine founded by Eugen Jakobson, or *Der Eisbär* (1918–20, The polar bear), a publication of Nordisk Film. Others were richly illustrated, for instance the biweekly *Film und Brettl* (1919–25), which, at the time of its demise, had a relatively large edition of 8,000, or *Die Filmtribüne* (1919–21), which presented caricatures and humorous reports from the film world.

While the consumer-oriented journals experienced the volatility of the market, the situation was different for technical journals, which responded to the great advances in film technology and production. Aimed at a professional readership, the weekly *Die Photo-Börse* (1919–31) published articles about new cameras and projectors on a regular basis. Together with Willi Böcker, the resourceful cinematographer Guido Seeber started the monthly (and later biweekly) *Kinotechnik* (1919–1940) as well as *Die Filmtechnik* (1925–1942), whose editor-in-chief, Andor Kraszna-Krausz, was largely responsible for the periodical's high journalistic standards. A specialist on the German art film, Kraszna-Krausz contributed regularly to the British film journal *Close-Up*. Seeber himself wrote the standard work on cinematography, the two-volume *Der praktische Kameramann* (1927, The practical cinematographer), and published extensively on technical questions such as lens systems, masking devices, and special effects (Seeber 1927, 1930).

Between short-lived popular magazines and journals with a strong technical orientation, the established trade journals faired exceedingly well, even assuming some of the functions of the popular press. Nevertheless, financial stability was often paid for with a loss of journalistic freedom and a growing influence over editorial decisions by the large film studios and new media conglomerates. After the move of *Der Kinematograph* from Düsseldorf to Berlin, most of these developments took place in the nation's capital. Part of the Scherl concern since 1923, the conservative *Kinematograph* was edited by Alfred Rosenthal (Tucholsky preferred to call him "Aros Hugenberg," referring to Rosenthal's pen name, "Aros," and the right-wing media mogul Alfred Hugenberg). The journal eventually became a semiofficial organ of the Ufa concern. Also in 1923, the more liberal *Lichtbild-Bühne,* then under Hans Wollenberg as editor-in-chief, began daily publication in an edition of 3,250 copies. Only one year later, the journal was acquired by Ullstein, one of the largest publishing houses in Weimar Germany (Sattig 1937, 77–94).

The contribution of print media to the dissemination of "cinematic consciousness" would have been unthinkable without the previous innovations in printing technology (e.g., rotary press, off-set printing, three-color printing), the acquisition strategies of the big media conglomerates, and the emergence of a new kind of mass journalism. Fan magazines, glossies, and promotional brochures like the *Ufa-Blätter* played an increasing role in the marketing of films, as well as in providing guidelines for culture consumption. The illustrated press, in a sense, provided the model of a new discursive order in which art and entertainment were no longer mutually exclusive, but instead part of a never-ending search for new diversions. By the early twenties, glossies like *Die Dame* or *Berliner Illustrirte-Zeitung* included articles on film on a regular basis. Others contained reports about the private lives of famous stars and directors, spectacular opening nights at the first-run theaters on Berlin's Kurfürstendamm, and the latest scandals from the set and the front office.

Many magazines and journals published special film issues, as did the popular *Illustrierte Zeitung* in 1919 (No. 153), the conservative weekly *Die Woche* in 1920 (No. 50), and the influential literary review *Der Querschnitt* in 1931 (No. 11.1). The range of approaches embodied by these three journals shows a growing diversification in film journalism. No longer a monolithic block, the cinema as a discursive subject reproduced the same kinds of divisions found in the areas of film production and exhibition; among others, it assumed various identities based on the readers' socioeconomic status and political convictions. A brief look at the contents of the special issues confirms this impression.

In the *Illustrierte Zeitung,* film is presented as a technical accomplishment, a clear sign of progress. Here an amusing history of the motion picture theater is followed by an informative article on cinematography by Seeber, and a report about film stars appears between popularized treatises about technical and economic questions; the illustrations add a frivolous touch. The well-known critic Rudolf Kurtz, in an essay on "Film and Culture," gives this special issue of *Illustrierte Zeitung* his blessings by calling film an "artistic accomplishment within limits."

The standard mixture of entertainment and information takes on quite a different function in the Scherl-owned *Die Woche*, where political themes predominate. While the 1920 special issue also contains the obligatory serial novel, two film poems, and numerous caricatures mocking the film world, the majority of contributors emulate reformist positions (e.g., in articles about film and school, film and science) or take an openly nationalistic stance (articles about cinema and the war). References to "German soul" and "German greatness" are ubiquitous. The nationalistic agenda becomes visible in the choice of events considered worthy of photographic representation, for instance a DVP (German People's Party) convention.

More than ten years later, a special issue of *Der Querschnitt* already uses film to strengthen its leadership role in matters of taste, made clear by the contemporary layout and the ads for Bauhaus-style furniture or retreats at Monte Verita, Ascona. The choice of topics and contributors reflects the journal's cosmopolitan orientation and its view of film as an international phenomenon. Articles by Blaise Cendrars, Georges Duhamel, Jacques Feyder, Jean Renoir, and René Clair and a short history of French film reveal strong Francophile tendencies. Critical positions are neatly divided among progressive artists, in this case George Grosz and Sergei Eisenstein, and the representatives of the industry, E. A. Dupont and Erich Pommer; glamour photographs of Hollywood stars add to the overall impression of fashionable modernity.

Special issues like those by *Illustrierte Zeitung, Die Woche,* and *Der Querschnitt* contributed to the public acceptance of film, but it was left to magazines like the *Illustrierte Kinowoche* (1913–25) and the popular *Filmmagazin* (1927–1930, renamed *Filmwelt*), published by Scherl in an edition of over 100,000 copies, to dispose, once and for all, of the old-fashioned prejudices and install the cinema at the center of modern life. Known for their appealing mixture of sensationalist reportage, glossy illustrations, and slick graphic design, these magazines placed critical essays about film side by side with articles about new consumer goods and luxury items, traveling and interior design, table manners, dress and hair fashions, and matters of the heart. They recreated, in the terminology of advertisement and within the confines of a desire that could never be fulfilled, the experience of fullness that was simultaneously promised and denied by the cult of the commodity.

The trade journals, on the other hand, promoted a kind of film criticism that, despite the institutional pressures, fulfilled some self-critical, self-regulatory functions. Apart from providing information to the various branches, writing in the trade press had to play two often conflicting roles. It had to create a positive image of the industry in which artistic consider-ations were primary and economic considerations secondary, and, at the same time, it had to evaluate its own products from the perspective of cultural consumers. The critics in the trade press argued simultaneously from the sides of production and reception, and their comments on specific films vacillated between the exigencies of advertisement and the myth of intellectual autonomy.

The *Film-Kurier* (1919–44), the first journal published on a daily basis, went furthest in combining professional concerns with a more serious commitment to film art (Sudendorf 1987). Its regular contributors included Willy Haas, who served as editor-in-chief from 1920 to 1921, Lotte Eisner, Hans Feld, and Béla Balázs. The editors of what was called a "daily paper for film — variety — art — fashion — sport — stock market" outlined their ap-proach in an early issue: "The main task of this new daily newspaper will be to inform audiences about all trends in the field of cinematography, and to convert wider circles to this young art form. . . . In addition, the *Film-Kurier* will serve as the main newspaper for the entire film industry, report-ing on a daily basis about everything new that might be of interest to the professional" (1 June 1919). The journal tried to improve communication between representatives of the industry and film audiences by emphasizing the interests shared by both groups. Contributors discussed the most urgent problems in the areas of film production and exhibition, but also paid attention to artistic questions. Hans Feld, who succeeded Haas as the journal's leading critic, cultivated a style that combined informed judgment with poignant remarks about a film's story or an actor's performance (Bock 1982). Feld would later describe the *Film-Kurier* team as "a tightly knit group of committed journalists set upon furthering experiments, the young avant-garde, and following a film-political line of a widening cul-tural horizon" (1982, 361). By the late twenties, *Film-Kurier* was the leading film journal in Europe, with a circulation of more than 12,000 copies. After Ernst Jäger assumed editorial control in 1926, the journal changed its editorial concept under the influence of conservative and right-wing groups.

During the same time period, film criticism in the daily press grew in importance both as a source of information and as a standard of evaluation for educated middle-class audiences. Newspapers with a nationwide readership, like the *Frankfurter Zeitung,* the *Vossische Zeitung,* and the *Berliner Börsen-Courier,* encouraged their film critics to cultivate distinct personalities. A well-known phenomenon in drama criticism, the figure of the star critic compensated for the disappearance of universally valid standards with an exalted subjectivism. Thus prominence was less an expression of critical excellence than a function of the increasingly competitive publishing industry. In responding to the growing professionalization, critics could either hold on to seemingly objective criteria of evaluation or treat writing as a marketable skill, with styles ranging from the dispassionate to the polemical. They could either try to produce the consensus associated with the liberal bourgeois public sphere, thereby confirming its emancipatory function but denying the existing institutional pressures, or they could embrace fully the subjectivism of the feuilleton and, in so doing, reject as old-fashioned the idea of the critic as a representative of the public. While those in the former position still believed in the utopian potential of criticism in spite of its crisis, the latter already recognized the discrepancies between its grandiose gestures and its limited impact on film production. The better-known Weimar film critics positioned their work somewhere between these two positions.

Among them, Herbert Ihering gained a wide reputation for unbiased reviews that represented the progressive, democratic spirit of the young republic (for reviews see Krull 1964; Krechel 1972, 48–51 and 292–306; Ebert 1987). Known as a theater critic and an early supporter of Bertolt Brecht, Ihering wrote for the *Berliner-Börsen Courier* from 1920 to 1932; he was voted "best film critic of the season" by the *Film-Kurier* in 1931. Rejecting all literary influences, but also opposing the trend toward specialization, Ihering argued that "the challenges in every field have come not from the specialists, but from the outsiders who maintained a distance. Film criticism has no tradition, no system on which it can build, like theater criticism. It knows no school. It is a beginning and that is its fortune. It still has to create the foundation on which theater criticism is built" (1961, 1:

405). Such remarks were meant to strengthen the cause — coming from the theater, Ihering could hardly have failed to see the critical and institutional restraints from which film was so desperately trying to free itself — but they also found expression in his own approach. Writing about films was a productive act, Ihering believed, and not an auxiliary in the promotion of new films. Rather than complain about the shortcomings of existing films, critics had to contribute to the making of better ones and, as he added in an ironic tone, assume the role presently played by the censors: "Through its judgments, through its ability to distinguish, film criticism creates a basis for the separation of good and bad, of imitation and real effects . . . and the film evaluation board will be relieved. Then the trash will peter out by itself" (1961, 1: 426).

Ihering's reviews show a strong belief in the revealing power of criticism, including its aesthetic and political implications. Two areas of concern stand out, the importance of actors and the quality of German films. While his experience in the theater gave him an unfailing standard for evaluating actors and discussing problems of mise-en-scène, Ihering never tried to compare film to the theater. Both explored new means of representation and therefore had to be measured against how successfully they translated the challenge of modernity into dramatic and filmic forms. As the older and more advanced of the two, he argued, the theater provided a good model. "That the film of today begins a new, and a radical, transformation has not only to do with technological progress or an understanding of its conditions. The transformation was only possible with the introduction of a style of stage acting that made creative use of a revived body consciousness, that concentrated, structured, and celebrated its own rhythms. . . . Film does not have a future because it advances technologically, but because its demands are in agreement with the demands of contemporary painting, architecture, and acting. Film exists, because the new actor exists" (1961, 1: 378).

Ihering's subsequent focus on the actor as a mediator between image and narrative responded to trends in theater and film to move from theatrical to more naturalistic acting styles. The centrality of acting, and of the body as the actor's primary tool, is captured in the term *expression (Ausdruck)* with its many variations (e.g., intensified expression, necessary expression) and qualities (e.g., precision, concentration, intensification, tension). Equating the human soul on the stage with the physical appearance on the screen, Ihering praised film as an unerring critic of acting and of actors. His fascination with film's expressive physicality influenced his evaluation of Germany's most popular film actors. On the one side were actors like Henny Porten, Fern Andra, Alfred Abel, or Albert Steinrück who, as Ihering saw it, simply repeated the old theatrical conventions ad nauseam or who treated film acting as a limited repertory of gestures. On the other side, there were actors who played with precision and refinement, and who included such stars as Asta Nielsen, Werner Krauss, and Fritz Kortner. A great fan of American slapstick comedies, Ihering always found confirmation for his ideas on acting in the films of Charlie Chaplin, Buster Keaton, and Jackie Coogan.

While actors play a crucial role in Ihering's reviews, the problem of national film culture must be described as his most persistently recurring theme. Time and again he mentioned the German inability to make good films. "A German film can be bad for a variety of reasons. It either fails to be a film or indulges in high-flown experiments. It either imitates literature or looks like a picture postcard. Its use of the material is either crude or sentimental. But when it is bad, then it is primarily because it is not a film in the first place. . . . The German film is often bad because it wants to be something other than film. The American, because it wants too much to be film. The German, because it neglects the filmic elements (the composition of movement). The American, because it exaggerates the filmic elements" (1961, 1: 435).

Often using the reviews for more extensive reflections on culture and society, Ihering explained these differences with regard to the relationship between dominant and popular culture in both societies. Whereas American film conventions originated in the culture and the sociopsychological needs of its people, they were bound to turn into empty formulas once introduced into a social setting without indigenous popular traditions. According to Ihering, these mechanisms could be found on the level of filmic styles and genres and they explained, among other things, the impossibility of a German adventure film. Ihering warned against the imitation of American methods but, at the same time, defended Americanization as a necessary part of the filmic condition. "Perhaps film requires an impersonal, homogeneous audience: America, and not an individualized one: Germany. In America the film audience already exists. In Germany it is still being created through each new film" (1961, 2: 493).

Precisely because film had first to create the conditions of reception and because the making of an audience was closely linked to changes in the social structure, Ihering spoke out in favor of a German cinema that reflected national styles. As his enthusiastic comments on Grune's film *The Street,* Pick's *Sylvester,* Dupont's *Variety,* and Murnau's *Last Laugh* suggest, he was thinking of a tradition reaching from German Romanticism and the realist novel to the more recent concerns of New Objectivity. What Ihering said about *The Last Laugh* probably holds true for all others, namely that it was international "because it is a *German* film hit, just as the American film is international when it is an *American* film hit" (1961, 2: 487).

Toward the end of the twenties, Ihering's enthusiastic comments on American culture gave way to a more critical assessment of a film industry that, in the meantime, had invaded the German market and lured away some of the most talented people. With the decline of the domestic film industry, the American film now represented to him a form of cultural imperialism. This change in attitude was partially caused by his encounter with the films of Eisenstein and Pudovkin. The new Russian films proved to Ihering that it was possible to make films with a popular mission and epic qualities, and to transform the audience into the agent and recipient of their revolutionary messages. While Ihering used the Hollywood-Moscow opposition to sketch the outlines of a democratic mass culture, it was his growing frustration with German films, including those by Lang, Murnau, and Pabst, that compelled him to distinguish more clearly between a national cinema striving for authenticity and a nationalistic cinema exploiting its own myths. The German cinema, in his view, belonged to the second group.

An exceptional figure like Ihering reveals little about the working conditions of most film reviewers. For the most part, the reviewers for the large regional and national newspapers worked under the pressures of the marketplace. Unlike journalists writing for the trade press, however, they denied such outside influences. Their insistence on autonomy — and their awareness of the illusionary if not self-defying nature of such beliefs — inspired a style of writing that on the surface treated film like the other arts, but without the usual attention and respect. Worried about the public image of this new profession, film reviewers tried to find a position between the sensationalism associated with the film world and the dignity of informed, responsible cultural criticism. They also had to define a critical position for themselves between the specialized trade journals and the politicized leftist publications. As a rule, reviewers in the daily press emphasized the formal qualities of a film and paid special attention to camerawork, set and costume design, and, above all, to performance. In a marked departure from the prewar years, technical details were rarely discussed; the obligatory mention of the studio's name gave way to extensive comments about the director or the star as the creative inspiration behind a film production. Rejecting the "tendentiousness" associated with leftist film criticism, reviewers in the mainstream press sought refuge in terms such as "universal value," "human interest," or "deep meaning." These established a critical framework in which films could be treated as the expression of a common interest that varied only in the form, style, or quality of its execution. Consequently, questions of artistic value were considered more important than those of content; likewise, social relevance was deemed less crucial than the emotional appeal to the audience. At times, films with provocative themes (social injustice, for example, or unemployment) elicited almost hostile reactions among reviewers, either because their depressing stories stood in the way of what they considered film's foremost mission, entertainment, or because their unmitigated realism was regarded as incompatible with the requirements of film art.

Out of opposition to these practices, such critics as Benjamin Brentano and Siegfried Kracauer for the *Frankfurter Zeitung,* Kurt Pinthus for *Das Tage-Buch,* and Hans Siemsen, Kurt Tucholsky, Rudolf Arnheim, and Axel Eggebrecht for *Die Weltbühne* explored new ways of writing about film. Self-criticism was a first step in this direction, and it will be the purpose of the remaining pages to examine the importance of self-criticism to film criticism in general and in one particular example, *Die Weltbühne.* During the first years of the republic, critics began to problematize the conditions under which film criticism had emerged as a discursive practice with often conflicting institutional affiliations and philosophical traditions. As the war years had shown, writing on film could be used equally well as a contribution to film promotion, nationalistic propaganda, or aesthetic theories. With the cinema's gradual integration into middle-class culture, however, any too-obvious links to state and industry were perceived as detrimental to the growth of film art. Given these circumstances, the need arose for a film criticism modeled on literary or theater criticism, especially since charges of greed and corruption represented a major obstacle to any plans for improvement. Listing some of the culprits, the filmmaker E. A. Dupont insisted: "In Germany, there are no other trade journals where the boundaries between journalism and advertisement have disappeared so completely as in the film trade press. In these journals, almost every single line is for sale" (1919b).

Some critics actually welcomed such practices, arguing that the introduction of higher critical standards would only destroy the cinema's "healthy" primitivism (Ickes 1919) or disrupt the balance of supply and demand (Alex 1922). As late as 1928, Arthur Rudolf claimed that film's mass appeal in no way justified the existence of reviews; on the contrary. "The bourgeois press . . . has no reason to pave the way for the film" (1928, 592–93), because, he concluded, film would either make it on its own or carry on in its present state of mediocrity, not even worthy of the most unqualified kind of commentary. Laroche, who had earlier compared film critics to psychopaths, argued in a similar vein. His conclusions are almost too extreme to be taken seriously. "If we want to save ourselves from this impending doom," he wrote, "we must at once pass a number of laws against the publishing of film journals, the writing of film reviews, the mentioning of film stars, the talking about films" (1919, 10). In his response to Laroche, Hans Pander spoke for the majority of critics when he confirmed their unyielding commitment to quality. "Preaching doesn't help. In order to take steps against the superficiality of film, one has to reform the film, and serious film criticism is a means to this end" (1919, 7).

Most film critics would have agreed with Alexander Kossowsky's formulation in the *Deutsche Presse,* the official organ of the professional organization of journalists, that high-quality film criticism was based on journalistic freedom and high professional standards; in other words, it required the "all-round educated writer, the critical man with life experience and artistic sensitivity, the man who knows what to demand of film, technically as well as artistically" (Kossowsky 1927). Yet opinions differed considerably when it came to defining the social and political role of the critic. Dismissing the endless discussions about film criticism as proof of its developmental shortcomings, Ihering offered a very general definition. "Criticism originates in the inner need to analyze the laws of an art form. Criticism means to experience the work of art through its distinct elements, and thus means instinctive confirmation of the productive, and instinctive rejection of the unproductive elements" (1961, 1: 445–46). Through the emphasis on form, Ihering offered a hidden critique of the feuilleton style practiced by star critics like Alfred Kerr and other self-appointed arbiters of taste, and presented film as an art form with clearly defined criteria of evaluation. His insightful comments on the specificity of filmic means suggest that he also perceived the critic as an artist in his own right. The term *productivity* thus referred equally to the complexity of a filmic text and the critic's ability to reproduce these qualities through and in writing; hence the importance of a solid educational background in literature and the arts.

Others saw film criticism in terms of social mediation. In the conservative *Der Kunstwart,* Roland Schacht described the critic less as a specialist in matters of taste than as an intermediary between the educated classes and the unsophisticated masses. Announcing the journal's new film column, Schacht wrote that "the cinema and the intellectuals need one another: the cinema, because it cannot improve without the intellectuals, and the intellectuals, because by ignoring film they only widen the dangerous gap between themselves and the masses. That is why we shall try from now on to inform the nation's cultural elite about the best, but also the most typical, new releases, in order to spare them the disappointment caused by spontaneous visits" (Güttinger 1984a, 488). As a protective device against the excesses of mass culture, film criticism was to guide the educated classes to the cinema and, through criticism and praise, impose their superior tastes on its products. Just two years later, Schacht admitted that such attempts were, more often than not, unsuccessful given the audience's continuous infatuation with cheap entertainment. The idea of the critic as a man of letters had to be discarded, he concluded, and the intellectual standards be lowered. "The task of the critic is here that of an honest mediator. . . . The most important thing is that audience participation increases, and here the critic can indeed serve important functions" (1927, 195).

The critics for *Die Weltbühne* contributed actively to the debate on film criticism. Hans Siemsen, who also wrote for such prestigious journals as *Die Neue Schaubühne* and *Der Querschnitt,* argued that film critics were partly responsible for the perceived crisis of criticism, because they had abandoned their original enthusiasm for a few profitable relationships with the film studios. The result: "It is not the critics who have gained control over film production; it is the other way around: the film industry controls the critics and, moreover, the entire daily press" (Siemsen 1921a, 102). These conclusions sparked a heated argument between Siemsen and Rudolf Kurtz about the generally low artistic quality of German films, the false ambition of many directors to produce art instead of solid entertainment, and the critic's responsibility to change this unfortunate situation. Their arguments replayed the old controversy over art and entertainment, and drew attention to the artist's simultaneous responsibility to his art and his audience. Supposedly expressing "the most innermost thoughts of the German film industry," Kurtz accused Siemsen of being a know-it-all who disguised his ignorance through hasty aesthetic judgments and trendy political arguments. Siemsen's arrogance was especially evident for Kurtz in his indifference toward economic issues. "Without money, without a lot of money, all these beautiful things don't help much; a cheap set and bad materials will be all that is left of them. The Siemsens don't know that, for they sit at their desks, have no idea about the costs of a film and insist on their naivete and their *bon sens*" (1921, 166–68; cf. Tucholsky 1921, 169). In his rejoinder, Siemsen dismissed Kurtz as "an employee protecting his company" (Ufa) and, citing several German films as proof of the prevailing lack of imagination, repeated his main point: "I love cinema. And that's why I am upset about the low quality of German films" (1921b, 254).[5] Despite their disagreement about the "creative" power of money, Siemsen and Kurtz nonetheless agreed that critical debates like these were necessary for the advancement of film, and that the representatives of the literary sphere should assume a leadership role in this process. In short, they still argued within the same critical paradigm.

By contrast, Willy Haas of the *Film-Kurier* promoted a quality-oriented, informative film criticism that differed equally from the political commitment of the *Weltbühne* critics and the moralistic appeals of professionals like Dupont (Kuhlbrodt 1987 and 1990; Jacobsen et al. 1991). Taking a strong antiliterary stance, the successful film scenarist called for greater attention to film's technological side. "In my opinion . . . reviews by a professional film critic are of greater relevance than those by the best drama or literary critic, even if the former is less known as a writer, intellectual, or public figure. Film criticism today has to be more than a mere criticism of effects [*Wirkungskritik*]" (1922; cf. Haas 1924). Opposed to what, for him, amounted to an obsession with narrative clichés and psychological effects, Haas introduced the perspective of the apparatus as a way of acknowledging the cinema's technological basis and making production the ultimate standard of critical evaluation. Reviewers without adequate qualifications, he argued, should not write about films, no matter how brilliant their styles may be. "Coming from literature, from the theater, the outsider [*sic*] critic — hence Siemsen, too — focuses only on the facts, never on the possibilities: because he doesn't know them, cannot know them" (1922). According to Haas, literary preferences prevented the nonspecialist from seeing film outside the traditional genre distinctions, and were largely responsible for the continual existence of films that mirrored this critical inadequacy in their theatrical settings and pretentious narratives.

This first round of critical exchanges inspired another one in 1927, in which the question of professional competence was discussed. Two years earlier, Siemsen had "revised" his opinion about the corruptibility of Berlin's leading film critics and emphasized their incompetence instead. "They think up everything you can think of, they think up more than all the other film critics in the world. They can write thick volumes about theory and philosophy, about the aims and the aesthetic laws of film. But they cannot see" (1925, 37). For a solution, Siemsen demanded more personal commitment. "He who loves film, disciplines it. Those under criticism, the studio bosses, should have an even stronger interest in independent, brutally honest criticism than the critics themselves. . . . However, it is my opinion that really free, really independent film criticism does not exist in Germany" (1927a, 147).

Siemsen's appeal to the critic's moral standards, and his calls for a radically independent film criticism, were based on the assumption that those writing for the mass press still had the power to claim such positions. They must be seen as programmatic statements, rather than realistic assessments of the situation. His insistence on self-reflection and his proposals for a professional honor code, after all, bear witness to the actual difficulties involved. Siemsen's numerous polemics on film criticism suggest to what degree its future depended on the ability of critics to communicate with their readers and clarify their relationship to the industry. Only higher critical standards, Siemsen concluded, provided audiences with an opportunity to influence the quality of films from the side of reception. The ultimate goal was therefore not to educate the public, but to engage in a critical exchange with the work and, indirectly, the artist. "Criticism, as we know it, is not really criticism. Real criticism only concerns the work and addresses those who created it and should continue to create" (1927b, 712).

Elsewhere, Siemsen used H. G. Wells's scathing review of *Metropolis* to speak about these problems in greater depth. After summarizing Well's comments on "the dumbest film of all times," Siemsen turns to those German critics who had showered the Lang film with praise and launched an all-out attack on what he painted as a megalomaniac industry and its inept scribblers. "The responsibility for such expensive, detrimental and shameful nonsense lies with those who made the film, the film producers and — how shall I say it? — the film artists, directors, set designers, writers, and so forth. But also with the film critics who will stand for such a thing without razing it to the ground. The fact that this review by Wells, this model of an uncompromising, concise, and sensible film review, is written in English is a scandal. The reasons why such a film review is not just unwanted in Germany, but simply not possible and being made impossible — they are even more scandalous. They are the main reason for the German film crisis" (1927c, 950). Again it was Haas (who in the meantime had left the *Film-Kurier* to start *Die Literarische Welt* with the publisher Ernst Rowohlt) who responded to Siemsen's polemics and argued for a "synthesis of high-brow conscience and low-brow possibilities" (1927, 7), thus using artistic compromise as the basis for a less confrontational relationship with the industry.

Despite the considerable differences between Ihering's close textual analysis, Schacht's emphasis on quality, Siemsen's notion of professional ethics, and Haas's attention to technical detail, all four critics realized that there was an urgent need for information and mediation. Hence the importance of reviews that were neither elitist nor simplistic, that took into account the needs of audiences, and that reflected the cinema's precarious position between art and industry through a similarly integrative style of writing. According to Haas, a thus-defined critical practice stood in sharp contrast to the criticism of taste associated with critics like Alfred Polgar and Alfred Kerr, who participated in the literary debates on the cinema only to affirm the superiority of the theater. Their contribution to film criticism, however, was not as destructive as Haas claimed. By writing regularly about film, they helped to determine its critical parameters, even though their involvement often took the form of writing "against," and they contributed significantly to the acceptance of film by the educated middle classes. In the process, these traditionalists even revised their opinions (cf. Kerr 1927, 11–25; Polgar 1927a and 1927b).

In 1913, Kerr had dismissed the cinema as a technical curiosity, asking: "Even the animals have facial expressions; man was given language. Why give that up for artistic expression? Why descend to the level of the deaf-mute?" (1991, 3:345). However, his contempt eventually gave way to real curiosity about an art form whose main advantage he now considered to be its profound silence. "One is deeply touched because the words are missing, because only visible facts are presented" (1991, 3:349). In 1912, Polgar had claimed that productive encounters between film and literature were not only undesirable, but impossible. But even Polgar succumbed to the inevitable by including film if not among the arts then among the various phenomena of modern life. In his reports from Berlin, the film-crazed city of the Weimar years, he not involuntarily assumed the role of the ironist unable to stop the tide. "Film occupies Berlin, deserters stream to it in masses, and the city's total capitulation is not far. Confused by klieg lights, the stranger often has the impression that the true Berlin, at this moment, could very well be a film vision built out of cardboard, and that the real houses are only placed there in order to feign a little bit of 'real city.' One could also say: one single film strip embraces all the peoples of Berlin, the strongest one since the dynasty collapsed. Its inscription: Millions — be embraced" (1926, 232).

To the degree that film criticism evolved into a literary genre in its own right, its questions reached beyond the domain of cinema. Writing about film became a way of discussing issues relevant to culture and society at large. In contrast to the prewar years, the cinema was more frequently used as a lever than as a target in the analysis of political processes. As critics looked for alternatives to the hyperbole of film promotion and the pretensions of the feuilleton, they confronted the conditions that had given rise to various discursive styles. The attempts by the big film studios to silence more outspoken critics drew attention to the material conditions of film production. Responding to such assaults on journalistic freedom, a group of Berlin critics, including Ihering, founded the Verband Berliner Filmkritiker (Association of Berlin Film Critics) with the explicit goal of preserving their independence (Kracauer 1979, 448–50).

The openness with which these conflicts of interest were discussed — in other words, the transparency of power relations — also explains the attraction of film criticism for some left-liberal intellectuals. Writing about film allowed them to put their opposition to bourgeois culture into practice and to contribute actively to the discourses that constituted modern mass culture. Similarly, the association with film enabled them to overcome their social isolation as intellectuals and establish closer contact with the masses, if only through writing about mass cultural phenomena. The results of such involvement were published in respected cultural journals and literary reviews like *Das Tage-Buch, Die Literarische Welt, Der Querschnitt, Die Neue Schaubühne* and, above all, *Die Weltbühne*.

The *Weltbühne* critics offered their views on a variety of topics, questioning accepted definitions of quality, underscoring the importance of film as a popular art, promoting noncommercial and progressive films, attacking the Hugenberg concern, and speaking out against reactionary tendencies in filmmaking (Deak 1969). Regular contributors included Roland Schacht

(1922–23), Kurt Tucholsky (1920–23), Hans Siemsen (1919–1928), Axel Eggebrecht (1926–27), and Rudolf Arnheim (1926–33); many supported progressive causes, but were unwilling to submit to the rigidity of party politics. Their writings on film, just like the *Weltbühne* as a whole, must be seen in the context of left-liberal politics and the growing marginalization of intellectuals in the later years of the Weimar Republic. The journal's not-always-unproblematic combination of political radicalism and elitist tastes, as well as the unyielding belief in the power of reason and the liberating but at the same time paralyzing sense of irony that characterized many articles, were as much a reaction to the intellectual's diminished influence in society as the result of an increasingly polarized political climate.

While the film critics of *Die Weltbühne* were highly effective in attacking bourgeois conventions and institutions, their critical analyses included many contradictions. Whenever associated with mass culture, film was celebrated as an alternative to bourgeois culture; but whenever it appeared in connection with something German, it was accused of cultural pretensions. "Rather than with German film production, one should concern oneself with the importation of goatskins. They are really more important" (Morus 1927, 187). This comment captures the mixture of anger and irony very well. Often Tucholsky, Siemsen, and Eggebrecht would write about German films, but only to enumerate their shortcomings in a way that conveyed a continuous disregard for "lowly" diversions. In the same spirit, they would mention the audience's need for good entertainment, but only to launch another diatribe against those who actually constituted the masses. Film theory regularly inspired diatribes against those involved in such esoteric quests. Referring to the discrepancy between theoretical claims (e.g., about the silent image) and technological innovations (e.g., the introduction of sound), Kraszna-Krausz once noted with derision: "It is the tragedy of film theory that it is trampled on by every new invention as soon as it seems to have proven its right of existence" (1932, 447). While remarks like these were meant to ridicule the typically German infatuation with speculative thought, they often sounded arrogant in light of the wider political implications of theoretical discourse. It was not until the late twenties and the rise of National Socialism that *Weltbühne* critics gave up their mocking style and summoned their rhetorical skills to fight the encroachment of reactionary politics in all areas of cultural life.

The critic most closely associated with *Die Weltbühne* and its sense of ironic detachment was Kurt Tucholsky. Writing about film under the pseudonyms Ignaz Wrobel, Theobald Tiger, and Peter Panter, Tucholsky offered his opinion on everything from the megalomania of directors like Lang to the shallowness of German film comedies, from the predilections of the petty bourgeois to the shady dealings of Hugenberg and his associates. With an unmistakable instinct for quality, he immediately recognized the uniqueness of *Caligari*: "But—the greatest of rarities: a good film. More of those!" (1987, 2:293). Writing as a cultural critic rather than a film critic, Tucholsky was best known for his satirical vignettes of audiences. In an article on cinema and daydreaming, he established a direct connection between the erotic scenes on the screen and the "private cinema" that unfolds in the minds of clerks and salesgirls (1987, 1:111–13). "Thus some films run in deep darkness," he wrote (1987, 8:112). Recalling a visit to the movies, he "confessed" a deep love for animals: "The program notes informed me that this film also had a story—I did not notice it. . . . Who wants drama? That ape, that beautiful ape!" (1987, 2:390). Tucholsky saw the ape's tricks as the sign of a new dawn in the "German cinematic sky" that had all too long been dominated by pretentious characters and bombastic stories. Almost on principle, Tucholsky dismissed German films as unimaginative, overly serious, and unsophisticated—qualities that, in his view, also described German audiences. Such disparaging remarks found an equivalent in the reverence with which he wrote about American films, praising their good sense of timing and their brilliant use of movement and action.

Perhaps it was the awareness of their marginal position in German society that caused Tucholsky and many other critics to renounce German films and to project their hopes and expectations onto another national cinema. Part of the widespread fascination with things American, the almost-childish love for the American cinema was at once an expression of protest and resignation. Embracing the products of mass culture with a vengeance, the intellectuals hoped to salvage the utopian potential of mass culture. The implications were spelled out most clearly in the Chaplin cult among artists and intellectuals (Hake 1990). The figure of the little tramp gave them a chance to forget Germany, its obsession with *Kultur*, its petty-bourgeois tastes, and its provincial atmosphere. As Tucholsky put it: "And we are grateful to you, Charlie Chaplin, for you show us that the world is not German (*teutsch*) and not Bavarian but very, very different. From the cellar, de profundis, be greeted!" (1987, 3:361). Tucholsky's enthusiasm was shared by many others, including Siemsen. "The national hero of the world is Charlie Chaplin. That is one of the main reasons why there is no longer an understanding between Germany and the rest of the world" (1922a, 368).

Chaplin not only represented the claims of the oppressed, he also showed the way to fight oppression through humor and mockery. His films were considered living examples of another, better life where the most basic human needs found expression in the most advanced form of mass entertainment. Tucholsky described the vacillation between resistance and submission as subversive precisely because of its lack of closure. "He [Chaplin] is able to mock other people merely through his appearance. He only has to appear, with the little hat, with the little stick, with the little mustache, waddling with his impossible legs — and suddenly everything around him is wrong, and he is right, and the whole world has become ridiculous" (1987, 3:230). That precarious balance was soon destroyed by brute force, however, and the love affair between Chaplin and an entire generation of German intellectuals ended with Tucholsky's terse note: "Chaplin has asked Hitler for the temporary surrender of his moustache. The negotiations continue" (1987, 10:52).

In this fictional encounter between Chaplin and Hitler the highly self-reflexive and often very heated debates on film criticism found an end as well. The representatives of the Other — American culture, popular cinema, irreverent slapstick humor — were pushed aside by the insidious propagator of German racial and national superiority, and the figure of the little tramp disappeared from Germany together with critical discourse.

# Chapter 7
## Toward a Philosophy of Film

The filmic representation of the body provided a first culminating point for the formulation of aesthetic questions outside of the paradigms of literature and the theater. However, reflections on the expressive quality inherent in gestures and facial expressions should not be confused with an actor's theory. For a better understanding of the concepts that gave rise to a philosophy of film, the discourses of acting and body must be separated from each other, just as aesthetics and politics must be brought into a new relationship so that they can illuminate these two often confusing sets of oppositions.

The fascination with the body reached back to the earliest writings on film, but it was in the twenties that writers began to discuss its significance in relation to filmic means. When they focused on a particular actor or on the differences between stage and screen acting, they did so in order to better understand the dynamic of absence and presence that structures the representation of the body. The actor functioned here as a heuristic device rather than as the focus of the investigation. It was the ontology of the image that inspired the interest in acting, and it was the metaphysical quality of a representation outside of language that prompted the comparisons to the stage. Therein lay the difference from theories of screen acting that simply equated film with a staged pantomime but paid little or no attention to camerawork or mise-en-scène.

This reassessment of gesture (*Gebärde*) in the theorizing of film took place under the influence to two simultaneous developments, the growing number of stage adaptations to the screen, which reintroduced dramatic considerations, and the modern dance movement, with its explorations into the language of the body. The widespread fascination with physiognomy in literature and the visual arts contributed to the process by making critics aware of the philosophical implications (Heller 1984, 176–96). In the prewar years, writers like Hofmannsthal and Lukács had commented on the spectacle of the body in their famous essays on cinema. While their discussion was informed by theoretical concerns, many Weimar critics approached the body with almost religious reverence, claiming it as an object for metaphysical reflection. As the most ancient form of human communication, they argued, gesture alone had remained unaffected by the crisis of meaning. The silent film proved essential to rediscovering gesture, the only antidote to the Babel of languages. Writers often described the face as the site where the body reaches identity and transcendence. As the mirror of the soul, they maintained, the face confirmed the anthropocentric perspective against the objectifying gaze of the camera. And as the center of the body, the face represented both spirituality and physicality — characteristics that preserved the unity of experience against the fragmentation of modern life and therefore confirmed their humanistic beliefs. Given this double movement, the writings on gesture were materialist as well as essentialist; deeply ambivalent in their relationship to modernity, they contained an antitechnological thrust as well as elements of technoromanticism. The discourses of the body allowed writers to reflect critically on their dependency on language and, at the same time, project their dreams of redemption onto the images on the screen, which were simultaneously so distant and so close.

It will be the purpose of this chapter to trace the beginnings of what, given these idealist underpinnings, will be called philosophy of film rather than film theory. As will be argued, the body provided a framework for dealing with the formal aspects of the filmic image and shifted the debates from questions of spectatorship to questions of representation. A comparison between two works by cinema reformer Konrad Lange will then be used to analyze the political implications of this shift, including the emergence of film as an academic subject. The main part of the chapter will be devoted to thinkers like Rudolf Kurtz, Rudolf Harms, and Georg Otto Stindt, who completed the return to normative aesthetics and, by using formal categories of evaluation, were able to identify film's unique qualities and inherent characteristics. To underscore the oppositions within the field of aesthetics, the chapter will close with the avant-garde (Hans Richter, Guido Bagier) and their contribution to the theorizing of the filmic image, and of non-narrative film in particular.

The face as a map that can be deciphered, the body as a site of profound meanings, the language of gestures, the return of the senses — it was an actress primarily associated with the Wilhelmine cinema, Asta Nielsen, who served as an inspiration for many of these thoughts. A comparison with another silent film idol, Charlie Chaplin, may be helpful in understanding the discursive function of the Nielsen cult. The admiration for Nielsen, whose films included, after the phenomenal success of *Afgrunen* (1910), classics like *Hamlet* (1920), *INRI* (1924), and *Die freudlose Gasse* (1925, Joyless Street), found expression in "Asta Nielsen theories" — critical writings that relied on acting and actors in the formulation of aesthetic principles. Significantly, it was foreigners like Chaplin or the Danish-born Nielsen who gave rise to these configurations, thus introducing national as well as sexual difference into the theorizing of the body. Both came to be associated with a decidedly filmic approach. Unlike the studied gestures of most German actors, their acting styles combined naturalness and an acute awareness of the camera.

Though equally removed from the theatrics of a Jannings or a Porten, Chaplin and Nielsen stood for very different traditions and, consequently, opened up different perspectives on the metaphysical status of the filmed body. Whereas Chaplin, the personification of America, represented the humorous answer to mechanization, Nielsen, as the corporealization of Nordic inwardness, was identified with an intense emotionality that found expression in the most subtle glances and gestures. In his mechanical choreographies of body parts and movements, Chaplin gave life to the alienated modern hero. By contrast, Nielsen upheld the promise of authenticity. "And precisely because Asta Nielsen speaks this language [of gesture], she has assumed the role of the great interpreter of mankind as such, the fulfillment of a primeval unity long foreseen, an apparition, a face, the countenance that everybody felt within themselves and that they welcomed in the very moment of her appearance" (Mungenast 1928, 27).

While Chaplin acted out the grotesque rebellion against social conventions, Nielsen's individuality found confirmation through the vacillation between self-revelation and self-restraint. In Chaplin's body, the crisis of male subjectivity was exposed through various strategies of distancing, whereas Nielsen opened up a space in which spirituality and eroticism could become one. The exalted tone with which Mungenast describes Nielsen's contribution to film makes clear to what degree certain film actors came to embody problems in modern culture. "Through Asta Nielsen, everything experiences a spiritualization. Everything becomes spiritual. All objects in her immediate environment become spiritual. Spiritualization of human beings and objects. Today Asta Nielsen has a mission to complete — that is, to prevent a catastrophe whose consequences cannot be measured: to fight the phantom that threatens to suck dry the soul of mankind. Not just for the sake of the future of film!" (1928, 114). Statements like these suggest that the human presence in film helped to dissipate fears linked to film as a means of mechanical reproduction and that it reinstated the creative individual at the center of meaning production and, implicitly, of the emerging aesthetics of film.

The literary writers used the notion of gesture to sketch an anthropocentric cinema in which faces conveyed secrets and in which bodies possessed a soul. Its elements are spelled out in an anthology with the programmatic title *Der Film von morgen* (1923, The film of tomorrow) and an eclectic mixture of vitalist, physiognomic, and modernist ideas. Setting the mood, editor Hugo Zehder defines gesture as the "royal road" to a new internationalism. Film, the publisher of *Die Neue Schaubühne* argues, is "a conqueror of time and space. It is filled with inspiration, surpassing the imagination, condensing all events, linking man, animal, and strangest fable, bringing together a family of nations, alliances, elevating the daily work to the realm of symbols" (1923, 32). As the primeval language shared by all peoples, gesture was the means by which this process of unification could be achieved. However, gesture is simply equated with the body, without any reference to the cinematic apparatus, and the body is conceptualized as an imaginary body without the markers of sex, race, or class and without any relationship to history or society.

Continuing in this vein, three other contributors speculate about the film of tomorrow in order to grasp the mysteries of the face, yet they, too, use the concreteness of the body only as a point of departure for disembodied ideas. Thus technopositivist and functionalist concepts become agents in the revival of metaphysics through film. Claiming that "the magic of the body is an artistic means that belongs exclusively to film" (1923, 36), the journalist Friedrich Sieburg begins his reflections on the body by praising the star system as the clearest sign of film's modernity. In an act of complete openness, the star presents his or her body to the camera and allows the soul to manifest itself in the image. Symptomatic of the entire anthology and its critical project, Sieburg's effusive description of the star phenomenon contains a quasireligious message that stands in sharp contrast to his almost mechanistic analysis of the sociopsychological function of film. The fascination with stars is, in his view, closely linked to the experience of want, and the desire to compensate for one's feelings of emptiness through the incorporation of an image of fullness. "He [the film star] is confronted with a new type of human being who expects completion, not just mirroring. Before, he had to present an image of fulfilled life. The only thing that counts today is the filling of that empty space created by an empty existence" (1923, 34). Thus the filmic image glosses over the experience of alienation and negates the divisions in society through the illusion of perceptual unity.

Arguing in a similar vein, Rudolf Leonhard welcomes the cult of surface phenomena as an integral part of modernity. The standardization of tastes, emotions, and beliefs through film represent for him the first steps toward a truly democratic art and a living internationalism. In the place of social and individual differences, Leonhard argues, film creates a pleasurable world of looking and being looked at, a world, in which all oppositions collapse in the face of physical beauty. Propositions like "appearance and essence are identical. Looks are always trustworthy, and to be beautiful is a distinction, a virtue, an obligation, and a task" (1923, 109) can therefore be considered paradigmatic of aesthetic theories based on physiognomy and the denial of the cinematic apparatus (see also Leonard 1920).

The more the body remains a theoretical construct that is called upon to facilitate a new film art, the more can the differences between real people be used to justify social discrimination. Ultimately, the rediscovery of the self in the beautiful faces on the screen is paid for through new divisions based on body types and an often disturbing mixture of racist and sexist ideas. Willy Haas, in his contribution to *Der Film von morgen,* introduces the notion of type and typage, a kind of modern physiognomy, to situate film in sharp opposition to the dramatic hero of the theater. He claims that "film is only capable of depicting one kind of human character, namely the passive one, the one affected by the world, not the one affecting the world" (1923, 28); hence its many images of women, hence its deep affinity with the feminine. Haas's conclusions show to what degree the body — and, implicitly, the cinema — continued to represent the Other, whether as threat or salvation, and with what intentions films were used to justify social and historical differences.

Carl Hauptmann, finally, covers the full range of meanings associated with gesture as he elevates gesture to be the source and ultimate goal of cinematography.[1] Time and again in *Der Film von morgen* he returns to the prefix "Ur" (primeval) to assert film's inherent spirituality, arguing that "the realm of gesture is a cosmic realm" (1923, 16) and "the whole world is a wide realm of meaningful gestures" (17). Film manages to "objectify the course of all significant movements, the deep gesture of all beings, of living and inanimate things alike" (1923, 12–13), and thereby establishes a link between the smallest gesture and the entire universe. Dreams of filmic internationalism, however, take the place of examples that suggest the possibility of their realization, and the liberating potential of the body disappears before the bloodless scenarios of a spirituality that only serves to hide the existence of other, more material differences.

With these implications, the contributions to *Der Film von morgen* make clear how film aesthetics emerged at the end of a complicated process of displacements within critical discourse, a process that began with studies on the actual spectators and that ended with speculations on the beautiful faces and bodies depicted on the screen. The change in tone and argument suggests a turning away from the physical body of the audience — those who constitute the masses — and a willing surrender to the illusionary, yet infinitely more seductive, body of cinema. Within these new scenarios of film aesthetics, film could then be theorized as a mirror, but a mirror where the reality of the original was gradually replaced by its own reflections and where a complete reversal of the relationship between image and reality could be achieved. At the end of this process, the spectator was often nothing more than a double of his favorite actor on the screen.

\* \* \*

A clear indication of film's social and cultural significance in the early twenties was the publication of numerous books on film, among them revised dissertations, monographs, and introductory texts, as well as the more popular yearbooks and anthologies. Just as films developed artistic ambitions, discourses on film became more philosophical, and just as the institution of cinema strove toward respectability, the critics aspired to the status of an academic discipline with its own methodology, terminology, and institutional framework. The search for what, in contradistinction to the film theoretical writings of Béla Balázs, Siegfried Kracauer, and Rudolf Arnheim, will be called aesthetics or philosophy of film motivated a number of writers to approach film in a more systematic fashion. Moving beyond the passions of the moment, whether of an artistic or a political nature, and eliminating all extraneous influences were first steps in this direction. The critics' goal was to determine the aesthetic laws that constituted the medium as such, and to develop standards against which all films, past and future, could be measured. The reliance on philosophical categories underscored their seriousness and importance, and the new art films supported their claim that the filmic image could be much more than the recording of a theatrical mise-en-scène. Though not the only influence, the new art films confirmed their belief that the filmic image should not be confused with the profilmic event. The resultant shift in the discursive practices from poetics to aesthetics, as it were, sealed film's emancipation from literature and theater.

The highly stylized films that have come to be associated with Expressionism showed that the camera was much more than a recording device, and that filmic reality originated from the encounter of technology and imagination, with the former realizing the ambitious visions of the latter. Through the new criticism's emphasis on frame composition, lighting, and editing, simplistic equations of film and narrative were replaced by formal analyses that concentrated on the image and accepted the artistic limitations of film. At the same time, questions of spectatorship were incorporated into this new order as the universal laws of perception. In trying to combine formal and perceptual approaches, the new film philosophies revealed the influence of late-nineteenth- and early-twentieth-century concepts, notably Johannes Volkelt's Neo-Kantian philosophy and its critical metaphysics, and Edmund Husserl's phenomenology with its investigations into the nature of human consciousness and self-awareness. While the concern with normative aesthetics continued a tradition reaching back to German idealist philosophy, and Alexander Baumgarten's writings on aesthetics in particular, it also provided the framework in which more contemporary perspectives could be introduced, including Oswald Spengler's exploration of cultural pessimism and discourse on national identity. It would be difficult to trace direct influences, except for the case of Volkelt and Harms. But since the shift toward philosophical questions in the writings on film also manifested the desire of yet another institution, the university, to take part in its constitution as a discursive object, film aesthetics inevitably reflected the concerns of academic philosophy and art history and of the methodological debates within these disciplines.

Unlike earlier studies, which focused on the productive and counterproductive aspects of cinema as a new public sphere, new works on film aesthetics approached film as a subject worthy of close scrutiny. With the rhetoric of shock and scandal exhausted, attention shifted from the spectator to the film and its formal properties. A group of academically inclined writers including Konrad Lange, Walter Bloem, George Otto Stindt, and Rudolf Harms began to study the elements of filmic representation, and laid down the rules under which film was to become, or continue to flourish as, an art form. The project of formulating a philosophy of film, indeed of conceiving films based on aesthetic principles, proved especially attractive to philosophers, who brought to the new medium a long tradition of reflecting on beauty and its fleeting definitions. Their goal was to extricate the mass medium from its lowly origins and, by using normative aesthetics as a kind of disciplinary measure, a controlling device, to create the conditions under which films would be deserving of the label "art." This was to be achieved through the exclusive attention to formal characteristics; anything referring to the production and reception of films had to be excluded. Technical considerations always drew attention to the conditions of production that, according to some aestheticians, were incommensurable with the goals of art. If technology had to be mentioned at all, then it had to provide the categories through which technical limitations could be transformed into aesthetic qualities — a process at the end of which technology was reborn on a higher spiritual plane. What is more, if audiences had to be taken into account, it was only as the worthy recipients of an art committed to universal concerns and eternal values.

In order for this new aesthetic object to emerge, a space had to be created, both real and imaginary, that existed outside the established spheres of film culture and politics, yet which did not contradict them in an antagonistic fashion. This precarious balance between exclusion and containment was achieved by borrowing from diverse philosophical traditions and combing their elements in an eclectic fashion, and by concentrating on film's future rather than on its present practices. Demonstrating their unyielding belief in the power of ideas, some philosophers claimed that the transformation of film into an art form could only be accomplished under their spiritual guidance. Only through aesthetic theory, they argued, was film able to finds its way between the Scylla and Charybdis of the technology of reproduction and the economy of capitalism, and to fulfill its true mission as a popular art.

The first task was, therefore, to distract attention from the cinema's industrial conditions of production, to suppress its historical origins, and to focus exclusively on the ideal film and its ideal characteristics. As a result, individual films were rarely mentioned; they neither gave rise to new theo-retical arguments nor did they serve to illustrate specific claims. The op-posite might be said about the casual yet almost obligatory references to terms like *universality* and *objectivity,* the spiritual value of films, or the artistic mission of the filmmaker. Ironically, a considerable number of these philosophers of film had close ties to the business, as film critics, cultural functionaries, public relations specialists, or film scenarists. The discrep-ancy between self-interest and the myth of objectivity made it even more important to confirm one's selfless dedication to unearthing the "true" nature of film. As might be expected, awareness of formal means came at the price of a growing ignorance about the relationship between visual pleasure and mass culture. The insightful comments on spectators and spectatorship that had characterized discussions in the prewar years gave way to rather crude definitions of mass manipulation, while, it might be added, the methods of mass manipulation themselves became more and more sophisticated. Similarly, the critical awareness about the cinema's social significance gave way to an almost fetishistic involvement with spe-cific filmic devices, such as the close-up. The search for a critical methodol-ogy transformed what began as a culmination point for cultural debates into an instrument of discursive order. Many of these works of film aes-thetics could be dismissed as marginal and unimportant, if not for the fact that the displacement of politics by aesthetics on the superficial level was partially invalidated by the return of political categories in the guise of aesthetic concepts and in the rhetoric of spirituality and universal truth.

The formulation of a philosophy of film was not only essential for pro-moting a product and attracting an audience, it also provided critics with a shared language and a fixed system of thought, the first signs of institu-tionalized discourse. First steps were undertaken to increase communica-tion between film scholars and establish the conditions under which casual references to other writers could develop into an ongoing critical exchange. An important part of every academic discipline, these exchanges can al-ready be found in the earliest writings on film. Thus when Emilie Altenloh referred favorably to Herbert Tannenbaum's work on film and theater, specific positions were confirmed and alliances forged. And when Tannen-baum reviewed Kurt Pinthus's *Kinobuch,* he did so in order to articulate differences and define boundaries. While discussions in the prewar years were structured by widespread opposition to the cinema, and characterized by the desire of its proponents to keep up a united front, the new philosophical writers disagreed primarily on issues relating to film and its formal properties. However, such disagreements, and the references to different schools and canons, were already a sign of confidence, just as the absence of justifications or lengthy explanations proved that the discourses of film, too, had become respectable.

These developments found expression in a more international perspective, as is evidenced by the translation of American and Russian film theoreticians. Hugo Münsterberg's influential work *The Photoplay: A Psychological Study* (1916) appeared in German in 1924; Vsevolod Pudovkin's handbook on film dramaturgy, translated as *Filmregie und Filmmanuskript,* was published in 1926 as part of a *Lichtbild-Bühne* series on film practice and received many positive reviews, including those by Kracauer and Arnheim. The internationalism of the film image, it seemed, prepared the way for the internationalization of film scholarship. Precisely this trust in the power of writing prompted Lange and Bloem to develop their arguments through frequent references to the work of others. To substantiate his position on the narrative film, Lange included in his second book a lengthy critique of Urban Gad, Victor Pordes, and Max Prels. Likewise, Bloem responded critically to the writings of Lange, Willy Rath, Erwin Ackerknecht, and Hermann Häfker, and used the thus defined reformist orthodoxy to align his aesthetics of film with conservative thought. Both examples reveal the growing need for film scholars to define their critical positions not only against a hostile cultural establishment, as it were, but also against each other.

A comparative analysis of two works by Lange may help to clarify what distances were, in fact, bridged by the philosophical discourses. Published in 1918 and 1920, respectively, the works document the smooth transition from politics to aesthetics. What in the earlier work belonged to the domain of class politics and mass culture is later inscribed into the framework of normative aesthetics. The qualitative differences between the works are, in this context, less important than the symptomatic nature of their discursive moves. An art history professor at the University of Tübingen and one of the more theoretical cinema reformers, Lange collaborated with other reformers on book projects (e.g., with the Tübingen neurologist Robert Gaupp) and was frequently mentioned in reformist publications as an untiring activist and inspiring thinker. *Nationale Kinoreform* (1918, National cinema reform) and his magnum opus, *Das Kino* (1920, The cinema), show his attempt to continue the reformist discourse within the framework of normative aesthetics.

Praising the war as the great purifier, the Lange of 1918 still believed that the cinema's future was dependent on the fate of German nationalism. Consequently, he called for the nationalization of the film industry, the founding of communal cinemas, the introduction of censorship laws on the national level, and the elimination of anything associated with art or aesthetics. The "art of cinema," Lange held, was a contradiction in terms. Providing pleasure without restraints, the cinema excluded an aesthetic experience from the outset; in fact, its sensationalist stories and its heightened sense of excitation reinforced rather questionable dispositions in the spectator. Real art, according to Lange, had the power to ennoble sin because it lifted the lowly content to the higher level of pure thought and aesthetic imagination. Cinema, on the other hand, was virtually indistinguishable from reality. That is why editing posed a threat to the spectator's physical and psychological well-being and "actually thwarts artistic effects. The mind of the spectator is expected to do something that it is unable to do under normal circumstances, given its physiological conditions. That is the reason for the great fatigue that takes hold of those members in the film audience who are not used to reflecting on what they see" (1918, 25).

To prevent the reality effect of cinema from controlling the masses, Lange developed ethical guidelines that were based on the inherent limitations of cinema, such as the lack of sound, color, and three-dimensionality. Only two categories of evaluation were available in this highly prescriptive aesthetics, the unacceptable (literary adaptations, psychological dramas) and the acceptable (nature scenes, pantomimes, fairy tales). Instead of inventing stories, Lange concluded, the cinema should capture the beauty of nature and the wonders of simple living; instead of imitating the drama, it should take advantage of its documentary potential. Only then could the nation be protected from this "art which in reality is no art" (1918, 58).

Faced with the undiminished appeal of the narrative film — by 1920, three and a half million Germans went to the cinema every night, Lange notes incredulously — the high hopes for a national education program had to be abandoned. The reformist activist repeated his claim that film would never be anything more than a mechanical reproduction of nature, and that filmmakers could easily do without creativity and artistic ambition. Yet in *Das Kino* he somewhat modified these statements in a chapter strategically placed between a discussion on the ethics of representation and one on cinema and the state. Within the proper boundaries, he now conceded, the cinema could obtain a few pseudoartistic traits, provided it followed in the tradition of the fairy tale, the burlesque, and the fantastic. The reality of cinema made necessary such compromises, Lange admitted; it demanded that "the cinema be brought closer to the arts — as much as is possible given the artistic means of this technology. After all, certain circles perceive the cinema as an art; in their lives, it has virtually taken the place of the theater and the visual arts" (1920, 133). This oblique reference to the working class suggests that even the most outspoken critics of the film drama felt a need to respond to the pressures of social reality, if only for strategic reasons.

This turn to film aesthetics — as a discourse exclusively concerned with objects — would have been impossible without the concentration process in the film industry and the increasingly important distinction between well-made entertainment films, expensive prestige productions, and ambitious art films. It would also have been less pronounced without the parallel attempts to provide aspiring cinematographers and filmmakers with professional training in an institutional setting that offered theoretical courses as well. For instance, at the Deutsche Filmschule in Munich, associated with the Emelka film company, the critic Ernst Iros lectured on film aesthetics, thus laying the foundation for his monumental study, *Wesen und Dramaturgie des Films,* published in 1938, which brought the ideas of Volkelt to new fruition (Iros 1928 and 1938). Precisely for these external reasons must it not surprise that, despite changes in attitude, aesthetic questions continued to play a subservient role compared to the large number of academic studies that addressed economic and legal issues. The institutionalization of film as an object of serious study remained, for the most part, limited to academic disciplines such as jurisprudence, economics, and business administration.

The shift from politics to aesthetics exemplified in the case of Lange characterized the entire discursive field, namely the purposeful separation of political, economic, and aesthetic perspectives under the disguise of specialization. However, there were no acknowledgments in the works of film aesthetics that the scholarly discourses on film actually originated in the fields of law and economics — a different kind of heritage indeed.[2] The earliest film dissertations in Germany dealt with legal questions, and the problem of censorship in particular. They included Hans Werth's "Öffentliches Kinematographenrecht" (1910, Univ. of Erlangen), Hans Müller-Sander's "Die Kinematographenzensur in Preußen" (1912, Univ. of Heidelberg), and Fritz Manasse's "Die rechtlichen Grundlagen der Theater- und

Kinematographenzensur" (1913, Univ. of Greifswald). Copyright protection laws played an important role in the prewar years, as the many dissertations on the topic prove. From 1912 until 1933 more than a hundred film dissertations were written, and by the late twenties film was generally recognized as an academic subject within the disciplinary boundaries outlined above.

Yet such developments hardly improved its precarious position in those disciplines traditionally concerned with aesthetic issues, philosophy, and art history. Through the sharp distinction between the specialized discourses that emphasized film's role as a commodity or a means of political propaganda, and the universalizing discourses that foregrounded its aesthetic and cultural values, conditions were established under which a particular aspect of film could be discussed without automatically summoning the others. This division of labor between the discourses of art and pleasure, on the one hand, and those of profit and control, on the other, became necessary with the cinema's increased presence in the public sphere and the continuous institutional reorganization along the principles of profit maximization.

The guiding principle in all these movements was to obscure the relationship between form and ideology, and to limit the more public discussions on film to aesthetic questions. What in the earliest writings on film still appeared in the same discursive space was now divided into different areas of investigation, all of which had their specific institutional affiliations and critical terminology. While the compartmentalizing of knowledge in the fields of law and economics reflected the growing specialization within the industry, the emergence of film aesthetics satisfied the need to recreate, if only within the framework of aesthetics, the kind of totalizing vision that had characterized the early discourses on film, though with often problematic results. That is also why film's coming into its own as a discursive subject — the appearance of the first academic books on the philosophy of film marked the successful outcome of this process — can only be examined against the backdrop of the specialization process that made necessary the illusion of unity provided by the framework of aesthetics.

The few dissertations that dealt with specific problems of film aesthetics — Bloem, in this regard, is really more of a popularizer — commented regularly on the state of scholarship and the problems of the field. Their choice of topics originated in the desire to develop interpretative tools outside of the established paradigms with which to analyze and evaluate the new art films. Underscoring the new sense of discursive maturity, Gerhard Zaddach stated as early as 1929: "The emancipation process from the model of literature seems to be concluded. Today film is no longer the servant of literature, but its own master" (1929, 3). The literary debate on film in the prewar years, Zaddach argued in a dissertation on literary adaptations, had to be regarded as a typically German phenomenon, that is, an indication of the great influence of writers and literary critics in the public sphere. According to Zaddach, their fear of losing these privileges was a stronger factor in the early debates than any real interest or expertise in the subject matter.

The recognition of these differences—between prewar and postwar writings, between literary and sociological approaches—increased the need for critical self-reflection, for an evaluation of the debates in historical terms. Above all, it was out of the desire to situate film within the present conjuncture that some academics for the first time returned to the beginnings of cinema. Writing a history of film involved the same competing discourses that characterized the relationship between film, art, and politics in the Weimar Republic. By giving film a history, scholars gave it an identity, and this historical identity turned out to be just as important for the formulation of future goals, since it enabled political and social groups to conceptualize their relationship to the new medium, if only in retrospect. The new historiography of film relied on categories such as origin and destination, and rise and decline, to make sense of the cinema as a historical phenomenon and to categorize what could eventually become film classics, that is, films that provided models for new genres or styles.

In one of the first film-historical dissertations, Walter Schmitt raised questions that still inform discussions on the historiography of Weimar cinema. His history of early German cinema and its origins indicates to what degree myths, generalizations, and clichés were, from the very beginning, an integral part of film's discourse about itself; it also shows how film history responded to these needs by reinventing the object of inquiry to make it fit the needs of the present. In this regard, two points are noteworthy in Schmitt's account, his conception of history as narrative, and his quest for the meaning of history and historiography. Rejecting linearity as an appropriate model for film history, he constructed a narrative that moved forward through errors, detours, and failures. "It is wrong to depict the rise of film genres as a straight, single trajectory where one genre developed in due time out of the other. On the contrary, an often-interconnected multitude is the most pronounced characteristic of all filmic development" (1932, 64).

Schmitt's description of the period prior to 1914 relied on the same discursive oppositions — art and technology, and art and entertainment — that were used in the context of film aesthetics to exorcize history, and with it all so-called external influences, and to establish a purely formal framework of evaluation. After stating that "film in these early stages was, on the one hand, a technological amusement and, on the other hand, a more or less unartistic, because only mechanical, reproduction of another original art form" (1932, 17), Schmitt projected these dichotomies back onto the beginnings of film, giving them a point of origin and truth. Once film had received a history and a theory, the need for legitimation was no longer as urgent and a new sense of confidence took over. In that spirit, Schmitt concluded. "If one wanted to divide the history of mankind based on the dominant art forms, our time would have to be called the filmic epoch" (1932, 131).

\* \* \*

To what degree the prewar debates laid the foundation for an emerging philosophy of film can be seen in a work that repeatedly emphasized its difference from the older sociological and pedagogical studies but, in introducing itself as "the first monograph of a new art genre," clearly profited from the poetological discussions about form and genre. *Das Lichtspiel* (1919, The film), in the words of its author, Victor Pordes, a professor from Vienna, was "the first standard work on the nature and on the artistic and technical structure of the narrative film [*Lichtspieldrama*]" (1919, 3). In order to substantiate his claim, Pordes developed his approach in opposition to the existing body of work, a critical move that soon became the rule among academic film scholars. He sharply rejected all comparative approaches — here Pordes singles out Lange, Häfker, and Lukács as particularly misguided — and expressed his desire to analyze film on its own terms. Following Tannenbaum and Rath, who commented repeatedly on the problem of terminology, the author argues: "Somewhere between the stage drama [*Bühnendrama*], which relies on the living word but exists in a limited setting, and the novel [*Romandrama*], which has both the word and the setting, but only in the imagination, the narrative film [*Lichtspiel*] emerges in its very uniqueness" (1919, 34).

The resistance to traditional categories provides the framework in which

Pordes formulates his theory of film art. Artistic properties play the central role. Referring to the predominance of the visual sense, he insists on telling a story through events rather than psychological processes, and calls for films that rely on everyday situations rather than dramatic scenes. A firm believer in the universal laws of film, Pordes takes an evolutionary approach when he argues that the silent film, with its technological means, has not yet fully reached its potential, that it still resembles the world as experienced by a deaf person. With technology's inherent perfectionism, he insists, these shortcomings are bound to disappear quickly through the addition of sound, color, and stereoscopy. While such speculations were widespread during this period of great innovation and economic growth, it was his emphasis on artistic production that distinguished Pordes's work from Lange's politics of representation or Bloem's metaphysical formalism.

Two areas, according to Stindt, can be identified in the transformation of film into an art form, scenario writing and directing. As for the scenarist, he must base his work on some basic dramaturgic rules and elements, including a logical narrative, positive identification of figures, and a dramatic structure that translates the classical drama's laws of exposition, climax, and denouement into the language of film. Whereas this emphasis on dramaturgy obliges film to follow the traditions of the theater, Pordes expands his definition of drama to include inanimate objects and landscapes, thus also recognizing the equalizing effect of the filmic image. In his comments on film direction, he argues in favor of a clear separation between scenarist and director, a position that shows his opposition to the literary-oriented *Autorenfilm*. The director, in Pordes's view, is responsible for guiding the actors and setting up the mise-en-scène; under his skillful direction, both become subject to the same filmic techniques and the same filmic perspective. Thus Pordes is able to conclude: "Cinematography is a new principle, and the narrative film, which has attracted most of the interest, is a new art form" (1919, 157).

For the same reasons that a pretheory such as Pordes's *Das Lichtspiel* reveals the continuous influence of the theater, the writings of Walter Bloem Jr., son of the popular Nazi author, bear witness to the continuous influence of politics. Dedicated "to the memory of Konrad Lange," Bloem's "Das Lichtspiel als Gegenstand der ästhetischen Kritik" (1921, Film as the subject of aesthetic criticism) was one of the first dissertations that focused exclusively on aesthetic problems. Its aims are spelled out in the introduction: "The following treatise has been written with the intention of supporting, at least in this one particular area, the defensive war fought by our culture against [the evils of] civilization" (1921, 2). Using the opposition of (German) culture and (French) civilization that dominated cultural debates before the war, Bloem examines to what degree film belongs to culture and its pure, spiritual aims, and to what degree it has already fallen prey to the delusions of external progress associated with civilization. Four basic questions — "Is film art? Can the representation of reality be art? Should film have intertitles? How can technical perfection be judged on aesthetic grounds?" — structure his investigation (1921, 45). After discussing the existing critical positions, Bloem arrives at what, for him, represents the central problem, film's lack of distance to reality and the conditions of mechanical reproduction. "The main characteristic of the reproducing arts is that the artistic *effect* is not attached to the actual work of art but to its reproduction, which is basically mechanical in nature" (1921, 71).[3]

A work of art, however, requires that all traces of reality be eliminated so that the will to abstraction can freely develop. Film, if it wants to be art, needs to suppress its technological basis and limit its artistic intentions to the pro-filmic event. Here Bloem envisions "an art form that can no longer be affected by the anti-illusionist tendency inherent in the process of mechanical reproduction, because it has already reached the level of art in its original form" (1921, 82). The question of art is therefore already decided prior to the intrusion of the cinematic apparatus; only by denying its means of production does film reach the status of art — namely as a kind of glorified set design, appropriately called *Außenregie* (external direction) by Bloem. In a way, Bloem substitutes the aura of the original work of art with the aura of the pro-filmic event, while relegating camerawork and editing to merely secondary functions. Such propositions make clear that the resurrection of the original work of art in the context of modern technology can only take place within the boundaries of the proscenium stage. Confirming such impressions, Bloem time and again appeals to the director and to the actor to protect film from the destructive influence of its own technology. As long as the false immediacy of the filmic image is counterbalanced by illusionism, exaggeration, and stylization, the question of film art can be resolved; as Bloem points outs, the names of Henny Porten, Conrad Veidt, and Ernst Lubitsch promised hope.

Under assault by the historical avant-garde, normative aesthetics had lost the very object of study, the original work of art. While many writers abandoned narrative with a vengeance, film seemed the only art form left where the laws of nineteenth-century realism were still intact. And while mimetic representation was abandoned as the central project in the visual arts, film took over its social and political functions. It was out of this retrogressive impulse that four critics, some of whom had little knowledge of actual films, each decided to write a philosophy of film. Their commitment to film art was superseded only by their attachment to aesthetic theories that had been put into question by cultural practices. Between the years 1924 and 1926, several monographs were published that tried to determine once and for all the artistic value of film: Georg Otto Stindt's *Das Lichtspiel als Kunstform* (1924, Film as an art form), Rudolf Harms's *Philosophie des Films* (1926, Philosophy of film), and, as the first study on an artistic movement, Rudolf Kurtz's *Expressionismus und Film* (1926, Expressionism and film). Each of the works presented a rigorous analysis of the narrative film, and each of the authors professed an almost religious belief in the image as the foundation of a world community no longer separated by language.

Some philosophers went so far in their desire for a future film art that they completely denied its links to mass culture. In *Das Lichtspiel als Kunstform,* Georg Otto Stindt presents a number of rather baffling strategies for negotiating the requirements of art and industry.[4] In the introductory remarks to this ambitious "philosophy of film, direction, dramatics, acting," the author proposes to "extract film's laws of form and effect from its spiritual content [*Bewußtseinsinhalt*]" (1924, 5), thus also relying heavily on idealist notions (Heller 1984, 211–17). It was the responsibility of the philosophers to protect the new art from the unqualified contributions of literary critics and political activists. Consequently, Stindt's arguments always refer back to the basic premise that art and politics must be separated, and that aesthetic questions should be left to the specialists — philosophers like himself. In contrast to Pordes, whose dependency on the model of the drama is all too evident, Stindt emphasizes the similarities with the visual arts, for instance when calling film "the translation of our thoughts and dreams into images" (1924, 7). Fixated on spiritual qualities, however, he fails to bring forth an aesthetic theory based on the analysis of film's inherent means or the critical engagement with actual films. He offers rather mysterious equations like "plot (pantomime + rhythm) = effect" (1924, 25), which demand that form laws (*Formgesetze*) be united with the appropriate consciousness contents (*Bewußtseinsinhalte*). At the same time, he makes very specific, almost formulaic suggestions on problems ranging from the need for short intertitles and original film music to problems of film author-ship. On the one hand, Stindt claims that the film director "only has to grasp and shape according to his stylistic will" (1924, 84), exerting total control over actors, set designers, and cinematographers. On the other, he criticizes those who pay exaggerated attention to the director, and calls for a more active involvement of producers, especially in questions of content.

Stindt's philosophical conviction does not in the least prevent him from making profitability the ultimate standard for art. He even criticizes Ger-man film companies for their lack of a good business sense. Rather than acknowledging the mutual interdependency of aesthetics and economics, he introduces the concept of nationalism to once again separate art, indus-try, and politics. Film as an art form is truly international, Stindt maintains, yet as a commodity it has to conform to national interests. Thus robbed of its utopian potential, film becomes, in Stindt's most revealing conclusion, indistinguishable from propaganda. "Every good film must lure the specta-tor out of the muddle of his egotistical little universe and convert him to the feeling that alone, he is a nothing, that he can become a useful member of human society only in relationship to his fellow human beings, to his nation" (1924, 35). As becomes clear in his lengthy comments on national film culture, Stindt, like Lange and Bloem, uses aesthetic concepts in order to reintroduce the political concerns that have only seemingly been elimi-nated through the self-imposed restriction to formal concerns.

Perhaps in opposition to the dominant discourse on film aesthetics and German nationalism, some thinkers limited their arguments to characteris-tics inherent in the medium itself. Their decision to ignore political or economic considerations originated in the belief that film could only be-come an art if it rejected all external influences as lacking true artistic effort. Taking just this position, Rudolf Harms argued that the art of film was synonymous with the creative use of its limitations. His influential work *Philosophie des Films* (1926, Philosophy of film) was based on a dissertation written under Johannes Volkelt, a professor of philosophy at the University of Leipzig and best known for his monumental *System der Ästhetik* (1905–14, System of aesthetics). Volkelt's attempt to classify aesthetic styles out-side any social and historical determinations inspired categories like sub-jective, objective, naive, sentimental, and realistic—categories, in other words, that transformed the historically formed positions of idealist philos-ophy into basic, invariable human dispositions. Opposing the reformist politics of Stindt as well as the anticapitalism of Balázs, Harms tried to apply Volkelt's systematics to the new medium of film — sufficient reason for Kracauer to dismiss his book as unoriginal, of use merely as a "treasury of quotations from Volkelt's *Ästhetik* and lesser-known works" (1927).

Harms placed the notion of style at the center of all film analysis. "The study of a specific art form is the more valuable, the more it gives attention to the specific qualities of the art form in question. . . . Every art, by its very nature, is subject to specific laws, since the characteristics of its mechanical means are different in every case" (1926, 33). This very simple rule, he elaborates, applies equally to the conditions of reception and production. To begin with, dependency on the photographic process propels film toward realism, although Harms's definition is wide enough to include naturalistic dramas as well as fantastic tales (Heller 1984, 217–21). Its primary means of expression include movement, the overcoming of space and time, and the kind of symbolism that originates in the sign character of the object as rendered visible by the cinematic apparatus.

At the same time, Harms insists, film art was determined by its collective mode of reception. "It should be noted that the film, as a result of its collective character, cannot spontaneously be taken from the shelf like a book and then be read whenever the individual feels a need for it" (1926, 36). This emphasis on the collective experience distinguishes film from the other arts and gives it meaning and direction. Harms's description here conveys the enthusiasm of the early years: "Out of the filmic movement arises the possibility of a communication between the new-born baby and the old man who is dying, between the most distant races, between man and animal. Gestures provide the most intensive means of communication. There is an extensive movement across space and time, a linking of primeval beginning and end" (1926, 186).

In order for this collective experience, this new internationalism, to be accomplished, issues of reception must become an integral part of film aesthetics. As one of the first to propose something akin to a reception theory of film, Harms devotes special attention to the cinema as an architectural space. He documents the short but significant history of cinema architecture and, after a sharp critique of existing practices, proposes higher standards for motion picture theater design. Concerned with providing the most intense sensual experience possible, Harms concludes: "As a mass medium, film needs a collective space. The darkened auditorium of the motion picture theater accommodates this need. Superficially, the goal and purpose of these facilities consists in bringing together a large, but not unlimited, number of people for the purpose of shared aesthetic and artistic pleasure. Their task is to guarantee that the work of art becomes the subject of the spectator's undivided 'concentrated attention' and 'intentional behavior.' This is going to be achieved by eliminating the lower senses (of touch, taste, and smell) and anything else that might prevent complete surrender to the work of art" (1926, 228).

As these remarks show, Harms had very precise ideas when it came to describing what he considered the total cinematic experience; he even offered detailed advice on seat arrangement and upholstery, projection facilities, lighting schemes, and lobby design. However, it is also obvious from his definition of reception that it did not include social conditions. In accordance with the new aesthetic paradigm, reception remained limited to its perceptual qualities and thus provided the essential link between Harms's formalist tendencies and his pragmatism.[5]

The growing interest in aesthetic questions led to specialized studies like Rudolf Kurtz's interdisciplinary study *Expressionismus und Film*. With Expressionist film as the main topic, Kurtz covers such diverse phenomena as art and literature, rationalization and mechanization, but he also comments on the totalitarian regimes of Lenin and Mussolini. Taking as his point of departure the aestheticizing of politics, Kurtz evokes an aesthetic modernism in which the artist mediates between art and technology, and where art eventually brings transcendence. Yet rather than focusing on its liberating potential, the successful film scenarist and editor-in chief of *Lichtbild-Bühne* longs for spiritual regeneration. His declared goal: to show how men can triumph over the photographic apparatus and assert their hegemony in the universe. That is why Expressionism remains to him the most important testimony to the glory of the human will. "Expressionism does not want to receive passively, it wants to create" (1926, 12).

Signs of this powerful impulse can be found in modern painting, sculpture, architecture, literature, theater, and the applied arts. Expressionist artists, who according to the author include such diverse figures as Marc Chagall, Alexander Archipenko, Georg Kaiser, and Valeska Gert, all share the strong belief that the new technologies should be used to celebrate human existence and to achieve the complete aestheticizing of reality (Zmegac 1970, 257 n32). Such statements, and Kurtz's frequent references to the glory of the individual, seem to be strangely at odds with the collective nature of film production. Likewise, such apodictic statements as "He [the Expressionist artist] does not look, he envisions!" (Kurtz 1926, 17) or "He organizes but does not explain!" (1926, 22) suggest a kind of creativity that requires only a sufficient amount of will power and inspiration to be deserving of this predicate.

On the basis of these general remarks, Kurtz ponders the significance of Expressionism for film. In his view, Expressionism can be an "important means of optically conjuring up effects that lie beyond the realm accessible to photography" (1926, 84), and it often provides a necessary counterweight to film's inherent mimetic tendency.[6] Thus the art of film must also be the art of resistance, for "effortless pleasure represents one of film's fundamental qualities. . . . Basically the Expressionist film opposes this" (1926, 126–27). Film as such is metaphysical, Kurtz insists, but only the determined rejection of its mimetic impulses and the use of all artistic means brings film closer to its essence. That is precisely why he rejects films that treat Expressionism merely as an assortment of stylistic ploys (e.g., subjective camera, stark contrasts). Even as he praises Expressionism as a unique way of seeing the world, he remains pragmatic enough to see the commercial limitations of the art film. This opposition between spiritual aspirations and financial rewards results in sometimes contradictory claims. A statement like "What does not win the approval of the masses is detrimental to the German film industry, for it reduces its capital investments" (1926, 129) now takes the place of the earlier assertion that "popularity always means: the autumn of life" (1926, 50).

Caught between film as commodity and film as art, Kurtz's study of Expressionist film therefore typifies the dilemma of aesthetic theories that are caught between their rejection of mass culture and their unwillingness to embrace the aims of the film avant-garde. It also shows the shortcomings of an approach to film art that relies on formalist principles, but remains too involved with questions of meaning and content to see film's inherent means as anything other than mere devices, techniques to be applied. With the possible exception of Kurtz, the four thinkers discussed on the last pages contributed more to the displacement of politics into spirituality than to the formulation of aesthetic laws; their definitions of film art reveal, more than anything, their actual distance to the most influential movements in modern art.

\* \* \*

Within these shifting contexts, the question of film art also attracted the interest of painters and photographers associated with the historical avant-garde (Kaes 1982; Elsaesser 1987a). Their writings about film, however, stand apart from other contributions and are usually excluded from historical accounts of Weimar film theory. As the byproduct of artistic endeavors, and as reflections from the vantage point of artistic production, they did not participate in the academic debates on film aesthetics. Yet precisely because they were conceived in a different context and for a different purpose, they provided a much-needed corrective to the overwhelming presence of the narrative film in the discourse of film aesthetics.

These writings introduced the perspective of the European avant-garde into a debate that had paid little attention to the most advanced positions on art and technology. Indeed, there could not have been a greater difference than between the academic writings on film aesthetics and the statements issued by the proponents of the so-called abstract film. Both groups rejected the entertainment film, but they did so for very different reasons. The philosophers sought to counterbalance the process of mechanical reproduction through the creative presence of an individual who firmly imposed his vision, his will to form, on the material. In contrast, the filmmakers rejected the narrative and documentary film in order to explore film's hidden potential outside mimetic representation.

While traditionalists like Bloem or Stindt adhered to the principles of normative aesthetics, including the belief in the incommensurability of art and mechanical reproduction, Walter Ruttmann and Hans Richter — to name the most vocal members of the Weimar film avant-garde — carried the challenges of early twentieth-century movements like Futurism, Constructivism, and Dada to their logical conclusion. Fascinated with the dynamism of the machine, with its rhythm and speed, but also aware of the perceptual changes brought about by modern mass media, they used the formal challenges of the avant-garde to develop the universal language of film. Coming from the visual arts, Ruttmann and Richter accused the mainstream filmmakers of having betrayed film's original mission, namely to liberate the human senses through the power of vision. In their view, only a strict separation of mass entertainment and film art could prevent the new medium from succumbing to the temptations of naturalism and commercialism. Therefore, they called for a systematic exploration of film's inherent qualities: form, light, contrast, movement, rhythm, color, and, given the strong affinities between film and music, sound.

While they shared with the later Arnheim a concern with the materials of film, their proposals were much more radical concerning the question of referentiality. Ruttmann and Richter not only rejected the narrative film, replacing the story with pure rhythm and the protagonists with the interplay of light and dark, they actually used a visual medium in order to defy mimetic representation. As is made evident by the so-called absolute film, developing the poetics of film meant developing animation techniques based on graphic rather than photographic processes. If documentary material was to be used, as in Ruttmann's cross-section films, then it was only according to the structuring principles of rhythm and montage. László Moholy-Nagy, the Bauhaus photographer and designer, once summarized these ideas succinctly in the notion of work-specificity (*Werkgerechtigkeit*). Specificity in the context of film was based on the conscious rejection of the traditions of painting and theater and the exploration of the optical, kinetic, and acoustic characteristics of film. The abstract sound film, for Moholy-Nagy, fulfilled perfectly this goal of an "optical-phonetic synthesis" (1969b, 255), the interplay of light and dark without the presence of an object.

While opposing film's "sanctification by a philological court of the arts," Ruttmann was well aware of the complicated relationship between film and theory. Known for his abstract film series *Opus 1–4* (1921–25) and for cross-section films such as the famous *Berlin — die Symphonie der Großstadt* (1927, Berlin — Symphony of the big city), Ruttmann viewed the absolute film with ambivalence, because it was founded exclusively on theoretical assumptions about film. At the same time that he rejected such approaches as too intellectual, the former painter proposed the establishment of a kind of "film laboratory" in which formal questions could be worked out, and where art and technology could find common ground. The underlying tension between the radical gesture with which Ruttmann asserted his innovative stance and his obvious reliance on the traditions of easel painting surfaces in scattered comments on film.

In lectures and articles on the film avant-garde and new technical possibilities like color and sound, the modernist aesthetic of film was outlined with its most basic characteristics (Ruttmann 1989, 73–89). Ruttmann's main approach can be summarized as follows: (1) film belongs to the visual arts; (2) mechanical reproduction is not art; (3) art originates in the exploration of formal qualities; (4) film must develop its possibilities out of the demands imposed by its material. Once these requirements were fulfilled, Ruttmann argued, film could become something like temporal painting. "An art for the eye that distinguishes itself from painting in that it takes place in time (like music) and in that the artistic focus lies not (like in the image) in the reduction of a (real or formal) event to a moment, but in the temporal development of the formal. Since this art evolves in time, one of its most important elements is the time-rhythm of the optical events" (1989, 74).

In the writings of Richter, the problems of film art appeared in the larger context of artistic and social constraints. His filmic work in the twenties, which included abstract studies like *Rhythmus 21, 23, 25* (1921–25) and the Dada-spoof *Vormittagsspuk* (1927, Ghosts Before Noon), were part of a larger attempt to introduce avant-garde ideas into a more mainstream context. Richter's interest in mediation is reflected in his writings for Theo van Doesburg's Constructivist journal, *De Stijl,* and the *Deutsche Werkbund* publication, *Die Form,* as well as in his involvement with the Gesellschaft 'Neuer Film' (Society for the New Film), which he founded together with Karl Freund and Guido Bagier to promote the cause of the film avant-garde.[7] Supposedly, Richter also wrote film reviews for the Berlin daily *Tägliche Rundschau* (Richter 1967, 173). In spite of these artistic commitments, even Richter made a sharp distinction between form and content, claiming that "to the degree that his [the spectator's] interest in the story and the appearance of objects diminishes, his interest increases for what a film . . . contains in spite of these — for what takes place on the screen behind the story" (1969, 230). This included everything — light effects, movement, and forms — that might contribute to the emerging universal language of film, to be understood here as a principle outside of human intervention, a structural quality inherent in the filmic medium itself. Such programmatic statements, of course, must be seen in the context of a film culture where mainstream and avant-garde film continue to be divided, without a chance for mutual inspiration. Richter complained repeatedly that the vast majority of films were not deserving of the name, because they ignored the laws of film. He remained, however, confident about a possible rapprochement of the narrative film (*Spielfilm*) and the art film (*Kunstfilm*) and stated. "It is absolutely essential for this new art to be composed of clear, unambiguous elements. Without them, it might well develop as a game — even a highly seductive game — but never as a language" (1971, 146).

In his first book, polemically entitled *Filmgegner von heute — Filmfreunde von morgen* (1929, Film enemies of today — film fans of tomorrow), Richter proposed a revolution in perception (see Wuss 1990, 266–83). He claimed that film "will create a new world. Film as a new creation, the poetics of film, is a pure play of the imagination" (Richter 1968, 31).Conceived for the important 1929 Film and Foto Exhibition in Stuttgart, the book supports its theoretical claims through the effective montage of film stills, photographs, filmstrips, typography, and bold captions. Through slogans like "We edit!" or "Expand vision!" Richter highlights those aspects of the visual world that usually escape the human eye but have now become available to artistic exploration. Subject only to the laws of rhythm, he declares, the films of the future will create imaginary worlds freed of the limitations of time and space; hence the importance Richter places on time-lapse, slow-motion, and freeze-frame photography.[8] Radical expansion of perception, reinvention of the time-space continuum, transcendence of the laws of relativity, suspension of everyday experience through the forces of the imagination — all of these qualities are central to Richter's definition of film art. Many of his ideas had already been presented elsewhere, but he was the first to bring them to their ultimate conclusion, that is, in the replacement of narrative by form.

Despite his avant-garde tastes, Richter never joined those who arrogantly dismissed the popular film as doctrinaire and stultifying. Instead, he argued polemically, "The more film enemies, the greater the chance for better films" (1968, 5), among which he included mainstream films. While a more extensive discussion of film and society would have to wait until 1939, when he completed his study on film, capitalism, and progressive cinema, *Der Kampf um den Film,* translated as *The Struggle for the Film,* (1979), Richter was well aware of the sociopsychological need for a narrative cinema and the social responsibilities of the film artist.[9] As early as 1929, he argued: "It makes no sense to condemn people for wanting visual pleasure or seeking excitement and distraction in the cinema; this doesn't change the circumstances that are responsible for the large number of film fans. Obviously, people need stimulation and distraction because they struggle with so many difficulties in real life yet are still left dissatisfied; hence the immense responsibility involved in what to offer those searchers. One could lead them into wrong, meaningless, or meaningful directions. One could betray and intoxicate them, or open their eyes, encourage them, educate, help them develop their most precious instincts" (1968, 46).

Looking for solutions, Richter called for more films based on simple stories and themes. Favoring the grotesque, the sensational, the antirealist, he referred to Chaplin as an integrative figure between the opposing trends of narration and abstraction. Last but not least, Richter hoped to increase the public's interest in non-narrative film by improving films in general. "If the narrative film is characterized by action and observation, then a true poetics of film must rely exclusively on the imagination. Then action becomes irrelevant. It will either disappear, or only play a menial role. There will be no intentions to produce 'the most detailed and complete image of an event' . . . but only the desire to imagine entirely new and unknown events. This process will take its inspiration from rhythm. For rhythm is not just an addition, but the foundation, of film poetics as such; it is the momentum on which its effects are more-or-less based" (1968, 47).

Similar positions on avant-garde art and progressive film politics can be found in Guido Bagier's *Der kommende Film* (1928, The coming film), which was also published in conjunction with the Stuttgart exhibition.[10] Through the probing half-title, "What was? What is? What will be?" and the modern typography and book design, the text's formal presentation defined the framework in which his argument was to unfold. Only film, the sound film pioneer and student of Max Reger argued, could achieve the longed-for unification of spirit and technology, for it represents the most satisfying compromise between high modernism and the psychological disposition of the masses. Now a new type of artist, the engineer, had put into aesthetic practice what he called the standardization and the normalization of human desire under capitalism.

Bagier called for films based exclusively on the formal exploration of movement and rhythm, but unlike Richter, he combined these modernist concepts with his peculiar brand of technomysticism. The new religion of the machine — the greatest symbol of modernism — will free man from the tyranny of nature, he argued, and defined film art accordingly: "Theoretically, the ideal content of film concerns the evolution of movement through abstract forms, liberated from the nature that we call reality. Practically, the actual content of film amounts to the revolution of movement, involving those objects available to an external action. . . . As an autonomous work of art, the coming film must follow only its own laws" (1928, 76). Without arriving at concrete proposals, Bagier closed on a hopeful note. "The forces of the mind and the material means of two continents [i.e., Europe and America] finally will come together in order to fulfill a mission which, like the forces of nature, will bring about the much-needed balance between technology and spirit, idea and reality, soul and matter. One, two, three, yes, many centuries mean nothing here; for to the savant, this development is certain to take place" (1928, 94).

This hope was not shared by Kracauer, who noted derisively in his review of the book that "general statements and amateurish definitions take the place of content. They do not become more weighty through the fact that they appear in sans-serif types of the most diverse sizes. . . . The best thing about the text is the pictures" (1928).

As the last remarks have shown, the distinction between mainstream cinema, with its dependency on narrative and mimetic representation, and the avant-garde film with its various attempts to move beyond narrative and beyond representation, was already firmly in effect in Weimar cinema — of course, with notable exceptions. A similar division between traditional aesthetics and avant-garde theory can be found in the writings on film as art. Whereas the former continued to be haunted by the fact of mechanical reproduction and mass culture even when the attempt was made to deny such influences through a retreat to more arcane philosophical pursuits, the latter avoided such problems by never really addressing the issue. However, the freedom of formal exploration — both in theory and in practice — limited their critical investigations to the realm of art and its elitist pursuits. The opposition of avant-garde and mass culture brought forth an almost absurd configuration in the writings on film aesthetics. The almost lifelike representation of moving images — an aspect of mechanical reproduction — made necessary a return to categories of authorship and self-expression associated with the traditional arts. At the same time, the politics of the avant-garde gave rise not to an alternative definition of film but to an emphasis on the very divisions between high and low culture that the philosophers of film tried to ignore. The marginality of the avant-garde in these critical discourses on film must, therefore, be seen as a result of the continual attempts to draw boundaries between art and mass culture, now in the domain of film itself.

# Chapter 8
## Fictions of Cinema

The previous chapter examined the resistance to film's modernity among critics with strong philosophical ambitions and showed their various attempts to use normative aesthetics as a protection against its transgressive qualities. Similar phenomena can be observed in the popular writings on film, though to a lesser degree. Some writers continued to use the other arts, especially the theater, as the ultimate point of comparison. Often ignorant about new filmic styles and technical developments, they cultivated a fear of social disintegration and cultural decline; aesthetic and spiritual purity remained their primary concerns. Yet no matter whether they defined cinema as modern folklore in order to reject existing practices or whether they opposed film on principle, their arguments facilitated an imaginary return to preindustrial, preurban conditions — but did so from the viewpoint of modernity.

In the early twenties, the prolific Friedrich Sieburg tried to recapture the enthusiasm of the literary debates by transferring the expectation of salvation from image to sound. His horror-vision of a dying world redeemable through music bears witness to the persistence of specific ideas from the prewar years that, in the context of Weimar culture, sounded antiquated and confused. "Bursting and dissolving, taking one's life, pressing into the void, music must save the filmic image, must expose this remaining power of three-dimensional imagination to the rays of eternity so that man, icily breathed upon by the decaying ghosts of his deadened world view, need not run away in fear from his world's soundless dance of death" (Güttinger 1984a, 419).

In light of the measured, objective tone that characterized much Weimar film criticism, such exclamatory statements sounded like a parody of the conservative resistance to film culture. The emphasis on the essence of cinema, without any regard for its actual practices, was an indication precisely of this marginality. Using the cinema as a projection screen for metaphysical speculations of dubious value, Sieburg deliberately avoided any direct engagement with films or audiences. However, his strategies of avoidance originated in an antimodernist sentiment that, in the last years of the republic, would give way to more reactionary pronouncements on the cinema and Germany's true spiritual needs.

Thus in 1932, the Russian novelist Fedor Stepun sketched a scenario of redemption that plotted the cinema, the agent of cultural decline, against the theater, the temple of metaphysics.[1] Much of the voluminous *Theater und Kino* (1932, Theater and cinema) was devoted to proving that the theater belonged to the world of religion, and that it stood in the service of a great mysterious spirituality. The cinema, on the other hand, had to be seen as a fact of life and could only be accepted like any other fatal strike: with stoic patience. Repeating arguments from the prewar years, Stepun conceded that the cinema, through its very depravity, contributed indirectly to the renewal of the theater and, more important still, to a much-needed religious awakening. However, the cinema would always be excluded from the higher goals of art. "Great art always means making the invisible visible. Film is able to show things that are otherwise invisible and, in so doing, surpasses the theater; but it has no inner relationship to the invisible. As much as film can, aesthetically speaking, be called a pure and true art, it remains, metaphysically speaking, not only anti-theater but . . . anti-art as well. And that makes the fight against the cinema a foremost duty for those men who know of the theater's religious and metaphysical roots" (1932, 95).

Appalled by virulent antimodernism, Rudolf Arnheim wrote: "Stepun belongs, as one sees, to the talkative secret society of those 'who know about the roots'; we know the tune" (1932b, 910). This preoccupation with roots—whether in the context of metaphysics or politics—was perfectly suited to accommodate other discourses of origin and descent, discourses with an explicitly political agenda. The configurations of cinema and fiction outlined in this chapter must be read against the backdrop of these conservative and reactionary texts and their ongoing fight against modern mass culture. Only then is it possible to appreciate the modern consciousness evoked in the essayistic and fictional accounts of Weimar cinema.

"The mechanization and acceleration of modern life-styles, the driven nervousness of modern souls, the false vitality of a nation that has degenerated into the 'masses,' the aberrations among social groups who have fallen prey to an unleashed sexus — these have brought forth a type of human being who looks at his reflection — in the cinema! Cinema man [*Kinomensch*] and cinema tempo [*Kinotempo*] are the predominant characteristics of our times" (Kern 1925–26, III). This is how the conservative Hans Kern described the gloomy state of modern culture in 1925. He conjured up the image of a society consumed by a longing for experience, a society where the divisions between art and life had been eliminated, a society where the reflections of life had invaded the experience of the real, and almost taken its place. Analyzing the formal qualities of a film, of course, revealed little about such processes, and even the customary references to urbanism and industrialization as the matrix of cinematic experience failed to explain how the cinema had come to effect so fundamentally the relationships between object and subject, self and Other. Here narrative assumed a central function, and it will be the purpose of this chapter to analyze the relationship between film theory and "film fiction" in this transgressive sense, that is, to show how narrative became an integral part of discourse formation. Moreover, the interpenetration of literary and critical genres and the growing importance of popular journalism for the consciousness industry will be studied in a number of popular books on film from the Weimar years. The notion of simulation has to be situated precisely in the changing relationships between film and film criticism.

With the new fictions of cinema — the film novels, the gossip columns, the films about film — came the recognition that the act of looking was no longer limited to evenings at the movies or the experience of the big city. Instead, the cinema now provided a paradigm for discourses exclusively concerned with imaginary relationships; it instituted spectatorship and fantasy as the organizing principles of modern consumer culture. The writer Arnold Zweig captured the psychological aspects of this culture of simulation in the term "functional pleasure" (*Funktionslust*), which he defined as follows. "The enjoyment of film is identical with man's enjoyment of experience (functional pleasure). To watch a tightrope walker and to safely live through the danger he is in; to take part in a competition and experience the pleasure of a speed reached and of resistance overcome; to share in the imaginary discovery of a new country and to enjoy the expansion of one's own limited existence; these are examples of functional pleasure, chosen from the perspective of the spectator" (Zweig 1922, 371–72).[2]

The filmic exploration of the object world, as described by Zweig, not only diverted attention from the work and its formal characteristics but, more importantly, resulted in the convergence of film and lived experience. This phenomenon played a central role in arguments about film's productive as well as transgressive qualities, its ability to produce feelings, attitudes, and identities rather than merely fulfill aesthetic or social functions. Writing on film itself became pleasure-oriented, an extension of the moments of pseudoexperience that punctuated modern life. Explaining "Why We Love Film So Much," Willy Haas turned to love as the emotion in which film and its discourses had finally achieved perfect harmony. He listed the standard arguments in favor of film as an international, democratic, and popular entertainment, but one stood out because of its unabashed relativism: "Because the film must really satisfy people in order to exist" (Güttinger 1984a, 456, 457, 458).

With personal gratification at its main purpose, film was suddenly transformed into a mechanism of pleasure and an object for consumption. No longer associated with the promise of social equality or the critique of bourgeois culture, the cinema instituted pleasure at the center of all social and cultural relationships. This transformation could not have been captured better than by Kasimir Edschmid, an Expressionist writer, who noted sarcastically: "Whoever throws sapphires into a cogwheel is a fool, whoever tries to infuse film with art should be expelled from society. I am for film if it gives me pleasure, and I am against it if it frustrates me. I do thousands of other things that have nothing to do with art; I travel, I play croquet, I play around with my dog, and nobody would use these situations to discuss art with me but politely stick to the subject" (Güttinger 1984a, 381). The obligatory references to the other arts were no longer necessary. In their place, the cinema emerged as a powerful intertextual practice, whose primary function consisted in simulating and restructuring human experience. Its movements were governed by the notion of pleasure, but it was a pleasure without the critical potential attributed to the "primitive" cinema of the prewar years.

Once they embraced the cinema as a phenomenon of modern life, the writers also paid more attention to the mechanisms of cultural consumption, and they studied the participation of audiences in a process that involved active and passive behavior. Their interest focused on two social groups, the working class, who represented the cinema's lowly origins, and the middle classes, who were to become its glorious future. Because of the ambivalent feelings many intellectuals had toward their own class, comments on bourgeois audiences were often full of resentment, even though they never exhibited the kind of contempt that characterized descriptions of working-class audiences. The German Philistine became their favorite target for polemics; as the scenarist Franz Schulz phrased it: "Repulsive — that's what the Philistine's attitude toward the cinema is!" (1921, 80).[3]

Others addressed the bourgeois spectator more directly, often exposing him to scorn and ridicule. Ernst Rothschild, in a call for more eroticism in the cinema, offered his condolences to the average man, because "his spouse, seated next to him at the cinema, gets to see all the things he'd rather see by himself" (1920, 317). In a place where artistic and educational interests played no role whatsoever, the presence of women, at least according to this author, had to be seen as an obstacle to the satisfaction of certain male needs. Others saw the eroticism of the cinema precisely in its regressive, polymorphously perverse qualities. Thus it was in recognition of the cinema's affinity with oral pleasures that Franz Reichwaldau emphasized its liberating effect on women. "The cinemas have unjustly been called the theater of the little man; in fact, they are the theater of the little and the big woman, the erotic equivalent of chocolate and whipped cream. A man has his beer and his cigar, a woman her chocolate and whipped cream. But the range of desires, in males and in females, cannot be fully satisfied by those alone. In order to satisfy other desires, . . . the man turns to an institution as old as the world. Striving toward emancipation, the woman finally recognizes her desires, too. The cinema satisfies them in the most tender ways" (1920, 85).

Even bourgeois slumming seemed to lose much of its attraction in light of the bemused indifference in which Willi Bierbaum, film critic for the *Neue Züricher Zeitung*, described his visit to the movies in 1923. Setting the tone for many reviews to come, he hardly lost a word on the film's story or any outstanding features. Instead, the cinematic experience was reduced to anecdotes about the latecomers, the relentless talkers, the ladies with their gigantic hats, the old men with bad habits, and, not to be forgotten, the animals. "Recently even dogs have taken an interest in the cinema, and it is amusing for animal lovers to observe how this new group of spectators gallops merrily through the darkness of rows, trouser legs and skirts, from the cheapest to the most expensive seats, looking for their owners" (Güttinger, 1984a, 183). As the harmless pleasures of diversion eliminated the dangers associated with visual pleasure, the masses, at least on the level of critical discourse, were replaced by fashionable and cosmopolitan city dwellers. The threat of a proletarian public sphere was banned; now one could turn to other, more "worthwhile" problems, including the unending, empty discourse of cinema about itself.

The cinema's integration into middle-class culture was nowhere more evident than in the area that had been expected to be affected most by the fetishization of the image, namely writing and book-publishing. Addressing this competition, the publisher Samuel Fischer spoke for many when he stated with resignation that "the book belongs to the most useless things in modern life . . . evenings are spent in front of the radio and in the cinema" (1926, 1). There is no doubt that Fischer had only specific books in mind, for the reading public, as a whole, increased continuously during the Weimar years; the same holds true for the number of books published, including books on film. Anthologies with short essays and glossy pictures presented the film world as exciting, fashionable, and glamorous. New genres such as the "book to the film" or the semibiographical film novel appeared on the market, and well-known literary critics were enlisted to create an air of sophistication. These projects resembled earlier efforts in the prewar years to cultivate the cinema from within, through the contribution and active involvement of the better-educated. However, instant commercialization may not have been what the Weimar critics envisioned.

The "literarization" of cinema did not have the desired effect of elevating the cinema to the level of literature. On the contrary, the strong links between art and advertisement introduced economic considerations into the practice of writing that, until then, had been dismissed as external disturbances, or means to an end. More important still, the commercialism of the cinema and its by-products drew attention to the conditions of literary production, including the impoverishment of many writers and the increasing economic pressures on publishers. The phenomenal growth of media conglomerates like Ullstein and Scherl proved to what degree cinema culture had already found entry in various literary genres (e.g., pulp novels, newspaper serials) and print media (e.g., paperbacks, glossy magazines), creating a new market for readers eager to learn more about their favorite entertainment.

The literary writers profited from this dissemination of "cinematic consciousness" into all areas of modern life, either indirectly through the inspiration provided by cinema as a new literary theme and stylistic paradigm or directly through the career opportunities that opened up in film journalism and scenario writing. Writers-turned-scenarists not only had the respect of educated audiences who were familiar with their literary work; they also bestowed on the cinema the mark of literary authorship that was still necessary for its acceptance by these social groups.[4] Not surprisingly, the film scenario, in Hans Kyser's words "the least known and least literary form of literature" (1928–29, 629), offered itself as a privileged space in which theoretical claims could be put into practice. Introducing the values of literature into a field often associated with blatant commercialism, film critics-turned-scenarists like Willy Haas, Willy Rath, and Rudolf Leonhard gave the cinema respectability. They personified the compromise between the calculated appeal of the industrial product and the creative vision of the writer in the traditional sense. In so doing, they stood as living examples of a new concept of film authorship that was neither exclusively literary nor filmic, but rather a product of the more fluid, instable configurations of cinema itself.

Interestingly, it was Bertolt Brecht who, in the "Threepenny Trial," used his own experiences with the legal system and the film industry to identify contradictions within the discourse on film authorship. When, in 1930, Brecht signed a contract with Nero-Film, the company that went on to produce *Die Dreigroschenoper* (1931, *The Threepenny Opera*) with Pabst as director, he took the opportunity to put his dialectical approach to mass culture into practice. Though Brecht had only "consultation rights"—the screenplay was written by Béla Balázs, Leo Lania, and Ladislaus Vajda—he turned the subsequent lawsuit and trial into a "sociological experiment," an exercise in applied film theory. Operating like a lawyer himself, Brecht staged a confrontation between an industry for whom literary sources were, quite literally, a property to be purchased and changed without any regard for its author outside of legal implications, and a legal system that protected the interests of big capital rather than its own notion of autonomous art. By insisting on his intellectual right of ownership, Brecht showed the inherent tensions in a system seemingly at odds with its own ideological constructs. To make his point, Brecht dismantled critical commonplaces like "The arts don't need film" or "Film needs the arts" and, instead of taking an affirmative or oppositional stance, pointed to their intentionally contradictory nature.[5]

Brecht used the bourgeois notion of authorship as a heuristic device in revealing the limitations of traditional standards of evaluation. "After all, the old forms of rendition do not remain unchanged by the new ones, nor can they exist side-by-side. Those who watch films read stories differently.

But those who write stories also watch films themselves. The mechanization of literary production cannot be reversed" (1967, 18:156). By interpreting the opposition between film and literature as a function of bourgeois ideology, Brecht moved beyond the rhetoric of cultural refinement; therein lies his main contribution to the early debates on film. In contrast, writers like Hofmannsthal, Mann, Kaiser, or Klabund may have written, or considered writing, proposals for film scenarios but their projects (significantly) never materialized.

Meanwhile, a new literary genre gained popularity that might be described by the term "book to the film" and that referred either to the novelization of a film or the compilation of promotional material, including snapshots from the set, anecdotes from the shooting, excerpts from the literary source, and personal statements by the director and the stars. This form of self-referentiality became a distinguishing mark of the megaproductions that allowed the film industry to present itself—its economic strengths as well as its cultural ambitions—to an affluent and discerning audience. Concurrently with, or even before, the national release of Lang films like *Metropolis* (1927) or *Die Frau im Mond* (1929, The woman in the moon), Scherl published the "novels to the film" written by Lang's wife and collaborator, Thea von Harbou. Turning film premieres into cultural events, these books created an atmosphere pregnant with meaning, from the leather-bound, hand-signed copies for the guests of honor—as was the case for *Die Frau im Mond*—to the celebratory reviews in the morning papers by Germany's leading critics. Deluxe editions seemed mandatory whenever famous writers were involved, for instance on the occasion of Paul Czinner's adaptation of Schnitzler's *Fräulein Else* (1929, Miss Else), with the celebrated Elisabeth Bergner in the title role. On anniversaries and for other commemorative events, the film companies gave away high-quality, lavishly illustrated portfolios, almanacs, and picture books, in which the glamour of the film world was reflected even in the high-quality paper and the gilded edges.

Some "novels to the film" also continued a film's story beyond the actual screening, for instance by adding episodes and characters, or by introducing a more philosophical perspective. The results can be studied in the books published after the release of Lubitsch's *Madame Dubarry* (1919) and *Anna Boleyn* (1920), two period films whose instrumentality in the discourse on national identity qualified them for such forms of literary reenactment. While the book *Anna Boleyn* (1921) was at least written by the authors of the film scenario, Fred Orbig and Hanns Kräly, Hanns Steiner's *Madame Dubarry* (1920) was only loosely based on the film of the same name. Both books were profusely illustrated with stills from the films, thus making the act of reading an extension of, or a substitute for, the cinematic experience.

Similar works on historical epics about August the Strong, Frederick the Great, and Bismarck skillfully combined entertainment and education, with Germany's great historical leaders thus revived as film stars and media celebrities. An abbreviated version of Walter von Molo's historical novel, *Fridericus Rex* (1919), was published in conjunction with the 1922 film by Arzèn von Cserèpy; additional promotional material included Fridericus engravings featuring the main actors, Fridericus postcards with scenes from the film, and the Fridericus musical score arranged for piano. In matters of national history, film journalists and publishers made sure that they showed the seriousness and respect required for such topics. But no matter whose stories were being told, the intertextual and intermedial relationships established by these popular books were a clear indication of film's growing significance as a discourse that interacted with, and contributed to, other, more established discourses, including those of literature and history.

A growing number of books also provided an opportunity for the stars themselves to speak, to present this fascinating world of film from within. Here the logic of simulation reached completion, disguising product advertisement as artistic biography and presenting iconography as authenticity. Rather than being written about, being evaluated from the perspective of the theater, the film stars confirmed the discursive autonomy of film through one of the founding myths of the classical narrative cinema: the identity of role and persona. Thus the figure of the star, and the discourse of stardom, completed the shift from a more traditional notion of film authorship, based on the separation of art and life, to the intrinsically modern concept of "life-style," in which such oppositions were no longer necessary. Representative of such publications, Stefan Lorant's *Wir vom Film* (1928, We film people) combined glamour photographs and star confessions in a way reminiscent of the most advanced examples of photojournalism. The book was hailed by critics as "a document of the time and a biography of filmic development" and considered to be "of topical and cultural historical interest" (Lorant 1986, n.p.).

Semifictional biographies and autobiographies by famous stars likewise enjoyed great popularity in the Weimar years. While the "books to the film" duplicated the cinematic event, facilitating an ongoing reflection about film and its contribution to modern culture, the literary genre of the biography contributed indirectly to the discussion on film authorship. By looking at "the new art as reflected in its artists" (Treuer 1928, n.p.), these works combined elements from the artist's novel and the theatrical biography for a celebration of unabashed commercialism. Concerned on the surface with the creative individual, the star biographies were often very outspoken in their portrayal of the film world as ruthless, greedy, and exploitative. Or, to be more precise, the narrative of "making it in the movies" provided a framework in which such qualities could be validated as part of the self-made mentality associated with American culture and, at the same time, be dismissed as antithetical to Old World notions of self-fulfillment.

Especially during the years of unemployment and political instability, film publicists took advantage of the overdetermined nature of celebrity and presented the star's life as something to be at once desired and disdained. The worsened economic situation may have led some readers to envision film careers for themselves, but the glaring materialism and the complete lack of privacy described in these books made it easy to give up such ideas and settle for the lower-paying jobs available in factories and typing pools. The example of those "who made it" dispersed feelings of social injustice and, rather than inciting resentment toward films' nouveau riche, confirmed the myth of film as a truly democratic medium. By denying the difference between character and role, the star biographies achieved much more than promotion of films. They introduced a concept of self into the relationship between cinema and audience that was neither imaginary nor compensatory, but that was maintained precisely through the indistinguishability between fiction and reality. Therein lay their contribution to the theorizing of cinema as the production site of modern subjectivity.[6]

Fern Andra's glamorous life story as told by herself in *Der Weg, der ins Glashaus führte* (1919, The road to the film studio) illustrates the tendency of star biographies to confuse public and private identity and to mix fact and fiction. As presented in this work, the American-born Andra personified the spirit of modern entrepreneurship as well as the pleasures of European decadence, including an aristocratic husband. She had started out in the circus, founded her own film company, the Andra-Film, produced and directed a number of sentimental film dramas, and reached great popularity in circus films where she could show off her acrobatic talents. Wiene's

*Genuine* (1920) is perhaps her most famous film. Only such a film star, it seemed, was still able to accomplish the integration of personal and public life that, until then, had been the privilege of the writer and the artist. The idealization of the star played a crucial role in the redefinition of cinema as a state of consciousness. However, by showing the underside of fame, for instrance in the form of public scandals, star biographies also helped audiences to accept the alienation in their own lives as the price to be paid for personal honesty. Reading about the liberating and oppressive sides of stardom was especially important for women, who, through identification with the star, could participate in the dream of an integrated life complete with economic independence and sexual freedom but, at the same time, reject these narratives as unacceptable or unrealistic.

A similar mechanism was at work in film novels, where biography and fiction are not clearly separated to begin with. Joseph Delmont, who became famous as the director of detective films, describes in *Der Casanova von Bautzen* (1926, The casanova of Bautzen) how his attractive male alter-ego becomes a success among the women of Hollywood. Rosa Porten's *Die Filmprinzeß* (1919, The film princess) may have presented itself as fiction but, since it was dedicated to the actress Henny Porten, the author's sister, it could do nothing but offer insights into the making of a real star.[7] The publication in the same year of a Porten autobiography, suggestively titled *Wie ich wurde* (1919, How I came to be), contributed to this impression, as did Rosa Porten's deliberate references to her sister's life in the phenomenal career of the fictional film princess Thea Lossen. Again film was described as a world of unlimited opportunities, but the allusion to aristocracy in the term *film princess* effectively undercut any beliefs in its democratic structure. "Thea Lossen, who a few months ago sat quietly at a typewriter . . . How was she ever able to endure this dreadful, meaningless life with its unending monotony ?!" (Rosa Porten 1919, 101). With this recognition by the main character, Thea Lossen, the novel identifies a problem in mass society and, at the same time, offers a fantastic escape into film stardom as the commodofied version of the old genius cult. Indicative of the cinema's personality cult, the title *Die Filmprinzeß* introduced, at least on the symbolic level, a system of social hierarchies founded on a person's public image, rather than his or her actual class position. This imaginary order was, of course, already firmly established on the screen — for instance, in film comedies about love between the classes — but it required the legitimating power of written discourse to introduce its beliefs into popular definitions of social status and identity.

Not surprisingly, a growing number of novels were set in the film world. Some had previously been serialized in the trade journals and illustrated magazines, others were published by small publishing houses who tried to profit from the cinema's insatiable need for supplementary discourses. Under the pretense of showing the film world "as it really was," these works contributed, in their choice of settings and characters, to the discourse on German and American culture that played such a central role in Weimar culture's ongoing reflection about itself. The negative characteristics of film were regularly associated with America and Americans, whereas its creative possibilities came to life in the figure of the German film director stranded in Hollywood, who symbolized the cultural decline of an entire nation. More often than not, the preoccupation in these novels with things American functioned as a smokescreen for the pressing question of German national identity (Kaes 1985). America as a fictional construct provided the foil against which the domestic film industry and the institutions of bourgeois culture had to prove their superiority. At the same time, Americanism as a cultural phenomenon promised the liberation from tradition that had not been realized in the political domain, and was thus used to express hopes for a more democratic society and culture, including unrestricted access to the means of cultural production.

Playing with these associations, Arthur Landsberger's *Miss Rockefeller filmt* (1920) uses the name of a legendary American dynasty to point to the close ties between film and money, whereas Arnold Höllriegel's *Du sollst dir kein Bildnis machen* (c. 1929, Though shalt not make an image) shows the deterioration of the marriage between a serious German writer and his actress wife once Hollywood success reduces her to "a shadow in the realm of shadows" (Höllriegel 1928, 362). At one point in Arnolt Bronnen's 1928 novel *Film und Leben Barbara la Marr* (Film and life of Barbara la Marr), two characters, director Al Green and his cameraman J. S. Friend, discuss the working conditions in a business not made "for tender souls." Nostalgically, Green reminisces about the past, noting "I, for instance, used to play Hamlet in the big cities of a small country called Germany, about which you probably know little" (Bronnen 1987, 26). By displacing the crisis of the bourgeois theater into the drama of individual biography and by equating cinema with the Hollywood studio system, Bronnen turns this rather trivial story into a morality play about American commercialism and cultural domination.[8] Furthermore, the identification of cinema with the feminine — a tradition established by the cinema reformers — enables him to formulate his critique along gender lines and makes what he perceives as the feminization of German culture the main reason for the nation's decline.

In *Filmgewitter* (1926, Film lightning) by Rudolph Stratz, similar mechanisms are at work. Here the American film star Olympia Moore of the Wide World Company enters the scene with the remarkable English sentence "Are you come at last [sic]?" and adds to the fear that America might "slowly and invisibly invade the soul of all peoples and hypnotize and Americanize the Old Continent through its moving images" (Stratz 1926, 237, 241). Fortunately, the chairman of the Germania-Gesellschaft in the same novel promises radical changes. Under the motto "The German film lives! The German film marches! . . . The German film leads the Old World!" (1926, 281), he confirms the German film's superior qualities — the emphasis on craft, the highly qualified actors and directors — and enlists director Götz Billing in the fight for a national film culture. Heroic German men turning the film business into a spiritual endeavor — this describes, in one sentence, the culture-political solution offered by Stratz, one of Hugenberg's better-known pulp novelists.

A similar kind of sexual politics — without the reactionary politics — is at work in Vicki Baum's *Leben ohne Geheimnis* (1932, Life without secrets), which features several Germans stranded in Hollywood. Disempowered and made feminine by an industry specializing in eroticism, they are the chauffeur Meyer, a former engineer, the ambitious but deeply frustrated director Eisenloh, and the unhappy stand-in Aldens. Thinking of Germany during a Hollywood gala, Aldens suddenly recalls his years as a young man "from a good family in Darmstadt, the youngest of four brothers, the four famous Aldenslebens, the most handsome boys in town. Three died in the war. When he, too, was finally drafted at seventeen, the mother took Veronal. The father, Court Counselor Aldensleben, died soon after without much fanfare. But then, with the end of the war, the soldiers flooded back to the homeland on rainy streets. Home! Aldensleben thought ardently, and he thought about it often — and always in German" (1990, 15). Baum uses the exoticism of the foreign setting to describe an entire generation, from the war experience and the collapse of the old system to the indestructible love for the language and the fatherland. The Otherness of America, ultimately, reaffirms the greatness and splendor of German culture. Ironically, as a journalist and novelist working for the Ullstein concern, Baum relied on the same methods of rationalization that she condemned as the embodiment of American materialism in her novels.[9]

The same might be said about Baum's famous predecessor in the world of fantasy, Hedwig Courths-Mahler, who in her later years wrote a heart-rending novel about a film star, *Harald Landry, der Filmstar* (1928). Belonging to an earlier generation raised on nineteenth-century values, Courths-Mahler was highly critical of the film industry's obsession with money, and she used the corrupting setting to underscore the importance of virtue and propriety. Likewise, Heinrich Eduard Jacob, in *Blut und Zelluloid* (1930, Blood and celluloid), explains the mass appeal of film through military metaphors—the projector as a machine gun, producing a salvo of images, "twenty shots a second" (1930, 31)—and presents an unlikely fable about profit and propaganda that covers the existing positions on film, from its nationalist to its internationalist goals and from its entertaining to its artistic values. No matter with what intentions these film narratives were told, the authors' willingness to address the topic at all proves to what degree the cinema had invaded public consciousness, whether in the form of hagiographical biographies, sensationalist tales, or moralistic parables.

Even the theater discovered the cinema as a dramatic subject. The fascination was especially pronounced in the lay theater, which, because of its closeness to popular culture, added film stars and directors much earlier to their list of dramatis personae than the institutionalized theater. From early examples like Hans Fischer's *Filmaufnahme in Krähenwinkel* (1915, Location shooting in Krähenwinkel), where a filmmaker by the name of Karl Fimmel and his unruly film crew invade a small village to recruit peasants as extras for a Western, to later comedies like Gustav Pfenning's *Der Filmautor* (1928, The film scenarist), ordinary people come in contact with the world of film and are always transformed. Pfenning's play, for instance, features an aspiring young doctor who decides to become a film scenarist and, after some confusion, ends up with a beautiful wife and the promise of great wealth—an indication also of the increased social status of those working in the film industry.

By contrast, the contributions by more serious dramatists show a more ambivalent attitude, vacillating between fascination and resentment. Precisely because they, in their own work, tried to move beyond the illusionism of the traditional stage, the modern dramatists were suspicious of the uncanny ability with which the cinema reproduced images of life and challenged the distinction between reality and representation. In Karl Kraus's monumental work, *Die letzten Tage der Menschheit* (1919, The last days of mankind), the day of reckoning arrives, typically enough, with the indignant call of cameramen: "That's out of the question, no way, that's not light / . . . . / Isonzofilm is unsurpassable, to be sure, / but we want more light for the 'Day of Judgement'" (Kraus 1957, 766). Kraus imitates cinematic techniques in order to represent the experience of war and the historical process as fragmented. Fritz von Unruh's semi-Expressionist drama *Phaea* (1924) may be set in a film studio — Phaea stands for Photographische Akustische Experimental Aktiengesellschaft — but only uses the technical paraphernalia to affirm traditional notions of creativity. More specifically, von Unruh transforms the film studio into a stage on which the rhetoric of interiority makes its triumphant return. When the mighty Samuel Morris defines the First Commandment of mass entertainment, "Thou shall serve us! Entertain us! Amuse us! Lift us up!" (1987, 1:730), he invokes the most clichéd oppositions of art versus commerce and literature versus cinema (Hake 1990a). And when the poet Uhle exclaims, "The way toward life leads only through ourselves," Morris bluntly replies. "No! The way toward life leads through the darkroom!" (1987, 1:793), thus announcing man's complete replacement by the machine.

Years after they had first argued about the cinema in essayistic form, writers finally began to use the cinematic in their novelistic work. Alfred Döblin in his novel *Berlin Alexanderplatz* (1929), Erich Kästner and his *Fabian* (1931), Arnolt Bronnen, Lion Feuchtwanger, and many other writers associated with New Objectivity all made the aesthetics of film an integral part of their prose style (Schütte 1971). Many Weimar authors presented fictional accounts of going to the movies and introduced characters who, like the readers, succumbed, all too willingly, to the attractions. In contrast to the dramatists, who used film to elaborate on problems of representation, novelists were primarily interested in the experience of cinema. They turned to questions of reception in the moment that the philosophers of film (Stindt, Bloem) abandoned the audience, so to speak, for the unambiguity of normative aesthetics. Such role changes in the relationship between critical and fictional texts were not uncommon in the formation of discourses about film and cinema. More than anything, they underscore the need to consider all kinds of discourse — criticism, theory, and fiction — and pay attention to their ever-changing configurations.

Since a fully developed theory of film seemed within reach, even the more respectable novelists sometimes allowed their protagonists to indulge in its illicit pleasures. Where the early pulp novels painted gripping tales of film addiction, moral degeneration, and erotic obsession (especially among women audiences), these new fictional accounts presented the cinema as a somewhat lurid but overall rather pleasant product of modern consciousness.[10] This change in attitude can be traced in two short pieces by the Swiss poet Robert Walser. The first, written in 1912 and significantly titled "Cinema," recounts an improbable film story involving a count, a countess, a scheming servant, and an unexpected inheritance. To underscore its absurdity, Walser's narration is punctuated by the voice of a vendor selling "beer, sausage sandwiches, chocolate, pretzel sticks, oranges anyone, ladies and gentlemen!" (1978, 1:276). The 1926 article, which, by contrast, is called "About a Film, " reviews a film drama based on Selma Lagerlöf's saga *The Story of Gösta Berling* (1891). Faced with a cinema that is obviously serious about its cultural mission, Walser shows good intentions — "This time I am going to be serious. Impossible for me to be funny here" (1978, 9:378) — but the ironic tone betrays an unchanged negative attitude that now has to look for more indirect ways to express itself.

Walser's example shows that writers with conservative attitudes had only one possibility at their disposal, namely to embrace film, but to do so with ironic detachment and disdain. In novels and novellas, the character's reaction to the cinema was often used as a measure of his or her individuality and commitment to bourgeois values. The fictional accounts of going to the movies played an important role in the portrayal of younger protagonists, the representatives of Weimar youth. And indeed, they regularly turned to the cinema to seek temporary relief from monotonous working conditions, and they watched the latest films to learn about life and its vicissitudes. The young Doris in Irmgard Keun's novel about female employees, *Das kunstseidene Mädchen* (1932, The artificial girl), for instance, wants to find an identity modeled on the stars on the screen. Daydreaming in bed, she reasons: "And I want to write [my diary] like film, for my life is film and will be even more so. . . . And later, when I read, everything is like cinema — I see myself in images" (1986, 4). Other authors stress the sheer pleasures of perception. "In the front, flashing and flickering, with bright lights and deep shadows, fleeting but still firmly outlined, it was passing by" (Zweig 1931, 79), is how Arnold Zweig describes the cinematic experience from the perspective of the young bookseller's apprentice Benno Bremm in his story "Cinéma," thus also acknowledging the impact of a fleeting phenomenon such as cinema on an established tradition such as the literary, represented by one of its more impressionable members.

Finally, two novels are worth mentioning in which the enjoyment of the cinema's simple stories and quickly moving images enters into a most harmonious relationship with the feeling of mild superiority that remains the hallmark of bourgeois consciousness. The moments that define this dynamic in detail involve a visit to the local Bioskop-Theater by the tubercular patients in Thomas Mann's *Der Zauberberg* (1924; *The Magic Mountain*, 1927) and Harry Haller's flight into the cinema's dark interiors in Hermann Hesse's *Der Steppenwolf* (1927; *Steppenwolf*, 1929). The programs in both novels feature historical dramas, which says more about the authors' perception of the cinema than about audience preferences at the time. Above all, the gaudy historical spectacles serve to confirm their cultural pessimism and to reintroduce the old hierarchies between high and low culture.

Thus Hesse describes Steppenwolf's experience in the cinema as follows. "As I sauntered along I passed by a cinema with its dazzling lights and huge colored posters. I went on a few steps, then turned again and went in. There till eleven I could sit quietly and comfortably in the dark. Following the attendant with the pocket light I stumbled through the curtains into the darkened hall, found a seat and was suddenly in the middle of the Old Testament" (Hesse 1961, 177–78). After giving a brief synopsis of the film, a biblical epic about the Exodus, the author concludes in the character's voice: "I found it so strange and incredible to be looking at all of this, to be seeing the sacred writ, with its heroes and its wonders, the source in our childhood of the first dawning suspicion of another world than this, presented for money before a grateful public that sat quietly eating the provisions brought with it from home. A nice little picture, indeed, picked up by chance in the huge wholesale clearance of culture in these days! My God, rather than come to such a pass it would have been better for the Jews and every one else, let alone the Egyptians, to have perished in those days and forthwith of a violent and becoming death instead of this dismal pretence of dying by inches that we go in for today. Yes indeed!" (1961, 179).

Whereas Hesse expresses his disgust openly, Thomas Mann is much more subtle. He describes the scene at the Bioskop-Theater as follows: "Life flitted across the screen before their smarting eyes: life chopped into small sections, fleeting, accelerated; a restless, jerky fluctuation of appearing and disappearing, performed to a thin accompaniment of music, which set its actual *tempo* to the phantasmagoria of the past, and with the narrowest of means at its command, yet managed to evoke a whole gamut of pomp and solemnity, passion, abandon, and gurgling sensuality" (Mann 1975, 316). While the women are deeply aroused—Frau Stöhr's "red, uneducated face" is consumed by pleasure — the narrator quickly regains control, once the feature film is over and the newsreels give rise to an extended reflection on cinematic representation. Interestingly, this discursive moment is inspired by the image of a Negress. "It [the charming apparition] seemed to see and saw not, it was not moved by the glances bent upon it, its smile and nod were not of the present but of the past, so that the impulse to respond was baffled, and lost in a feeling of impotence. Then the phantom vanished. The screen glared white and empty, with the one word *Finis* written across it. The entertainment was over, in silence the theatre was emptied, a new audience took the place of that going out, and before their eager eyes the cycle would presently unroll itself again" (1975, 318).

Years later, Mann related his own visits to the cinema in the following gentleman-of-the-world manner: "For now only so much that my interest in this phenomenon of modern life has grown into a real concern over the last years, indeed, has assumed the character of a serene passion. I very often go to the cinema and, for hours, I don't get tired of the visual spectacles spiced with music" (Kaes 1978, 164). But he then qualifies his remark. "I spoke of a 'phenomenon of life,' for film in my opinion (forgive me) has very little in common with art, and I find it inappropriate to approach it with criteria taken from the sphere of art." A coy confession of weakness is then added by the author to hide, or rather emphasize, his individuality. "The tear tickles in the dark, and in dignified secrecy I rub it from the cheekbone with my fingertip" (Kaes 1978, 165). Thomas Mann's tear, in a way, symbolizes the ambivalence with which the middle classes made the cinema their own, as a form of entertainment and a place of self-confirmation.

\* \* \*

With the defiant spirit of the early years giving way to resigned acceptance of the inevitable, critical writings changed in form, and style, as well as in mode of address. Contributions increased in length, and, as a result of the growing specialization within the industry itself, became more diversified. The previous chapter has shown how the process of economic concentration gave rise to the first theories of film, which used normative aesthetics to elevate film to the status of an art form. The resultant shift in the critical paradigm, from the conditions of reception to the formal characteristics of the work, did not extend to all discourses on film, however. While the trade journals approached the cinema from a variety of perspectives, the literary writers and critics continued to emphasize the side of reception, thus also representing the interests of spectators. During the same time, the cinema emerged as a subject of critical inquiry in academic disciplines as various as economics, law, psychology, and public health. These studies were aimed at a small group of specialists, but the nonpublic character also resulted directly from their great public relevance. No matter whether the topic concerned contract law or new import regulations, the definition of cinema in such specialized terms affected the theorizing of film as an art form, if only through its absence from public debate. What at first glance seemed diametrically opposed — the philosophical speculation of a Bloem or Stindt, say, and the numerous dissertations on film censorship — contributed to the same project of constituting a discourse for cinema, and constituting a cinema through discourse.

However, the second part of this chapter will also show how the consequences of specialization were magically erased by the popularizers of film, who restored the unity of cinematic experience by using the experience of cinema as the foundation on which its practices had to be defined. The inclusion of film in theatrical productions, the appearance of cinema as a fashionable topic in novels and plays, and the almost casual reference to its pleasures in the essays of respectable authors would not have been possible without these controversies and debates. They constituted the cinema as a discursive subject and, in combination with changes in production and exhibition practices, prepared the ground for its integration into middle-class culture. At the same time, middle-class culture itself was transformed into a heterogeneous field of cultural practices, where the traditional arts existed side-by-side with an all-encompassing consumerism. Whether in relation to the objects of everyday life or as a new way of perceiving reality, consumption determined the parameters of modern existence to an unprecedented degree. It played a crucial role in the definition of class identity, especially for those members of the impoverished middle class who relied on fashion to reattain the social status that was no longer theirs. As proved by the cinema and the illustrated press, images were all-important. Establishing a connection between the laws of the marketplace and the laws of desire, consumption dissolved the boundaries between art and commodity, and created an imaginary space without borders. Its power was founded upon the promise of happiness, but its fulfillment was inextricably bound up with the principles of advertisement. From the elation with which the modern city-dweller entered the department stores to the casual attitude with which films were consumed in the splendid motion-picture palaces, one unifying force ruled the products and productions of mass culture.

The implications of this transformation process can be studied in the popular books on film and the film world. These so-called film books (*Filmbücher*) were published by trade journals like *Lichtbild-Bühne* and big media conglomerates like Ullstein and Scherl, or they were offered by small publishing houses that had been founded specifically for such purposes. On their pages, the cinema was no longer portrayed as a popular distraction or an aspiring art; instead, it became a measure of the successes of modern mass culture, and a metaphor for its precarious position between gratification and compensation. While Stindt, Harms, and Kurtz continued aesthetic discussions begun before the war, and while Lange and Bloem tried to combine normative aesthetics with nationalist politics, the Weimar cinema brought forth its own discourse. Its parameters were defined by the conditions of reception, and its intended readers were mainstream audiences rather than intellectuals. Above all, the new brand of film books sought to confirm the cinema as the paradigm of modern existence.

Through writing, the cinematic experience was prolonged beyond the duration of a visit to the cinema and became part of everyday life. The new popularizers of cinema simply translated the cinematic effect into another medium, the medium of language; this effect was achieved through the means of duplication and imitation. Their pseudo-intellectual style required only moderate intellectual effort from the readers, yet showed enough expertise to convince them of the "seriousness" with which cultural criticism was being practiced. Mixing sensationalist journalism with philosophical excursions and bold literary experiments, the authors of the popular film books reproduced the cinema's very own eclecticism and, in so doing, established the conditions under which all kinds of relationships between high and low, the sacred and the profane, became possible. Suddenly all boundaries seemed dissolved; only the imagination remained as the ultimate limit of the cinema and its critical fictions.

With the apologetic tone of the prewar years a thing of the past, coffee-table books like Resi Langer's *Kinotypen* (1919, Cinema types) began to flood the market. Frequently written in the first person, these books offered little more than pleasant platitudes on everything from current film trends and famous stars to the details of cinema etiquette. Catering to the growing number of women in the audience, Langer presented female role models like the film diva, who had glamour and eroticism as well as professional success. As the author stressed repeatedly, the identification with the emancipated screen heroine provided only temporary relief from the discrimination experienced by women in the modern workplace. Ultimately, "the look behind the scenes" (according to the book's half-title) only confirmed the audience's dependence on the illusion. "Accompanied by music, everybody streams to the exits; and what had just been a whole dissolves, for now, into atoms . . . perhaps tomorrow the individual will again become part of a whole and surrender to another 'light oasis' [*Lichtoase*]" (1919, 31). Erwin Magnus's *Lichtspiel und Leben* (1924, Film and life) refers precisely to the close relationship between reality and the skillful staging of what he calls *Lichtspiel* (literally: light play). The cultural ambitions expressed in the term are captured in the calm, relaxed scenario that has little to do with the frenzy of early reports from the movies. "I sit in a soft chair. An orchestra plays a soft, insinuating tune. Then silence. The mysterious, church-high space darkens. Now the large silver screen lights up" (1924, 9).

Defeatism turned into an aesthetic experience — that these sweet addictions could also be caused by economic hardship was suggested by Herbert Lewandowski who, in the illustrated film almanac for the year 1921, describes Berlin's "other" film fans with bitterness. "Berlin is the most beautiful city in the world! When there is nothing to bite and nothing to wear, one goes to the movies, becomes sated with viewing [*sieht sich satt*], seeks amusement in the dark, and forgets about the bad times" (Skolnar 1920, 23). Displacing social reality into the realm of pure fiction, Heinz Salmon goes so far as to think up a discussion among film fans and film enemies that not only features stereotypical characters like the intellectual, the poet, the industrialist, and the stockholder, but also introduces such venerable figures as the Muses and allegorical representations of "Public Opinion" and "Censorship" (1924, n.p.). Salmon's collection of prose pieces — *Film-Götter (Frechheiten aber Wahrheiten). Eine durchaus ernsthafte Betrachtung einer lustigen Angelegenheit* — bears a title that unwittingly reveals the incoherences of cinema culture in its set of oppositions. The main title, *Film-Götter* (1924, Film gods), refers to the degree of idolatry that makes film the subject of public worship and the object of almost indiscriminate consumption. The lengthy half-title then defines the conditions under which both sides of cinema are to be negotiated. The comment in parentheses, "Indolent Remarks, But Truths," prescribes the attitude of disrespect with which the cinema, and this book, too, should be approached, whereas the following explanation, "More or Less Serious Thoughts About a Funny

Affair" expresses the cinema's desire to be taken seriously. It is just this impossible position between gossip and philosophy, as defined by the title of Salmon's book, that constituted the cinema as an impossible object: as a truth without depths, and as a diversion without shallowness. To emulate this intermediary, noncommittal state in their writings was the foremost goal of the popularizers of film.

The more ambitious authors tried to enlist the fascination with scandal in the writing of philosophy. Catering to the educated middle classes, they satisfied the need for information, all the while providing sufficient titillation to make the reading worthwhile. These works are perhaps characterized best by the prefix *pseudo:* they present pseudoconcerns, set pseudostandards, and divulge pseudotruths. As if repeating a litany, authors mention the velocity of modern life, the overwhelming stimuli, the need for distraction. Complaints about the low quality of films appear side by side with derisive comments on film art; proposals for improving the reputation of the film business share the page with the worst examples of yellow-press journalism, and ecstatic hymns to technology alternate with hackneyed metaphysical phrases.

Curt Moreck's *Sittengeschichte des Kinos* (1926, The cinema's history of manners and morals), with its peculiar mixture of sensationalism and cultural pessimism, represents a totalizing vision of eclecticism and is just as riddled by contradictions as the title chosen to define its project. In accordance with the genre of "the history of manners and morals," Moreck comments on virtually everything from popular genres, audience psychology, film eroticism, and famous stars to future developments in the industry and problems of film censorship. Celebrating the cinema as the essence of modernity, and praising the inventor as a kind of modern Saviour, Moreck simply declares aesthetics and technology to be identical; hence his conclusion "that only technical inventions will decide the fate of future generations and that they alone bear within themselves the possibility of completion" (1926, 9). All his later comments — "cultural small talk," to quote Kracauer (1927) — offer variations of this technopositivist theme. He explains the predominance of erotic subject matter with the cinema's dependency on the visual. Similarly, the large number of protagonists from the upper class is explained through the "primitive technical means" that can only depict extreme conditions; the sound film, Moreck speculates, might give voice to a new group, the "chatting middle class."

Linking the cinema to the ongoing struggle for spiritual redemption,

Moreck rejects all comparisons to the drama and proposes an alternative genealogy, one based on the spectacles of the fairground and the masses' inexhaustible need for distraction. "Instead of finding peace in immersion, he [modern man] longs for distraction" (1926, 12), Moreck argues, thus using the classic opposition of immersion and distraction for an alternative history of cinema developed in analogy to the history of the printing press. Through its collective mode of production, the cinema carries on the tradition of the medieval guilds and triumphs as the cathedral of the modern masses. Its collective mode of reception, however, must be seen as a product of modern mass society. "Thus the tendency of contemporary man and that of cinema move in the same direction, and both equate mankind with the masses" (1926, 68). Only the cinema, Moreck explains, is able to overcome the Babel of languages and to reunite all peoples through the internationalism of the image. Only the cinema recognizes the "primeval, immediate forms of expression of the human spirit" (Moreck 1926, 54) and, in so doing, creates meaning through "one of the most powerful and vital drives" (1926, 63), visual pleasure (*Schaulust*). The darkness in the auditorium may, for a while, eliminate moral restraints, but Moreck insists that the visual experience of cinema will eventually lead to a heightened sense of humanity once its lowly instincts are under control, and once its cultural qualities prevail over its merely civilizing forces.

With these implications, the cinema becomes the mirror in which the masses encounter themselves. "The life depicted by film is our own existence. The strange, vibrating atmosphere of our days, the nervous, fast, hurried existence of modern man is extricated, if only for the short moment, from the dance of changing stereotypes and experiences a moment of eternity. . . . We watch ourselves live. . . . Like in a mirror we recognize our own restlessness, our own lack of balance. The pressure of being yields, if only for a moment, to a peculiar tranquility. How precious is this moment, how quickly does it pass. But this is more than mere escapism, more than intoxication followed by disenchantment. The cinema allows us to embrace our existence without succumbing to [it and] . . . , as a future cultural document, gives a more profound and complete picture of our time than all the chronicles written with the pens of Clio" (1926, 265). The association of cinema and life, as evoked by Moreck in the celebratory ending, describes a cinema based on experience, and therein closer to modern consumer culture than to the traditional arts. However, his notion of "life," which reveals the strong influence of *Lebensphilosphie*, stands outside all definitions of class and gender and gives precisely the illusion of freedom that makes the cinema so appealing in a society held together by distinctions and boundaries.

While Moreck's consumerist dream of cinema satisfies the need for an affirmative discourse, other film books assume a much more aggressive position; they attempt to reunite the politics of pleasure with politics proper. In *Grossmacht Film* (1928, The world power of film), Curt Wesse constructs a history of cinema that takes loans from the history of science and technology to prove its cultural legitimacy—citing the astronomer Ptolemy and Athanasius, bishop of Alexandria, as well as the photographer Eadweard Muybridge and Oskar Messter, the German film pioneer—but, unlike Stepun, he sents his metaphysical speculations within a modernist framework.[11] Evoking Futurism both in its fascination with technology and in its later sympathies for fascist ideology, Wesse's book describes film as "a new Antheus," born in the marriage of Art and Technology. By renouncing individuality, he argues, film gives rise to a new collective spirituality. "In film, and through film . . . mankind inexorably moves toward the solution of the great social problems that can never be solved through the fair distribution of material wealth, but only through the spirit of the individual who controls his extravagant demands by submitting to a new idea of human community" (1928, 275).

Wesse's scenario at once denounces political movements that offer a critique of private property and magically erases social tensions through his notion of a higher, more spiritual community. The new temple of mass culture, the phoenix that will rise from the ashes—imbued with such religious imagery, film promises not just redemption but another kind of society, whose rudimentary forms are already prefigured in the medium's formal qualities and its conditions of reception: "A force close to the great force, a force which has to destroy itself in order to fulfill its own nature, which animates every measure through excess, which dissolves all individuality in favor of a higher form of communality: a triumphant struggle to reconcile men with their deeds" (1928, 294). In the process of this deification, the cinema became a testing ground for explicitly political forms of mass spectacle in which the renunciation of individuality meant the first step toward totalitarianism. The spirituality of cinema, which was summoned by progressive as well as conservative writers to counterbalance its inherent "materialism," thus paved the way for another kind of spiritual revolution that would soon turn the cinema into a means of indoctrination.

Not surprisingly, Rudolf Arnheim saw in Wesse only "the symptomatic coquettishness of an author who adorns himself with a bricklayer's apron and an enamel flask in order to coyly indulge the spirit in the shadow of these film props" (1928b, 926).

When leftist writers used the format of the popular film book, they often made their reflections on cinema part of a more general analysis of capitalism. The best example for this kind of popular Marxism is Ilja Ehrenburg's *Die Traumfabrik* (1931, The dream factory), when it transforms political and literary concerns into a riveting narrative of exploitation and despondency. The German-Russian novelist and critic presents his critique of the film industry alongside millenarian visions and gossip from the Hollywood studios. He celebrates technological progress while at the same time calling for spiritual redemption through increased alienation. He attacks film for its false internationalism, which is based on total exchangeability, but at the same time accuses the industry, in truly humanist fashion, of exploiting the workers and their need for distraction. He follows the vicious circle of lack, desire, and compensation that paralyzes the modern mass individual, preventing him or her from developing forms of resistance, yet describes this process in a fatalistic fashion — that is, as a vicious circle. Ehrenburg's report from the dream factory employs strong metaphors and repeated ellipses, and his consistent use of the present tense prompted Tucholsky to dismiss the book as monotonous (1987, 10:25). Kracauer sharply criticized Eherenburg's attempt to present a literary representation of capitalism as objective reportage. "It [the form] is all too novelistic and often one doesn't know where reality — which is the topic, after all — ends and where imagination begins to have a free hand" (1932).

As a literary simulation of the cinematic experience, the following passage from *Die Traumfabrik* is worth quoting at length: "In the evenings, the jungle of the cities lives. The people rush along, passing each other, like animals running to the watering holes. The people rush to the silver screen. . . . She has typed 280 letters today, he has installed 3,000 screws. What now? How to save oneself from the emptiness and the yawning? At home, canned food waits, and silence. At home, you have to think and thinking is difficult! All gossip is exhausted, the last cigarette smoked. Three more hours. Then sleep. Then the alarm clock: Typing and screwing. How bored each is of the other. He says nothing: 'Damned screws! Today they took something out of my salary again!' She doesn't even manage a smile: 'The new stockings are torn. . . .' To sink deeper! To forget! Not being!" (1931, 302).

Ehrenburg's description of a world ruled by General Electric, Metro-Goldwyn-Mayer, tired prostitutes, and weeping shopgirls bespeaks a secret fascination with American culture. Behind his apprehension about the effects of rationalization and the crisis of meaning in late capitalist society lies an even greater infatuation with the power of modern mass media. "During the day — the running conveyer belt; at night — the cinema. That is the law of being" (1931, 32). Ehrenburg's sarcastic conclusion — "The cinema should be open twenty-four hours a day, like a pharmacy" (1931, 178) — acknowledges an almost physical desire for something else, while at the same time evoking associations of illness and pathology. In *Die Traum-fabrik,* the image-starved workers, neon-lit streets, and profit-hungry film investors, therefore, become characters in a morality play of capitalist culture that, despite all good intentions, is almost quaint in its simplicity.

For René Fülöp-Miller, the plight of film was inextricably linked to American culture, which had invaded the German consciousness to become "archetypes on the stage of our existence." In his "saga of greed," *Die Phantasiemaschine* (1931, The fantasy machine), Fülöp-Miller argued that the cinema had to be regarded as truly American in origin and orientation, and that it had to be rejected together with all other phenomena of Americanism. It was the obsession with material goods, he claimed, together with a general a lack of sophistication, that had given rise to the emotional equivalent of the modern factory, the cinema. "Today cinematography provides the industrial satisfaction of psychological needs, just as the physical need for clothes and food has been satisfied before by manufactured goods" (1931, 31). Based on this central thesis, Fülöp-Miller presented a number of complaints that, given their lack of specificity, equally applied to other phenomena of mass culture.

The cinema, he argues, reduces human feelings to prejudices and preconceived notions. It promotes hypocrisy by arousing forbidden passions while at the same time upholding moral standards. It increases ignorance, since its prefabricated dreams require no intellectual effort on the part of the spectator and can be consumed like any other product. It gives rise to an infantile eroticism by exploiting voyeuristic tendencies. It creates an artificial world where human beings are portrayed through a few physical features like height, shape, weight, or skin color and where entire lives are reduced to the most simplistic oppositions of good and evil, yet it always has a happy ending. It caters to people who can only deal with the lowest levels of abstraction and who only want to satisfy their most primitive needs.

Needless to say, Fülöp-Miller opposes the idea of film as art. "Like a curse, the unartistic desire for fulfillment at any price rests on all expressive forms of cinema. Its effect has been, from the very beginning, that film could not free itself from the slavish imitation of nature" (1931, 141). Art, in his view, means production, and not the kind of reproducibility that characterizes these slavish imitations of nature. Art, moreover, requires mature audiences, and not a homogeneous mass that behaves like children and adolescents. Fülöp-Miller's final verdict on film, with the exception of very "physical" genres like slapstick and comedy, is devastating: "After all, real life consists of more, and of something else than even a meticulously organized card catalogue of bald heads, hunchbacks, and skin colors, and a production that relies on a central office that does not have the the key to all the world's secrets in its hands" (1931, 131).

These four works, by Moreck, Wesse, Ehrenburg, and Fülöp-Miller, in a sense represent the discourses of film and consumer culture and the aesthetic and political positions available to them. Those who accepted the power of cinematic consciousness either sought refuge in a kind of spectatorial hedonism (Moreck), or tried to imagine a new modernist metaphysics (Wesse). Those who opposed the transformation of cinema into an instrument of cultural and economic domination either focused on American capitalism (Ehrenburg) or American culture (Fülöp-Miller). The positions taken by Moreck and Wesse functioned like a mirror to the film industry, reflecting its image, but ultimately confirmed the communal experience of cinema as pleasurable and redeeming. The analyses by Ehrenburg and Fülöp-Miller became vehicles with which to move behind the smooth surface of the finished products and examine the sociopsychological and economic processes that constituted them. To quote Kracauer, their works "originated in the need that has become more and more pressing, namely, to explain the film wares offered to the consumers in all countries out of the conditions of production" (1979, 530). In all cases, however, the rejection of aesthetic categories in the traditional sense prepared the ground for a repoliticization of cinema in the wider sense: through the convergence of visual pleasure and consumerism, through the affinities between cinematic modes of reception and other mass phenomena, through the relationship between work and leisure, and through the equation of cinema and Americanism.

# Chapter 9
## The Politicization of Film

n 1922, Carl Einstein wondered about the mass appeal of the cinema. "That a crowd of two thousand people is being formed remains one of the more recent film secrets, all the while the police manage, since thousands of years ago, to disperse even assemblies of two people" (Kaes 1978, 158). While Einstein seemed perplexed by the fact that the cinema, as a place of public assembly, was no longer perceived as a threat to the social order, a growing number of leftist activists and critics made sure that political concerns were reintroduced into the debate on film, and that the cinema did become an important means of political propaganda. As has been pointed out in an earlier chapter, the organizations on the left initially showed little interest in the cinema, rejecting it like the cinema reformers as an enemy of the working class. These attitudes changed dramatically after World War I.

One of the purposes of this chapter is to describe leftist film criticism during the Weimar years as part of a more far-reaching critique of capitalism and bourgeois ideology, and in relation to leftist filmmaking and media initiatives. Film criticism differed in the Social Democratic, Communist, and independent leftist press, and these differences found expression in the approach to bourgeois and proletarian cinema, narrative and non-narrative film, and the respective models of criticism and propaganda that informed them. Given the extreme polarization of Weimar politics, the second purpose will be to point to the continuities in the rightist discourses on film, from the books on the *Kulturfilm* to the appearance of nationalistic film publications and ultra-rightist authors like Buchner or Kalbus. The notion of film criticism as a political intervention continues some of the concerns discussed in chapter 6, while the political divisions themselves recall similar confrontations over the cinema and the nation from the prewar years, discussed in chapter 2. Indeed, it might even be argued that the philosophy of film and the fictions of cinema, outlined in chapters 7 and 8, provided the backdrop of denial and displacement against which the repoliticization of film in the late twenties took place.

After the October Revolution in Russia and the collapse of the Wilhelmine Empire, Germany had to find both a new political order and a new political identity. The Spartacist uprisings in Berlin and the short-lived Bavarian Soviet Republic created a situation where, for a short moment, everything seemed possible — until the political reaction triumphed again and high hopes gave way to disillusionment. The founding of the Weimar Republic in 1918 was, in this regard, the work of fear and compromise. In the years that followed, leftist critics gradually developed an interest in the cinema and discovered in its sentimental stories and lurid effects an emotionality not dissimilar to the revolutionary spirit that had fueled their own longing for radical change. This shifting of revolutionary energies from the realm of politics to that of cinema accounts for the ecstatic tone with which many writers envisioned the future of film. While the military and political defeat of the old order put an end to reformist plans for a national cinema, it meant the beginning for a revolutionary cinema. Suddenly, very different images occupied the leftist imagination: "An age in which Soviets visit a palace is no longer interested in the inhabitants of a palace. In the future, Bolsheviks and Spartacists will have to play the roles of the obligatory counts and barons. The revolution is the future empress of the film world!" (J. Roth, quoted by Kinter 1985, 176). Filled with joy, Rudolf Leonhard proclaimed in 1920: "If Schiller were alive today, he would be a Communist and . . . he would write films" (1920, 196). The Expressionist dramatist and revolutionary socialist Ernst Toller praised film's importance "as a weapon of immeasurable value" (1978, 1:115) for all socialists, and he demanded the production of "a film about the German revolution" (1978, 1:117), a historical documentary of great emotional appeal, and with workers as the main protagonists.

The sudden change in attitude was not limited to the representatives of a revolutionary Expressionism. A comparison of two statements by Clara Zetkin, a founding member of the Independent Social Democratic party (USPD), shows how important the postwar years were for the formulation of leftist film politics. In 1919, Zetkin still sounded very much like a conservative reformer when she argued: "The movie plague takes hold of the few free hours, thereby destroying the most precious energies needed in the struggle for a classless society. . . . And the biggest scandal: They [the workers] leave these shows with diminished strength, with besmirched souls, and a fever-ishly intensified perception of things" (1983, 95). By 1924, she was calling for more productive approaches. "We must develop the great cultural potential of film. In a revolutionary sense — that does not mean that we should simply reverse the characteristic schemes of the bourgeois film and show the bourgeois as a devil, the proletarian as an angel. . . . The film with a revolution-ary content must provide information about the proletarian situation, must advance proletarian class-consciousness, and awaken and strengthen the determination and readiness for self-sacrifice in the revolutionary struggle" (Hirschbach 1980, 80). Putting such demands into practice, the leftist orga-nizations began to study the historical conditions under which the cinema had become the main source of entertainment for the urban masses.

It was not until the mid-twenties that leftist organizations used film for their own purposes. From then on, they paid attention to the psychological effects of film instead of rejecting it as detrimental to the development of a proletarian consciousness. As a first step in this direction, a number of organizations were formed with the explicit goal of producing, distribut-ing, and promoting progressive, noncommercial films. To be sure, most leftist critics still believed in the primacy of the economic base, and some continued to doubt the possibility of creating a revolutionary cinema under capitalism. Faced with the overwhelming success of commercial films, the leftist parties, labor unions, and cultural organizations were more or less forced by the political conditions in the Weimar Republic to reexamine their culture-political strategies and reassess their definitions of art and mass culture. These projects took on very different forms in the context of Social Democratic, Communist, and independent leftist organizations.

Generally speaking, the Social Democratic party (SPD) pursued a more conservative approach, stressing the need for education and reform. If no cure against the film plague could be found, one speaker had already argued at the 1913 party convention, then the progressive cultural organizations should at least try to utilize film in educational projects. Like the cinema reformers, the representatives of Social Democracy consistently empha-sized the usefulness of educational films and documentaries. An official declaration from 1922 explained this approach: "As a medium of popular entertainment, film has become very important. However, its products are for the most part inferior, and often very detrimental to people's tastes. The good things film does have to offer — for the documentation of nature and the arts, as an art form in its own right, and above all as a means of illustration and education — remain largely unexplored given the present structure of the film industry. Thus it is the task of the workers' education movement to support all serious initiatives for film reform and to stop the flood of inferior products by making available to the public the good films that do exist" (quoted by Kinter 1985, 200).

Similar arguments stood behind the founding in 1922 of the Volksfilm-bühne (People's Film Theater) which, like its model, the Volksbühne, was committed to educating the masses in cultural matters; the articles on film published in *Vorwärts,* the Social Democratic party organ, usually supported such initiatives (Murray 1990, 93–98, 168–79). It was not until later that its critics paid more attention to the narrative film, calling it a vehicle of bourgeois ideology and a major obstacle to social change; even then, their interest in questions of narrative remained limited. Siegfried Nestriepke from the *Volksbühne* Berlin simply equated the cinema's technical and artistic features and used such a mechanistic model to explain its mass-psychological appeal. Advocating a more pragmatic approach to film, he demanded: "It is necessary that all those who want to prevent cultural damage involve themselves actively in today's business of film production and exhibition, even if they are basically unable or unwilling to accept film as an art form" (1926, 1). As is made evident by this statement, the discovery of film by leftist critics was primarily motivated by political considerations, namely, to reverse the growing alienation between the masses and their political representatives. Speaking at the 1929 Sozialistische Kulturtag in Frankfurt, whose participants had assembled to discuss new mass media like film and radio, Nestriepke referred to their scandalous lack of knowledge of mass-psychological processes as the greatest shortcoming of socialist film politics. "The masses rush to see films that show ridiculous situations and unbelievable happy endings, and do so with the most primitive methods and against all psychological and dramatic logic. Yet these masses, including the class-conscious workers, eagerly suck in the glorifications of the bourgeoisie, even the glorifications of militarism" (Nestriepke 1929, 20).

Though Social Democrats rarely opposed narrative films on principle, they refused to study the psychological dispositions that made specific genres so appealing and specific stars so enormously popular. The discrepancies between the reality of people's lives and their desire for other images of reality were no longer ignored, but the old distinctions between popular and proletarian culture still remained firmly in place. Thus Nestriepke's own list of valuable films — with such classics such as *Phantom, The Nibelungs,* and *So This Is Paris* in the "of little value" category — revealed not only the limitations of normative aesthetics in general; more importantly, it revealed strong Social Democrat biases against formal experimentation and daring subject matter.

While the Social Democrats tried to improve the quality of film production by appealing to the filmmaker's artistic responsibility, the Communists chose a more aggressive strategy. They approached the problem simultaneously from the sides of production and reception (Happel and Michaelis 1980, 91–102). Founded initially for the distribution of Russian films in Germany, Prometheus Film in the late twenties produced *Mutter Krausens Fahrt ins Glück* (1929, Mother Krausen's Journey to Happiness) and *Kuhle Wampe* (1932, Whither Germany?), perhaps the best-known examples of leftist filmmaking in the Weimar Republic (Lüdecke 1973; Korte 1980; Perry 1982; and Murray 1990).

Behind many projects stood Willi Münzenberg, who, since his early involvement with the International Workers' Relief Organization (IAH), had continuously expanded his area of influence through the publication of newspapers, critical journals, and illustrated magazines (Gruber 1965 and 1966; Surmann 1982; Heller 1984, 145–56). Münzenberg's pamphlet *Erobert den Film!* (1925, Conquer the film!) encapsulated the leftist approach to film criticism as it combined theoretical insight with a clear practical purpose, including detailed information on how to organize media events. Praising film as an important tool of Communist propaganda, Münzenberg called for the full utilization of its artistic possibilities in unmasking the class enemy and promoting the revolutionary struggle. He argued that "film is not only useful in fighting and castigating the enemy, it also affords the opportunity to represent, in a positive light, the goals and the struggles of the Communist movement and the revolutionary workers' organizations. There is no doubt that a film will have a strong influence on thousands of adolescents when it deals with the life of a youth who is beaten in school, mistreated by his master, who suffers, starves, but finally gets in touch with the Communist youth movement, finds protection, shelter, and solutions to his problems, who is attracted to the mass movement, gets to know the world of political meetings, participates in rallies, etc. . . . Such a film would bring large crowds to the Communist youth movement" (1925, 86). Thus Münzenberg concluded: "Film does not only stand in the service of entertainment — although it primarily serves this end — but to an increasing degree, it also educates. . . . It is therefore in the best interest of the revolutionary workers' movement that it devotes great attention to this extremely important problem, and that the movement finds ways to make use of this effective, vital means of propaganda and agitation" (1925, 88).

However, even in Communist circles, the problems of the narrative film were rarely addressed, either in relation to issues of spectatorship or in the context of people's working and living conditions. In their analyses of mass entertainment, leftist critics seemed unable to move beyond moral appeals to the class-conscious worker, or to reconsider the basic tenets of economic determinism. Instead a certain helplessness prevailed, as Martens noted matter-of-factly: "The capitalist mode of production, with its oppressive and exhausting working conditions, has induced a state of nervous tension and mental exhaustion in everybody . . . a state that, without doubt, provides the most fertile soil for the proliferation and prosperity of the cinema" (quoted by Kinter 1986, 157). The author of this rather typical article on cinema and youth neglected to take into account the willingness of this "most fertile soil" to see films that, objectively speaking, stood in sharp contrast to their class interest.

While the more dogmatic positions on the narrative film disappeared as critics shifted their attention from the problems of film reception to those of film production, many asked themselves whether independently pro-duced films could provide a valid alternative to bourgeois cinema, econom-ically as well as ideologically. If big film companies like Ufa were able to influence audiences through film, the writer, physician, and activist Frie-drich Wolf argued, then the organizations of the working class should do the same. "Especially in the case of film, it has become more than obvious to what degree art today is a weapon! . . . Film: an invisible weapon in the class struggle, a taste- and odorless combat gas that confuses and dulls the people with kitsch and stupefaction, with fulsome Rhinegold and colorless Nibelungs and Faust films!" (Kühn 1975, 1:71). Only a dispassionate analysis of the existing films, Wolf argued, could stop this flood of lies and decep-tions; hence his appeal to the film critics to abandon the idea of art as something precious, hence his suggestion to the film directors to find their stories among real people and in everyday life. Once this was achieved, Wolf claimed, all obstacles to using film for the revolutionary cause would be eliminated. The result would be something similar to what one of the proponents of Proletkult, Platon M. Kerschenzev, described in glowing terms: "For the first time, cinematography will be the platform from where to propagate the ideas of socialism" (Kühn 1975, 1:44).

Yet because of their instrumental approach to film, and culture in general, most Communist critics continued to insist that real revolutionary films could never be made in a bourgeois capitalist society. Since the cinema had been conceived under capitalist conditions, it derived its forms and functions from the close association with bourgeois ideology. Consequently, all films contributed, more or less, to the existence of false consciousness. Film criticism could, at best, draw attention to these mechanisms and offer its services to the propagation of Communist ideas. However, as Alfons Goldschmidt stated emphatically: "Only a noncapitalist economy will liberate the film" (1928, 1).

Here the independent leftist Volksfilmverband (People's Film Association), which counted among its members Heinrich Mann, Käthe Kollwitz, and Erwin Piscator, took a more pragmatic approach (Murray 1990, 228–32). Based on the motto "The enemy is on the right — even the enemy of film," the association tried to organize groups in the fight against reactionary films and oppressive censorship laws.[1] Especially during the last years of the republic, its primary goal was to unite the divided left against the common enemy, the growing conservative and ultraright forces. The association offered seminars about film-theoretical questions, started noncommercial distribution networks and production companies, published a journal devoted exclusively to film, and practiced what could be called a revolution from below. In a speech given at the 1928 founding assembly of what then was stilled called the Volksverband für Filmkunst (People's Association for Film Art), Heinrich Mann spoke of intellectuals who, through their elitist attitudes, had indirectly contributed to the abysmal situation. "In Germany there is little talk about the art of film. . . . Art has a responsibility to present as well as future generations and is held accountable for the most distant consequences. Truly popular art does not seduce, it educates. It is not for sale, it does not lower itself in order to seduce the people instead of teaching them how to see and think. To teach thinking, to serve the spirit — every serious art approaches this task in collaboration with the people" (1928, 4).

The different attitudes toward film and society continued in the different approaches to film criticism, as the following examples will show. Making the mass appeal of cinema the nodal point, film criticism in the

Communist press was more or less synonymous with political agitation. While articles about film could also be found in *Die Arbeiter Illustrierte Zeitung, Kulturwille,* and other Communist publications, it was *Die Rote Fahne,* the official paper of the German Communist Party (KPD), that took a leading role in the debates (Brauneck 1973; Murray 1990, 42–52, 113–18, 188–95). Regular contributors to *Die Rote Fahne* included Axel Eggebrecht, Heinz Lüdecke, Alfred Durus, Otto Steinicke, and a number of women critics such as Alice Lex, Trude Sand, and Gertrud Alexander. Especially after 1928, critical essays and reviews played an important role in the party's campaigns against film censorship and the powerful Hugenberg concern. The public reaction to films like *Battleship Potemkin* and *Kuhle Wampe,* from their temporary ban and negative reception in the conservative press to the many rallies organized in their support, became case studies for analyzing the contradictions between the bourgeois notion of freedom of speech and what Communist agitators called "the true face of the ruling class." Articles about noncommmercial films and film events sometimes provided an occasion to attack the Social Democrats for their reformist compromises and to promote the idea of a truly proletarian cinema. Critical writing in general served the overriding purpose of radicalizing the working class and creating a political situation conducive to revolutionary change. Through an emphasis on character and plot analysis, the various strands of argument, from the critique of filmmaking under capitalism to the proposals on media education, came together under the unifying idea of filmic realism.

Often the controversy over realist tendencies in literature provided a blueprint for discussions about realism in film. For instance, *Die Linkskurve,* the journal of the Bund proletarisch-revolutionärer Schriftsteller (BPRS), from 1928 on tried to recruit and organize writers from the working class and wanted to develop a theory of literature from the perspective of the proletariat. The debate on realism between Brecht and Lukács had its origins in these efforts. By emphasizing narrative at the expense of visual spectacle, and by insisting on typicality rather than psychological motivation, the leftist films critics established a conceptual framework in which filmic reality could be directly related to the social conditions, either as a reflection or as blatant falsification. Film reviews in *Die Rote Fahne* usually summarized a film's story and then examined the ideological function of its story elements, main protagonists, and central themes. Measured against the reality of working-class life — and not the reality of workers' desires —

the majority of bourgeois films, with their shallow protagonists and escapist stories, could, of course, not live up to these standards. The dogmatic tone of many reviews made it virtually impossible to explore the complex relationship between working conditions and forms of entertainment, between the mechanisms of sensory deprivation and need for visual pleasure. The adherence to the realist paradigm also prevented any detailed assessment of the avant-garde movements, which were regularly dismissed as a product of bourgeois decadence.

More constructive approaches, especially toward mainstream films, could be found in *Film und Volk* (1928–30), the official publication of the left-liberal Volksverband für Filmkunst. Contributors to the journal included Alfons Goldschmidt, Max Brenner, and the *Weltbühne* critic Hans Siemsen, famous directors like Eisenstein and Pudovkin, men with technical know-how like Edgar Beyfuß and László Moholy-Nagy, and — evidence of the many contradictions in Weimar radicalism — later Nazi sympathizers Arnolt Bronnen and Walter Ruttmann. Many articles were published anonymously or signed with initials. In 1930, the journal merged with *Arbeiterbühne* to form *Arbeiterbühne und Film,* "no longer treating the problems of the revolutionary workers' theater and the revolutionary film separately, but in connection with each other," as *Die Rote Fahne* noted approvingly (Kühn 1975, 2:272). *Arbeiterbühne und Film* ceased publication in 1931 (Frey 1980).

Because of their strong interest in film, the journals associated with the Volksfilmverband were more open to formal and technical problems. Whereas a party organ like the *Rote Fahne* focused almost exclusively on questions of content, the contributors to *Film und Volk* were frequently professionals in the film business and therefore very knowledgeable about the practical side of filmmaking; this can be seen in articles about the importance of dynamic editing, the use of nonsynchronous sound, or the problems with film color. Concerned about the return of theatrical conventions in some early sound films, Hans Spielhagen, for instance, called for "a radical transformation that would establish a connection between visual and spoken style" (Spielhagen 1929, 7). Edgar Beyfuß expressed ideas developed further by Rudolf Arnheim when he spoke in favor of a coexistence of silent and sound film. "The silent film as a work of art will remain and must remain, no matter how many new inventions will give rise to other art forms or art genres that we cannot even imagine today" (Beyfuß

1929, 4). Discussions, however, always returned to the economic and political conditions that, in the view of most critics, prevented the making of good films. Thus Ebbe Neergard argued that "it doesn't do any good when incidentally quite intelligent and perceptive astheticians and critics present their theories about how to make a good and artistically valuable film. Those who could are not willing, and those who would are not in a position to do so" (Neergard 1929, 5).

Despite the limited influence attributed to film criticism, the discussions about film criticism were quite extensive. They provided a means for addressing more fundamental questions about criticism, ideology, and the public sphere, thus serving the same metadiscursive function as debates in the trade press and in left-liberal journals like *Die Weltbühne*. In the Communist publications, such self-reflexivity fulfilled an additional purpose, namely to define one's critical practices in opposition to the conservative and Social Democratic press, and to determine the possible contribution of intellectuals to the building of a proletarian cinema. Their political beliefs did not prevent the critics from denouncing the close links between film studios and film journalists, a criticism based on decidedly bourgeois notions about the autonomy of critical discourse. When leftists wrote about corruption and favoritism, they not infrequently assumed an attitude of moral righteousness that ultimately weakened their argument. Edwin Hoernle's description of the typical bourgeois critic is typical in this regard: "These well-trained and well-paid little animals are adaptable, like chameleons, and the film studios reward their reviews, not only by quoting them in film advertisements. One idea brings them all together: business. Bourgeois film criticism is one of the worst signs of decadence in today's society. What most critics — with very few exceptions — have to say is rotten to the core, and would be completely useless if everybody knew how things really are with this 'art.'"

Instead of celebrating film's artistic value and universal appeal, the leftist critics drew attention to the underlying social and political issues and, without hiding their intentions, argued from a particular perspective: that of the working class. Their strategy was to take the most popular commercial films, uncover their hidden messages, and, in so doing, prove the urgent need for other films, as well as for another society. Since they saw film criticism as a form of political activism, the emphasis was on the characteristics shared by all bourgeois films rather than on the qualities that distinguished the few artistic masterworks. However, many argued that such rigid critical standards should not be implemented at the expense of the masses and their legitimate need for entertainment. As Werner Illing pointed out, the revolutionary film critic had to reject the majority of films because of their reactionary content; yet he also had to study them in order to improve the critical abilities and aesthetic standards of the workers. In other words, the critic had to "frankly and ruthlessly unmask the art products of capitalist reaction and to educate the comrades about their functioning" (Kühn 1975, 1:91–92). Such considerations stand behind the the extensive comments on the reactionary *Fridericus* films and the organized protests against film censorship; they explain the in-depth analyses of American films and what was frequently referred to as the cult of possessive individualism; and they point to the strategic reasons behind the lengthy reports about new Russian films and the many attempts to build an effective leftist propaganda machine. In all these instances, the leftist critic was called upon to take a position, that is, to show the right "tendency" that, according Lukács, promoted class consciousness and prepared the ground for a revolutionary art.

The goals of proletarian film criticism were defined in sharp opposition to what Hermann Hübner described as "one single big scandal," namely the "undisguised terrorism of the film capital" and the resultant "leaps and contortions of the reviewers" (Hübner 1928, 8, 9). Heinz Lüdecke wrote a series of articles that delineated in great detail the tasks of the film critic in the service of the working class. Reviewers, according to Lüdecke, had to provide information about the conditions under which films were produced; this included institutional politics as well as economic cycles. They had to expose the "antiproletarian propaganda" behind seemingly apolitical entertainment films and draw attention to the filmic means that made possible the insidious manipulation of the masses. Time and again he insisted that the critique of bourgeois cinema was only effective in combination with "a proletarian self-critique of the proletarian film" (Kühn 1975, 2:301).

The ultimate consequence of what might be called the politics of class identity was the replacement of the professional critic by the proletarian-as-critic, a proposal modeled on the Arbeiterkorrespondenten (workers' correspondents) who wrote about books and plays from the worker's standpoint. The "real experts" (i.e., the spectators) replaced the capricious star critic and the overly educated specialist—"Dr. Arrogant, Dr. Shop Talk, and Dr. Blind Man," to quote Durus (Kühn 1975, 2:314) — and transformed film criticism into a participatory event. The readers of *Arbeiterbühne und Film* were invited to express their views on pages set aside for this purpose. Education through active participation, this was Lüdecke's program, and it is worth quoting at length. "We want to destroy one of the enemy's strongest weapons, that of manipulating the masses through the moving, and now also the sounding, image! Let's go to work! Everybody goes to the movies once or twice a month! Because it's easy, because it offers cheap entertainment, because it's dark or because there is nothing else to do! From now on your and your and your visit to the movies will take on new meaning. You will no longer leave the class struggle at the cloak room. You will show the gentlemen from Ufa, Paramount, and Warner Bros. that you are a swell proletarian even in the dark, someone who can't be fooled easily and doesn't take a war film for an antiwar film. And the next day, when you rethink the whole thing, you will say: 'The man from *Arbeiterbühne und Film* was absolutely right. These people lie through their teeth! Where did I leave my eyes for such a long time?' Then you are in the right frame of mind! Then you take a piece of paper, write your review and send it to the editors of our journal" (Kühn 1975, 2: 303–4).

Yet these lay reviewers — put down by the *Film-Kurier* as children playing with a new toy — experienced censorship problems even in the Communist press. Not only were they reminded by the editors not to visit the expensive first-run theaters and write about the newest film releases (since that would increase the studio's profits), they were also informed that there was no need for extensive comments on an actor's performance, and that only the important parts of a story needed to be mentioned. As Lüdecke emphasized in subsequent articles, the goal was not to use writing as an outlet for indignation and rage, on the contrary. "The writing and publication of reviews is supposed to intensify the anger many workers legitimately feel toward the bourgeois film trash and to bring them to express their anger through actions!" (Kühn 1975, 2: 307). Marxist criticism, for Lüdecke, meant the ruthless exposure of bourgeois ideology through the instrument of dialectical materialism. But he admitted that it was not enough to have the right consciousness: "The critic must provide the worker with the tools for revealing hidden indoctrination" (Kühn 1975, 2: 310). In other words, Marxist criticism had to formulate its critical agenda on the basis of social practices, and not on other philosophical traditions; only then would the workers be able to take their fate into their own hands and assume the leadership role assigned to them by world history.

Now that the various approaches to film criticism have been identified, it might be illuminating to look more closely at the leftist writings on the bourgeois and the proletarian film and draw attention, through the example of a film called *Mutter Krausens Fahrt ins Glück,* to the continuous presence of traditional categories of evaluation in leftist review practices. As a way of strengthening their oppositional stance, leftist critics devoted much of their writings to mainstream or bourgeois film and what they called dominant "film ideology." For obvious reasons, the historical films, with the spectacular military parades and the "enlightened" monarchs, became a favorite target for attacking totalitarian structures and authoritarian attitudes in Weimar society. Focusing on the *Fridericus* films, critics drew attention to the conflation of historical events and contemporary concerns and analyzed the correspondences between specific genres and political dispositions. In order to stop the use of cinema as as instrument of the ruling class, they employed a range of critical strategies: detailed plot analysis, summary of predominant themes and motifs, references to the high production value, and, not infrequently, disparaging comments about the director and the actors. The critical reception of the *Fridericus* films in the leftist press even included detailed reports about the boycotts organized by Berlin workers and the participation of Social Democratic officials in quelling these riots.

The campaign against bourgeois films, however, was not limited to these obvious examples of reactionary ideology. Romantic comedies and melodramas with a contemporary setting were regularly criticized for the ways in which fantasies of social climbing were used to replace social analysis and stories of social decline were automatically linked to personal failure. At the same time, the attempts by progressive filmmakers to create films of universal human appeal were sharply rejected by the suspecting leftist critics; hence the negative reviews of Lamprecht's drama of human suffering, *Die Verrufenen* (1925, The notorious), of *Westfront 1918* (1930) and its inconsequential pacifism, and of thrillers like *M* (1931) that, supposedly, only introduced social themes for sensationalist effects.

Sometimes reviewers abandoned their rigid standards and (unwittingly) admitted to pleasures that were perfectly legitimate but that, in the context of a narrowly defined social realism, sounded like relapses into a subjective criticism of taste. For instance, the critic who ended a review of Arnold Fanck's *Der heilige Berg* (1926, The sacred mountain) with the statement "excellent . . . because of the beautiful skiing and the climbing in the mountains" (Kühn 1975, 1:180) in fact repeated a standard element of uninvolved criticism, the distinction between form and content. And the critic who concluded his description of *Madame wünscht keine Kinder* (1926, Madame doesn't want children) with the suggestion "Let's be entertained by such films — but let's be ready for the class struggle at the cultural front" (Kühn 1975, 1:181) in fact gave new meaning to the bourgeois insistence on the separateness of politics, art, and everyday life.

Demanding a "conquest of the film," the critics of the *Rote Fahne* and *Film und Volk* tenaciously promoted the cause of the proletarian film. This included the promotion of films with a progressive content and of films produced by the organizations of the working class; it also resulted in Alfred Piepenstock's redefinition of art "as an expression of life, as a motor that activates social forces and propels them toward action" (1928, 5). No longer a "thing in itself, but a thing for us," to quote Alfred Piepenstock, this new class-specific art was to give an accurate reflection of social reality, and to enable the masses to change their lives. A critical exchange in *Die Rote Fahne* between Béla Balázs and a representative of the Communist Youth by the name of Stephan dealt with these demands from a variety of perspectives. Stephan had argued that the existing films were of no value for the purposes of the revolutionary proletariat, even those that featured working-class characters. While he agreed that film should show differences between characters as class differences, Balázs insisted on the autonomy of the fable and the power of imagination. In order to make use of "the agitative power of film," the leftist organizations had to be productive, not prescriptive, wrote Balázs. "We must start our own film factories that produce *our* films. And they must do more than illustrate sociological lectures. Otherwise we will never lure the tired, entertainment-needy proletariat away from the spell of the bourgeois prestige films. Our films must at least be as interesting and exciting. And above all inspiring! In order to increase class consciousness and combativeness!" (Kühn 1975, 1:36).

The characteristics of a revolutionary cinema, almost everybody agreed, could be studied best in the new Russian films that received an enthusiastic reception in Weimar Germany. Not surprisingly, the films of Eisenstein and Pudovkin played a central role in converting a number of left-liberal intellectuals to the ideas of socialism. As the first films to be produced under noncapitalist conditions and as the most advanced examples of Marxist aesthetics, films like *Battleship Potemkin* (1926), *Strike* (1927), *The Mother* (1927), *Ten Days that Shook the World* (1928), and *Storm Over Asia*

(1929) were reviewed everywhere, with special attention being paid to their model character in the advancement of a proletarian cinema. In her reviews for the *Rote Fahne,* Gertrud Alexander spoke about the great emotional appeal of documentaries about the Soviet Union and confirmed their importance for strengthening international solidarity. Otto Steinecke even emulated the Russian montage style in his film reviews, using direct quotes, short sentences, and exclamation marks. In so doing, he relied on formal qualities to translate the power of Russian cinema into the medium of language which was, at least for leftist film critics, a rather unusual but nonetheless highly effective approach.

While the Russian films represented the future of cinema, *Mutter Kraus- ens Fahrt ins Glück* was regarded by many as the first German revolutionary proletarian film. The Jutzi-Prometheus production received considerable publicity before its release, since critics debated whether the film would be yet another milieu study or a realistic portrayal of Berlin workers and their living conditions. Announced as the first social drama that did not romanti- cize poverty, director Piel Jutzi's gripping tale of a poor working-class family proved to be a great success—perhaps because it relied for its emotional appeal on the same identification processes that were exploited by the so-called street films (*Straßenfilme*) and film melodramas. A brief look at some reviews may illustrate the discrepancies between the notion of criticism as the anticipation of a utopian state and the actual review prac- tices in the leftist journals and newspapers.

Applying rather traditional categories, the reviewers for the Münzen- berg newspapers *Die Welt am Abend* and *Neue Berliner Zeitung* praised the convincing performances of the actors and the documentary quality of the images. Focusing on the film's extraordinary realism, the *Film und Volk* critic noted: "Here nothing is distorted, here someone has actually taken a look. The bright floodlight shows reality and the things that lie hidden behind it. Piel Jutzi knows this, he looks with the precision of his optical instrument" (*Film und Volk* 3.1 [Jan. 1930]: 7]). Others mentioned the accuracy of the *Milljöh* (Berliner dialect for *milieu*) and recounted the film's most memorable moments of working-class solidarity; again others praised it as a dignified monument to the social caricaturist Heinrich Zille and working-class culture. Some critics, however, complained about the de- pressing ending and, in so doing, indirectly confirmed the logic of compen- sation according to which entertainment had to make up for deprivations in real life. "The gas tap is never, ever, the 'way to happiness.' In order for the poorest of the poor to attain 'happiness,' they themselves must find another solution" (Kühn 1975, 2:127). Hardly anybody mentioned the film's rather traditional narrative structure or the consistent use of visual clichés and melodramatic effects. While conservative reviewers complained about "a few party-political gaffes," *Mutter Krausens Fahrt ins Glück* was perceived as so universal in its depiction of human suffering that even they conceded that "despite the International and the Communist propaganda, it remains artistic" (Kühn 1975, 2:116). Just these few examples indicate to what degree the critical reception of "the first proletarian film" followed the basic principles of mainstream criticism (e.g., references to quality, originality, tradition) but neglected the more problematic aspects in favor of a demonstration of political power. Ultimately, the chance for a more far-reaching reassessment of the relationship between production and reception remained unexplored, and the leftist film critics continued to be an intermediary between films and their audiences — nothing less, and nothing more.

As a result, the shortcomings of leftist film criticism are most evident in their unwillingness to address the question of mass entertainment and mass media, in their ambivalent relationship to the masses as spectators, and in their general disregard for formal experimentation. Fixated as they were on the conditions of production, most leftist film critics failed to grasp the potentially subversive quality of visual pleasure. Very few wrote about the revolutionary potential of laughter, and even fewer analyzed the deficiencies of bourgeois films in this light. The maudlin stories of the cinema, Axel Eggebrecht argued in a moment of great insight, were dangerous for "the tired proletarian woman and the young proletarian girl" precisely because they failed to satisfy their entertainment needs. The problem was not too much, but too little diversion: "It is a sign of the decline of bourgeois culture that it does not utilize this wonderful medium according to its possibilities but lets it . . . go to waste from the very beginning" (Kühn 1975, 1:85).[2]

Whenever critics did pay attention to audience psychology, they invariably became more aware of the correspondences between the spheres of production and reproduction. Then entertainment need no longer be dismissed as mere escapism, a psychological problem, in other words; rather it could be recognized as the sociopsychological foundation of capitalism. Walter Pahl noted: "Through its inner nature and particular effects, film compensates very effectively for those harms inflicted upon the proletarian masses by modern working life. It is the emotional substitute, indeed, one could almost say the side product of the capitalist-industrial work conditions" (quoted in Kinter 1985, 340). As an expression of their humanity, and as a reminder of their right to a more human life, the workers' laughter in the cinema thus was essential for the preservation of their critical skills. "In the cinema, they experience adventures, stunts, and exploits otherwise not within their reach. . . . How gladly, how badly, how frequently do these people want to smirk, smile, laugh, explode in laughter! Life no longer offers many such opportunities; in this case, too, the cinema must provide a substitute" (344). As someone who believed in the revolutionary potential of laughter, Hoernle even demanded: "The proletarian film should pull the laughs onto the side of the revolution, should systematically use laughter as a revolutionary means. . . . The proletarian film should be suggestive, should be realistic and exciting. Only then does it fulfill its purpose — only then may it be called art" (Kühn 1975, 1:50).

Secondly, leftist critics often wrote about the masses with the same expressions of condescension and "concern" used by more conservative critics. No matter whether these attitudes originated in their own precarious class position as middle-class intellectuals or whether they were based on Leninist ideas about the leadership role of the Communist party, the sharp distinction between the class-conscious proletarian and the faceless masses resulted in a moralistic style that was well-intended at best. Arguing in this vein, leftist women frequently emphasized the need to protect the weakest members of the working class, the women and children, who seemed to succumb more easily to the cinema's false promises. Trude Sand, for instance, asked class-conscious parents to watch over their children. "We ourselves must go to the cinema with our children! Like the husband with his wife, like [political] cells and groups, in order to discuss the program afterwards" (Kühn 1975, 1:121). And Alice Lex, the progressive journalist and experimental photographer, accused women of yearning for romance, beauty, and luxury without ever questioning the reasons for such longings. "Misled by the 'ideals' of the bourgeois cinema, the wife wants to look like a well-situated, well-educated bourgeois woman when she really should be a class-conscious proletarian. But this desire for appearances takes a bitter revenge. The husband, coming home tired from work, does not want to be changed. The children, guided by a healthy opposition to good manners, live in constant opposition to their mother. The household money, not even enough for the most basic things, cannot pay for the hats worn by Greta Garbo, not even for their cheapest copies" (Kühn 1975, 1:118). Lex's attention to the problems of working-class families was certainly justified in light of rising unemployment and worsening living conditions. Yet she, too, was unable to explain why even the correct political orientation failed to satisfy emotional needs other than the basics of everyday life—needs that subsequently attached themselves to material excess in every shape or form in order to experience a brief moment of paradisiac abundance.

Last but not least, leftist film critics focused almost exclusively on plot structure and character development and had little interest in challenging the formal conventions of the narrative film. Experimental and non-narrative films were regularly attacked in the Communist press. The following description of an abstract film stands out through its almost hysteric tone: "On the screen, conic sections, hemispheres, all kinds of conceivable squares and triangles do gymnastics . . . all of mathematics, geometry, stereometry, trigonometry meet for an absurd rendezvous. Scribbles or the nightmare of a badly prepared pupil before a math exam? The workers' educational organizations and theater subscriber's organizations, as much as they usually like to support innovative enterprises, should be warned about such poor and tedious bluff" (quoted by Kinter 1985, 334). Measured against the dogma of Socialist Realism, even Russian films with strong formalist tendencies were not spared the scorn of the self-righteous. One reviewer of Vertov's *Man With a Movie Camera* put it succinctly: "Now we really must ask: are we opticians or revolutionaries?" (quoted by Kinter 1985, 337).

While official cultural politics in the Soviet Union and the German KPD were increasingly characterized by antiformalist tendencies, some critics refused to abandon the dialectic approach to questions of form and content precisely because of their commitment to the class struggle. Two are worth mentioning in this regard—not in order to state the critical failure of much leftist film criticism, but to point to the coexistence of polemical, didactic, and theoretical positions, all of which fulfilled important functions in defining political propaganda, media education, and a materialist film theory, respectively. The relationship between film and ideology was central to these projects, but, as the two following examples indicate, the significance of technology as an aesthetic force had not yet fully been recognized by most leftist critics and activists.

Speaking out against prevailing attitudes, the writer Klaus Neukrantz rejected the distinction between original and reproductive arts as unproductive and saw film's main task precisely in mediating ideas and facilitating critical exchanges. "Film can never communicate 'art', but the communication can be an art form, a technical art" (Kühn 1975, 2:52). Film, in his view, possessed a unique ability for representing things that in reality were separated in time and space, and for documenting processes captured only inadequately by words or still images. According to Neukrantz, the revolutionary film had to explore these possibilities to the fullest and, in so doing, make the formal qualities of film the basis of its stories and themes.

Arguing along similar lines, the Marxist critic Lu Märten rejected the proletarian versions of standard bourgeois narratives and called for a cinema true to its material qualities (Schütz 1973; Heller 1984, 157–65). Märten demanded that the proletarian film take advantage of its visual possibilities, instead of limiting itself to storytelling. Film, after all, was "not just a picturebook machine gun, but also provided critical commentary and conveyed purely visual values" (1928, 235). Unlike the traditional arts, Märten argued, film made the machine an integral part of artistic production. By relying on a new technology to explore the boundaries of the possible, film had a liberating effect on the senses as well as on existing interpretations of reality. As the new relationship between art and technology made possible a materialist approach to aesthetics, the traditional aesthetic categories were replaced by those of experience and pleasure. Introducing into the realm of the aesthetic the senses and their historically formed qualities, Märten concluded. "After all, if the claim that things determine our consciousness and not the consciousness the things is rightfully part of our scientific foundations, we must conclude that our sensory reactions, too, can change, and do not forever remain the same. This means: It is not an absolute, but only a historically significant fact that an image or a figure, indeed any artistic form, should necessarily result in the experience of pleasure" (1925, 667–8).

\* \* \*

Conservative cinema reformers dominated the debates in Wilhelmine Germany, but it was leftist film criticism in its various forms that contributed most visibly to the politicizing of cinema during the last years of the Weimar Republic. The leftist critics developed their views on film and the masses not only through a radical critique of bourgeois film but also in confrontation with the reactionary forces that increasingly controlled the film industry and suppressed all oppositional practices. Thus the critical reception of films like *Battleship Potemkin* and *Kuhle Wampe,* and the enthusiasm generated by Chaplin, were not only important as moments of self-affirmation in the liberal and leftist press; they also served as crystallization points around which ultraconservative and National Socialist critics could present their ideas on national and racial superiority (Rauh 1984). In these highly politicized constellations, the remaining reformist writers were often associated with a nationalistic position that had exhausted itself in pedagogical initiatives and educational projects without really understanding the power of film. Their contributions sounded increasingly outdated and, given their failure to come to terms with the narrative film, played only a marginal role in the film-political discourses of the twenties. However, reformist assumptions about cinema continued to influence public opinion in less noticeable ways. Many statements about cinema and society in the mainstream press bore the distinct mark of reformist rhetoric, and many of the assertions about the usefulness of film and other mass media for the cause of German nationalism would soon be taken up in the context of National Socialist film politics. Even as the reformers vanished from the stage of public controversy, their critical concepts lived on in the terminology of media pedagogy, providing the theoretical basis for many future discussions on cinema and society. Their disappearance from the political arena in a way prepared the ground for the return of reformist concepts in the form of common sense; examples include the popular theories of mass manipulation or the standard arguments about media and violence that are still in circulation today.

After the collapse of the Wilhelmine Empire, the reform movement lost much of its institutional support structure. Those still active in educational and cultural associations had to come to terms with the narrative film and the seemingly ineradicable need for diversion. Some reformists adopted a conciliatory stance and presented more realistic strategies. While still insisting on the educational mission of film, they now demanded quality instead of dry instruction. "We must make *good* films; then public education will follow suit without any extra efforts," Wolfgang Schumann claimed in 1924, only to end with a surprisingly unreformist admission: "This yearning doesn't need education and instruction but entertainment and — art" (1924, 12). Despite these obligatory gestures to film art, he then focused on a documentary film about Africa and used the reaction by various members of the audience to praise the cinema's unique ability to provide both an individual and a collective experience. This reference to cinema as the construction site of national identity was ominous in many ways, for Schumann went on to evoke a "yearning for the homeland [*Heimat*] of tomorrow. It forms the soul's view of life, and happy the man in whose inner self the chorus of the earth resounds" (1924, 31). The "chorus of the earth, " of course, recalls the terminology of blood and soil, in whose propagation the cinema would soon play a significant part, and the "yearning for the homeland of tomorrow" was enlisted in fantasies about a Greater Germany that did not remain limited to the cinema.

Presenting similar arguments, Eugen Guerster called for more sociological studies on film and its yet unexplored possibilities of mass suggestion. Film sociology, in his view, was ideally suited to accelerate the process of social leveling and standardization and to turn the cinema into "an effective instrument for creating the psychological foundation of the coming standard man [*Einheitsmensch*]" (1928, 211). Obsessed with the future, Guerster completely ignores the social and political measures necessary to reach this forced state of unity. It also remains unclear whether his concept of "standard man" relies on older theories of mass psychology, or whether it already voices the concerns of a new racial science. However, these few examples illustrate well the problematic position of reformist discourse between depoliticized "good" entertainment and more insidious visions of national film culture.

National Socialist film criticism remained a marginal phenomenon during the Weimar years, but many of its proposals and propositions can already be found in the writings of a firmly established group, those critics working for the film industry and related organizations. Writing from the side of production, they focused all their attention on the German film industry and its contribution to rebuilding the nation, be it through favorable legislation, aggressive export strategies, or promotional tools like the *Kulturfilm*. These concerns found expression in the shared fight for a strong national cinema and its attendant discourses. To mention the most obvious example, the influx of foreign films in the postwar years inspired in a conservative critique of the commodity that was both anticapitalist and nationalistic in orientation. At the same time, conservatives often used economic competition as a smokescreen for identifying tendencies that they considered detrimental to the goals of German nationalism, just as they resorted to nationalistic slogans to justify the expansionist tendencies of Ufa and other major studios. Obliging audiences to see more German films and planning a broad assault on foreign markets were, therefore, two sides of the same thing.

In the realm of film criticism, the ultimate goal was a restructuring of the debate on film and society around the unifying concept of nation, rather than class, and a reassessment based on the exigencies of politics rather than aesthetics. There is no doubt that the arguments against rampant internationalism expressed economic concerns, especially in regard to the growing influence of American companies. Yet the foreign films also provided the backdrop against which German values and traditions could affirm superiority; in a way, economic necessities were turned into ideological constructs so that they could become political reality. In an anthology with the ominous title *Lichtträger im Chaos* (1925, Visual media in chaos), for instance, Richard Muckermann demanded more attention to the economic side of cinema and, in a daring move from theory to practice, reminded his readers of their patriotic duty as audiences and citizens. The educated classes, Muckermann maintained in familiar fashion, were partly to blame for the low quality of films. Now they had to participate actively in Germany's spiritual awakening. "At home, the nation thirsts for a new ascent to power; new energy streams into withered trunks, the nation needs direction and confidence. . . . Abroad, everybody is in keen anticipation of German spirit and German morality. After all, one does expect more from an old cultural nation than hymns to urban gentlemen and fallen shopgirls" (1925, 65). A first step in this direction, suggested Muckermann, would be the closing of all the seedy theaters in working-class neighborhoods, those reminders of the cinema's humble beginnings. New and better motion picture theaters needed to be built, with excellent projection facilities, attractive neon advertisements, and luxurious theaterlike interiors. The detailed attention to theater design shows to what degree Muckermann perceived architectural spaces as the mold in which, and through which, the cinema could fulfill its bourgeois aspirations. It also clarifies why film's integration in middle-class culture required the disinfection of this space, literally and metaphorically speaking, and it gave an indication of how the reformist discourse continued to evoke to the unspeakable — the existence of class society — while exorcizing its traces in the name of popular entertainment.

The genre in which many of these arguments came together was the *Kulturfilm,* which included documentary, educational, or scientific films and dealt with such diverse topics as nature, geography, science, and, most importantly, German customs and traditions. Promoted as an educational tool by the cinema reformers, the *Kulturfilm* acquired new meaning in the twenties once the film industry discovered its usefulness for self-promotion and self-legitimation. Writing about the *Kulturfilm* amounted to a declaration of moral sincerity, social responsibility, and deep commitment to German culture — categories that virtually demanded political interpretations. While its history includes remarkable examples of documentary filmmaking, the discursive function of the *Kulturfilm* within the debate on German cinema was more or less limited to political and economic concerns, yet it was also overdetermined in its symbolic function. The many anthologies on the *Kulturfilm* and related topics published during the twenties indicate to what degree the return of normative aesthetics had already brought about the reification of theory. From the elaborate design and the famous contributors to the peculiar mixture of reformist fervor, philosophical speculation, and business pragmatism, every detail was subordinated to the logic of integration and co-optation. Thus writing about the *Kulturfilm* strengthened the bond between conservative cultural criticism and the film industry, while at the same time introducing nationalistic ideas into the discourse of film as commodity.

One of these anthologies, *Das deutsche Lichtbildbuch* (1924, The book of German cinematography) was published by the Deutsche Lichtbild-Gesellschaft (Deulig) and August Scherl, the media conglomerate with strong connections to the Ufa concern (via Alfred Hugenberg and Ludwig Klitsch). Its editor, Heinrich Pfeiffer, presented a wide range of articles, including many by members of the film industry (Emil Jannings, Ernst Lubitsch), the reform movement (Albert Hellwig), and the academic community (Walter Bloem). Behind the appearance of critical diversity, the reformist perspective returned triumphantly, as can be seen in the theorizing of social problems. Rejecting party politics for the (equally political) myth of universal truth, Peter Grassmann demanded: "Give the working man excerpts from the life of his people, show him the contributions of the most varied professions so that he learns to understand and appreciate how others feel, show him his own country and foreign, distant countries, introduce him through images to the history of other nations, of mankind in general — but show him everything without makeup, without bias [*Tendenz*]! Or, with the only bias desirable: the truth. Have the worker leave the cinemas as he would leave a good stage production: wiser, better, purer!" (Pfeiffer 1924, n.p.).

This scenario captures perfectly the rhetoric of authenticity and reconciliation behind which a totally instrumentalized approach to film took over. Accordingly, some contributors proposed to use the *Kulturfilm* in improving Germany's image abroad and replacing prejudice with greater understanding. Others raised the possibility that the *Kulturfilm* could help Germans to regain a sense of national identity, provided they were willing to give up their emotional resistance to the ideas of nationalism. Concerned with mass appeal, the editors of another anthology, *Das Kulturfilmbuch* (1924, The book of the culture film), proposed a wider definition that allowed them to claim aspects of popular culture for the project of national education. In the introduction the editors, Edgar Beyfuß and Alexander Kossowsky, argued: "Every film that has cultural ambitions, that educates its audience, that ennobles the nation, and that has one's own ethics, is a *Kulturfilm* for us (and for every educated person, too)" (1924, viii).[3] Precisely this combination of political rationale and cultural philosophy transformed the writings on the *Kulturfilm* into a rehearsal of the cultural significance of cinema and the power attributed to its products. The contributions by famous directors like Fritz Lang and Richard Oswald, on the one hand, and unknown specialists from zoology, geography, medicine, and physics on the other, confirmed the possibility of diversity through identity on the level of editorial politics; as a result, the *Kulturfilm* came to personify the integrationist tendencies in cinema as well as politics.

The strange affinities between the discourses of anticapitalism, racism, technoromanticism, and nationalism also prepared the ground for openly reactionary works that, as a rule, emphasized political rhetoric over critical analysis. In these works film represented the perfect propaganda tool, since it eliminated the traditional distinction between art and politics. Whereas the literary opposition to the cinema was fueled by the fear that the voice of reason would soon give way to the sheer emotionality of the image, some reactionary writers decided to take advantage of this hidden force and to complete the instrumentalization of the filmic image by the existing power structures. The implications can be studied exemplarily in Hans Buchner's *Im Banne des Films* (1927, Under the spell of film), which offered an analysis of what was really at stake in "the world rule of film," as the half-title suggests. To begin with endings, Buchner summarizes his ideas in the by-now-familiar language of nationalism: "Today film does not address the nation but only the masses. It is not yet a mystery, but only intoxication and stimulation. It will only fulfill its true mission when it attempts to represent reality, the fate of nations. The struggling, celebrating nation, not the vegetating proletariat; the individual as the member of an organic whole-ness, not as a part of subversive multitudes. Only then may film be regarded as an art for the nation, a nation that right now is threatened by the arrival of the masses" (1927, 185).

On the preceding 185 pages, Buchner has blamed the cinema for virtually every problem in modern society, including prostitution, murder, perver-sion, fetishism, miscegenation, urbanism, internationalism, sensational-ism, Americanism, Fordism, materialism, capitalism, and so forth. He repeatedly refers to the "Bolshevist-Jewish world conspiracy" as the ulti-mate reason for the crisis of German culture. It is Bolshevism, with Chaplin as a leading man, that, to the author's chagrin, has seduced the masses. Corrupting the soul with intoxicating spectacles and relying on mecha-nisms not dissimilar to hypnosis, Buchner asserts, the cinema is the embod-iment of evil in this world — even worse, it promotes the idea of class struggle. "With great determination, a dark, mysterious power systemati-cally projects the oppositions of life onto the screen: the poles of rich and poor, master and slave, good and bad" (1927, 41). That is why the cinema's mass psychological possibilities, as Buchner stresses repeatedly, have to be explored by the "right" people. His conclusion — the need for a restructur-ing of the film industry — already implies the elimination of all Jews and politically suspect individuals from leadership positions in the film indus-try, and therefore offers a perfect example of the smooth transition from conservative discourses about national film culture to the anti-Semitic, anti-Communist politics of National Socialism. After all, Buchner con-cludes, wasn't it shocking that in a popularity contest the film star "Harry Liedtke received the majority of votes, not the political and creative celebri-ties like Mussolini, Hitler, Hauptmann, or Stresemann" (1927, 156).[4] As is evident by this disturbing remark, the ground was prepared for a new kind of cinema reform.

The political oppositions in Weimar film criticism can be studied in the exemplary career of Oskar Kalbus.[5] After an early beginning in the trade press, where he wrote for *Der Kinematograph* and *Film-Kurier,* Kalbus was appointed head of Ufa's *Kulturfilm* department only to later make a name for himself as a Nazi film historian. His *Vom Werden deutscher Filmkunst* (1935, On the rise of German film art) was described by Kracauer as "a Nazi-minded product with some remnants of pre-Nazi evaluations" (1947, 52), a characterization that reflects these shifts between commercialism and fascisms very accurately. In Kalbus's view, film originated in the "technical principle of cinematography" and, given its ability to represent events, was inherently dramatic. Compensating for the lack of language through superior technology, films were able to translate the most complex psychological processes into images. Kalbus expressed his early ideas on the silent film through one of Balázs's favorite language metaphors: "Film stands apart from the Babel of languages, it is the only real means of communication between the nations, the Esperanto of the soul. Created by a true artist, film can heal the wounds of the world war and spread the ideas of humanism. That is the undeniable merit of film's muteness" (Kalbus 1920c).

Kalbus's most ambitious contribution to the debate on film and politics was a three-part article published in *Kinematograph,* in which he proposed to extend the term *political* to seemingly unpolitical genres like the society comedy and the crime film. His goal, of course, was to explore the possibility of using film for political purposes. "However, political propaganda needs planning, programs, goals. Since these treasures are lacking in our times, and will continue to be lacking for some time to come, any exertion of influence on the national psyche through film is out of the question in Germany" (1922b, 2). Rejecting the openly propagandistic film, Kalbus called for more indirect approaches. "It would be a good thing if the German film, in addition to the typical political film, presented an inconspicuous picture of German essence, thereby promoting Germanness in a subtle way" (1922b, 12). He outlined what would soon become official National Socialist film politics as he praised film as a means of social pacification, emphasized its separation from party politics and daily politics, and contributed to political and cultural education.

Not surprisingly, the formulation of a theory of film legitimating the National Socialist takeover of the film industry and the redefinition of the German film based on racial and national categories was already in full process by the mid-twenties. Its was evident in publications that upheld the spirit of cinema reform, or in the writings of critics who promoted reactionary works and authors. Its growing influence became noticeable in the changing ownership of established journals and the appearance of new journals with a clear political agenda. For instance, *Der Deutsche Film,* the National Socialist film journal founded in 1932 in Berlin, used criticism almost exclusively to build opposition to the alien film industry and to reintroduce racial categories into the discussion on film. Openly anti-Semitic and very militant in their approach, the journal's editors proclaimed in their inaugural first issue: "The German film must again become German! We will make sure that German men make the films for the German nation" (Kühn 1975, 2:128). Their anger focused on what they considered the disproportionate number of Jews in the German film industry, and at Ufa in particular. These economic motives, however, were hidden behind verbose proclamations about the German soul that, among other things, found an outlet in relentless attacks on Chaplin as the personification of a decadent Jewish internationalism. Offering an alternative to what National Socialist critics considered an unhealthy preoccupation with appearances and visual sensations, the German film was supposed to be like filmed theater, including a strong emphasis on dialogue. However, Wolfgang Ertel-Breithaupt, the editor of the "first nationalistic film journal," *Filmkünstler und Filmkunst* (1929) pointed out that "a reemergence of film-artistic creativity can only be achieved on the basis of a truly German world view" (quoted by Dunger 1978, 164). What these critics demanded was nothing less than a return to the prewar paradigm, but under conditions where theatricality now represented the future of film, not a past that had to be overcome. The same reversals took place in the relationship to politics, where the National Socialist film journals, together with journals like Goebbels's *Der Angriff,* ransacked the legacies of cinema reform in order to revive its film-political and pedagogical concepts on the context of a decidedly modern approach to mass media and mass manipulation. Again film criticism had been turned into a weapon, but a weapon of racial hatred and political indoctrination.

# Chapter 10
## Béla Balázs

**U**ntil now, this study has concerned itself with the formation of discourses, that is, with the question of how the cinema was constituted as a subject of critical inquiry and how its parameters changed in turn. By tracing this movement through the destabilizing moments that accompany all technical innovations, the last chapters have focused on institutionalized discourse and the power structures behind them: the film industry, the educational system, the literary establishment, the academy, the publishing industry, and the political parties. Because of the public character of these institutions, individual critics have been treated as contributors to a larger debate on cinema, mass society, and cultural politics. Because of their often controversial tone, particular texts have been analyzed in relation to other texts and textual practices, or been discussed in the context of important literary and philosophical traditions. And because of the metadiscursive function that ties the writings on cinema to the crisis of legitimation in modern society, greater emphasis has been placed on the historical configurations, the multitude and diversity of voices, than on the so-called masterpieces that might admit their authors into the pantheon of great film theoreticians.

The remaining chapters will show how these traditions were continued by three thinkers whose names have become synonymous with classical German film theory: Béla Balázs, Siegfried Kracauer, and Rudolf Arnheim. It was in their critical writings of the twenties and early thirties that a theory of cinema first appeared — a theory attending to the entire cinematic experience rather than to an isolated aspect. Balázs and Kracauer initiated what might be perceived as a return to earlier notions on cinema as a public sphere, but they did so in order to develop an alternative to the increasing fragmentation of discourses (e.g., film as art versus film as entertainment, film as commodity versus film as political propaganda). Likewise, Balázs and Arnheim renewed the interest in questions of reception and perception, but did so by shifting the center of inquiry from sociological to psychological and aesthetic concerns. To various degrees and with different implications, all three theoreticians reintroduced a political perspective into the debates. They also attempted to define the hierarchies between high and low culture from the perspective of film and to develop a theory of mass culture based on the experience of modernity. And in rejecting the distinctions provided by normative film aesthetics, they made film's vacillation between subversion and co-optation an integral part of their critical project. In short, Balázs, Kracauer, and Arnheim established the conceptual and methodological framework in which the cinema could assume its rightful place in modern mass culture and, from that position, realize its emancipatory potential.

Until recently, the early writings of Balázs, Kracauer, and Arnheim were more or less unknown among English-speaking readers. While the name of Balázs is associated with his most comprehensive work, *Theory of the Film* (1945, English translation 1952), Kracauer's reputation rests primarily on his sociopsychological study of Weimar cinema, *From Caligari to Hitler* (1947), and his impassioned argument for a realist cinema, *Theory of Film: The Redemption of Physical Reality* (1960). Arnheim continued the Gestaltist investigations of *Film als Kunst* (1932; *Film as Art,* 1933) in numerous works on the psychology of art, including *Art and Visual Perception* (1954), *Towards a Psychology of Art* (1966), and *Visual Thinking* (1969). In one way or another, these books bear the mark of exile, having either been written in exile or otherwise affected by the rise of National Socialism. The loss of all social and cultural reference points, which made Balázs, Kracauer, and Arnheim spiritually homeless, was repeated for a second time in the critical reception of their work. Most traces of their early intellectual biography were obliterated, most references to the formative influence of Weimar culture overlooked. Their writings on film came to be identified with the heroic project of a universally valid theory of film.

In other words, the admission of three Weimar film critics into the realm of high theory took place in the context of a decidedly ahistorical approach. Dudley Andrew's comments in his survey *The Major Film Theories* (1976) are rather typical in this regard. Focusing on their late work, Andrew places Arnheim and Balázs in the formative tradition, whereas Kracauer is introduced as a representative of realist film theory. Andrew's presentation of

Balázs emphasizes the affinities with Russian formalism, but dismisses his politics as "standard Marxist rhetoric" (1976, 92). Kracauer is characterized (following a description by Peter Harcourt) as "the kind of man who decided after forty years of viewing film that he ought to work out and write down his ideas about the medium; so he went straight to a library and locked himself in. There, reading widely, thinking endlessly, and working always alone, always cut off from the buzz of film talk and film production, he slowly and painstakingly gave birth to his theory" (Andrew 1976, 107). Arnheim's narrow definition of film art and its raw materials may have inspired a few handbooks on visual literacy but, as Andrew sees it, also makes his ideas seem rigid and sterile. While assessments like these — numerous others could have been cited in their place — have some validity for the later works of Balázs, Kracauer, and Arnheim, they fail to take into account the complicated process of theory formation and, in so doing, present as closed systems of thought that which is really the product of intellectual development under specific historical conditions.

All three critics formulated their ideas in a society where the question of cinema had been politicized from the very beginning, and where film functioned increasingly as a catalyst in the struggle for political dominance; hence the often polemical tone in their articles. To minimize the continuous opposition to cinema by the bourgeois arbiters of taste and to ignore the impending threat of National Socialism means to deny writing one of its main functions, namely to make a critical intervention. Thus the post-1933 works by Balázs, Kracauer, and Arnheim can also be seen as different attempts of coming to terms with the failure of their original projects.

From the perspective of intellectual biography, one can discern surprising similarities between three theoreticians who are often placed in opposition to one another. Balázs (born 1884 as Herbert Bauer in Szeged, Hungary) and Kracauer (born 1889 in Frankfurt am Main) were almost the same age; Arnheim (born 1904 in Berlin) was considerably younger, a fact that he "compensated" for through an almost stubborn attachment to the silent film. Their formative experiences must be considered rather typical for a generation of Central European intellectuals who came of age during World War I and whose adult lives were deeply affected by the coming of the Third Reich. Sharing a Jewish middle-class background, all three exhibited a strong belief in the power of intellectual discourse and, in their student years, received strong impulses from the philosophical movements of their time: Balázs and Kracauer from the phenomenological writings of

Husserl and Bergson and the sociology of Simmel, Arnheim from the founders of Gestalt psychology, Max Wertheimer, Wolfgang Köhler, and Kurt Lewin. During the twenties, all three worked as film critics for liberal daily newspapers and leftist journals and experienced the last years of the republic in the center of cultural and political life, Berlin.

Because of the direct contact with films, their critical writings lacked the prescriptive tone of the scholarly treatises discussed in chapter 7. Likewise, the distance from purely academic interests and the greater involvement in daily politics increased their awareness of the importance of critical discourse. The silent cinema, and the encounter with American and Russian films in particular, provided the backdrop against which their ideas on film as the art of the masses developed, just as the Weimar Republic determined the conditions under which they had to make a living as left-liberal intellectuals. In that regard, the later theoretical works can also be seen as a kind of reception history of Weimar cinema written by three participating observers. While belonging to different circles, Balázs, Kracauer, and Arnheim shared friends and acquaintances; however, closer personal relationships did not develop between them. And while *Die Weltbühne* was used by all three to express their political concerns, they reacted very differently to the developments after 1933: Balázs embraced the Marxist ideology, Kracauer used writing to work through the trauma of Weimar, and Arnheim turned to more scholarly pursuits. All three were forced into exile, with Balázs leaving for Moscow, Kracauer for Paris and eventually New York, and Arnheim slowly making his way to the United States via Rome and London. The trajectory of these exile routes not only betrayed their allegiances at the time, but also prepared the ground for the subsequent importation of Weimar film theory into very different discursive fields.

In light of so many overlaps, it must not surprise that Balázs, Kracauer, and Arnheim commented publicly on each other's work. Kracauer, who once referred to Balázs as "a German film writer of Hungarian descent" (1947, 78), reviewed his books in the *Frankfurter Zeitung* and mentioned his theoretical writings in *From Caligari to Hitler* and *Theory of Film,* though only in passing. More detailed comments were reserved for Balázs's film scripts. Of the script for the cross-section film *Die Abenteuer eines Zehnmarkscheins* (1926, The Adventures of a ten-mark bill), for instance, Kracauer wrote that "Balázs was not yet sufficiently bold or indifferent to substantiate his idea to the full" (1947, 181), a statement that also summarizes his opinion of Balázs as a theoretician. Arnheim was much more outspoken in his views on Balázs, for instance when he reproached him for confusing the quality of a film with its content and for presenting mere speculation as systematic thought (1977, 226–27); however, he did include a work by Balázs in a short list of "decent" books on film aesthetics. While Arnheim wrote a favorable review of Kracauer's *Theory of Film* in 1960 and while he quotes Balázs and Kracauer repeatedly in *Film als Kunst,* there are only brief references in his later work to the two thinkers who played such an important role in advancing the cause of film criticism. Balázs, whose main contacts in Berlin after 1926 were with film professionals and political activists, remained surprisingly noncommittal in his remarks about Kracauer and Arnheim. Perhaps he did not consider it worthwhile to engage with critics who had no practical experiences with film — the inaccuracy of many quotations would support such a claim — or perhaps his growing involvement with the Communist Party made him contemptuous of bourgeois intellectuals and what he once dismissed as their "negative rebellion."

Not surprisingly, Balázs, Kracauer, and Arnheim offer very different definitions of film criticism.[1] Balázs's approach is based on the notion of film as modern folklore. This is already evident in his first contribution to the liberal Viennese newspaper *Der Tag* when he raises the question "Why is there no cinema criticism (*Kinokritik*) in Vienna? Why is a cultural event made out of every operetta and why do none of the self-appointed judges of culture pay attention to film? Why does nobody pay attention to the *art of the people*?" In order to change this despicable situation, he wrote, the film critic must eliminate the misconceptions about the cinema and draw attention to its social and cultural significance. "No matter how problematic the products of this art form may have been until now, its possibilities are immense. And perhaps much depends on serious, qualified, engaged criticism. From now on, we want to open our columns to such qualified, systematic criticism" (Balázs 1982, 149, 151). Two years later, enthusiasm gave way to more concrete analysis. Responding to a group of motion picture exhibitors who had questioned the need for film reviews, Balázs stressed the advantages to be gained from a better communication between film producers, exhibitors, and audiences. Far from being a hindrance in a free market economy, as his detractors had argued, the qualified critic could be a valuable source of information for theater owners. "Forced to accommodate audiences, they [the theater owners] should be well aware that the

future of film art — indeed, the fate of this new, great, aesthetic culture —
depends on the refinement of their tastes" (1982, 318). In bringing together
educational and commercial perspectives, Balázs concluded, film criticism
contributed to the emergence of a democratic culture.

In 1932, at the end of his association with the liberal *Frankfurter Zeitung,*
Kracauer offered a definition of film criticism that bore the signs of disillusionment and obstinacy. Unlike Balázs, Kracauer no longer insists on
finding exemplary films or educating the audience. Based on the material
experience of cinema, he wants to effect a shift from the mere evaluation of
films to a detailed analysis of the processes underlying modern mass culture. Kracauer's point of departure is the surface appearance of things and
not, as for Balázs, the unyielding belief in film's populist mission. His
critical strategy involves a reversal of hierarchies rather than an embrace of
traditional value standards. Film criticism for Kracauer means to analyze
the social function of films, especially of popular ones. "In fact, the less film
operettas, military films, film comedies etc. have in content that could
withstand strict aesthetic evaluation, the more important is their social
function" (1974, 9–10). Thus mainstream cinema, because of its industrial
mode of production and its mass appeal, emerges as his privileged field of
inquiry. Where the old value judgments fail, the criteria of social relevance
become doubly important as a replacement and alternative. In order to take
full advantage of this potential, the film critic must not only provide
information but also proceed like a detective. "In my opinion, the task of
the competent film critic consists of analyzing those social intentions hidden in the average film, and pulling them into the daylight which they often
eschew. . . . The professional film critic can only be thought of as a social
critic" (1974, 10–11).

Professionalism, however, could mean very different things. Like Kracauer, Arnheim demanded greater expertise from reviewers, but he was
referring to a broader knowledge in technical matters. The professional
film critic, in his view, had to analyze the shortcomings of a film from the
side of production; in other words, the task was to "consider the production process, thus also taking into account whether or not the artist had full
control over his artistic means" (1977, 168). Here production establishes the
framework in which the critic finds the categories of evaluation and standards of good taste that enable him to identify the great masterpieces of
film. Arnheim's definition of artistic production marks the audience as

passive recipients and insists on the universal validity of formal categories. Criticism ultimately becomes synonymous with aesthetic judgment. "The film critic perceives the film production of the entire world as one homogeneous body of work in which every single work has its place. The task of the critic is to assign this place" (1977, 171).

Arnheim's insistence on boundaries in this 1929 essay has its origins in a very specific problem, his opposition to the sound film. The magic formula of filmic means not only helps to keep in check what he describes as the excesses of contentism and aestheticism, but also, and more importantly, excludes the sound film from any claims to excellence and originality. Even the call for more professionalism is now used by Arnheim to defend the silent film. "Professional in the good sense means that a critic is able to recognize whether an action is translated 'into images' in a skillful or awkward, original or conventional manner; that . . . he does not deny a film's mediocrity out of enthusiasm over its unusually beautiful theme; that one or two single shots, no matter how picturesque, do not seduce him into believing that the style is first-rate as well. It is not professional when the critic, out of pure enthusiasm over sensational novelties, but without any awareness of the laws and limitations of filmic means, welcomes the advent of the sound film" (1977, 170–71).[2]

To what degree these definitions influenced the practice of reviewing can be seen in the case of Pudovkin's film *The End of St. Petersburg* (1927), which was used by all three critics as a sounding board for more theoretical problems. Kracauer begins his review by confirming politics as the foundation of aesthetics and introducing the category of social relevance. Pudovkin's film, he argues, succeeds because "its artistic value is tied to a specific attitude. . . . The work of art is not reduced to the illustration of a tendency. Rather it is conviction that makes possible artistic achievement" (1974, 79, 80). Kracauer examines every aspect of the film — its symbolic use of buildings and objects, the diversity and complexity of social types, the emphasis on associative montage — for how they express a revolutionary consciousness, and he identifies those few instances that depend on "mere tendency." His critical strategy is aimed at replacing the traditional distinctions between form and content, and surface and depth, with a materialist aesthetic that focuses on relationships rather than hierarchies.

Balázs, too, used a political category, the concept of *Einstellung* — in German, the word denotes both a camera position and a critical position —

to discuss the Pudovkin film in a lecture for the Berlin Association of Cinematographers. There he spoke of the cameraman's responsibility to fill with meaning the wordplay on *Einstellung,* that is, to visualize the poetic and political qualities of the single shot. Balázs argued that "if every camera position can mean something, then every camera position should mean something. The possibility obliges" (1984, 239).[3] In this equation, the formalist concept of making strange, of undermining everyday perception, joins forces with emphatic calls for a political art. But where Kracauer proposes a dialectical relationship between aesthetics and politics, Balázs collapses both terms and reduces the power of film to the question of correct positions, both in the literal and figurative sense. This mechanistic approach is based on the assumption that all meaning originates in the single shot and that its poetic qualities are always in agreement with its political implications. The problem with defining *Einstellung* in such a way becomes evident once Balázs illustrates his point, arguing: "In Pudovkin's *End of St. Petersburg* something is added to the mere content of the fable when the little peasant with his old mother look increasingly small and forlorn among the huge city tenement houses. The story is told not by itself, but with a strong personal opinion" (1984, 241). As the expression "something is added" suggests, Balázs defines *Einstellung* within the logic of the supplement. Yet while the term provides the central category for evaluating the film's political contribution, it plays only a marginal role in the assessment of characters and story line; form, narrative, and politics remain strangely at odds.

The opposite is true for Arnheim, who separates these terms from the outset and makes their separation the basis of his evaluation. "People always say that the Russians are only able to make such good films because the revolution provides them with a universally valid topic. To be perfectly honest, I don't believe it" (Arnheim 1977, 197). What Arnheim does believe in is the Russians' extraordinary ability to use the medium. For him Pudovkin's greatest achievement lies in the fact "that he creates his work out of the limitation of the filmic means and that the exciting stories become meaningful through the surface characteristics of the material" (1977, 198). Like Kracauer, Arnheim praises the director's ability to depict social types, and he expresses admiration for the many carefully composed frames. Yet ultimately, his comments only serve to highlight Pudovkin's personal triumph as an artist. Making artistic mastery the prerequisite of political art and aesthetic judgment the foremost task of the critic, Arnheim is therefore able to conclude about *The End of St. Petersburg* that "This is film art" (1977, 201).

＊ ＊ ＊

Balázs's contribution to film theory rests on three major works: *Der sicht-bare Mensch* (1924, The visible man), *Der Geist des Films* (1930, The spirit of the film), and *Iskusstvo Kino* (1945), first published in Russian and translated into English in 1952 as *Theory of the Film*.[4] These works accumulate and systematize the insights Balázs gained while contributing film reviews and short essays to *Der Tag, Die Rote Fahne, Die Weltbühne,* and *Die Filmtechnik.* Written over a period of two decades, they attest to his search for a system of thought that brought together aesthetic, anthropological, sociological, and political perspectives in the description of a medium already distinguished by its heterogeneity. Like Stindt, Pordes, and Harms, Balázs avoided the customary comparisons to the other arts and concentrated on the specificity of filmic means instead. While the notion of gesture as the universal language of man played a central role, he did not content himself with glorifying its representations as a kind of secret world spirit or the true soul of man. On the contrary, his theory of film originated in the examination of actual films; important critical points are supported by examples, and technical remarks are often illustrated by scenes from the most outstanding, as well as the most mediocre, films of the time. A similar commitment to the practice of theory characterizes his political position. Through the new medium Balázs hoped to forge a link between the existing traditions of popular culture and the new urban masses whose demand for adequate forms of entertainment could no longer be satisfied by trivialized versions of high culture. He tried to achieve this goal by making technological innovation the basis of all cultural development, and by focusing on the socioeconomic conditions that constitute film as an industry and an art form. The result was the first systematic analysis of film under capitalism.

In the late twenties Balázs further specified the circumstances necessary for promoting film's inherently revolutionary potential. Striving for universal truth in a world characterized by fragmentation, he naturally experienced difficulties in adjusting his critical project to new technological inventions such as film sound. To compensate for this systemic instability, he resorted increasingly to dogmatic statements in matters of taste and adopted a rather crude schematism in the more theoretical contributions—

despite the fact that the study of Marxist theory should have revealed to him the nature of dialectical processes. These shortcomings become evident in the repetitiveness of his arguments, the frequent self-quotations, and the peculiar mixture of metaphysical speculation, revolutionary pathos, and detailed technical analysis that distinguishes Balázs from his contemporaries. The essayistic style and the innovative layout make his first two books look less academic and more "filmic" than comparable works by Lange or Bloem, but they also serve to hide a certain degree of intellectual stagnation. The fact that entire sections of *Der sichtbare Mensch* reappear twenty years later in *Theory of the Film* and that *Der Geist des Films* is largely made up of film reviews and previously published essays suggests that Balázs was more interested in perfecting his theory than in exploring new avenues of thought. Guido Aristarco once commented on his unique ability to synthesize ideas, noting that "if we regard Canudo and Delluc, Dulac and Richter as the forerunners of film aesthetics, then we should regard Balázs as the first systematizer of film aesthetics" (quoted in Ralmon 1977, 26).

As an "all-round educated personality without steady income," to quote Koch (1987, 167), Balázs personified the uprooted intellectual of the twenties, a sociopsychological character described in his semiautobiographical roman à clef, *Unmögliche Menschen* (1929, Impossible people), and in numerous sociological studies on the growing "intellectual lumpenproletariat" in Weimar Germany, including Alfred Weber's *Die Not der geistigen Arbeiter* (1923, The plight of the intellectuals). The discrepancies between the high esteem in which German society traditionally held its writers and their actual economic status and waning influence in the public sphere become nowhere more apparent than in a characterization offered by Balázs biographer Joseph Zsuffa. Characterizing Balázs as "an *international artist* and a humanist beyond national boundaries" and "a true *uomo universale,* one of the most distinguished intellectuals and progressive artists of the twentieth century" (1987, xi, 373), he chooses attributes that Balázs may have used to describe himself.[5]

However, after the postwar years these extraordinary qualities no longer found a basis in reality; increased specialization and ongoing commercialization had made the *uomo universale* obsolete. The difference between Koch's and Zsuffa's characterization, then, bears witness both to the breadth of Balázs artistic, critical, and political interests and his impossible desire to excel in all of these areas; yet precisely this ill-fated attempt makes his contribution to film theory so unique. Balázs's longing for integration can be seen in direct relationship to the Austro-Hungarian Empire and its failed attempts to bring together various nationalities in a single political realm. The attitudes and beliefs associated with the term *fin-de-siècle* remained the decisive influence in his approach to intellectual matters, just as the rediscovery of Hungarian folk culture in the fight for political independence provided the matrix for his theorizing of political movements. In Budapest, Balázs made a name for himself as the author of dramas and poems in the symbolist tradition. The growing interest in folklore not only resulted in several collections of fairy tales, but also found expression in his collaboration with Béla Bartók on the opera *Duke Bluebeard's Castle* (1911) and the ballet *The Wooden Prince* (1914). Balázs was a founding member of the so-called *Sonntagskreis* (Sunday circle), an informal discussion group consisting of such writers and scholars as Karl Mannheim, Georg Lukács, and Arnold Hauser.

Because of his participation in the short-lived Soviet Republic of 1919, Balázs was forced to leave Hungary and settle in Vienna. There he discovered the cinema, which from then on provided the center of his creative and theoretical endeavors. In 1922, Balázs assumed the position of film critic for *Der Tag* — becoming "a professional carper," in his own words (1982, 283) — and wrote the first film scenarios for Alexander Korda, another Hungarian emigré. Balázs was the first critic in Austria to pay attention to a film's artistic qualities. Through the more than two hundred reviews that he wrote until 1926, he exerted a strong influence on film audiences and film culture in Vienna. In a self-portrait published in the *Film-Kurier,* Balázs would later describe these years as follows: "For me film criticism, which I introduced in Vienna, paved the way for an in-depth study of film. These preliminary studies resulted in the first film dramaturgy ever written, *Der sichtbare Mensch*. It became known all over the world, was adopted as a textbook in Russian film schools and brought me the first invitation to Berlin" (1984, 360).

From 1926 until 1931, Balázs lived and worked in Berlin, where he pursued his career as a film scenarist and actively involved himself in leftist media initiatives, including the People's Association for Film Art.[6] His participation at the initial 1929 meeting of the International League of Independent Film in La Sarraz led to a first meeting with Sergei Eisenstein, with whom he would later conduct a well-publicized debate on montage. No longer reviewing films on a regular basis, Balázs now wrote longer, more specialized essays that were published in technical journals like *Die Filmtechnik,* contributed political analyses on film under capitalism to *Film und Volk,* and presented his ideas in numerous lectures for professional organizations, progressive media initiatives, and evening schools like the Marxistische Arbeiterschule (MASCH), organized by the KPD.

The growing preference for didactic forms of writing was occasioned by his firsthand experiences in the film industry and his involvement in leftist politics. Balázs's most successful film scenarios from these years include *Madame wünscht keine Kinder* for Alexander Korda and *Die Abenteuer eines Zehnmarkscheins* for Berthold Viertel. His participation in the screen adaptation of Brecht's *Threepenny Opera* made him the target of many accusations of opportunism in the left-liberal press, including Ihering.[7] Balázs's mixed reputation among his contemporaries — an unmistakable sign is his exclusion from what Koch calls the "mutual footnoting circuit" (1987, 172) — may have been influenced by their contempt for his ability to function in the intellectual marketplace but is caused, above all, by his own ambivalences. Balázs's association with Communism, his romantic vision of a new folk culture, and his rather conservative ideas about art and culture result in a conception of revolutionary film art not without inconsistencies and contradictions. His own practices are very telling in this regard. On the one hand, Balázs collaborated on stage productions with Piscator, whose influence is noticeable in a section of *Der Geist des Films* on the use of film in stage productions. On the other, he worked with Leni Riefenstahl on *Das blaue Licht* (1932, *Blue Light*), a film set in the mountains that very much expressed his own fascination with the romantic and the mystical. In 1931, Balázs responded to an invitation by IAH-affiliated Meshrabpom-Rus and left for the Soviet Union, where he would later accept a teaching post at the Moscow Film Academy. His qualifications as a Marxist thinker elicited rather critical comments from Lukács, who claimed that his comrade from the 1919 Hungarian Soviet was only called a Marxist film critic because Marxist film theory did not yet exist.[8] It should be noted, however, that the relationship between Balázs and Lukács was not without its own misgivings.

After this short overview, the development of Balázs's critical style can be traced more easily. Passion and partiality characterize his relationship to film from the very beginning. His early reviews are subjective, polemical, speculative, witty, often unrelenting in their defense of film, and sometimes peppered with amusing anecdotes from the screenings. Balázs's love for the cinema becomes evident in the enthusiasm with which he presents his favorite films and the scorn and derision that erupt in the few scathing reviews. Of one particular film, he writes: "Lya de Putti is beautiful and Luciano Albertini is strong. The Riviera, too, is splendid, as is well known, and those wild cliffs that appear in the film under name of the Cordillera are wonderful. Even the ocean makes an appearance, including huge ocean liners, and in order for everything that filmed nature has to offer to be clearly visible, cows, horses, goats, and even geese appear in cameo roles. In other words, the film is so full of beautiful nature and natural beauties that we hardly ask for anything else. And this is good. For with the beauties of art, things are not so good" (1982, 264).

While Balázs's comments on technical details are well-informed and to the point, his observations about a particular frame or actress are often surprisingly poetic. Then noncommittal phrases like "nice details of direction," "many beautiful images," or "well-constructed and with good timing" give way to the confessions of the aficionado; then adjectives like "soulful," "profound," and "expressive" predominate. Balázs frequently uses scenes from the films to elaborate on theoretical points but, as someone responsible to his readers, also complains repeatedly about inferior projection facilities, uncomfortable seats, and the bad quality of prints. In his likes and dislikes, Balázs makes the choices typical of an entire generation of critics whose views on cinema were formed in the early twenties by the films of Griffith and Chaplin, and in the late twenties by the films of Eisenstein and Pudovkin. While his high political expectations made him, at times, more critical of Russian directors, American films received his undivided attention, even those with simplistic stories and rather cheap effects. Their refreshing lack of literary ambitions inspired the confession that "yes, we dream of a great synthesis: European art united with American technology" (1982, 155). Concentrating in his reviews on films with popular appeal, Balázs supported the good entertainment film; hence his continuous praise for Lubitsch, from *Die Austernprinzessin* (1919, The oyster princess) and *Die Flamme* (1922; *Montmartre*, 1924) to *The Marriage Circle* (1924) and *The Student Prince* (1927). Among German films, *Die Straße* and *Die Nibelungen* also received a positive mention; Murnau's *Nosferatu* (1921) was hailed for its fairy tale elements and *Phantom* (1922) characterized as a "good German film."

Many reviews show his great emphasis on acting. When Balázs writes of the admired Asta Nielsen, "Lower your flags before her, for she is incomparable and unequaled" (1982, 159), or when he describes her face as a "lexicon of gestures," he demonstrates an understanding of film that hinges, to a large degree, on the actor's ability to hold together story and image through facial expressions and body movements alone. When he refers to Chaplin as a film poet, "the master of that nonliterary film-specific substance that clever European theoreticians dream of" (1982, 194), he unmistakably identifies the actor as the most important creative force in film. Such programmatic statements, and the numerous panegyrics to actors like Lillian Gish, Gloria Swanson, Sessue Hayakawa, Conradt Veidt, and Emil Jannings, explain why Balázs's early film theory is often characterized as an actors' theory (Diederichs in Balázs 1982, 37–38). However, the relationship between actor and close-up—in the first reviews they are almost indistinguishable—points more than anything to the creative role of camerawork. Its importance is underscored by the fact "that pantomime and film are very different art forms and so very unique that a filmed pantomime ceases to be a pantomime even when filmed in a very realistic manner" (Balázs 1982, 341).

The reflections on great actors in the early reviews give rise to the notion of physiognomy as the true language of the body. Predisposed to physiognomics through his familiarity with phenomenological ideas, Balázs first introduces the term as a function of the close-up and elaborates on its implications in a comment on the filmic representation of the masses. There he argues that "the masses are not a chaotic, unformed element of nature. They always are like an ornament and always have a physiognomy" (1982, 181). Later he also applies the term to buildings and objects of everyday life, for example when speaking of the face of an elevator or a factory. Because of its ability to unite objects and human beings under the primacy of expression, physiognomy assumes a crucial role in Balázs's poetics of film. In an article appropriately titled "Physiognomy," he explains its function by distinguishing between physiognomy and facial expression: "After all, every face has a distinct physiognomy that we can change as little as the color of our eyes, and within that distinct physiognomy we find the constantly changing facial expressions. Their relationship to each other, their struggle with each other, reveals everything: soul, character, fate" (1982, 206).[9]

Physiognomy, according to Balázs, represents nature and the unconscious, whereas facial expressions reflect a person's character, occupation, and social background, thus in a way cultivating the face. The tension between nature and culture, and between race and individual, constitute a face and make it the site of ever-changing meanings. Because film offers privileged access to the visible world, Balázs concludes, it provides the "material for a comparative physiognomic science," thereby also ending the artificial separation between the humanities and the natural sciences. For the same reason, the centrality of the face underscores film's natural affinity for specific themes and genres and make it "the art of physiognomy" (1982, 229). Delineating these origins of physiognomy in Balázs's early writings is crucial for a better understanding of his later theory of film. Physiognomy is never limited to the human realm; as mentioned above, it often manifests itself in inanimate objects and must, therefore, be seen as participating in a materialist pansymbolism, as it were. While the projection of human categories onto the outside world originates in a subjectivity that wants confirmation of its perceptions and beliefs, the re-presentation of the visible world in human terms also puts an end to the experience of fundamental separation. Thus the process is anthropomorphic as well as anthropocentric. Outside reality is animated by the desire to find resonances of the human in what is increasingly perceived as foreign, alien, Other; therein lies the provocation of Balázs's earliest contributions to film theory.

His first major work, *Der sichtbare Mensch,* appeared at the end of his first two years as a critic in Vienna. The book's explicit goal was to place contemporary filmmaking in the larger context of social, economic, and philosophical concerns and design a future for this new art form. Not all of the ideas presented were new; the interest in gesture can be traced back to the prewar years, and comparisons to folklore can already be found in the writings of many cinema reformers. However, in Balázs's book they became part of a more ambitious project of establishing a connection between aesthetic, social, technical, and economic perspectives (Wuss 1990, 134–48). As was to be expected, *Der sichtbare Mensch* was welcomed as the first theory of film and its author praised as someone who had developed his ideas through extensive film viewing and not, like Bloem or Stindt, through rigid classification systems. Alfred Polgar referred to Balázs as "the exact evangelist of a new art," Leopold Jessner praised the book as "an almost scientific systematic," and Karl Grune, a well-known film director, saw "the unexpected beginnings of a universal dramaturgy" (all quoted by Gersch in Balázs 1984, 33).

Kracauer was one of the few to object to Balázs's speculations about an emergent visual culture and his categorical rejection of language as inadequate and obsolete. "The making visible of man through film is the opposite of the movement toward real concreteness in that it only confirms, and holds on to, the bad rationality of capitalist thinking. Only through the insights that come with language can radical change take place" (Kracauer 1927). The writer Erich Kästner, on the other hand, saw this transgressive quality already realized in the presentation of the material. "Balázs's book is one of the most interesting essayistic books of the last years. An unusual mixture, he combines the abilities of the critic with those of the poet, and this rare double talent not only has a favorable effect on his films, but also on his dramatics of film, *Der sichtbare Mensch*" (1949–50, 178).

Balázs's preference for sentence fragments, colorful metaphors, and shifting modes of address that simulate the cinematic experience, the use of short paragraphs and bold headings in the book's innovative design, and the many references to famous Expressionist films may be responsible for its critical reception as a study of Expressionist film (Eisner 1977, II; Palmier 1977, 36–44). While his background as a poet predisposed him toward the open-ended and the multileveled, Balázs nonetheless made every effort to present a coherent, conclusive system of thought. It is perhaps because of this striving toward universal applicability that the external characteristics often amount to little more than fashionable embellishments. Departing from the single shot that symbolizes film's aesthetic potential, Balázs relies on the appearance of fragmentation to achieve discursive closure and develops his argument though a sequence of discrete "textual shots." The need for control had its productive side, however. It brings to the fore the author's own subjectivity as a critic and spectator and, in undermining any totalizing tendencies, compensates for his conventional judgments and rigid definitions. Moving from celebratory remarks on actors to detailed descriptions of specific scenes, and combining political analysis with confessions of personal enjoyment, Balázs takes the expressive qualities of film and transforms them into a theory of expressiveness. Thus he must be characterized as one of the first film critics to write from the perspective of a spectator, and, in that regard, one of the first film theoreticians to continue, on the basis of a thorough knowledge of films, the discourse on visual pleasure begun in the prewar years.[10]

*Der sichtbare Mensch* opens on a note of urgency as Balázs presents the case of film before the representatives of high culture. "Like the disenfranchised and despised mob in front of the manor, film stands before your parliament of aesthetics and demands entry into the august surroundings of theory," he writes, and goes on to explain why: "Because film is the popular art of our century (1924, 10–11).[11] Fighting for its social and cultural empowerment, the author appeals to the three groups that influence public attitudes toward film: the filmmakers, the philosophers, and the audience. Still excluded from official culture, the cinema and its supporters have risen to demand a theory that could assess the present situation and, like a compass, show the direction for future developments. In order to underscore film's great cultural significance, Balázs then compares its invention to that of the printing press. "Now another machine is at work to move culture toward the visual and to give man a new face. It is called cinematography. It is a technology for the reproduction and distribution of products of the human spirit; its effect on human culture will be no less than that of the printing press" (1924, 24).

The introduction of the printing press is often linked to cultural progress, and has had a direct effect on the institutions of knowledge and power, but the rise of narrative film in a society driven by technical innovation produces a peculiar double movement in Balázs's argumentation. He claims that film is destined to bring about a return to the primeval grounds of humanity and introduce new forms of communication based on the body. Here the most advanced technology of mass entertainment makes possible the (imaginary) return to a preindustrial culture and an idealized definition of folklore.

It would be misleading, however, to characterize this argument as retrospective, for in Balázs's constellation of terms folklore is inseparably linked to the language of the body and its inherently equalizing, unifying qualities. Against the divisions introduced by language, film comes to fulfill the ancient dream of a communication without and beyond words. The universal language of the body shows the way to a communal paradise, a social utopia. Film provides the means to this end because of its secret affinity with the body. In a very basic sense, it brings people together in a specifically designated space, the motion picture theater, and, on a more theoretical level, it reaches beyond the representation of the individual to become the new art of, and for, the masses. Not as isolated individuals but as types, classes, and races do people communicate through film as the first international language. However, this ideal version stands in sharp contrast to the reality of cinema. By promoting internationalism, Balázs admits readily, film also complies with the expansionist tendencies of late capitalism. To make his point, he resorts to the kind of biological metaphors that more often than not weaken his political analyses — or, to be more precise, that show them to be grounded in antimodernist rather than anticapitalist sentiments. Accordingly, evolution now assumes the discursive position within the paradigm of folklore that is later assigned to the term *revolution* in the context of class analysis. This is how film in Balázs's account receives its legitimating prehistory: "Physical expression is always the last stage in a process of cultural evolution. Thus even if the film of today sounds like primitive barbaric stammering in comparison to contemporary literature, it nevertheless contributes to the process of cultural evolution, because it is the unmediated embodiment of the spirit" (1924, 30).

This process has aesthetic as well as political consequences. The aesthetic categories that for Balázs develop almost naturally out of the body — which, interestingly, is equated with nature in a way that precludes all social influences — replace the idealist notion of a disinterested enjoyment of the beautiful with the critical directives for the long-awaited merger of the aesthetic and the social. It is in this context that the coming of film reverses the effects of abstraction brought about by the printing press and an elitist book culture. When he describes the process of civilization through the oppositions of body and mind, and perception and conception, Balázs implicitly characterizes the cinema as being at once anti-intellectual and deeply metaphysical. Such combinations are bound to create a constant slippage in terminology. For instance, his frequent use of the Babel of language metaphor makes linguistic discourse seem superfluous but, at the same time, relies on its rich connotations for assertions such as "the origin of language is physical expression" or "the language of gesture is the original mother tongue of man" (Balázs 1924, 26).[12]

Having claimed a discursive place for film, if only in the form of programmatic statements, Balázs returns to the status quo, so to speak, and explains his oppositions to comparisons with the other arts. While many of his points recall earlier poetological controversies, they already comprise, as in a photographic negative, the basic elements of what *Der sichtbare Mensch* promises — namely the illumination of the human condition through the relationship between actor and camera. In contrast to theater, Balázs argues, the actor in a film creates meaning; his or her facial expressions do not merely add form, but are its very content. In contrast to literature, he continues, stories are secondary in a medium more accurately described by references to texture — Balázs, deceptively sounding like Kracauer, coins the term *surface art* (*Flächenkunst*) — than to text, which implies the existence of layers. By making surface the locus where all processes find representation, film facilitates the rapprochement of the animate and inanimate world that is all but revolutionary in its effects. "In their shared silence they [the objects] merge with man and, in so doing, gain life and meaning. Since they do not speak any less than men, they also speak just as much. This explains that special atmosphere in film which exists outside of all literary possibility" (1924, 48).

Similar considerations determine film's relationship to theater and dance, for the facial expressions of a film actor are equally removed from the gestures that accompany speech on the stage and the stylized movements in the art of dance. Even pantomime bears no resemblance to film, according to Balázs. Whereas the former communicates through silence and celebrates the art and soul of silence, the latter simply exists without sound; as Balázs points out, speech continues to be expressed through facial expressions. Free of all external constraints, film must, therefore, concentrate on its inherent possibilities; it is with such goals that the central chapters discuss the formal principles of film.

Not surprisingly, the following "Sketches for a Dramaturgy of Film" shift from the actor and facial expressions to the close-up and the face of things and, in so doing, affirm the essentially anthropocentric framework of the book.[13] However, by grounding his spiritual quest in the human and technical materials of film, Balázs takes an approach that might be more accurately described as anthropomorphism. Notwithstanding such nuances, the widening of his definition of physiognomy offers a good opportunity for an examination of his intellectual debts. Balázs's description of facial expression as the poetic substance of human life, a category preceding language, can be placed in a philosophical tradition that reaches from Johann Kaspar Lavater and Goethe to the then-influential *Lebensphilosophie*.[14] Many ideas about the correspondences between inner self and external features recall Lavater's *Essays on Physiognomy*, while others are more specifically modeled on Goethe's scientific writings on morphology.

The influence of phenomenological thought on Balázs is evident in the great attention he pays to the expressive potential of gesture. It also results in similar aesthetic concepts; to quote just one example, Simmel's claim that "except for the human face, there is no other form that could bring together such a great diversity of shapes and surfaces in such an absolute unity of meaning" (1957, 154) could have been taken directly from *Der sichtbare Mensch*. Last but not least, Gestalt psychology left its traces in the formulation of the part-whole relationship. The term *microphysiognomy,* which appears later in *Der Geist des Films,* recalls the Gestaltist notion of microphysics and refers precisely to the universal principle of holistic determination.[15] Balázs's main contribution to the tradition of physiognomic thought, then, lies in introducing into its various configurations a new technology and a new subject. Through the scintillating term *collective face,* he provides the urban masses with the critical and aesthetic means to reach self-awareness both as a class and a civilization; therein lies the revolutionary potential of film.

On a more problematic note, *Der sichtbare Mensch* also places physiognomy in a conceptual framework that invites, among other things, a stronger emphasis on race. Moving from the images of the body to those living bodies that are always already determined in relation to gender and race, Balázs repeatedly proposes to use the new medium for anthropological purposes. To put it in somewhat exaggerated terms, he sees film as a useful tool in studying the relationships between character and fate, individuality and race, type and personality. Because of his belief in a universal body language, Balázs seeks to eliminate racial difference and its implicit notions of "superiority" and "inferiority," but defines the coming standardized human being in very problematic terms. "Here we find the first living scion of that white man who, as the synthesis of the different races and nations, will rise in the near future. Cinematography is a machine, creating, in its own way, living and concrete internationalism, *the one and only psyche of white man*" (1924, 32; my emphasis).[16] Questions of gender are ignored entirely in these scenarios. This glaring omission, in combination with the lengthy descriptions of individual female faces (e.g., of Asta Nielsen, Lillian Gish), confirms the impression that, whereas the examples may underscore the diversity of human existence, the actual representatives of the Other are excluded from any theoretical pronouncements.

It is with these shortcomings that physiognomy functions as a structuring device in Balázs's theorizing of acting and its filmic manifestations. While distinguishing between performance and camerawork, he still places key concepts such as "facial expressions" and "close-ups" on the side of physiognomy, with the result that the boundaries between reality and representation become blurred. The profilmic event provides the critical framework in which even the close-up appears as an aspect of acting rather than of camerawork; it predetermines the genres, themes, and styles in which film as a narrative medium is thought to be most convincing. The actors only provide the raw material, so to speak, that makes possible this ongoing celebration of expressivity; even in passages devoted to performance, they hardly ever appear as agents of the narrative.

Film's total reliance on the expressive qualities of the face, in Balázs's view bring it closer to the lyric than to the epic. The extensive comments in *Der sichtbare Mensch* on music and musicality serve to confirm this somewhat surprising comparison. Balázs not only uses such musical terms as *polyphony, tempo,* and *rhythm* to describe stories unfolding on a face or exploding in a gesture, he even coins phrases like *chords of emotions* to describe the layering of different emotions, or juxtaposes the *legato* effect created by the succession of facial expressions to the unpleasant *staccato* associated with spoken language. These comparisons may be useful for distinguishing expressive registers, but they hardly constitute a language, complete with grammar and lexicon. Yet it is on the basis of such suggestive analogies that Balázs defines the close-up as "the technical condition for the art of facial expressions and thus of all high film art" (1924, 71). As the art of emphasis, detail, and nuance, the close-up makes possible the rediscovery of the face. For Balázs, this most intimate of all shot sizes provides both the foundation and the materials for the poetics of film. Its formal qualities — he does not really discuss other shot sizes — are determined by camera angles, lighting, and principles like *pars pro toto;* yet its meanings originate from the laws of physiognomy and greatest expressiveness.

For the most part, Balázs's discussions focus on the poetic qualities of the single shot. It is from this perspective of formal unity — again: the physiognomy of the visible world — that he analyzes the connections between images. The term used here is *Bilderführung* (literally, "image direction"), and he describes it as follows: "Editing, that is the sequence of images and their speed; it corresponds to style in literature. Editing is the living breath of film, and everything depends on it" (Balázs 1924, 121). As his reference to breathing suggests, the main function of editing seems to consist of providing temporal continuity. Balázs's technically well-informed discussion of ellipses, transition shots, and parallel editing, as well as his remarks on the duration and rhythm of shots, all stress the importance of smooth transitions. He insists that editing — here the comparison to breath is indeed fitting — should facilitate vital processes but not draw attention to itself. Fixated on the single shot as the first step toward "living physiognomy," Balázs argues almost like the proponents of the film drama, who based their analyses solely on the long shot as a representation of the theatrical mise-en-scène. Other forms of artistic expression seem inconceivable from within Balázs's system of thought, as his hostile reactions to the montage theories of Eisenstein and others indicate. Meaning, for him, arises from the still image, and from movements within the frame; there is little room for the tensions created in the encounter of two adjacent shots.

The theoretical implications of this emergent "dramaturgy of film" based on physiognomy become apparent as soon as Balázs shifts from the human face to the world of objects. Then expression and expressiveness become vehicles for the redemptive project of art. Pointing to the growing abstractness in all areas of modern life, he argues: "Like bashful women, the objects usually wear veils in front of their faces. The veil of our traditional and abstract view of things. Artistic Expressionism removes that veil. . . . There is no doubt that film is the origin of Expressionism, perhaps the only legitimate home of Expressionism" (1924, 88). Balázs finds evidence of such developments in the fact that filmmakers turn away from nature and naturalism and move into the controlled environment of the studio. Expressionism—here to be understood as a specific attitude toward the world—reintroduces the category of language into a world made illegible by the process of civilization. Stylization, then, means nothing less than the rediscovery of that hidden language. While its manifestations are most powerful in relation to the human body, its principles, according to Balázs, apply equally to landscapes and cityscapes, revealing their soul and freeing their spiritual impulses. Thus he concludes that "the stylization of nature, no matter whether Impressionistic or Expressionistic, is the precondition for film becoming a work of art" (1924, 94).[17]

Statements like these originate in a kind of pansymbolism, the belief that all things, without exception, are necessarily symbolic; here the influence of German Romanticism and its theory of language (Schlegel) is evident. Ultimately, physiognomy is destined to restore the equivalence of all phenomena on the level of expressiveness. "For all things, whether we are conscious of it or not, leave a physiognomic impression on us. All and always. Just as time and space are categories of our perception and an integral part of the world of our experience, so does physiognomy inhere in every phenomenon. It is a necessary category of our perception" (Balázs 1924, 103). In light of such remarks, it should not be surprising that film holds a special attraction for Balázs. Close enough to the visible world to evoke its presence but removed enough to draw attention to its symbolic function, it bears within itself the utopian quality which still awaits realization as the folklore of the urban masses. The secret of film's popular appeal resides in the life — the "matter and substance of concrete life" (1924, 74) — that unfolds before the camera in all its nuances, and that communicates through the visual expression of its essence. Film's preferred subjects try to capture this miracle: hence the fascination with nature and everyday life; hence the great enjoyment of movement, chases, sensations; hence the enormous appeal of animals and children.

Such theoretical pronouncements also provide the point of departure for Balázs's analysis of film under capitalism and its designation as inherently revolutionary. The glaring discrepancies between film's contemporary practices and its true mission provoke this programmatic statement: "Film may well be the only art that was born as the child of capitalist industry, and it does bear its spirit. But it need not stay that way" (1924, 147). The historical alliance of film and capitalism, Balázs argues, can be studied exemplarily in the genre of the detective film. As the guardian of private property, the detective personifies the spirit of capitalism; he makes visible its effects. Although the origins of film are capitalist and its association with American culture an essential part of this genealogy, Balázs is convinced that film will eventually destroy capitalism through its own means. "The spiritual atmosphere of capitalism stands in opposition to the essence of film, which, despite these origins, longs for the concrete, sensual, immediate experience of things. . . . The reasons for its manifold imperfections are to be found in this contradiction. And it will only become the great art form that lives up to its immanent possibilities when the changed social conditions provide a more favorable spiritual atmosphere" (1924, 152). Instead of furthering the precise analysis of class society, however, such blanket statements open the door for sentimentality and nostalgia. Balázs's definition of class continues to be colored by his desire for a revival of folklore through film and the attendant cult of authenticity and immediacy. Likewise, his concept of revolution cannot be separated from physiognomy and its unifying powers and, therefore, often appears more metaphysical than political. These influences must be kept in mind if Balázs's romantic anticapitalism is not to be dismissed as a faulty Marxism, but seen as the most adequate expression of his belief in the "visible man."

The dream of a film culture based on images of the body and the language of gesture proved so appealing to contemporary critics that *Der sichtbare Mensch* inspired reviews with the weight of philosophical treatises; it also produced misreadings that simultaneously challenged and confirmed Balázs's main propositions. Robert Musil used the book to reflect on a wide range of issues, including the opposition between what he saw as the ruling principle of modern life, rationality, and what he describes as "daylight mystics" in his magnum opus, *Der Mann ohne Eigenschaften* (The Man without Qualities). By making sensory experience the basis of critical reflection, Musil argues, *Der sichtbare Mensch* provides a critical model for literary criticism as well. For the new medium has the power to overcome existing divisions through the necessarily symbolic function of the image, the physiognomic nature of all things. Thus Musil welcomes Balázs's assertion of a deep human truth inherent in filmic representation and confirms his view on physiognomy as an experience of unity, both on the individual and social level. Speaking of a "mystics of film," he maintains: "It is this state in which the image of every object ceases to be merely functional and becomes an extralinguistic experience. The descriptions of the symbolic face of things and their awakening in the silence of the image . . . clearly belong to its field of influence. Interestingly, a volatile trace of these experiences can be found in the territory of film which, after all, provides a territory for speculation in the most common sense. It would be a mistake to see the newly discovered physiognomy of things merely as astonishment at an isolated optical experience. Those are only the means; what is really at stake is to explode normal experience. And this is a basic ability of every art" (1978, 1,144–45).[18]

However, in order reach this state, Musil cautions, art has to emphasize its difference from life. Only through the formal means of condensation and displacement, and only through the spectator's active participation, can the mystical origins of art be reclaimed and the limitations of everyday life be expanded. Then, film will pave the way for a "new sensual culture" based on visual pleasure. "Through the art of seeing, film reclaims the eternal and inexpressible that lies at the heart of every existence — as if placed under glass through the mere fact that one can only see it" (1978, 1,148). Through the metaphor of reality fossilized by the camera's intrusion, Musil arrives at a definition of film that stands in sharp contrast to Balázs's explicitly political frame of reference, but also reveals its internal contradictions. Musil takes Balázs's ideas on facial expressions and incorporates them in his own conception of a purely aesthetic experience. What for Balázs promises to become a genuine expression of the masses now serves to legitimate bourgeois subjectivism. Musil proves, with Balázs, that infusing the filmic image with metaphysical significance represents one way of fighting reification through the radical transformation of its elements. However, this process either allows film to challenge the conditions by embracing alienation with a vengeance instead of denying its effects, or it introduces a metaphysical quality that has little to do with the social origins of film and stands in sharp contrast to its industrial mode of production. Balázs meant to pursue the first possibility, but Musil, in his reading of Balázs, foregrounds an underlying essentialism that weakens film's revolutionary potential (Heller 1984, 240–43).

Measured against its own claims, there is indeed much left to be desired in *Der sichtbare Mensch*. As a contribution to the emerging theory of film, the work was flawed by the author's effusive declarations about mankind's salvation through film, while as a political manifesto its radicalism was undercut by antimodernist tendencies. The provocation of a term like *physiognomy* disappeared, once its implications were spelled out in the context of aesthetic preferences that more or less confined film to narrative. Behind the appealing scenarios of nonverbal communication, the liberation of the masses was, once again, reduced to a matter of intuition and trust, and the flight from intellectual discourse found justification in the cult of specularity. Moreover, the linking of spirituality and class struggle within a formalist framework was not without its problems. While physiognomy predisposed film toward the masses, it also confined its effects to the profilmic event. In spite of such shortcomings, Balázs's impassioned calls for a return to visual culture, and his notion of a revolutionary cinema based on the process of making visible, of unmasking, did pose a challenge to traditional aesthetics and the formal ambitions of art cinema. As will be shown in the chapter's third part, these ideas prepared the ground for his later statements on film and working-class culture.

\* \* \*

Balázs's writings between the publication of *Der sichtbare Mensch* and *Der Geist des Films* reveal the growing influence of Communist orthodoxy. While earlier comments on the double meaning of *Einstellung* showed his interest in ideological questions, they remained within the paradigm of folklore and its assumption of a harmonious, homogeneous society. Balázs's analysis of capitalist society, and his discussion of fragmentation and reification in particular, was informed by the essentially Romantic belief in a primeval unity behind all things, and a longing to restore this original plenitude. To what degree these desires laid the foundation for a

"Marxist" film theory can be seen in a lecture given by Balázs at the 1928 founding meeting of the People's Association for Film Art. Here earlier formulations on film and capitalism are rephrased in strong political terms. "The film works for us. Despite everything. Even in the hands of nationalist and imperialist big capital, it works against them. Cinematography revolts by means of its inner destination. The spirit of this technology rebels against its creators. That is an exciting and instructive spectacle. They own the film. But it belongs to us. It stands under their command but is secretly aligned with us, as it were. They produce it. But it is meant for us" (Balázs 1984, 228). Indicative of the changes in Balázs's approach, the former "child of capitalist industry" now appears as the product of specific social and economic conditions. Instead of developing his analysis of film under capitalism around the notion of ideology, however, Balázs continues to appeal to spirit as an intangible quality that manifests itself equally in the "spirit of capitalism" and the allegedly revolutionary "spirit of film"; at times, these residues of *Lebensphilosphie* weaken his argument.[19]

A similar ambivalence characterizes Balázs's fervent attacks on left-liberal intellectuals published in *Die Weltbühne* under the title "The Intellectuals' Fear of Socialism" (1932). In this series of articles, he accuses left-liberal intellectuals of rejecting capitalism without being willing to give up their privileges in bourgeois society and embrace the only alternative, socialism. He interprets their defense of individualism, their insistence on the freedom of the arts and sciences, and their contempt for tendentious art and working-class culture as signs of a continuous resistance to the reality of class struggle and the leadership role of the Communist Party. Despite the dogmatic tone, it would be wrong to conclude, with Congdon, that Balázs "sacrificed his talent and judgment on Communism's altar" (1991, 136) when he joined the KPD in 1931. Just as the solidarity with the masses was an integral part of Balázs's work even before he turned to film, his film-theoretical writings revolved around ideas that, whether in the context of modern folklore or Socialist Realism, validated the great tradition of bourgeois art and literature.

Because of Balázs's growing interest in the relationship between aesthetics and politics, the masses began to play a central role in his writings on film: first the masses depicted on the screen, then the masses that would realize the dream of a new classless society. Significantly, it was in the context of an extended reflection on facial expressions — in other words, through physiognomy — that the masses first appeared on the center stage of Balázs's film aesthetics. He asked: "Is it conceivable that the soul of the masses could be as profound, as deep, as emotional as that of the individual? Is it possible that the individual does not disappear when joining the masses? It is possible that the masses obtain a face and eyes and look at you like a friend to whom you could open your heart?" And he answered with an enthusiastic *yes:* "And this crowd has *one face* that smiles and cries, a face so deeply inspired, inspired by *one* emotion, as only the face of the greatest actor in the moment of deepest emotion could be" (1982, 361). By blending the individual and collective face, Balázs was able to include audiences in his politicized approach to film and to utilize physiognomy for the project of a revolutionary cinema.

Earlier reflections about film's innate internationalism took on a new dimension as its actual limitations were made evident in the context of specific genres and styles, revealing film to be "a dirty swamp that clings heavily to its forms" (1982, 281). Enthusiastic statements about its ability to remove the veil of illusions gave way to a more detailed investigation into the processes by which the capitalist film industry had turned this "art of looking" into an "art of illusion." Aware of their enormous appeal, Balázs began to focus on sensationalist and escapist films and suggested that their psychological mechanisms be used for, and not against, the masses. His definition of filmic realism in this context reveals the influence of the leftist debates on literature, as do his proposals for radical change. "The cinema is its only source of distraction," Balázs said about the working class, only to conclude that "our films must show action and gripping personal fates. Otherwise they waste the captivating qualities of the fable which we have to use, just as the capitalist film abuses them" (Kühn 1975, 1:36).

Balázs's often conflicting interests as theoretician, scriptwriter, and political activist found a common ground in the call for films that used convincing stories and strong identification figures in order to win audiences for the revolutionary cause. At the same time, his strong belief in classical forms, together with an equally strong aversion to New Objectivity, made him reject, in one breath, such diverse phenomena as jazz, advertisement, Americanism, and urban life-styles. "No, this New Objectivity has nothing to do with revolution, socialism, or the proletariat. On the contrary. It is the embodiment of a fully rationalized world held together by the power of corporate business. It is the aesthetics of the conveyer belt" (1984, 237). The aesthetic preferences that inspired such statements found an equivalent in Balázs's rather traditional views on the education of the masses. Questions of reception had only played a marginal role in *Der sichtbare Mensch,* but the political situation in the late twenties required more concrete proposals. Balázs's pedagogical models were based on the notion of compensation (i.e., the belief that mass entertainment compensated for social inequity and economic exploitation), a standard element in Socialist debates on bourgeois and working-class culture. Convinced that education was the first step toward social change, and that knowledge about the functioning of ideology automatically led to a change in aesthetic preferences, Balázs placed his entire trust in the spectator who, supposedly through his critical judgments, determined the future of film. "The audience must already be susceptible. As paradoxical as it may sound, film presupposes an understanding of things that do not yet exist; one must see its beauties so that they can develop. Thus in order to have good films one must first have a certain theoretical and aesthetic understanding" (1982, 349).

While concentrating his efforts on film and politics, Balázs also developed a very practical interest in questions of cinematography. Moving to a position behind the camera, as it were, he began to equate the art of film with the art of cinematography. Consequently, the cameraman emerged as the center of artistic control, for "it is his work that we see in the film. Not the performance and not the direction, but the visual representation of the performance and of the direction" (1984, 210). Balázs's sharp distinction between profilmic event and camerawork marked a radical departure from the scenarios of unmediated presence he described in *Der sichtbare Mensch.* Its implications were far-reaching, as his reflections on film as art indicate. "Film could only become a work of art in that highest sense if it were photographed in a productive and not a reproductive way, if the ultimate and determining creative expression of spirit, soul, and emotion would develop not through performance and mise-en-scène but only through the shooting of the filmic images themselves, if the cameraman, who in the final analysis creates the film, would be the spiritual creator, the writer of the work, the actual filmmaker" (1984, 210).

Balázs first developed these ideas in an earlier article on style and the historical film, when distinguishing between the artificial world of the set and the aesthetic qualities of the shot. Again, style appears as an inherent feature of the filmic image. Balázs distinguishes between style-conscious films (*Stilfilm*) that are "authentic representations of a style, but have no style themselves" (1982, 342) and films with a distinct visual signature. Film style (*Filmstil*), then, has to be thought of as something like a painter's brush. The growing emphasis on the camera is captured in the word *Auf-nahme*, which, like *Einstellung*, means two things, shooting and reception. Balázs uses these homonyms to draw attention to the identity of art and ideology and to foreground the relationship between film and the masses. Accordingly, the cameraman's personal style, which expresses itself in the composition and selection of shots, converges with what Balázs calls the "objective style of contemporary life" (1982, 344). The camera, he explains, fixates this elusive social phenomenon — *zeitgeist* might be an appropriate translation — as it conveys a sense of authentic objectivity and increases the appreciation of things usually ignored in everyday life. Just like man's sensory and critical faculties come together in the act of seeing, reality in Balázs's wish scenario gets translated into filmic realism almost automatically: "To photograph means to see. And even in the naturalistic shot the living rhythm of the present, so to speak, is uncovered and revealed. Thus style becomes visible" (1982, 345).

As someone "raised" on silent films, Balázs naturally regretted their disappearance and complained about the low quality of most early sound films, yet unlike Arnheim he recognized the possibilities of sound from the beginning. His openness to technical innovations expressed itself in a strangely repetitive move, however. Theorizing sound, Balázs turned to the same argumentative strategies that characterized his approach to the visible world. Thus his enthusiasm about the widening of the field of perception and the continuous exploration of the material world recalls ideas first formulated in the context of visual culture, including the belief that the sound film would bring deliverance from the chaos of noise. Again Balázs insisted that "the acoustic film will open up for us the language of things, just as the optical film revealed the face of things. It will teach us to hear the world, just as the optical film taught us to see. It will reveal to us man's deep, mysterious relationship to the voices of things, as the optical film continues to explore their appearance" (1984, 235).

Separating the innovative sound film (*Tonfilm*) from the mere talking picture (*Sprechfilm*), subsequent lectures and articles focused on the techniques necessary for the successful transformation of this new technology into a creative tool. The often detailed observations on the acoustic close-up or the montage of sound effects show Balázs to be a man with practical experience. It was not without self-interest that he talked repeatedly about the importance of good dialogue. In order for the sound film not to imitate the theater, it had not only to explore all aspects of sound (sound effects, music, speech) in an imaginative manner, but also to win the best writers for the emergent art of screenwriting. That the latter should indeed be considered an art form is borne out by the fact that mediocre novels often make the best screenplays, Balázs argued, whereas the screen adaptation of literary masterpieces is more often than not fraught with problems.

If, as the author maintained, *Der sichtbare Mensch* was a kind of "pre-theory," then *Der Geist des Films* may be characterized as a continuation and critical revision of earlier ideas in light of the sound film. "Please change here!" This is how Balázs announces the paradigm shift in one of his chapter headings. On the one hand, his approach remains very much the same; the book opens with a programmatic introduction, followed by an extensive discussion of formal questions, and ends with a chapter on film and ideology. On the other hand, the paragraphs with the sloganlike captions are considerably shorter and more prescriptive in tone. While earlier arguments reappear in revised form, there is a greater emphasis on specific films than universal truths. In a mosaic manner, Balázs puts together the pieces, thereby realizing his desire "to sketch a kind of grammar for this language [of film]. A study of style and, perhaps, a system of poetics" (1930, 7).

His ambition to design a closed theoretical system and the problems that accompany such a project may have been among the reasons the critical reception of *Der Geist des Films* was reserved, if not unfavorable. T. K. Fodor, in the journal *Linkskurve,* criticized the book for its lack of a "well-developed historical-materialist basis" (1932, 35).[20] Kracauer, who praised the author's materialist approach but objected to the often simplistic explanations (e.g., of petty bourgeois ideology), summarized his reservations in the (Balázsian) image of an *"Einstellung* suffering from lack of focus" (1930). In his review of *Der Geist des Films,* Arnheim introduced some of his own ideas about film art, for instance when criticizing Balázs for failing "to start with the elements and develop a system upwards out of the concrete psychological analysis of the 'character traits' of film. This is the only way to arrive at sufficiently exact and universally valid rules and provide the reader with the solid knowledge that he needs" (1977, 318). Thus Arnheim concluded: "Balázs offers the complete materials for a unique film aesthetic. The book that he did not write is extraordinary" (1977, 317).

In accordance with his plan to write a grammar of film, Balázs concentrates on the three basic elements of its "optical language": the close-up, which shows things in microscopic detail; the shot, which, through framing and camera angles, conveys the attitude of the filmmaker; and montage, which is responsible for the composition of a film. Like *Der sichtbare Mensch, Der Geist des Films* departs from the close-up as the point where the camera and the visible world meet, and where the one reveals itself to the other. However, there are numerous signs of a greater awareness of film as a constructed, second reality. The face disappears into the formal characteristics of close-up and mise-en-scène, and the physiognomic aspects of the close-up are integrated into a wider range of possibilities, including shot sizes, camera angles, and frame composition. The implications of this process are captured in the term *visual gesture* (*Bildgebärde*) which makes the camera part of an all-encompassing filmic anthropomorphism. With facial expression and visual gesture thus made equal, Balázs's poetics also produces its own critical impasses.

In order to reverse the flight into the "intimacy of hidden details" that, in his view, mars bourgeois film, and in order to overcome the lacking dynamism of the shot, Balázs turns to montage as the main facilitator of narrative continuity, tempo, and rhythm. This sudden interest in the possibilities of montage — he no longer uses the term *editing* — is undoubtedly due to the enormous influence of Russian films, and the work of Eisenstein in particular.[21] In spite of their political affinities, Balázs never quite agreed with the theoretical thrust of Eisenstein's "montage of attractions." His rather mechanical description of montage as "the final precision work on a film" bears little resemblance to the great power afforded it by Eisenstein, and while many of the examples in *Der Geist des Films* seem to validate the Russian approach, the more general comments aim in the direction of continuity editing. Resorting again to his language metaphor, Balázs argues against intellectual montage: "But an image cannot be conjugated like a verb. It only exists in the present. It itself does not indicate its temporal position. The position of the image in the film indicates the time of the represented event" (1930, 49).

To what degree montage remains a function of narrative can be seen in his handling of its technical aspects. In addition to fade-out and superimposition — he calls them "montage without cuts" — Balázs includes camera movement (pans, traveling shots) among the various modes of transition, which, in turn, are all associated with montage. Among its best techniques, he even counts associative montage which "can force us to associate in a particular direction. . . . Montage can let us conjure up emotions, meanings, thoughts that become perceivable without becoming visible themselves" (1930, 51). This quality, Balázs is quick to assert, also extends to what he describes as the "highest spiritual sphere" reached by the silent film, intellectual montage (*Gedankenmontage*). In such rare cases, montage loses its essentially supportive function; rather than provoking ideas, it strives to represent them. Balázs's general resistance to what he dismissively calls "ideograms and treatises in hieroglyphics," however, supports the impression that his conception of montage stands closer to music than film, and that it has little in common with the theories of Eisenstein.

While he does explore the musical side of montage, Balázs remains highly critical of non-narrative film. What he polemically describes as a "flight from the fable" and "a separatist tendency toward 'pure' form" (1930, 85) represents, in his view, really nothing but the privileging of formal aspects — grammar, in other words — at the expense of content. Balázs's failure to see the contradiction between his own formalism in aesthetic matters and his hostility toward certain kinds of non-narrative film is more than disconcerting here. Above all, it undermines his politically motivated critique of New Objectivity, and makes his insistence on filmic realism sound like mere lip service to the dogma of Socialist Realism. Though an advocate of classical narratives, Balázs does not reject films without heroes on principle. Genres such as the documentary, the newsreel, the film essay, and, of course, the cross-section film provide him with positive examples for how to transform reality through the presence of a human consciousness. His objections are aimed at what, from the perspective of romantic individualism, looks like the systematic eradication of all subjectivity and its replacement by a cult of objectivity.

Fighting again what Lukács would have described as typical signs of bourgeois decadence, Balázs directs his criticism against two artistic movements. First he accuses the absolute film — its main representatives include Wilfried Basse and Joris Ivens — of presenting "unconstructed, raw life material," that is, a "matter without form," and of reducing reality to visual phenomena without meaning, according to Balázs. Once the images take on an existence of their own, the external world becomes what he calls its "reflection in the consciousness. Not the thing as such but its psychic representation is recorded by the camera" (1930, 114). Balázs is quick to concede that such films do fulfill an important purpose, namely to test the boundaries of the art of film, as long as they establish a psychological connection between the images and as long as they model themselves on dream images and the unconscious. Balázs's assessment of the abstract film by Viking Eggeling, which he describes as a self-involved play with forms, lines, and tonalities — a "form without matter" — is much more devastating. Claiming that "abstract film is born out of theory, meaning: parthenogenetic. Such a thing is never healthy" (1930, 132), Balázs rejects the lack of all human reference points and, in so doing, draws a clear dividing line between "healthy" experimentation and the "unhealthy" fetishizing of technology.

A similar obsession with boundaries informs Balázs's position on technical developments such as the sound film. The overly positive attitude toward technology is immediately put into question by the self-deprecating gesture with which he apologizes for an earlier statement on the color film. "What I wrote ten years ago is completely wrong. I had not freed myself entirely of traditional aesthetic notions and, in this case, applied the formal principles of the visual arts to film" (1930, 135). That bears the marks of political rationale, and not of critical insight. Instead of reexamining his formal categories, Balázs merely exchanges the anti-Naturalist sentiment for the orthodoxy of falsely understood montage. Subsequent statements on color, wide screen, and stereoscopic film follow in this tradition; they leave the author-director as the only remaining fixed point in an ever-changing system of signification. With him as monteur, adapter, and visionary — these equations are already problematic — the notion of montage deteriorates into a kind of magic formula for dealing with technological innovation. In place of impassioned appeals to the image, which tend to reduce film to beautiful still photography, Balázs now explores spatiotemporal relations. In place of a voluntary limitation to the single shot, he now celebrates the dynamics between image, sound, and color.

With technology as a seemingly inexhaustible source of inspiration, the sound film receives its legitimation as yet another stage in the rapprochement of two previously separated needs, expression and communication. Repeating arguments first tested on the silent film, Balázs takes formal characteristics such as framing, perspective, and focus as his point of departure; their technical aspects are discussed in brief sections on aural close-ups, sound montage, image-sound relations, asynchronous sound — and silence. His prognosis on the sound film follows almost naturally out of these formal characteristics. "If the sound film should become a new art form that can well hold its own next to the other arts and the silent film, then it must treat sound not only as a supplement, an addition for dramatic scenes, but as the central and decisive dramatic event and treat it as the main motif of the narrative" (1930, 177).

In addition to theorizing the sound film, *Der Geist des Films* also continues some of Balázs's earlier discussions on the amorphous masses by introducing the notion of class. His analysis of the ideology of bourgeois cinema begins with the petty bourgeoisie, which for him represents the most problematic group among audiences. The growing influence of Marxist theory on his thinking can be seen in the way Balázs delineates the relationship between cinema and class. Standing at the center of the most dramatic changes in society, he argues, the petty bourgeois emulates bourgeois life-styles and tries to improve his living conditions, if not through more prosperity then at least through his conservative attitudes. Lacking class consciousness, his main concern is not to fall into the quagmire of proletarization, even when he has already done so economically. Because of their ambivalent class position, the members of this new social group are particularly susceptible to political ideologies, mythologies, and other kinds of fictions, all of which satisfy their longing for an identity. It is on the basis of this analysis that Balázs examines the affinities between mainstream cinema and the petty bourgeoisie, thereby also bringing the spirit in the book's title closer to the classical Marxist definition of ideology. He finds traces of petty-bourgeois consciousness in the cult of private property, in the emphasis on romance, family life, and personal comfort, and most of all in the preference for stereotypical characters and formulaic stories.

Yet in the end, Balázs is quick to point out, the progressive element inherent in the technology of film will prevail, and the utopian vision of a new society changed through film will be realized. He never accounts for the discrepancies between theory and practice outside of a rather crude economic determinism. Instead he simply insists that the orientation toward material reality distinguishes film from all other art forms and determines its true political mission: to become the new art for the revolutionary masses. Its inherent collectivism extends from the conditions of production (i.e., film as collective effort) to those of reception (i.e., film as a popular art). Thus any serious study of film, according to Balázs, calls for the perspective of sociology, rather than art history; after all, "never before has an art form been as strongly influenced by such factors as film is today. No spiritual product, aside from the vernacular, has been capable of documenting the thoughts and feelings of the masses" (1930, 186). On the basis of these aesthetic and political commitments, film is assigned its place within the coming order of things. In a concluding scenario that expresses perfectly the unresolved tension between materialist and idealist thought in Balázs's entire work, the spirit of world history already waits in the future to welcome the classless society that personifies its inner being. "The spirit of film that I have tried to describe in this book is the spirit of progress. Despite everything! This spirit obliges film to become the art of the people, of the world's people. And if the latter will ever come into being, it will find film prepared to be an adequate means of expression for its spirit" (1930, 217).

Produced over a period of almost ten years, Balázs's early writings on film are not exceptionally innovative or profound. Similar explorations into the nature of gesture or into film's revolutionary potential can be found in the essays of Lukács or Hofmannsthal, who are more rigorous in their analysis and less nostalgic in their tone. However, Balázs's contribution to film theory stands out because of the ambitious attempt to unite political, aesthetic, and philosophical perspectives in one theoretical framework. While the associative style that characterizes much of his writings undermines any claims to a coherent theory, it leaves room for specific examples and the concreteness of filmic experience. Precisely these incommensurabilities distinguish *Der sichtbare Mensch* and *Der Geist des Films* as productive and engaging texts. Balázs resolved the seemingly insurmountable opposition between art and the masses by developing an aesthetic theory based on the capitalist origins of film and its inherently anticapitalist nature. He tried to link poetics and political praxis, thereby also identifying his own precarious position between creativity and activism. Balázs's propositions were often marred by romanticized depictions of class struggle, the continuous presence of phenomenological ideas, and his dependence on a formalist terminology. With radical politics and traditional aesthetics forging an unusual alliance, Balázs ultimately remained oblivious to the ruptures brought about by the historical avant-garde. However, that does not diminish his contribution to the theory of film and the formulation of its revolutionary potential.

# Chapter 11
## Siegfried Kracauer

**D**espite the similarities in their intellectual biographies and despite their commitment to a realist cinema, the differences between Balázs and Kracauer are considerable. However, they cannot be explained through traditional oppositions. The previous chapter has shown that Balázs's writings were extremely diversified and included poems, fables, novels, dramas, screenplays, and librettos. Notwithstanding such variety of form, his discussion always returned to the central theme of spiritual redemption. With the exception of a semi-autobiographical novel, *Ginster* (1928), and the posthumously published novel, *Georg* (1973), Kracauer was involved with criticism and philosophy. Yet by crossing the boundaries of traditional disciplines, Kracauer covered a surprising number of topics, including the history of music, sociology, literary criticism, and the philosophy of history. His idea of a "redemption of physical reality" through film, which first appeared in articles on the sound film, was predicated on complete immersion in the experience of modernity. Where Balázs's theory of film remained committed to the traditional view of art as sanctuary and counterdesign, Kracauer's materialist theory of cinema took the analysis of the ephemeral as a starting point from which modern mass culture was to be transformed into a culture for the masses.

Politically active throughout his life, Balázs thought of himself as the first Marxist film critic. Nevertheless, his formal analyses more or less validated the classical narrative cinema, including its anthropocentric perspective. Rejecting the artificial distinctions between form and content, and surface and depth, Kracauer initiated a reassessment of such subjects as distraction, visual pleasure, and mass entertainment. In contrast to Balázs, Kracauer shied away from direct political involvement, even though he was associated with the Frankfurt Institut für Sozialforschung and had many critical exchanges with Theodor W. Adorno, Max Horckheimer, and Walter Benjamin.[1] But it was he, and not Balázs, who made the dramatic changes in modern culture and society the point of departure for his thinking, striving not just toward a new theory of cinema but to an awareness of the state of theory under cinema.

From 1921 to 1933, Kracauer worked for the liberal *Frankfurter Zeitung,* contributing film and book reviews as well as short articles on a wide range of cultural phenomena, including sports events, art openings, photography, detective novels, jazz, tourism, café society, and modern architecture. It seems that his first contribution on film was an anonymous review of Buchowetzki's *Danton* in 1921 (Levin 1990, 231).[2] After 1926 Kracauer began to write regularly on film and became known as a critic with a precise understanding of the social function of the entertainment film. Reviewing the new film-theoretical books by Balázs, Harms, Bagier, Richter, Ehrenburg, and Fülöp-Miller made him acutely aware of the need for new critical concepts. In 1930 he replaced Benjamin von Brentano as head of the newspaper's cultural editorial office in Berlin.[3] Reminiscing about these years, Kracauer would later maintain, "I was the first in Germany to offer serious film criticism and analysis in the *Frankfurter Zeitung,* whose editorial member I was until March of 1933 — an assignment the boundaries of which I tried to expand toward the aesthetic as well as sociological side and which I continued for thirteen years. I was without doubt the most renowned film critic" (Levin 1990, 242 n.10). While the latter statement may be somewhat exaggerated — Ihering's reviews for the *Berliner Börsen-Courier* were considered exemplary by many contemporaries — Kracauer is certainly correct in underscoring the innovative nature of his approach.

The majority of film reviews in national newspapers and literary reviews continued to rely on aesthetic categories, no matter whether these were developed in agreement with or in opposition to the traditions of drama criticism. By contrast, Kracauer's critical method was based on what might be called the transgressive quality of cinema, to be understood here in the generic and conceptual sense; comparisons to the other arts were conspicuously absent from his writings. This balancing act between representation and critical analysis involved on the one hand a greater attention to the ideological function of mainstream cinema and on the other a fundamental reconfiguration of the discursive space defined by its products. Kracauer's reviews stand out through what Adorno once referred to as

a *"parti pris* for the insoluble" and an unresolved "conflict between experience and theory" (1984, 393, 395), qualities that precisely reflected the cinema's uncertain status as a cultural practice. Many leftist critics, including
Balázs, focused on the relationship between film and ideology, but they
usually developed their critical approach within an analysis of class society.
Criticizing bourgeois films from the perspective of the working class, they
formulated their standards of evaluation in the context of revolutionary
politics. By contrast, Kracauer's revolution was one of cinema. He conjured
up a cinema that expressed the needs of audiences as well as its own inherent materialism, and he chose a strategy that prefigured this utopian state in
critical discourse. Writing about film was not a means to an end, but an
integral part of the process.[4]

To describe Kracauer's method as sociological or sociopsychological
would only do justice to one side of his search for a new cultural theory.
Kracauer returned the debates to the original concern with cinema as a
public sphere, and affirmed its close ties with the world of public spectacle
and lived experience. The traditional aesthetic categories, however, were
not simply replaced by the empirical methods of modern sociology. His
*Soziologie als Wissenschaft* (1922, Sociology as a science) attests to an interest
in epistemological questions that reaches beyond scientific methodology,
and *Die Angestellten* (1924, The white-collar workers) shows the author's
awareness of his difficult position as participant observer and bourgeois
essayist. Instead of providing certainty, the categories of an established
discipline like sociology are mobilized to highlight the complexity of modernity. The dissolution of all boundaries that lies at the core of the modern
experience finds an equivalent in Kracauer's discursive style, namely, in the
reclaiming of experience for theory. Accordingly, the empirical framework
of "Die kleinen Ladenmädchen gehen ins Kino" (1927, The little shopgirls
go to the movies) and the phenomenological undercurrent in "Das Ornament der Masse" (1927, "The Mass Ornament," 1975) must be seen as two
sides of a critical project that thrives on such productive tensions.

Kracauer's film reviews are characterized by a deep affinity for the cinematic experience, which for him is of a social rather than metaphysical
nature, and a desire to capture its uniqueness through the means of critical
discourse. His intentions find expression in opening sentences such as "The
way Ufa envisions someone loved by the gods defies description. I will
nonetheless describe it" (1979, 444). Just this determination to describe
what escapes description laid the foundation for a critique of ideology that

moves by analogy and substitution, rather than in dialectical leaps. Illuminating the relationship between film and society, however, required a new approach to the topics discussed in the average review. Thus Kracauer discusses formal and technical characteristics in the context of the ideological constellations that produce them and, in turn, are produced by them. Actors are mentioned only insofar as their public persona spills over into their dramatic role, and vice versa, and the comments on performance always refer back to the importance of visual spectacle. Narratives are not reduced to questions of psychological motivation or probability, but measured against the way they make use of filmic possibilities. Last but not least, the spectators, who enter the discussion via the popular reception of a film, are raised to the level of their real needs, instead of being compared to that unattainable ideal, the public sphere.

Perhaps because he believed in the utopian quality of criticism, Kracauer convinces the most in the negative reviews. While Balázs had his best insights when writing about admired films and beloved actors, Kracauer became surprisingly inarticulate when called upon to identify the positive in the present — with the exception, of course, of slapstick comedies. Noteworthy German films, including classics like *Girls in Uniform,* inspired such noncommittal statements as "a decent, clean film," "a clean, skillfully arranged entertainment film," "a relatively pleasant surprise" or "a charming distraction." Whenever there was an occasion for polemics, Kracauer tended to be more direct and outspoken, as if the "good" cinema could only be grasped through the outlines of its negativity. Of Lang's *Die Frau im Mond,* he derisively asked: "When will they ever come down to earth in our country?" (1979, 414), thus using the film's cosmic setting as a metaphor for the aloofness of German producers in general. Other reviews offered maxims — "The more expensive the production, the cheaper the taste" (1979, 423); "The more sounds the sound film produces, the quieter its critic should be" (1979, 448) — that convey an unexpected sense of bitterness.

Bodily metaphors became one of Kracauer's favorite ways of expressing outrage and indignation. Their corporeality reflects the fetishizing of the body in the cinema's own quest for concreteness, but it also protests against the discourses of quality that hide direct personal involvement behind seemingly objective value categories. Accordingly, one film proved to him how "all known drugs are not simply passed by the spoonful, but mixed into a punch that will even bring down strong men" (1979, 511), another was counted among those films "that gradually poison the audience by providing them with the cheap pleasure of intoxication" (1979, 511), and a third prompted the remark that this "hypocritical and ostentatious stuff tastes rancid, like a rotten meal" (1979, 487). Sometimes his highly suggestive images reach the complexity of allegories and generate a stream of associations. For instance, Kracauer compares *Der blaue Engel* (1930, *The Blue Angel*) to a glove turned inside out: "That's how it's supposed to be: if the external conditions of our existence are to disappear from consciousness, then interiority must of course fill up the external world and develop into a splendid facade behind which the actual outside can disappear unnoticed. A glove turned inside out: the inside turns into the outside so that the latter becomes invisible" (1979, 420). The functioning of ideology is captured in a simple image — an object of everyday use — that makes visible the invisible and reveals its underlying mechanisms through an allegorical reading. The reversal of interiority and exteriority in this particular instance applies equally to the practice of criticism, for like the glove turned inside out, criticism must attend to the trivial in order to grasp the full meaning of things.

Making precisely this point, Kracauer once responded to the charge that "I take a trivial topic too seriously" with the assertion that "actually, real triviality withstands any pressure" (1979, 505). Such resilience, however, is not just the manifestation of some inherent density or opaqueness. Above all, the trivial shows, by analogy, the power of those institutions that distribute cheap mass entertainment as a substitute for, and not an expression of, the real. Once the reference points disappear against which triviality plays out its deceptive games, the possibilities for subversive readings become limited as well. Faced with a cinema under siege, the Kracauer of the early thirties thus resorted increasingly to unambiguous statements in which quality judgments again joined forces with sharp political analysis. Disillusioned, he wrote: "It isn't worth talking about most of the films. They are industrial productions, they have their audience or they don't, and that's that" (1979, 429). The difference between these two models of criticism — one concerned with future possibilities, the other with present limitations — makes Kracauer's reviews important points of negotiation in the formulation of a theory of cinema.

The predicament — that is, to fight for different films or for a different kind of film criticism — is most pronounced in relation to German films and the German film industry. Like most left-liberal critics, Kracauer spoke out repeatedly against direct and indirect film censorship and the overt and covert attempts by the big studios to influence reviewers. And like many others, he protested the politically motivated banning of *Battleship Potemkin, Whither Germany?* and *All Quiet on the Western Front.* However, the analysis of mainstream cinema and its ideological function remained his primary concern. From the perspective of popular culture, Kracauer rejected as ostentatious such well-known literary adaptations as *Die Weber* (1927, The weavers), based on the Hauptmann play, and Jutzi's *Berlin Alexanderplatz* (1931), based on Döblin's famous novel of the same title. Experimental films like Eggeling's *Diagonal-Symphonie* (1921, Diagonal symphony) or Ruttmann's *Berlin — Symphony of the Big City* were dismissed by him as mere arts and crafts. Their purely formal explorations, as Kracauer saw it, contributed to the fetishizing of the cinematic apparatus and aestheticized the equalizing force associated with modern technology. His opposition to the historical film, and the Fridericus series in particular, was relentless; these big-budget films showed him how people's longing for a sense of community and self-pride was reduced to mere sentimentality, and exploited for reactionary purposes. Other "typical" German genres like the operetta film confirmed Kracauer's worst fears about the calculation and cynicism with which old formulas were recycled, whereas entertaining detective films and unpretentious adventure stories often elicited favorable comments.

During the more than ten years that Kracauer wrote for the *Frankfurter Zeitung,* he concentrated on films that, unlike the so-called classics, represented mainstream tastes and values. By reviewing films "that are above the average, which, however, is below average" (1979, 474), he maintained a balance between originality and typicality that was necessary for his ideology-critical approach. As a result, questions of authorship played a secondary role. One of the few directors who received continually good reviews from Kracauer was Pabst, whose *Westfront 1918* (1930) and *Kameradschaft* (1931) he praised as outstanding examples of filmic realism. But whenever the cult of the film director justified exorbitant costs and pompous subjects, or came to be associated with a mythologizing of the present, Kracauer could be very sharp and belligerent; among the recipients of such attacks were Lang and Murnau.

In contrast to many German films, whose shallowness proved to Kracauer the shallowness of German culture as a whole, foreign films allowed him to articulate the pleasures of cinema and to outline aspects of a cinema yet to come. While many early American and French films were indeed outstanding, Kracauer's taste for foreign films must also be seen as the result of displacement. Like so many of his contemporaries, he overcame his ambivalence toward mass culture by reserving critical praise for films too different from his own cultural environment to require a confrontation with established traditions and ingrained prejudices. The "bad" cinema was identified with the domestic film industry, whereas the exoticism of foreign films provided the framework in which the "good" cinema could develop. To what degree these divisions were informed by a continuous disregard for the products of low culture is difficult to ascertain; undoubtedly Kracauer's enthusiasm for minor American films originated in the same attitude that made him reject German art films on principle.[5]

Within this configuration, Russian films came to represent a cinema that was revolutionary in form and content, whereas American films embodied the spirit of modernity. Thus Kracauer described the uniqueness of *Potemkin* in terms of an intellectual and visual revelation: "It [the film] has broken through the wall that those [other] films fail to penetrate. It aims at a problem that is real, it involves the truth that should govern everything. . . . The wall is pierced, a real content emerges" (1979, 73). In Kracauer's view, Eisenstein did not simply reverse the process of externalization described above as the main characteristic of the bourgeois film. Moving beyond the surface-depth opposition, he used montage to explore the formal qualities of surface and thus removed the veil of ideology from the representations of social reality. This distinction, between the provocation of superficiality in a discursive formation obsessed with profundity and the salvaging of truth by means of a medium that depends, quite literally, on "the wall" to project its images, is crucial for an understanding of Kracauer's concept of realism, particularly his dialectics of form and content. It also explains his growing disillusionment with Russian films. Soon after the Russian films had first been screened in Berlin, he accused Eisenstein's *Ten Days that Shook the World* (1928) of didacticism — "Instead of the images replacing the text, a text is being illustrated" (1974, 77) — and found signs of artistic and political stagnation in Pudovkin's *Storm over Asia* (1928). "The primitivism of its arguments has been surpassed by the events of the last years. It is high time that Russian film art kept up with reality" (1974, 83). The same reasons that occasioned these critical remarks made Kracauer praise Vertov's *Man with a Movie Camera* (1929) for the way it foregrounded the cinematic apparatus in a self-critical fashion.

American films, on the other hand, were treated as synonymous with modernity in its enlightening as well as disturbing aspects. The silent film comedy became Kracauer's preferred genre for reflecting on the convergence of the human body and the machine, and for pointing to the growing separation between individual and society. Time and again, he praised Charlie Chaplin, Buster Keaton, and Harold Lloyd for translating the experience of alienation into a physically founded humor that made visible its hidden mechanisms. By acting out the experience of lack — a lack of ego, as Kracauer expressed it — these comic actors held on to the promise of plenitude and defended it against the claims of reason and rationality. Especially Chaplin, who stood out because of his sharp social criticism and his sympathy for the oppressed, balanced these critical and pleasurable aspects of cinema with unsurpassed mastery. What Kracauer once wrote about Chaplin's idiosyncratic laughter — "that laughter which melts together madness and happiness in one flash of lighting" (1974, 179) — attests to an almost uncanny ability to embrace and express ambivalence. No wonder intellectuals made "the little tramp" their hero.

In the later twenties, and especially after the introduction of the sound film, it became increasingly clear for Kracauer that the American cinema often dealt with problems of identity in a very different way, namely, by cloaking them in the exaggerated emotions of the melodrama or the spectacle of props and effects in the historical film. In a scathing review of *Ben Hur* (1925), Kracauer used his earlier assessment of *Potemkin* to identify the false relationships that sustained this simulation of meaning. "The inadequacy of content creates an abyss between *Ben Hur* and the *Potemkin* film. Here emphasis is placed on reality, which finds expression in the aesthetic medium of film, there a small private affair is painted large against the backdrop of world historical events" (1974, 164–65). The kind of individualism that required the world to be a reflection of the self undermined the original project of cinema which, according to Kracauer, involved the rediscovery of the world of objects and man's place in its changing constellations. The coming of sound only exacerbated this situation since, as he argued repeatedly, the growing dependence on dialogue brought with it an onslaught of unmitigated sentimentality. That is why Kracauer dismissed the Lubitsch musicals *The Smiling Lieutenant* (1931) and *One Hour with You* (1932) for their total lack of substance, and that is why he branded Sternberg's *Morocco* (1930), *Shanghai Express* (1932), and *Blonde Venus* (1932) as manifestations of pure kitsch. As for the dream of a "good" cinema, the effect of realism that the slapstick comedies produced through their grotesque movements and absurd situations now gave way to the sound film's allegedly greater proximity to reality; only sometimes would there be films like King Vidor's *Hallelujah* (1929) and *The Champ* (1932) whose expressive realism continued the traditions of the silent film.

Such judgments might imply that Kracauer held on to the aesthetics of the silent film. The opposite is true; the range of positions in his early writings bears witness to the complexity of the problems at hand. To begin with, Kracauer repeatedly emphasized the difference between technical possibility and creative use. The sound film, he argued, was not a continuation of the silent film, just as sound was much more than a mere supplement. "Sound has its own time, its own space. Only after the successful fusion of the distinct aesthetic worlds of sound and image will the word in film take on form" (1979, 417). At the same time, the importance of continuity should not be underestimated. "The sound film can only find itself when it makes use of the possibilities of the silent film instead of simply pushing them aside" (1977, 438). As he elaborated in numerous reviews, one of the greatest dangers was to fetishize technological innovations that, more often than not, brought with them the wholesale rejection of existing conventions and a deep disregard for the filmic image as image. The new musicals and operetta films compelled Kracauer to remind readers of the obvious, namely, that film was a visual medium after all. "Actually, the sound film is as much film as it is sound, and only when the visual and the acoustic become equals can it find itself as a genre" (1977, 447).

While attentive to artistic as well as technical problems, Kracauer located the real problems of the sound film in the domain of ideology. The addition of sound, he argued, put an end to the indeterminacy of meaning that protected the silent film from being instrumentalized in the ideological struggles carried out through and in language. "While the silent film was able to move beyond conceptual fixations unhindered, the sound film must make use of language. Thus it is pulled into the crisis that today affects all spoken expressions, whether in the theater or in literature" (1977, 455). While the characterization of the silent cinema as a realm of freedom suggests a romantic view of the visual as unmediated, Kracauer was careful to prevent such associations. Thus he reversed the cause-effect relationship that located the international appeal of silent film in the universality of the image, and focused instead on the economic basis, the source of a very different internationalism. Against the essentialist claims of many contemporaries, conservatives as well as leftists, Kracauer asserted that "the internationalism of the silent film did not arise automatically from the universal accessibility of the images, but was the result of a methodologically executed distribution of images. . . . The silent film, in a way, did not originate in the internationalism of visual impressions; it moved toward it" (1977, 469). That is how the distribution of images, given its dependence on the laws of the market, brought into focus the relationship between film and ideology.

It was on the basis of such observations that Kracauer introduced realism as a notion reaching beyond genres and technologies. The insight that filmic reality never was, and never would be, identical with lived experience enabled him to avoid the pitfalls both of technopositivism, according to which the total simulation of reality is indeed possible, and of cultural pessimism, where technical innovation invariably means the end of film poetics and the triumph of mere imitation. Distinguishing between narrative time and experienced time — the reference here is to Bergson's concept of *durée,* or experienced duration — Kracauer confirmed film's affinity with narrative time and concluded: "Man will only master technology if he preserves the life that only appears in the memory, and not in the camera lens" (1977, 4II). This statement defined, for all times, the boundary separating lived experience and filmic reality, a boundary that cut through Kracauer's assessment of filmic styles and genres as well as through questions of spectatorship. Their precarious relationship was determined by his understanding of reality and his theory of filmic realism, both of which stood at the center of the reflections on the sound film. Emphasizing its productive side, Kracauer argued that "the possibilities of the sound film lie much more in representing and forming a previously unrecorded reality — that reality which has not been spoken on the stage until now" (1977, 4II). With regard to the artistic contribution of sound film, that meant: "It would be idle playing around simply to repeat an experience that is already aesthetically mediated; the sound image film will only reach its true meaning when it opens up a previously unknown existence, the sounds and noises around us which never before communicated with the visual impressions and always eluded the senses. In parentheses: "The sound image film is thus far the last link in a series of great inventions moving toward the complete recording of human reality with blind certainty and as if guided by a secret will. In principle, it could afford the possibility of wresting away life in all its totality from transitoriness and imparting it to the eternity of images" (1977, 4II).

This emphasis on reality as a construction, and the recognition of the deep human need to encounter the real, played a central role in Kracauer's comments on the social function of cinema.[6] Arguing from a sociopsychological perspective, he focused on the process by which the audience's desire and the formal conventions of film came together to produce an almost uncanny reality effect. Questions of authenticity and productivity were all-important in the evaluation of its constructive and destructive aspects. Based on his sociological studies, Kracauer maintained that the need for a social identity, no matter how contrived, was greater in Germany than in any other country, and especially urgent among the group most closely associated with social change, the *Angestellten,* or white-collar workers. Their values and ideas were the result of what many critics described as false consciousness. White-collar workers continued to believe in individuality, freedom, and progress, even as these notions ceased to have any relevance for their lives. In *Die Angestellten,* a study originally conceived as a newspaper series on the loves and lives of young office workers, Kracauer defined the dilemma of this social group with great accuracy. "Most white-collar workers distinguish themselves from the worker's proletariat in that they are intellectually homeless. At the present, they are unable to join the comrades, while the house of bourgeois concepts and feelings, which they did occupy, has collapsed, losing its foundations as a result of economic development. At the present, they live without a theory to turn to, and without a place to find answers" (1971, 23).

The dilemma of the white-collar workers who made the cinema their shelter for the homeless was indicative of a more fundamental problem. As the gap between social identity and economic position widened, film audiences took refuge in strategies of imitation and simulation. "While actors elsewhere personify types who exist in the flesh, many people in Germany model themselves on actors. The living space that we inhabit is fake, the air is impregnated with ideologies and the ground below our feet is about to give" (1979, 510). Kracauer observed a similar phenomenon in the way documentary material was presented in the newsreels. Challenging their claims to truth, he pointed to the many omissions. "But the world in these newsreels is no longer the world as such, but that which is left of it when all important events are eliminated" (1974, 11). Elsewhere he also argued, very much under the influence of Russian montage theories, that the newsreel of the future "would fill with substance only when its construction is radically altered. The change in sequence is almost more important than the filming of meaningful events" (1974, 15).

On the basis of a thus defined relationship between realism and ideology, Kracauer developed an understanding for the "false" needs of audiences. Discussing the popular *Fridericus* films, he exclaimed: "How much must the people lack security that they believe to have discovered it in such a glossy war piece! For the enthusiasm is not just artificially produced; rather, the real desire searches for an object to which it can hold on. . . . The masses are misguided, and yet they want to be guided in the right direction. If we don't succeed in giving them good, decent goals the explosion of their longings will be frightful" (1979, 462). Kracauer's analysis of the mechanisms of desire conveyed a sense of urgency that would soon dominate his writings. With his growing attention to the reality of simulation also came the recognition that the process of commercialization had progressed beyond all reasonable limits. "The average films in our country and probably in the entire world," Kracauer stated with bitterness, "have their commodity character so clearly imprinted on them that they hardly fulfill other, more practical functions" (1979, 463).

Instead of calling for educational measures, Kracauer now evoked myth to describe the double movement of demystification and remystification that allowed film to maintain its double status as art and commodity. "A revival of myth, in other words? On the contrary, its irrevocable destruction and, moreover, film's embarrassing flight from itself" (1979, 397). Presenting a reading of myth that in some ways resembles Adorno's Enlightenment critique (Adorno and Horckheimer 1972), he spoke of a tendency (present in the films of Lang) to "relinquish myth in order to mythologize the present" (1979, 499). Nonetheless, the oscillation between commodification and redemption inspired an image of decline that showed the utter depravity of mainstream cinema, but also offered hope about its eventual destruction from within. "First the foundations of our our social existence are flooded with a Rhine stream of ecstasy and then they are once again drained out of sheer negligence. One piles up drunks and other ruins in front of reality to render it invisible and afterward shows its bare skeleton. To spread ideologies and, in the same breath, reveal their economic basis — that means nothing but to expose these very conditions" (1979, 429).

\* \* \*

While the first part of this chapter has tried to situate Kracauer's work in a historical context and to establish his film reviews for the *Frankfurter Zeitung* as the foundation of his theory of cinema, the second part will take a different approach. Based on his writings on a variety of cultural phenomena, it will map the movements of his thought in relation to specific issues such as class and gender and discuss his notion of distraction in relationship to theories of modernity and mass culture. Reflecting this diversity, Kracauer's critical style always involves a double movement. He foregrounds the fragmentation of modern life by rejecting conventional approaches that strive toward unity and, at the same time, sets up unexpected analogies between the ephemeral and the profound that simulate the unifying power of mass culture. Within these configurations, his self-reflexive use of language prepares the ground for a critical simulation of modernity. Mainstream cinema, vacillating between the critique of high culture and the affirmation of dominant ideology, establishes the parameters in which Kracauer's approximation of theory and experience takes place. The products of the entertainment industry become main protagonists in his investigation of modernity because their "essence" lies so close to the surface. The titles of essays like "Cult of Distraction" and "The Mass Ornament" suggest to what degree the old ways of thinking have been abandoned for new and often surprising confluences and intersections. Even when the cinema is not explicitly mentioned, it provides the backdrop against which concepts such as experience, visual pleasure, and distraction are theorized with the tools most appropriate to their fleeting nature. Together with the early film reviews, these essays on modern culture outline a theory of cinema that receives its aesthetic and social categories from the experience of modernity.[7]

The cinema, in Kracauer's view, was exceptionally qualified to perform this metadiscursive function. By confirming the individual at the center of the narrative, it provided a link between the cult of bourgeois individualism and the experience of social disintegration. Through the equation of animate and inanimate worlds, it reinstated objects in all their power. Depending almost entirely on the visual as a channel of communication, the cinema explored new forms of representation while at the same time giving inspiration to theater and literature. Based on the unstable relationships associated with looking, it validated the desire for pleasurable surrender and loss of control, yet also exercised the ability — of great relevance in the postindustrial workplace — to move back and forth between passivity and activity, concentration and distraction. Uniting people in the shared experience of a film screening, it provided a communal experience and functioned as a substitute for actual exchanges. With its diverse offerings, the cinema compensated for monotonous everyday life and, at the same time, used the appearance of fullness to perpetuate this situation of need. While expanding the experience of the self and inviting multiple identifications, it functioned as a tool of social control and psychological manipulation. In short, the cinema represented modernity in its most oppressive and most liberating aspects. As the boundaries between the traditional disciplines of knowledge and interpretation dissolved in its presence, Kracauer used the cinema to develop a heuristic method that captured these movements through what might be called mimetic thinking.

This willingness to engage the phenomena of modern mass culture is most evident in Kracauer's reliance on critical categories that are themselves formed under the new conditions of production and consumption. The notions of *surface* (*Oberfläche*) and *distraction* (*Zerstreuung*) stand out in his reconceptualization because of their extremely visual quality as well as their wide and diversified field of connotations. *Surface* refers equally to the appearance of things and the site of truth, that is, the point where the hierarchies of inside and outside are reversed and where the fleeting phenomena acquire specific traits, whether as visual ornament, narrative pattern, or rhetorical schema. Above all, *surface* evokes the things in *statu nascendi,* that is, the moment of emergence and least ossification; it is also the state in which ideological determinations are most evident. "Distraction," on the other hand, introduces its sociopsychological equivalent, that is, the attitude or disposition through which these perceptions and experiences are processed. By replacing immersion with distraction as the dominant mode of cultural appreciation, Kracauer sets up a critical framework that mirrors the conditions of culture consumption in mass society and that accounts for, among other things, its remarkable ability to disperse and disseminate without losing momentum.[8]

The implications of this process are first spelled out in Kracauer's 1927 essay "The Mass Ornament." Taking as his point of departure the human ornaments formed by the Tiller-Girls, a popular twenties dancing troupe, Kracauer uses choreography to arrive at a process-oriented definition of his method. He writes: "An analysis of the simple surface manifestations of an epoch can contribute more to determining its place in the historical process than judgments of the epoch about itself" (1975, 67). From the legs of the Tiller-Girls, a surface phenomenon, to the hands on the assembly line, the same aesthetic principle of serialization reigns. Instead of searching for a hidden structure that connects seemingly unrelated phenomena, Kracauer examines their interrelatedness on the level of appearances, thus, in a way, mirroring the shift from hierarchical to spatial relations that makes each new cultural trend or fashion a reenactment, rather than a mere product, of the underlying principle.[9] This critical strategy attests to a deep affinity for the trivial, fragmentary, and transitory — for the rubble of history, in other words — and a strong belief in the importance of salvaging the scraps of the historical process for a radical transformation of society. Not surprisingly, Benjamin once characterized Kracauer as a "rag-and-bone man, early — at the dawn of the revolution" (1980, 3:225).

With his interest in distraction, Kracauer was not alone. First mentioned as a psychological disposition by the literary critics of the prewar years, and often described with horror and concern, distraction seemed to capture best the spirit of what has often been romanticized as the "golden twenties." With changing meanings, *distraction* expressed bourgeois disdain for the new forms of mass entertainment as well as the continual appeal of pleasures that required no special knowledge or particular effort. Other critics before him had pointed to its subversive qualities, but Kracauer was one of the first to analyze the ambiguity of distraction as a function of its cultural significance. Rather than confirming the term's traditionally negative connotation, he used it to challenge the overly sharp distinctions between high and low culture. This also meant rejecting the belief that art — or all serious endeavors, for that matter — was, and always would be, irreconcilable with more superficial pleasures and less permanent involvements. However, distraction not only represented a valid alternative to the paradigm of high culture; its practices also demanded a redefinition of mass culture based on the ideological nature of such distinctions.

The fascination with the ephemeral may be traced back to the Dadaists and Surrealists and to the sociological writings of Simmel, but the essays of Kracauer — and Benjamin belongs to the same critical configuration — raised it to the level of an epistemological principle and discursive strategy. For Kracauer, adherence to the old rules of interpretation amounted to an effacement of the modern condition. Similarly, the insistence on linear relations obscured in his view the central role of analogies in translating the experience of modernity into critical terms. Only the study of ephemeral phenomena, with their ever-changing appearance and their secret mechanisms, could shed light on the deceptive reversals of cause and effect, interior and exterior, reality and simulation. Earlier approaches to mass culture, Kracauer argued, still presupposed a stable, hierarchical relationship between these categories; they were based on the belief that the surface existed to conceal and protect an inner truth. With the advent of modernity, such cherished notions as *essence* and *substance* disappeared into the marginal, the superficial, and the vernacular, whereas objects and practices usually considered unworthy of close scrutiny emerged as culmination points for the new critical paradigm. Reflecting on the resultant uncertainties, Kracauer once described his excursions into the spaces of modernity as more adventurous than African jungle expeditions. Made strange by the explorer's gaze, the products of consumer culture came to divulge their most threatening Otherness and radical challenge. By analyzing fashion, revues, sports events, interior design, and film, and by focusing on the aesthetic preferences of white-collar workers, Kracauer filled in the lacunae of a yet-unwritten theory of modernity and revealed its fragmented, divergent nature in the process.

The cinema played a key role in these investigations, for it already practiced, through the means of filmic representation, what Kracauer set out to reproduce in critical discourse. Because of its industrial mode of production, which led to growing standardization and serialization, the cinema provided a place within society where the experience of alienation could be represented under the distancing, and more pleasurable, conditions of visual pleasure. Furthermore, because of its inherent affinity to the real, the cinema promised redemption, even if only in the realm of the imagination. Whether or not this promise could be translated into actual social change depended on audiences, filmmakers, and, last but not least, the film critics.

If Kracauer's contribution to an appreciative, though critical, understanding of modern culture needs to be located in a grid of political and intellectual affiliations, it is Walter Benjamin who seems closest to him, and not just because of their shared preference for essayistic writing. Like Kracauer, Benjamin examined modernity in light of the intricate relations between cinema, visual pleasure, and modern life-styles. Both critics first studied its characteristics in reflections on the big city, using it as source material, metaphor, and heuristic device. Significantly, it was Paris, the capital of the nineteenth century, that inspired the topographic approach of Kracauer's *Orpheus in Paris: Offenbach and the Paris of His Times* (1937) and Benjamin's Arcade Project as presented in "Paris — Capital of the Nineteenth Century" and "Some Motifs on Baudelaire."

Outlining what has been called an archaeology of modernity, both critics demonstrate how nineteenth-century Paris prepared the ground for the emergence of cinema. First signs of a distinctly filmic consciousness can be found in the figure of the flaneur, a precursor of the more distressed film fan, and his propensity for flirtatiousness, gossiping, and window shopping. Benjamin's Paris of the shopping arcades, boulevard society, iron constructions, and world exhibitions in a way provides the backdrop for Kracauer's sociological-musical reconstruction of Offenbach's biography, which examines the desperate need for distraction that made his musical parodies of bourgeois existence such an enormous success with Parisian audiences. Tracing the operetta's rise and decline, the study's narrative format duplicates the historical conditions constitutive of bourgeois society — and, indirectly, of modernity. A similar dynamic sustains Kracauer's essays on famous European cities, Berlin streets and landmarks, and places of public assembly like the department store, the hotel lobby, and the working-class pub. As in the later writings of Benjamin, the spatial order of the modern metropolis is evoked as the mold for, and the expression of, more elusive social processes, and the structuring principles of superimposition, simultaneity, and discontinuity are employed as the privileged means of making palpable the experience of modernity. The following description of a white-collar worker brings together its social, cultural, and psychological aspects in the experience of boredom. "In the evenings one strolls through the streets, filled with a frustration from which no fullness can sprout. Over there, flickering words pass along the roofs and immediately one is projected from one's own emptiness into this exotic advertisement. The body grows roots in the asphalt, and the mind, which is no longer ours, escapes with these enlightening light slogans, endlessly out of the night into the night" (1977, 322). At this point, the modern flaneur may enter a cinema.[10]

The method of approaching a subject from its surface structures bears witness to Kracauer's professional training as an architect. The systematic study of architectural forms and structures — his dissertation dealt with the art of wrought iron — provided him with a critical model for reformulating the relationship of surface and depth in the context of modern mass culture. Thus on the one side in his topography of cinema, one finds spectacular movie palaces like the Ufa-Palast am Zoo, the Capitol, or the Marmorhaus catering to the entertainment needs of the middle class. In "The Cult of Distraction: On Berlin's Movie Palaces," Kracauer uses details such as interior design, programming, and the rituals of attendance to explore the transgressive forces within distraction. Guided by the observation that "in the streets of Berlin, one is frequently struck by the insight that one day all of this will explode into pieces" (1977, 315), he turns the surface character of things into a kind of secret code that, once deciphered, reveals their hidden meaning.[11]

The study of the ephemeral draws attention to the decline of high culture, at least in regard to its function as a dominant model, and its substitution by an industrialized mass culture based on "the *homogeneous cosmopolitan audience* that, from the bank director to the sales assistant, from the diva to the typist, is of *one* mind" (1977, 313). Welcoming this development, Kracauer appeals to audiences to take seriously their need for distraction, and to seize their only chance for understanding the world in which they live. By reproducing the workday's empty tension in the prevalent forms of mass entertainment, they are able to maintain the honesty of their existence.

It is just this vacillation between a compliance with and a critique of mass culture that shows distraction at its most productive — and its most political. Even Kracauer's call for a cinema outside of traditional genre categories includes the utilizing of its pleasures for political ends. "But the movie theaters have more urgent tasks than to take care of the artsy-craftsy. They will only be able to fulfill their vocation — an aesthetic one only when attuned to its social vocation — when they stop flirting with the theater, anxiously trying to restore a bygone culture. In fact, they need to free their products from all impairing factors and radically aim at a form of distraction that unmasks the disintegration instead of masking it. This could be done in Berlin, home of the masses who are only so easily intoxicated because they are so close to the truth" (1977, 317). According to this scenario, the uniformity of mass society can be turned into a means of democratization, just as the formulas of dominant cinema can give rise to alternative readings. The possibility of disrupting the vicious circle of commoditization, however, depends on the spectator's willingness to embrace fully the products of modernity, and to see their effects as part of a dialectical process that is propelled forward by the longing for a better world.

Kracauer makes clear that the theorizing of distraction is closely linked to issues of gender and class. Thus on the other side in his spatial reconstruction of mass culture, second-run cinemas like the one in the Münz-strasse provide shelter to people who gather in "forced boredom," either because they are homeless or unemployed. Kracauer's description of these disenfranchised participants of cinema culture and his atmospheric account of the screening — the stale air, the bad print, the false laughter — make palpable the problematic association of cinema and society; it is captured in the image of "the unemployed who stand outside of the work process and thus gradually lose their power of discernment" (1987b, 70).

In addition to these two paradigmatic sites of consumption that bring to the fore the social divisions within Weimar society, Kracauer introduces yet another setting that stands equally removed from the splendor of the picture palace and the squalor of the second-run house, and yet is inextricably tied up with their pleasures as the original site of production. In "Kaliko-Welt" (1926, Calico world), his description of the Ufa lot at Neubabelsberg invites an exploration of the division of labor, and of forms, that gives rise to the filmic reality. (Prümm 1992, 122–30).[12] The opening image of a haunted forest is suggestive. "In the middle of the Grunewald lies an enclosed area that one is only allowed to enter after several tests. It is a desert in the oasis. The natural phenomena outside . . . have lost their rights inside its boundaries. To be sure, the world returns again — in fact, the whole macrocosm seems assembled in this modern-day Noah's Ark — but the things that congregate do not belong to reality. They are copies and distortions torn away from the flow of time and mixed together" (1977, 271). As the intruder moves around freely among the ruins of past and present productions, admires the different historical periods and visual styles, and notices the fragments and façades that simulate a wholeness that never was, references to magic and exoticism give way to the more probing gestures of the archaeologist. The identification of different layers and precious finds enables Kracauer to reconstruct the process of production; here the comparison to a laboratory serves to foreground its synthetic if not alchemical character. With unification as the final goal, he concludes that "instead of leaving the world in its crumbled state, one returns it into the world. After having been removed from their context, the things are reinserted into it, the traces of their isolation erased, their grimaces smoothed out. From the silly graves, they awake to an appearance of life" (1977, 278).

However, Kracauer is quick to point out that distraction cannot be considered subversive as such; its qualities must be determined within the historical process. The more Weimar cinema moved away from its original intentions, the more Kracauer focused on its escapist tendencies and, closely related, the numbing effect of distraction. Invoking Wagner, the master of spectacle, he writes: "Out of the cinema crawled a glittering, revue-type creature — the *Gesamtkunstwerk* of effects" (1977, 312) and produced a totality of effects in which cultural innovation gave way to sensory overstimulation. As the cinema developed bourgeois ambitions, it forfeited the chance for a radical cultural transformation. Instead the new aesthetics gave rise to an almost fetishistic attention to theater architecture and design. The logic of presentation included celebratory newspaper reviews, splendid opening nights, and the idolization of famous stars.

Responding to the changes, Kracauer reads architectural spaces as social spaces into which specific modes of pleasure are inscribed; the concerted efforts by film exhibitors to redesign the cinema and, implicitly, its audience only confirm his assumptions. The movie palaces promise distraction but, by imitating the theater, undermine its critical potential. While the storefront cinemas are driven out to suburban neighborhoods with a predominantly working-class audience, the new cinemas seduce the audience with all their modern trappings, transforming themselves into a total spectacle, and attracting as much attention as the films themselves. Their appeal, to paraphrase Kracauer, is based on the exploitation of the cultivated splendor of surfaces. Good taste reigns, he notes; the sacred reverberates and transfigures the production's unified look. Through changes in programming practices, the screening becomes part of a sequence of effects, including light shows, orchestra music, and the cameo appearance of artistes and impresarios. Framed by an attractive setting and part of an ongoing program, film no longer poses a threat to bourgeois society. It appears domesticated; as a result, all hopes for a democratic mass culture perish. Even distraction falls prey to the respectful awe that has always been part of the traditional arts. From the glass of champagne and the symphonic sound of real violins to the glamorous evening gowns and the appearance of celebrities, the "gentrified" cinema simulates a fictitious wholeness against the confusion and isolation that rules outside.[13]

The definition of distraction along the lines of gender played a crucial role in the distinction between its critical and escapist functions. Most of the negative characteristics, including the specter of regression, pointed toward women as a new audience, as individuals with a specific psychological disposition, and as a convenient projection screen for the cinema's scenarios of seduction and surrender. "Girls and Crisis," this is how Kracauer apostrophized the link between women and modernity in a reflection on the popularity of girls' dancing troupes and on girlishness as the inevitable fate of modern femininity. The contribution of women to the trivialization of cinema inspired his 1927 newspaper series on contemporary film production, "The Little Shopgirls Go to the Movies." Introduced by a caption that vaguely recalls a genre (e.g., "Nation in Arms" evokes the war film, "Modern Harun al Rashid" a sentimental love story), each of the eight parts summarizes a "typical" film plot and then describes the "typical" reaction by female spectators. Using as a point of departure the observation that films always reflect society, Kracauer shows the contradictions within the narratives and, supported by specific rhetorical devices like irony and exaggeration, draws attention to their ideological function.

But instead of making the notion of gender part of the strategy, his conclusions — in the style of "if the little shopgirls are later in the evening approached by an unknown gentleman, they probably think he is one of the famous millionaires [from the film]" (1977, 291) — merely confirm the discrimination of those characterized elsewhere as the vanguard of bad taste and the personification of false consciousness. Through the presence of women, the relationship between reality and simulation is thus reversed, and distraction turns into mere daydreaming. "Film story and reality usually correspond to each other because typists model themselves after the examples from the screen; perhaps the most hypocritical examples are stolen from life" (1977, 280). Because they are lacking both in critical skills and emotional detachment, Kracauer argues, women succumb to this false reality without being able to use the trivialities as a means of critical analysis.[14]

As a bourgeois male intellectual who was threatened by the very subject of his studies, Kracauer obviously failed to resolve the contradiction between distraction as a subversive act and the disqualification of women as passive cultural consumers. In its function as a theoretical construct, distraction was saved for the realm of theory and its utopian promises, whereas the notion's inconsistencies were equated with the deficiencies of women, and not of theory. Speaking of distraction and associating its negative aspects with femininity therefore amounts to nothing less than an operation of displacement (Schlüpmann 1982, 50). Kracauer ignored the sensual, regressive aspects that had always been a constitutive element of distraction and that now returned to the surface in the problem of female spectatorship. It might be argued that women only seemed more "stupid" because they were not yet fully integrated into the industrial work force. What appeared as a deficiency actually pointed to an emotionality that, notwithstanding its distorted nature, still resisted co-optation. The shopgirls' reaction to a film on love and revolution, then, expressed but a true feeling. "Love is stronger than money, when money is used to buy sympathies. The little shopgirls were scared. Now they sigh with relief" (1977, 294). Such was the emotionality of women, and such was the power of cinema. Their reactions upheld the unfulfilled promise of a society based on human relations. In so doing, the little shopgirls acted out what Kracauer only dared to admit through others. As Adorno once noted: "He himself has something of the naive visual pleasure of the moviegoer; even in the little shopgirls who amuse him he encounters a piece of his own reaction" (1984, 397).

These changes in Kracauer's attitude toward film and mass culture, especially during the last years of the Weimar republic, were politically motivated and should be evaluated accordingly. The original project of reading popular culture against the grain—from surface to depth, from superficiality to meaning—had to be revised once the political conditions made such critical distinctions difficult to maintain. Instead of analyzing the various manifestations of mass culture, Kracauer focused all of his attention on the ideological function of film, and the necessary politicization of film criticism in particular. The insistence on clear categories of evaluation also affected aesthetic questions and led to a further reevaluation of distraction. Reviewing a musical comedy in 1931, Kracauer complained about the unnecessary expenditure of talent and money. "Such a procedure, absurd already in itself, virtually contradicts the true nature of distraction. It does not want to be treated carefully, like a momentous, thematic proposition. On the contrary, it wants to express its ephemeral qualities through formal characteristics as well," he argued, only to translate this imbalance into ideological terms: "It is self-evident that there is a connection between the strained expression with which entertainment is produced and the larger context. Seriousness is being displaced, as it were. It is diverted from those subjects that deserve its attention and directed onto topics devoted entirely to recreation" (1979, 501, 502). Consequently, Kracauer began to use the traditional standards of evaluation as a form of resistance that not only revealed the emptiness at the center of all this commotion, but also pointed to its ideological function as a smokescreen and a chimera. The new/old distinctions between high and low culture served to highlight the absence of any distinctions in a world of total commoditization. "Over are the times of jazz, the girlie show, the high life in hotel lobbies: all that is over. The entire culture of distraction, systematically created by the film industry, was, after all, only possible as long as the masses could be intoxicated. In the meantime, they have been awakened from their half-sleep by the incessant noise; this does not mean that they have seen the light" (1979, 518).

Now the streamlined, superficial products of the entertainment industry appeared as a dangerous form of indoctrination. These films, Kracauer noted, fulfilled the same ideological function as the propaganda films, which, at least, did not try to conceal their true motives. The combination of total styling and lack of substance turned out to be an ideal vehicle for hidden political messages. Hence Kracauer's critical self-quotation: "'Distraction is pleasant and possibly useful . . . but if it turns into a leitmotif and prevents all true learning, its good intentions become useless. By cheering up the somber soul, it only contributes to growing indoctrination and the relaxation, provided to the audience, leads simultaneously to their blindness.' . . . In fact, this kind of distraction has the same effect as the above-mentioned tendencious film genre" (1979, 531). Kracauer rejected the false distinction between entertainment and propaganda, but he reconceptualized their differences by coming down on the side of distraction. This departure from earlier formulations, however, suggests less a theoretical inconsistency than the need to adjust the practice of criticism to the changing political situation. In a way, distraction always meant both the critique of bourgeois culture as elitist and outdated, and the critique of mainstream cinema as superficial and stultifying. Alternately claimed for the discourses of mass culture and radical politics, the notion of distraction allowed Kracauer to recognize the subversive potential of cinema and to insist on the emotional truth behind its false emotions.

The productive tensions that constitute Kracauer's early writings on cinema and mass culture may be conceptualized in one of his most suggestive images, that of boredom and, closely related, expectancy. In an important essay on the virtues of boredom, Kracauer argued for its usefulness as a method of gaining self-confidence and fighting the pervasive sense of crisis. While he neglected the fact that boredom was a luxury available only to those who could afford it, he was right to emphasize its distance from the breathless search for new stimuli. Behind the individualist attitude and the elitist underpinnings stood the legitimate desire for a world of substance and relevance. Accusing the cinema of inducing social amnesia and of reducing human existence to a continuous flow of shallow sensations, Kracauer describes how "one forgets oneself in staring" and how "the dark hole revives itself with the shadow of a life that belongs to nobody and consumes everybody" (1977, 322). Boredom remains "the only activity that may be called proper, because it still guarantees the possession of an existence. Without boredom, one would probably not even exist, or only exist as another object of boredom . . . flashing over rooftops or running as a filmstrip" (1977, 324). The motif of boredom returns in a different essay in the figure of a lower-class woman, but with radically different connotations. There, in a scene near the Münzstrasse cinema, boredom comes to mean unconditional surrender to the offerings of mass culture. In combination with a kind of waiting that is without aim and purpose, the previously idealized state of mind reveals an undeniable element of despair: "A woman in an imitation fur stands in front of the movie theater and chews. She chews silently, neither looks to the right or the left and waits. She is middle-aged, a common woman, who has nothing to do and therefore simply stops somewhere on the sidewalk. If nobody comes and takes her into the darkened movie theater, she will just stay there and continue chewing" (1987b, 71).

These two alternatives, the pleasures of bourgeois ennui and the hopelessness of working-class misery, are once again transformed in a more encouraging reflection on waiting. Against the *horror vacui* that contaminates everything with a ubiquitous relativism, Kracauer places his last hopes in those who are still waiting. "What remains is perhaps only the attitude of *waiting*. He who decides to wait neither closes himself off from the possibilities of faith like the stubborn disciple of total emptiness, nor does he force this faith like the soul searchers who have lost all restraints in their longing. He waits and his waiting is a *tentative openness*, but in a way that is hard to explain" (1977, 116). This quote captures the complicated movement described by Kracauer's writings.

# Chapter 12

## Rudolf Arnheim

t seems appropriate that the last chapter be an assessment of Rudolf Arnheim's contribution to Weimar film criticism and theory. Not only is Arnheim the third in a group of critics who have become synonymous with the concerns of an entire period, his early writings also bear witness to a particular shift in the discourses on film, this time from film as mass entertainment to film as art. Balázs and Kracauer continued to explore the ideological nature of film in their later work, though not always without problems. By contrast, Arnheim focused increasingly on the relationship between art and perception and dismissed content-related questions as secondary. His unyielding commitment to the silent film and his growing interest in the psychology of art, however, cannot be separated from the conditions under which they first developed. Just as Gestalt psychology — the major influence on his thinking — was a reaction to the emergence of other human sciences (e.g., psychoanalysis, behaviorism), so were his aesthetic theories inextricably tied to the silent films that inspired them. Arnheim's early writings on film will therefore be examined for the way they reenacted, and resolved, the tension between aesthetic, psychological, and social categories of evaluation. To counter the widespread perception of Arnheim as a formalist, the emphasis will be on his contribution to the cultural and political debates of the late twenties.

This historical approach places his work among various attempts at the end of the Weimar years to protect film from the infiltration by reactionary politics and rampant commercialism. Earlier chapters have shown how the rise of National Socialism coincided with a renewed interest in film as an instrument of German nationalism and a reevaluation of traditional notions of art in the context of national film culture. Confronted with such developments, Weimar critics either turned to political activism, introduced a stronger political perspective into film criticism, or sought refuge in formalism and microanalysis. Arnheim's preference for the silent film was not just an aesthetic choice, but also an attempt to hold on to its possibilities, including the promise of individual and collective expression. While Haus Richter followed the avant-garde aesthetics of his *Filmgegner von heute — Filmfreunde von morgen* (Film enemies of today, film friends of tomorrow) with the polemics of *Der Kampf um den Film* (The struggle for the film), Arnheim chose the opposite direction — he tried to make a critical invention on the basis of the universally valid laws of human perception.[1]

Arnheim wrote his first reviews for the satirical journal *Das Stachelschwein* while still studying psychology, philosophy, and art history at the University of Berlin. He contributed film reviews and eyewitness reports from the cinema to *Das Stachelschwein* and *Die Weltbühne* until he was appointed cultural editor of *Die Weltbühne* in 1928, just having completed a psychological dissertation under one of the founders of Gestalt psychology, Wolfgang Köhler. The association with the well-known left-liberal journal, which resulted in more than eighty reviews and articles, was abruptly ended in 1933 when the *Die Weltbühne* ceased publication and Arnheim was forced to leave the country. He later wrote about these years: "It was indeed the film that, after the dissertation at the University of Berlin, made me pursue journalism until the end of my German years. All my striving was concerned with art theory and especially the visual arts as an experimental field for the principles of sensory perception" (1977, 10).

This statement sets up an opposition between film and art that, in their respective affiliations with journalism and academic scholarship, reveals more of Arnheim's later approach to film than of his actual Weimar activities. Even though he confesses a preference (as a reader) for the high-spirited *Weltbühne* articles, Arnheim now, forty years later, associates film with low culture. Emphasizing the distance between the young critic and the mature professor, he points to the external circumstances that produced these differences. "What strikes me especially in the effusive comments of the young film critic is how closely and completely he was connected to all expressions of then-contemporary daily life, the art world, politics, the protagonists and anecdotes of the big city" (1977, 11).[2]

Such influences indeed left a mark in the ironic if not satirical tone of many of his early articles and reviews. They show their author as a modern city-dweller who uses his perceptions at a gala premiere, a screening of one of the new sound films, and, of all places, a public swimming pool to reflect on popular tastes and the quality of mainstream films. To what degree New Objectivity influenced his writing style can be seen in the short sentences and sloganlike phrases, the paratactic sentence structure, the effective play with oppositions, the matter-of-fact description of actors and actresses, the laconic summary of film plots, and the seemingly disengaged perspective of the reviewer-turned-reporter. While Arnheim wrote regularly about Russian films and more experimental genres like the cross-section film, his true passion lay with what he referred to as *Konfektionsfilm* (literally: ready-to-wear film) — films that admitted to their use of prefabricated forms and standardized contents without shame. Adventure and detective films were his favorites; the enthusiasm with which he welcomed simple but original ideas was only surpassed by the contempt he had for pretentious psychological dramas and shallow prestige productions. While rejecting most of the early American sound films because of their theatrical mise-en-scène, he was unceasing in his praise of Chaplin and Garbo, two actors who embodied for him the unlimited possibilities of the silent film.

The following examples may illustrate what Arnheim once described as "the cheerful foil-fencing style of the *Weltbühne*" (1974, 2), and show to what degree fantasy and provocation were an integral part of his critical style. Under the title "Psychotic Montage," Arnheim turned his views on German culture and society into a truly absurd scenario. "On the dark nightly skies the smiling face of broadcasting director Alfred Braun stands yellow and round, carefully pushing aside all clouds, pouring his faint light over all mortals, whether they like it or not. But the smiling face is in reality only an optical illusion, for as one gets closer to the heavenly body, one notices that its surface is covered by fantastic craters after sketches by Thea von Hartburg (Germans, carry German names!) and executed in delicious sugar frosting by Hans Poelzig as the decoration for a film scene Fritz Lang is shooting here for the Opel newsreel. . . . For the ending, as the apotheosis, a gigantic globe appears in the form of an Edam cheese out of whose door climbs Otto Gebühr. His mission is to fight the decline of German culture through dictatorial Nordification and to do so by replacing the Reich's Constitution with Günther's 'Racial Science'" (1929b, 378, 381).[3]

While this scenario — inspired by one of the most successful German films of 1929, *Die Frau im Mond* — relies on parody to draw attention to the connection between film and politics, Arnheim usually resorts to a more serious tone when describing the economic mechanisms that require conveyer-belt film production. "A decent motion-picture palace needs films that play there. That is why films are playing every night. And of course always new ones . . . new releases arrive three times a week, and one always, always, sees the same things. That is sometimes pretty, most often boring, and always the same" (1929a, 774). Such comments suggest a notion of quality that is neither modeled on traditional value categories (e.g., originality, preciousness) nor limited to specific genres or styles (e.g., the art film). They aim at an understanding of film that, instead of reinstating the divisions between high and low, supports its artistic aspirations.

While never defined in positive terms, filmic quality becomes the standard against which Arnheim measures all films — not to judge them, but to arrive at an increasingly precise definition of what constitutes film as an art form. The presence of a structuring absence, so to speak, effects his critical practice in two ways. First, the assumption of an evolutionary model of filmic development enables him to relate the imperfections in then-contemporary films to a stage of emergence in which flaws become directives to a potential still unfulfilled. These unrealized possibilities find expression in the assumption of a "not yet." Thus Stroheim is characterized as "a great poet in whose time the language [of film] was not yet developed" (1977, 208) and his most famous film, *Greed* (1923), described as "not a perfect work of art but a splendid compost heap of art to burrow in. This film is a good example why it is inappropriate in the early stage of an art to completely dismiss a work as 'bad' instead of emphasizing the pieces that point toward future perfection" (1977, 207). Second, the appeal to a standard of quality that exists in a state of permanent revision would allow filmmakers to explore the new medium on their own terms. Precisely by dismissing the clarity associated with normative aesthetics is Arnheim able to respond to new developments and unmask the mere appearance of quality as arts and crafts. He identifies the shortcomings of existing films and thus contributes, through the means of criticism, to the production of better films. His assessment of the Siodmak-Ulmer documentary, *Menschen am Sonntag* (1929, People on a Sunday), expresses this attitude very nicely: "But it doesn't matter that there is so much to be criticized in this work — on the contrary, that precisely is its purpose, and what these newcomers did wrong is a thousand times more important than what a group of nimble-fingered, greedy film producers do right" (1977, 225).

The kind of arguments that buttress his definition of filmic quality can also be studied in a 1931 review of three newly released films, William van Dyke's adventure film *Trader Horn;* the Charell-Pommer prestige production about the 1814 Congress of Vienna, *Der Kongreß tanzt* (The Congress dances); and Fritz Kortner's first directorial effort, *Der brave Sünder* (The honest sinner), written in collaboration with Alfred Polgar. "Partly Expensive, Partly Good," as the review is called, opens on an ironic note that describes the filmic experience in terms of good and bad investments. "The Ufapalast had a bad streak, if one can say that about a palace. It offered Africa once, Vienna once, boredom twice" (1977, 244). Like Kracauer, Arnheim takes details from the actual screening to substantiate his claims and uses the reaction of the audience to support specific theoretical points. Because sociological questions are of little interest to him, he does not use films to elaborate on ideas about visual pleasure or spectatorship; everything remains subordinated to the filmic text. The spectator becomes part of Arnheim's reconstruction of the aesthetic effects only insofar as the film realizes its expressive quality through the way it is perceived. In his comments on *Trader Horn,* description and narrative serve to highlight the limitations of the sound film; hence the references to the inaudible dialogue, the pandemonium of sounds, and the indignant reactions by members of the audience.

To underscore his point, Arnheim shifts the level of the argument from the aural to the visual realm as soon as he turns to another film, *Der Kongreß tanzt,* and what he describes as its intolerable mixture of conspicuous consumption and lack of imagination. "No sooner was the screen cleared of all the mistreated animals and Negroes than it filled up with many hundreds of extras in Viennese costume who began to waltz with great conviction, as if a new art form was to be propagated" (1977, 244). Arnheim is not interested in historical accuracy — an argument traditionally used when quality is at stake — but only in how the historical material is adequately translated into filmic material. Diagnosing the failure of this transformation, he repeatedly uses the impersonal pronoun *man* (one) in order to emphasize the absence of a creator that could have given the film structure and direction.

Not surprisingly, the refreshing quality that, in his view, distinguishes a "small" film like *Der brave Sünder* is linked to the participation of well-known artists. Because of the originality of their approach, the film is spared a representation in acoustic and visual terms, the objects of fetishization in the first two films. Instead, a comparison to culinary pleasures gives rise to an intriguing textual metaphor: "This film is stuffed like a Christmas goose, stuffed like a stocking; the threads have been placed tightly together throughout, so that a firm, somewhat nontransparent weave could be created. . . . Those who expect something easy to digest will only upset their stomachs" (1977, 246, 248). While Arnheim provides sufficient evidence for why *Der brave Sünder* succeeds in being substantial as well as light-hearted, it is above all that rich metaphor that links this ordinary review of three films to the more far-reaching project of mapping a future for film.

The relationship between film and technology stands at the center of Arnheim's definition of film as art. A double movement can be discerned in his reflections on mechanical reproduction, one that moves away from the mere imitation of reality and one that uses the new technology for a reconfiguration of art and reality. From the beginning, Arnheim perceived film in a continuum of scientific innovations and as the result of technological progress. He rejected "certain theoreticians"—the reference is obviously to Balázs—who claimed that its invention was necessitated by specific social conditions, such as the fast pace of modern life-styles or the rise of the urban masses. At the same time, Arnheim ardently defended the new medium against those who dismissed it as a technical curiosity. "But we speak of the apparatus. Unlike the printing press, it offers more than just a mechanical reproduction. It provides the creative means for the art of film" (1977, 20). Whereas Balázs compared film to the printing press in order to illustrate its revolutionizing impact on mass communication, Arnheim emphasized their differences in order to underscore film's artistic potential. In his view, its inherent closeness to reality required film to create a distance and cultivate its antimimetic tendencies. Thus he argued: "Painting and sculpture provide products of art that depict reality. By contrast, film is a product of reality that is artistically formed" (1977, 21).

Notwithstanding the fact that this proposition excludes nonrepresentational art, it drives home the point that film, though a reproductive art, need not be equated with the mechanical process and, because it is a reproductive art, should not be compared to the other arts. Arnheim's definition, which extends to photography and broadcasting, is worth quoting at length. "What distinguishes this reproductive art? That reality represents itself. It is as if the model took the brush away from the painter when the light rays engrave light and dark on the silver bromide emulsion, when the sound waves inscribe themselves in the wax layer or the film strip! Now, we already know that this is not about a purely mechanical process of reproduction. Then we would be dealing with a technical process like printing that has nothing to do with the creative acts of the human spirit. No, even in the case of reproductive art we are dealing with a creative work. The fact that reality represents itself only shows us where we have to look for the specific characteristics of this new art. Its strength lies in *representation,* and its specific formal means originate in the representation from a *particular perspective* and through a *particular selection*" (1977, 22).[4]

By insisting on the particular, Arnheim confirms the uniqueness of filmic perception, but his reference to film's ability to depict reality also reveals a surprising side. The metaphorical role reversal between model and painter endows reality with an active quality usually missing from his discussion on film and technology. Especially the phrase of "reality representing itself" attributes to film an affinity with the visible world and, implicitly, with realism that seems to precede any filmic means. The act of representation, which Arnheim elsewhere denounces as unnecessary duplication, is here described as a taking possession of reality for a second time. Moreover, the word *inscription,* and its association with writing, suggests that the objects in front of the camera participate actively in this process, even establishing the framework in which film's specific qualities are to be explored. As a reproductive art, film therefore exists in a field of tension constituted by the mechanical act of recording and the inherent qualities of the material. Though *Film as Art* suggests otherwise, this relationship is not necessarily defined as hierarchical, for the particular can only emerge from the unmeasurable wealth unfolding in front of the camera.

The need for a clear vision accounts for Arnheim's extensive comments on film directors, especially in his early years as a critic. His understanding of authorship is, again, most evident in the negative — that is, in highly critical remarks and deliberate attacks. Their defamatory nature — he once compared René Clair to a "circus horse trained in the haute école" — frequently originates in his admiration of that particular director's work. Similar to the elusive category called quality, the notion of authorship is developed through a complicated process of inclusion and exclusion, and situated within a constantly changing framework of artistic and theoretical accomplishments. Arnheim, like Kracauer, utilizes the spatial and political opposition between Hollywood and Moscow to express disappointment and attribute blame.[5] Of Josef von Sternberg, he wrote that if "he lived in Russia, he would make the most splendid films in the world. But, unfortunately, he lives in Hollywood" (1977, 250), and about Lubitsch, he said: "One doesn't want to envision what kind of films he would create if he smoked his cigars in Moscow instead of Hollywood" (1977, 263). Behind the political sympathies confessed in such remarks lay an acute awareness of the external conditions that either furthered or hindered creativity. To what degree these scenarios of dislocation must be read as ciphers, communicating an artistic rather than political dilemma, can be guessed from Arnheim's equally critical remarks about Russian filmmakers. Exceptions notwithstanding, he found much to fault in "the strange way in which Russian film artists ruin the great chance of visualizing things through their penchant for theoretical constructions. The Russians are real fanatics of film theory. They have thought up almost cabbalistic systems; yet the application to the actual work of art is for the most part not very satisfactory" (1977, 233).

What Arnheim dismissed as "stuck-on Marxisms," however, only belonged to another fundamental opposition in his conceptualization of film authorship, that between theoretical ambition and filmic imagination. In his view, rigid theories only gave rise to good intentions, while their absence was generally conducive to the exploration of film's inherent qualities. Both oppositional pairs, the one between talent and circumstance and the other between intention and imagination, established the framework in which Arnheim evaluated most film directors. In his view, the worst possible combination, that of great financial resources and even greater spiritual ambitions, was personified by the Lang-Harbou team. Accordingly, Arnheim characterized *Metropolis* (1926) as a combination of "the extremeness of engineer-Americanism" and "the dust-collecting craftiness of the European psyche" (1977, 185). *Spione* (1927, Spies) reminded him of the "luxury edition of a cheap detective story" (1977, 204), and *Die Frau im Mond* inspired the observation that "Fritz Lang films are parvenus: nouveau-riche backstage novels" (1977, 221).

What Arnheim despised most about Lang films — their triviality, their pretension, their insincerity — also guided his extensive comments on actors. He played the role of the connoisseur often enough, for instance when describing Lya de Putti "as beautiful, dumb, snakelike, and lascivious." But for the most part, Arnheim was more concerned with the demise of character actors like Asta Nielsen, Fritz Kortner, Paul Wegener, and Emil Jannings. As he saw it, they were being replaced by the pretty, nice types — the human equivalent of the Lang films. The art of film, Arnheim insisted, required another kind of beauty, a beauty aiming at the universals. "Art shows the universally valid manifestations of human fate through the concrete individual case that is cleansed of all coincidence, and precisely this concreteness, this validity, this pure recording of the essentials we call beauty" (1977, 115). Not surprisingly, Arnheim opposed everything that interfered with the vision of the creative individual, whether it was the director or a character actor.

Arnheim's position on film as a mass medium confirms this emphasis on self-expression and formal exploration. Frequent references to the "Philistine hostility toward art" and the "dumbness" of the audience suggest a division among appreciative spectators who expect to expand their mental and perceptual horizon through film and the masses who oppose anything vaguely reminiscent of intellectual effort; as is to be expected, Arnheim's sympathies lay with the former. His disregard for pleasure — "Where is it written that pleasure should play a greater role in the arts than in other sensible activities?" (1928c, 97) — justified these social divisions on the level of cultural practice. Arnheim hardly expected his definition to be universally valid, but he did call for sharper boundaries. "Especially in the case of film and theater, let us separate art and entertainment so that the artist is no longer inhibited by the demands of those longing for distraction, and the exhausted professional is no longer confronted with massive aesthetic tasks in his spare time" (1928c, 100). Rejecting the aesthetic excesses of *l'art pour l'art* and the instrumentalizing of art for political purposes, Arnheim refused to limit himself to specific styles or genres. Instead, the characteristics of film were outlined in contrast to existing practices: against the masses, against pleasure, against traditional categories. To call Arnheim's program elitist would be missing the point, however. His arguments were aimed at a diversity that allowed film to evolve as an art form and that put an end to what, for him, represented the tyranny of the average.

Because Arnheim had little emotional investment in questions of mass culture, he was also less susceptible to romantic pronouncements about its subversive potential. With a bitter comment — "Film is not an art of the masses [*Massenkunst*], except [in the sense] that quantity [*Masse*] alone counts at the box office" — Arnheim began his long campaign against the sound film. These talking pictures, as he preferred to call them, destroyed all expectations that he might have had about a progressive film culture. Yet despite their destructive influence, they also provided the obstacle through which his ideas about film, art, and technology could come into focus. The advent of sound made necessary a model of artistic development that allowed for continuity and coexistence; this becomes clear in Arnheim's speculations about its purifying effect on the silent film. While it would be wrong to give the silent film a privileged place in this aesthetic order, it undoubtedly marked a moment of perfection against which all later forms were measured. By describing a trajectory of rise and decline, with the silent film as the high point of artistic development, Arnheim presented ideas reminiscent of the classicist Winckelmann, who, during the Enlightenment, proposed a similar theory of historical cycles based on the model of Greek antiquity. Though never stated explicitly, the silent film was to play a comparable role.

Convinced that the boundaries between the arts were fluid and that new art forms were constantly evolving out of older ones, Arnheim maintained that "the silent film is not ripe for replacement. It has only lost its profitability, not its fertility. Especially if one realizes that the sound film is more than an addition, that it is an artistic activity *sui generis,* one should really oppose the popular claim that it represents 'progress.' . . . Sound film is not progress, but only a new thing — and that is something different after all" (1977, 402, 404). Such pronouncements were rather typical of the time. Emphasizing the dynamic qualities of the silent film, Ihering wrote elsewhere that "the talking picture [*sprechende Film*] is nothing more than a reproduction of reality. The moving picture [*Bewegungsfilm*], through its own laws, stands apart from reality as something new" (Ihering 1961, 1:429). Likewise, the composer Kurt Weill demanded that "the sound film must find its own, autonomous forms of expression" (Witte 1982, 188).

While Arnheim shared their hopes about a peaceful coexistence of silent and sound film, he disputed claims that they actually derived from different aesthetic paradigms. The laws of the silent film, he argued, represented the essence of film. Accordingly, the contribution of the sound film could at best be compared to a difference in instrumentation (i. e., like a symphony arranged for piano). At times, he went so far as to deny the sound film any artistic value outside the documentation of theater performances; and at times, he painted nightmarish visions of a film culture obsessed with technical novelties like sound, color, and stereoscopy. With such beliefs and attitudes, Arnheim emerged as the most radical proponent of the silent film — and his complaints were not only directed against the unproductive union of film and reality. The aesthetic reservations against the sound film also influenced his assessment of economic factors. Arnheim was convinced that the introduction of sound technology accelerated the process of economic concentration, and brought with it an impoverishment of artistic means. For this reason, the future of film could only be described as bleak, with "millions of listeners who understand nothing and still endure, and are forced to endure, everything for their money's worth" (1977, 19).

While Arnheim shared many of his reservations against the sound film with other film critics, he went furthest in analyzing the sound-image relationship. Avoiding the nostalgia that characterized other contributions, he focused instead on the specter of simulation, a form of reality that was no longer kept in check by the limitations of a particular art form but that, ultimately, took its place. He thought the consequences were fatal, for "in the moment that this happens, film loses its arduously conquered position to the good old peepshow" (1977, 59). The presence of sound, Arnheim concluded, returned film to the aesthetics of the proscenium stage. It made the image look three-dimensional and reduced the frame to a mere opening, without any particular characteristics. Sound burdened each scene with an unnecessary naturalism, thereby preventing the play with other realities and making impossible quick transitions between shots; in short, film became a "technically perfected theater." To strengthen his argument, Arnheim distinguished between the talking picture (*Sprechfilm*) and what he called the sound film (*Tonfilm*). Whereas the latter — a confusing term in light of today's usage — referred only to the mechanical recording of a musical score, it was the former that, in using sound effects, music, and dialogue to create a veritable cacophony of sound, received most of Arnheim's criticism.

There are grounds for the assumption that many of his statements were as much meant as a polemic intervention as they were supposed to indicate perceptual and aesthetic impasses. For instance, his claim that off-screen sound, when combined with rapid editing, elicited reactions from the spectator similar to those caused by the first close-ups in film history, namely shock and confusion, could have hardly been meant in earnest. What Arnheim did want to emphasize here was the artistic inability "to transfer the montage technique of the silent film to the sound film. Because the superiority that we have painfully reached for the silent film, which constructs a scene out of the multitude of single shots, cannot be utilized in the sound film. An acoustic presentation always appears in the form of a temporal process, whereas an optical one must be described as a static scene" (1977, 64). Arnheim related this aesthetic problem to a basic psychological law according to which vision represents a state, and sound perception an action. Thus, for the duration of an acoustic phenomenon (e.g., a song, a dialogue), no editing or changes in camera position should take place. Elsewhere, he described the shifts from a close-up to a long shot as "painful monstrosities" and rejected film music as "melodramatic" and "unbearable." Often the defense of the silent film prompted Arnheim to make statements that were unexpectedly dogmatic. This rigidity in aesthetic matters was most evident in his critique of Russian film theoreticians like Eisenstein, who had introduced the notion of asynchronous sound. The only conclusion that could be drawn from such "aberrations" was, according to Arnheim, "that sound and image should not be combined" (1977, 69).[6]

\* \* \*

In 1932, the same year that *Film als Kunst* was published in Germany, Arnheim described the task of the film critic. "Since he has to deal with such novel things, the film critic of today must proceed in the opposite direction from the paleontologist, who deals with ancient things. He must preconstruct the art of film from the occasional ossifications, and from the imprints of not always precious parts — in other words, those laws of construction that the film of the future will perhaps, in rare moments, bring to full fruition, but that must be applied to the film of today for just this reason. The 'Shakespeare of film' is still to come. The laws of his work, however, are already valid" (1977, 255). *Preconstruction,* then, means the establishment of artistic standards based on future practices but tested on present examples; given its utopian element, it also means the first step toward a theory of film (Koch 1990, 169–70).

The term also might be used to describe Arnheim's first book. *Film as Art,* the first summary of his critical writings, was conceived as a book of standards that developed film's artistic potential from its inherent possibilities and limitations. Unlike the American edition published in 1957, which contains only sections from the book, the first German edition (and its 1933 British translation) is a product of its time, beginning with the choice of topics and examples. Influenced by modern book design, Arnheim uses sloganlike page captions such as "Bubble Gum," "False Reality," or "Metaphors for the Eye" to simulate a filmic consciousness. While these captions recall Balázs's use of chapter headings, the organization of the chapters themselves, which are grouped under large headings like "How to Film" and "What to Film," follows didactic principles published in 1928 by Guido Bagier in *Der kommende Film* (The coming film). The deferential mention of Goethe, Lichtenberg, and Thomas Mann places *Film als Kunst* in an intellectual tradition that made the bold claims about film art more acceptable to middle-class readers. Many examples are taken from earlier articles and reviews but adjusted to the theoretically more ambitious framework; there are few of these kinds of repetitions found in Balázs's *Der sichtbare Mensch* and *Der Geist des Films*.

Despite the methodical approach, *Film as Art* reveals a very personal agenda, namely Arnheim's strong belief in the silent film, the main influence on his formation as a film theoretician, and his equally strong resistance to the sound film and what he perceived as a dangerous trend toward naturalistic imitations of reality. The interspersed comments on radio and television, then still referred to as radio film (*Rundfunkfilm*), served to confirm his suspicion that the proposals for a coexistence of silent and sound film as two independent art forms with the same laws, but with different applications, might not be very realistic after all. Perhaps because of the elitism associated with such positions, Arnheim's book received mixed reviews. Kraszna-Krausz called it "the most mature, extensive, and outstanding" film theory but voiced some reservations about Arnheim's critique of the sound film (1932, 449). Similarly, Kracauer praised the author's systematic approach to the form laws of the silent film, but found fault with his use of content analysis. "His interpretation of the 'mass-produced' film is not really original, and I would argue that he lacks the necessary sociological categories" (Kracauer 1932). In a review of the first English translation in 1933, Lewis Jacobs also mentioned Arnheim's formalist tendencies when criticizing his "ivory tower approach" (Jacobs 1934, 48). A more extensive critical reception of *Film als Kunst* in Germany was prevented because of its ban by the Nazis in 1933, and its reception in the United States until now has taken place from the perspective of Arnheim's later works.[7]

The main argument of *Film als Kunst* is deceptively simple; its premises may be summarized as follows: (1) not all films can be considered art; (2) film and photography are not mechanical reproductions; and (3) filmic perception differs from normal perception. As Arnheim describes his project, "the basic elements of the film medium will be examined separately and compared with the corresponding characteristics that we perceive 'in reality.' It will be seen how fundamentally different the two kinds of images are; and that it is just these differences that provide film with its artistic resources. We shall thus come, at the same time, to understand the working principles of film art" (1957, 9). This goal dominates the work's first part, in which Arnheim explores the difference between the camera and the human eye under headings like "The Projection of Solids Upon a Plane Surface,"

"Reduction of Depth," "Lighting and Absence of Color," "Delimitation of the Image and Distance From the Object," "Absence of the Space-Time Continuum," and "Absence of the Nonvisual World of the Senses."

With the exception of the last two categories, which introduce the elements of time and movement, Arnheim's discussion focuses on the photographic qualities of film. Here the influence of New Photography, with its emphasis on formal exploration, is undeniable, beginning with the book's only illustration, a press photograph reminiscent of Umbo's "Die unheimliche Straße" (1924, The uncanny street). The following quote, taken from the section on two-dimensionality, illustrates Arnheim's method in its very simplicity: "Let us consider the visual reality of some definite object such as a cube. If this cube is standing on a table in front of me, its position determines whether I can realize its shape properly. If I see, for example, merely the four sides of a square, I have no means of knowing that a cube is before me, I see only a square surface. The human eye, and equally the photographic lens, acts from a particular position and from there can take in only such portions of the field of vision as are not hidden by things in front. . . . We have, therefore, already established one important principle: If I wish to photograph a cube, it is not enough for me to bring the object within range of my camera. It is rather a question of my position relative to the object, or of where I place it" (1957, 9, 10).

Building his argument around such examples, Arnheim refers to what Gestalt psychologists call constancies of size and shape in order to account for the differences between the human perception of space and its photographic representation. He mentions the phenomenon of partial illusion to explain the ease with which the spectator translates shades of grey into color and accepts the sudden changes in time and place that constitute filmic narrative. And he points to the kinesthetic reactions of the body when he discusses the artistic possibilities of the moving frame. Paying little attention to the objects being represented, Arnheim concludes that film's significance as an art form resides in the creative use of its material limitations, which are photographic in nature. Consequently, the frame emerges as the main organizing principle. Aesthetic experience is equated with its difference from everyday perception and described as an ongoing confrontation with the artistic and cognitive implications of that difference. The resulting inconsistencies are easy to discern. Film's future as an art form, Arnheim argues, is dependant on the proper use of material limitations that are to a large degree historically determined; examples include the absence of three-dimensionality, spatiotemporal continuity and, above all, of color and sound.

Concluding the first part of *Film als Kunst* with the assertion that "the images we receive of the physical world differ from those on the movie screen" (1957, 34), Arnheim devotes the second part to translating the laws of perception into aesthetic categories. His presentation deliberately mirrors the structure of the first part when, to mention only two examples, the defamiliarizing effect of extreme camera angles is discussed under the heading "Artistic Use of Projections Upon a Plane Surface" and the powerful symbolism of light versus darkness is examined in conjunction with the "Artistic Use of Lighting and the Absence of Color." Again, Arnheim's formalism is most evident in an example used to underscore the importance of specific camera positions. "In Chaplin's film *The Immigrant* the opening scene shows a boat rolling horribly and all the passengers being seasick. They stagger to the side of the ship pressing their hands to their mouths. Then comes the first shot of Charlie Chaplin: he is seen hanging over the side with his back to the audience, his head well down, his legs kicking wildly—everyone thinks the poor devil is paying his toll to the sea. Suddenly Charlie pulls himself up, turns around and shows that he has hooked a large fish with his walking stick" (1957, 36). This quote shows to what degree Arnheim relies on the single shot and the characteristics of shot size and frame composition to present his ideas about an art form that, supposedly, stands in sharp opposition to the theater. Furthermore, it proves to what degree he emphasizes cognitive effects—in this case, the discrepancy between expectation and reality—to endow the act of perception with aesthetic significance.

Although much of his discussion focuses on the formal properties of the single shot, Arnheim also uses the section on spatiotemporal relations to analyze the principles of montage. In his view, montage is less a means of juxtaposition than of emphasis, and instead of promoting theoretical arguments, it represents formal concerns; hence Arnheim's extensive discussion of specific features like duration, similarity, contrast, synchronism, and asynchronism. As an alternative to Pudovkin's and Timoshenko's rigid principles of montage, Arnheim proposes a system that integrates montage into the larger framework of visual phenomena. In an observation that sounds almost absurd in its consequences, he uses the Gestaltist notion of illusionary movement to characterize film as an act of montage made invisible by what is commonly known as persistence of vision. "For actually, objectively, there is nothing but a succession of single motionless images, phases of motion, on the celluloid strip. It is only because the images succeed one another so rapidly and because they fit one another so exactly that the impression of continuous movement is given. Fundamentally, therefore, film is the montage of single frames — imperceptible montage" (1957, 99–100.) While he recognizes the surprise element associated with the shot–reserve shot pattern, Arnheim denies montage a privileged position among the filmic means. Equated with the succession of single frames on the film strip, montage remains are excluded from the creative effects achieved through camerawork and is reduced to what, in deliberate opposition to the Russian model, is referred to as editing. Thus editing, rather than montage, becomes part of the filmic techniques which, according to Arnheim, constitute the standard elements of film language: the traveling shot, tilt, and pan; backward, accelerated, and slow motion; fade in, fade out, dissolve, and superimposition; and, of course, special effects.

This list of techniques makes Arnheim sound like a true formalist. However, recurring references to the "partial illusion" provided by film, and to the necessity that film be "denuded of its realism" also attest to an understanding of form that recognizes the physicality of the objects represented. Arnheim's fascination with how the texture of ordinary material is translated into filmic properties and his disappointment about how the pale, ethereal beauties on the screen have nothing in common with the pink-faced actors of flesh and blood indicate to what degree he longs for a fusion of form and content — a process, to be sure, that requires a clear distinction between representation and imitation. Likewise, his comments on specific techniques make clear that these only serve a larger purpose, namely people's inherent need for representation (*Darstellungstrieb*) and ornamentation (*Ornamentiertrieb*) — two powerful drives that seem to defy the antimimetic rhetoric that usually accompanies such discussions.[8]

Given the "unlimited possibilities of molding and transforming reality" (Arnheim 1957, 132), even the notion of film authorship now appears as a function of the material's inherent drive toward expression. While *Film als Kunst* does not follow Arnheim's early reviews in placing all trust in the director, his powers are represented in romantic terms. This is apparent in the repetitive sentence structure that designates the male creative subject as the point of origin and the center of artistic control. "He shows the world not only as it appears objectively, but also subjectively. He creates new realities. . . . He calls into existence magical worlds. . . . He brings into being symbolic bridges between events and objects. . . . He intervenes in the structure of nature. . . . He arrests the progress of the world and of things. . . . He breathes life into stone. . . . Of chaotic and illimitable space he creates pictures that are beautiful in form and of profound significance, as subjective and complex as painting" (1957, 133).

Arnheim makes clear that this expressive potential can only be realized by a strong director figure. At the same time, expression, which for him represents the ultimate purpose of art, remains a function of the material and its inherent limitations. It is, therefore, not surprising when he rejects the so-called complete film (*Komplettfilm*) for succumbing to cheap illusionism. By disregarding the formal principle that "what counts are not the boundaries of an artistic field but its center" (1957, 235), the complete film, according to Arnheim, advances only through the principle of addition; its goal is to copy, not to create and interpret. While he is aware of the human need for imitation, he refuses to accord these urges any deeper value. Reproductive arts like photography and film are even more dependent on cultivating their antimimetic side than the other visual arts, he concludes, for it is precisely in the differences between the image and the physical world that they find their aesthetic and cognitive challenges.[9]

*Film als Kunst* utilizes very different theoretical traditions, such as the aesthetic writings of Enlightenment thinkers like Gotthold Ephraim Lessing, the turn to formal analysis in late-nineteenth-century art history and, most importantly, the rise of Gestalt psychology with its extensive research on the psychology of perception. The influence of Lessing's *Laocoön* — acknowledged in the title of the 1938 essay "A New Laocoön" (1957, 199–230) — is most evident in the assumption that the various art forms are different in character and must choose their styles and subjects accordingly. Where Lessing sets out to free poetry from the dictates of painting, Arnheim proposes to limit the formal explorations of film to its innate properties and thereby liberate the new art form from literature and theater. Where Lessing locates the meaning of an art form in its material limitations, Arnheim forges a link between film and art based on the very expressiveness of form. This becomes clear in his discussion of spatiotemporal relations in film.[10]

The absence of a historical perspective, and the shift from questions of representation to those of perception, can be traced back to the art theoretical writings of Heinrich Wölfflin who, in works like *Kunstgeschichtliche Grundbegriffe* (1915, Art historical terms) proposed to eliminate historical and biographical elements from the study of art and focus exclusively on autonomous laws. In combination with the emerging psychology of perception, Wölfflin's emphasis on style and transepochal categories like grandeur, lucidity, and the sublime reduced all artistic development to a kind of formalist history of seeing.

While such precursors provided Arnheim with the critical tools for elevating film to the status of an art, it was the scientific perspective of Gestalt psychology that allowed him to canonize this new art form around the central terms of form and perception. Notwithstanding their often contradictory nature, these influences came together in the concept of *Materialtheorie,* defined by Arnheim as "a theory meant to show that artistic and scientific descriptions of reality are cast in modes that derive not so much from the subject matter itself as from the properties of the material — or *Material* — employed" (1957, 2).

This mixture of idealist, formalist, and cognitive concepts makes *Film als Kunst* a unique contribution to Weimar film theory, but also accounts for some of the resultant tensions and incommensurabilities (see Wuss 1990, 233–47). The scientific perspective was already strongly developed in Arnheim's dissertation "Experimental-Psychological Studies on the Problem of Expression" (1928a, 118–19), in which he analyzed the perception of visual phenomena like handwriting and facial expressions in an experimental setting, a controlled environment whose theoretical implications still reverberate in the sometimes clinical tone of *Film als Kunst*. Arnheim chose graphology and physiognomy, two pseudosciences that establish analogies between physical expression and an inner self, because of their formal qualities. In contrast to Balázs, for whom physiognomy was the royal road to a democratic internationalism, the actual meaning of these physical manifestations remained secondary to him. Describing form as the expression of material-specific qualities, rather than of psychological dispositions or aesthetic traditions, Arnheim relied heavily on one of the main concepts of Gestalt psychology, the interdependency of form and perception.[11]

Developed in the twenties by Max Wertheimer, Wolfgang Köhler, and Kurt Lewin, Gestalt psychology departs from the assumption that the whole is more than the sum of its parts, and that each part is determined by the intrinsic laws of the whole. Important areas of inquiry include the study of the visual field and the perception of movement. Both resonate in Arnheim's distinction between normal and filmic perception and inform his decidedly cognitive approach to the act of looking. Reflecting on the evolutionary nature of the senses, he writes: "We must get a feeling for how imprecise and inaccurate our senses are, so that we can cure ourselves of the presumption that the senses are the highest instance, the real world, and the results of science are to be measured against how far they accommodate this seemingly 'real.' For progress points into the opposite direction. The senses must learn. They will grow not poorer, but increasingly more profound, more meaningful, more sensitive, more human" (1932a, 216).

Arnheim's objection to mechanical reproduction and the mimetic impulse in general also departs from the Gestaltist notion, "according to which even the most elementary processes of vision do not produce mechanical recordings of the outer worlds but organize the sensory raw material creatively according to principles of simplicity, regularity, and balance, which govern the receptor mechanism" (Arnheim 1957, 3). As these statements show, Gestalt psychology provided Arnheim with the theory of perception that became the basis for his analysis of film's specific means. In fact, the very notion of *Gestalt* (form) suggests an affinity to the visual arts, whose influence can be seen in his almost exclusive preoccupation with camerawork, often at the expense of all other aspects of filmmaking. Even the cognitive qualities of *Gestalt* — Arnheim's appreciation for Chaplin is based on the notion of productive thinking — seem to legitimate a disregard for anything associated with the profilmic event despite his extensive comments on film and ideology.

Until now, the discussion of *Film als Kunst* has been limited to those chapters included in the German editions of 1932 and 1974 (a re-edition with a new preface by the author), and the British edition of 1933, as well as the American edition, *Film as Art* (1957). For the remaining pages, attention will focus on the substantial revisions and omissions through which the original 1932 German edition — one of the most influential contributions of Weimar film theory, a work marked by history — was transformed into a canonized text of the formalist tradition. The 1957 American edition included a new preface by the author, parts of the original edition, and a number of later articles. Arnheim, who by 1957 was mostly known in the United States for his writings on art and psychology, said the changes were necessary because "some of the chapters tangled with tasks for which respectable techniques are now available, such as my sketchy 'content analysis' of the standard movie ideology; others dealt with temporary questions — for example early fumblings of the sound film. . . . I have eliminated details that sounded redundant or untenable, built qualification into brash assertions, tightened loose reasoning. But nothing substantial is changed" (1957, 4).

A closer look at the "missing" parts of *Film as Art,* however, reveals an interest in questions of content that cannot be dismissed so easily, and in fact Arnheim used the 1974 German edition of *Film als Kunst* for revisionist purposes, acknowledging his political and philosophical debts. "The influence of *Die Weltbühne* also made me aware of the ideological-political nature of film production, although I was already convinced then that the analysis of the formal means is not at all irrelevant . . . but must necessarily precede any ideological analysis" (1974, 3).[12]

The 1957 American edition eliminated all traces of a political consciousness and deleted numerous contemporaneous references. In the place of a detailed analysis of film and ideology and a long chapter on the sound film, Arnheim added four texts written after 1933.[13] The point here is not to claim Arnheim for socially conscious film criticism but to draw attention to the unity of a work in which formalist tendencies exist side by side with an acute awareness of the functioning of mass entertainment. For the same reasons, Arnheim's later writings, which include the self-reflexive prefaces to various editions of his collected works, should neither be praised as the product of a logical evolution in his thinking nor be dismissed as a kind of revisionist attempt to silence the voice of youthful radicalism. The purpose here is to draw attention to the existence of two strands of thought in Arnheim's work, both of which were important precisely because of the tension between them.

While Arnheim was certainly no Marxist — he sharply rejected the idea that the work of art was determined by social and economic conditions — he commented repeatedly on the relationship between the artist and his need for self-expression and a society that replaced this need with economic considerations. Similarly, while Arnheim showed little interest in questions of narrative — he often referred to narrative as a mere instrument — he was acutely aware of the ideological function of specific stereotypes and genres. In the original edition of *Film als Kunst* (1932), he in fact offers a remarkable analysis of the relationship between form and content that dissolves the problematic opposition of formalist and realist tendencies into a truly "material theory" of film. Arguing for an identity of form and content, Arnheim begins with an example that immediately evokes leftist politics. "One can call the same thing either form or content, depending on how one looks at it. The story of Director B., who falls in love with his secretary,

Miss C., could be called the *content* of a film. But it is *form* if one conceives of it as the dramatizing of an abstract idea: the clash between rich and poor, the struggle between class difference and human desire" (1974, 159).

The implications of this argument are considerable. By eliminating the distinction between form and content and making each a function of the other, Arnheim draws attention to the illusion of illusionism, so to speak, which in his view accounts for the widespread mistake of "consider[ing] as raw material what in reality is already the product of an artistic process" (1974, 160). At the same time, the application of formal principles to narrative and thematic concerns allows him to analyze these within the same critical framework and, therefore, to establish representation as the ultimate reference point. To what degree the comments on film's proximity to concrete, physical events profit from this formal, if not formalist, approach to questions of narrative can be seen in Arnheim's proposals about effective film openings or his discussion of filmic acting styles.

Ultimately, the form-content relationship makes possible a notion of film and reality that, instead of focusing on the mechanics of photographic illusion, accepts that film reflects ideological positions. "Film is the art closest to reality — if we understand as reality the totality of everything that our eyes and ears communicate to us. . . . Whatever the camera records is reality, the most authentic reality. However, everybody knows how often films are *unnatural,* that is, they do not show the world as it really is. In such cases, a higher notion of reality is involved. Imagine the following scene: In front of a factory gate, an expensive private car drives up at the end of the shift; a worker leaves the factory, the car's driver jumps out of the car, greets him, opens the door, the worker gets in, the car drives off. Or: a woman laughs as she watches a stranger grab her child and thrash it! We call such scenes unnatural because they contradict the economic and psychological laws of our world" (1974, 182, trans. indebted to Sieveking and Morrow). Arnheim makes up these absurd examples to illustrate his claim that film must always represent the characteristic and the typical (i.e., not the millionaire-turned-worker or the psychotic mother), that it must focus on the essential and leave out the unnecessary.

The construction of what might be called realism — Arnheim never uses the term, but the combination of "reality and necessity" points in this direction — requires a continuous process of reduction, limitation, and emphasis. Not life as it is, but film as it can be: perhaps this formula describes best an approach to film in which quality and topicality are no longer mutually exclusive terms. Arnheim's critique of the mass-produced film, then, eludes accusations of elitism through the fact that it moves upward from the materials that constitute narrative, and that it measures all genres, respectable as well as the disreputable ones, against the high standards of film art. He makes no distinctions between subject matter and filmic representation, and his objections to the escapism of most entertainment films are not invalidated by the conclusion that the "question of subject matter is almost exclusively a political one. Artistically, it is pretty uninteresting" (1974, 188). Just as the so-called Zille films prove to him that "good" content alone fails to raise social consciousness, so do the Russian films present themselves as instructive examples why disproportionate attention to formal aspects can weaken the political issues at stake.

On the basis on these equations, Arnheim offers a critique of the mass-produced film based on its industrial mode of production. Comparing the inventory of stereotypical characters, narrative motifs, and dramatic constellations to a periodic table, he describes the work of the scriptwriter as a constant rearranging and combining of standard elements. These include the stock characters of the drawing-room comedy (e.g., the old baron, the elegant detective, the painted whore, the jealous husband) and the many visual conventions that reduce images to abstract symbols (e.g., the champagne glass shattering on the floor, the ripples on the water). Arnheim objects to such standardization, because it negatively affects filmic techniques and turns original ideas into empty formulas. However, he knows that the reasons for the continuous appeal of the mass-produced film must not be sought in a lack of education or good taste. Even in his comments on a film's content, Arnheim points to the positions, literally and figuratively speaking, that determine frame composition as well as political tendencies. "Almost all of these films contain, whether consciously or unconsciously, a certain tendency in their *story* [sic]. Not that somebody is preaching — no, the dangerous thing about this tendency is that nothing is formulated theoretically, nothing is postulated. Instead, the position from which the things of this world are viewed, the selection of stories and their underlying moral standards are one-sided" (1974, 193). Such attention to ideological questions seems to contradict earlier efforts to formulate universal rules and objective standards; not surprisingly, Arnheim calls his investigation a "foray into extra-aesthetic areas." He obviously conceives of the mass-produced film as an obstacle to the emergence of film art, not an integral part of film's role as a modern mass medium.

Many details in his analysis recall Balázs's writings on film ideology, including the assertion that the mass-produced film manipulates the audience, that "it makes sure that dissatisfaction does not explode in revolutionary action, but dissipates into dreams of a better world" (1974, 194). Notwithstanding the political tone, Arnheim's definition of ideology remains suspended between mass psychology, the psychology of perception, and a critique of mass culture that, despite the attention paid to films' formulaic stories, barely conceals the secondary role attributed to narrative. It is psychology, in this case the psychology of Everyman, that establishes the critical framework and, in the process, blurs the boundaries between socially conditioned preferences and basic human dispositions; the dialectical process associated with the term *false consciousness* falls out of this rather schematic analysis. The result? In addition to envy and hatred, which are listed as class-related responses, Arnheim cites lack of initiative and sheer laziness as reasons for the audience to appreciate false renditions of reality and accept them as substitutes for actual experience. On the basis of a few typical stories, he analyzes how bourgeois films exploit the hopes and fears of average people, for instance by offering individual solutions, resolving conflict through simplistic oppositions of good and evil, and catering to a widespread fascination with wealth and eroticism. In so doing, these films help to strengthen social institutions like the state, the church, and the family — institutions, according to Arnheim, that represent the mentality of the petty bourgeois (*Spießer*). He points out that this mentality can even be found among the workers who constitute the majority of the audience, but who hold on to bourgeois values even when they develop class-consciousness.

Significantly, Arnheim identifies the supporters of the mass-produced film as a social type that has become synonymous with narrow-mindedness in cultural and ethical matters. Whereas Balázs and Kracauer develop similar analyses around the petty bourgeois (*Kleinbürger*) as a social class, Arnheim focuses on a psychological dilemma, the difference between knowledge and desire, which for him makes possible the smooth functioning of film ideology. Thus the term *petty bourgeois* and its changing association with a class position and aesthetic preference encapsulates what can be described as a similar wavering between formal analysis and critique of ideology in Arnheim's analysis of film as a whole. The traces of this process have been eliminated in his rather unproductive search for theoretical clarity and unambiguity.

Not surprisingly, the German and the American versions of his film book end on very different notes. Whereas the American edition concludes with somber thoughts about the triumph of the complete film and the inevitable disappearance of the silent film as an autonomous art form, the German edition explains why art and the masses are still at odds with each other. The reference is, unmistakenly, to the world outside as Arnheim concludes: "He who wants to improve the film must first improve the social order. . . . The future of film depends on the economics and politics of the future. To predict them does not come within the scope of the present work. What will happen to film depends upon what happens to ourselves" (1974, 327, 330).

The interdependency of art and reality, which is kept in suspension through the explicit references to the power structure and the autonomy of film art, also structures Arnheim's contribution at the end of a formative period in film criticism. Written in the era of sound film but primarily concerned with silent film, *Film als Kunst* must be regarded as a work of retrospection and transition. Its main ideas were conceived in the heated cultural and political debates of the Weimar years, but some of the conclusions already aimed toward a theory of film existing outside such determinations. The concept of intrinsic filmic means and qualities was developed in the encounter with the silent German cinema, an influence most noticeable in the great attention placed on camerawork. Yet these examples also served to justify the neglect of anything associated with the profilmic event, including narrative, acting, and set design. What in the reviews began as a passionate engagement with films and their audiences — an approach not always free from the idiosyncrasies of taste — gave way to a search for universally valid laws. Displaying these divergent influences, Arnheim's writings bear within themselves the productive tensions that characterize Weimar film theory as a whole.

# Afterword

I t is not possible to summarize more than twenty-five years of writing about film and cinema in a few concluding remarks. Since the main purpose of this study has been to establish a historical body of work that has thus far only been available in fragments — at least in American film scholarship — it would be premature to offer any further speculations about its place in the history of film theory. Likewise, since the focus has been on the productive force of critical discourse across a variety of disciplines and in a variety of contexts, little can be said at this point about its concrete influence on particular configurations (e.g., the cinema reform movement, leftist film politics). What can be achieved in these concluding remarks, however, is a somewhat schematic definition of the field of forces in which early German film theory and criticism must be situated.

It is an area characterized by specific continuities and oppositions. A direct line extends from the earliest articles in the trade press and the first treatises on cinema reform to the Communist polemics against bourgeois film and the amusing reports from the film world. One of the driving forces behind such astounding productivity was the deep trust in the power of critical discourse that has been an integral part of intellectual debates in Germany since the Enlightenment. By carrying on in this tradition, the contributing writers and critics affirmed not only that the conditions for the free exchange of ideas still existed and that social and political change could be effected through writing; they also hoped actively to influence public attitudes toward the cinema and establish themselves as opinion leaders in their respective fields. Such assumptions continued to structure the debates even as critics moved beyond comparisons to literature and theater and established a framework that included proposals about visual pleasure and the specificity of the new medium. Therefore, in spite of the often heated controversies, early German film theory and criticism can be described as a homogeneous body of work, defined by the social, political, and economic conditions of the time. As a discourse with precise functions, it was held together by the continuing belief in the bourgeois public sphere and the leadership role of intellectuals in society.

At the same time, early German film theory and criticism developed through the ongoing negotiation of two critical paradigms, cinema as a public sphere, and film as an aesthetic experience. Writing about film and cinema represented a field of contention — with rhetorical styles ranging from lyrical and declamatory to ironic and defamatory — in which language functioned as a conduit for controversies imported from other areas and an instrument for consolidating the cinema's own claims to power. The linguistic opposition of *cinema* and *film,* in fact, stood for two sets of oppositions, that between the discursive practices in Wilhelmine Germany and Weimar Germany on the one hand, and that between the notion of cinema as an event and film as a product on the other. Historically speaking, *cinema* evoked the masses and mass culture and brought with it decidedly negative connotations, such as cultural decline and social disintegration. In contrast, the term *film* promised the emancipation of the new medium from bourgeois prejudices, while at the same time preparing the ground for its integration into middle-class culture. As theoretical positions, however, the preference for *cinema* implied a greater attention to audiences and questions of spectatorship, whereas *film* made possible an involvement with the text that resulted in detailed formal and narrative analyses.

While none of these linguistic definitions can be associated with a particular political position, they all were highly politicized — whether in relation to the nation, literature and the theater, or the film industry. The surprising lack of controversy over specific film genres or styles — with the exception, of course, of films associated with leftist causes — only confirms the description of early German film theory and criticism as a discursive field divided over political rather than aesthetic questions; if aesthetics played a role, then it was primarily as a function or a form of cultural politics.

As the last three chapters have shown, the continuities that made possible the formation of film/cinema as a discursive subject reached a point of completion in the work of Béla Balázs, Siegfried Kracauer, and Rudolf Arnheim, whose inclusion in the canon of great film theoreticians reflects the originality of their contribution. This rare moment of mastery of, and love for, the subject also marked the end of all critical discourse in Germany. With the rise of National Socialism, any film criticism that defined its purpose in the original sense of the word—that is, to judge and to discern—was regimented and repressed precisely because of its inherently political nature. At the same time, however, film experienced its total instrumentalization in the name of fascist politics.

From the perspective of a history of film theory, there are two ways of looking at early German film criticism and theory, as leading toward a theory of silent film or a theory of mass culture. Both utilize critical insights developed in the historical conjuncture of film/cinema and politics, and both define their positions through emphasis and omission. Part of two distinct academic endeavors—scholarship on silent cinema and on Weimar culture, respectively—they contribute to very different areas of knowledge. Like the critical positions associated with *cinema* and *film,* their discrepancies bring to the fore the tensions that made writing on film/cinema a field of contention in the first place. The label "silent film theory" defines the boundaries without question. Its field of influence is limited to the period of silent cinema; thus its evocation after 1927 is bound to denote historicity, if not nostalgia. The critical framework remains limited to the individual film and its double existence, so to speak, as industrial product and work of art. Such limitations are useful in providing focus, but they tend to distract from the conditions under which these films were produced and seen. Speaking of a theory of silent film draws attention to those features that already preoccupied the critics in Wilhelmine Germany. They include the absence of language and, closely connected to that, the utopian vision of a world reunited by the international language of gesture; the emphasis on spectacle and, as a result, the reconsideration of "lowly" pleasures like visual pleasure; the elimination of the traditional laws of aesthetics and, for that reason, the desire to conceive of film as a new art form.

Arguments in favor of such distinctions can be found in the contributions of the literary writers, the critics in the daily newspapers and literary journals, and the representatives of an emergent philosophy of film. However, their writings also point to the discursive function of the silent film as a historical concept in relation to questions of spectatorship and mass culture. Especially the chapters on film and politics and the modern fictions of cinema make clear what little impact the transition from silent to sound film had on film-political strategies, and how little it affected the dissemination of cinematic consciousness into all areas of modern life. Structuring the history of film on the basis of technical innovations theory, then, brings out the same romantic perceptions that characterized the literary contributions to the cinema debate: the construction of silent cinema as a place outside of language and, therefore, outside of power relations; the association of silence and Otherness; and the attribution of essential qualities to this decidedly historical art form.

Early German film theory and criticism can also be characterized as a theory of mass culture. This term consciously neglects the differences between film and other cultural practices and places the new medium among a wide range of modern phenomena and pleasures. Film in this context assumes the function of symptom and cause, at once reflecting and engendering the new configurations in modernity. The aesthetic qualities of film are, of course, of little significance in a critical paradigm primarily concerned with questions of production and reception. In their place, the urban masses take center stage as the active pursuers of needs that cut across the boundaries separating high and low culture, as the passive recipients of mass-produced products whose shallowness is only superseded by their calculated exploitation of human desires, and as a projection screen for the most diverse fantasies, including the return to a pre-industrial folklore, the rise of a truly nationalistic cinema, and the anticipation of a genuinely proletarian culture.

As the study's first part has shown, the beginnings of film criticism were inextricably tied to the rise of the urban masses and the decline of the old political order. This connection, which places the question of cinema within a social and political framework, can be traced from the cinema reform movement to National Socialism, despite their very different definitions of Germanness and German nationalism. Between these two points, various groups during the Weimar years tried to cultivate, suppress, or divert the energies brought into being by the powerful association of the cinema and the masses. Visual pleasure, the product of this association, became the testing ground where bourgeois culture was to assert its power, either by radically changing its systems of thought, or by integrating the cause of controversy into its expanded field of influence. Discussions on national versus international culture, high versus low culture, education versus diversion, and manipulation versus agitation played a crucial role in the search for new demarcation lines that bore witness to the real struggles taking place outside the motion picture theaters.

The historical material presented in these chapters suggests that early

German film theory and criticism must be described as both a theory of silent film and a theory of mass culture. The critical energy in the texts originates precisely in the vacillation between two traditions of thought, one committed to the legacy of the Enlightenment, the other influenced by critical debates on national literature during the nineteenth century. Their negotiation took place against the backdrop of the most important philosophical movements of the early twentieth century: cultural pessimism, modern sociology, psychoanalysis, phenomenology, Gestalt psychology, and, of course, Marxism. The present study maintains that this process can only be reconstructed, can only become accessible to critical analysis, under very specific conditions. They include a historically informed approach to film theory, an interdisciplinary approach that brings together economic, legal, pedagogical, and academic discourses, and a theoretical approach that emphasizes the metadiscursive qualities inherent in critical writings on film and the complicated process of discourse formation.

Thus defined, writing must be characterized as an act of appropriation, that is, a mode of representing difference while integrating difference into existing systems of thought. At the same time, it must be seen as a production, an active intervention into the course of history with the purpose of affecting change or maintaining the status quo. Accordingly, the literary debate can be described as an attempt to master the problem of spectatorship through recourse to the discursive strategies of comparison and exclusion, while at the same time adjusting to new cultural phenomena. The search for aesthetic systems can be characterized as a withdrawal into normative aesthetics, which includes the denial of the presence of the cinematic apparatus and the spectator, and as a first step forward in film's emergence as an art form in its own right. Usually excluded from serious consideration, the articles in the trade press can be identified with a promotional discourse that simultaneously legitimates and denies film's economic basis. The cultural critics can be described as using the cinema as a means for coming to terms with radical changes in the public sphere, and leftist criticism as bringing about the testing of film as a weapon in the revolutionary struggle. The writings of Balázs, Kracauer, and Arnheim participated in these various strategies of recognition and denial, but also moved beyond them, as they laid the foundations for a theory of cinema yet to come.

Traditionally, film criticism has been treated as an integral part of film production, exhibition, and reception; it is usually perceived as a supplement, an organizing device, a method of attributing meaning and value. Although criticism bears the traces of this historical moment, film theory is often regarded as something that exists outside of history, that gives birth to new critical concepts in the self-generative act of thinking. Early German film criticism and theory renders such distinctions problematic and introduces other participants in the process of theory formation, including the discourses of nationalism, mass culture, and modernity. In order to accommodate these influences, this study has avoided linking film criticism exclusively to film, as the product and the production, or to the cinema, as the larger context in which the experience of film is organized. Instead, film criticism and film theory have been treated as discourses in their own right, not just as mere reflections of film production or film politics at a particular historical juncture.

That is not to say that writing represents an autonomous practice. As in the production of films, the act of writing involves the negotiation of conflicting positions, institutional restraints, and economic and political interests, and therefore simultaneously resists and conforms to the structures that facilitate these exchanges. Writing, however, through the power of imagination, also makes possible the representation of concerns absent or excluded from the cinematic spectacle. Through the diversity of contributions — a diversity that includes philosophical movements, organizations, and individual authors — the materiality of discourse becomes palpable.

Early German film theory and criticism demonstrate exemplarily how writing about film/cinema established a context for coming to terms with modern mass culture and its new paradigms of interpretation. What the films could not address in their stories and images found a new home in the textual productions surrounding them. Critical writing, therefore, established itself as the underside of production as it revealed the "unconscious" of representation and marked the fallout of the historical process. Recovering that unique quality is only possible through approaches to film theory and criticism that emphasize their historical nature, but do so from the perspective of discourse formation rather than film history. Ultimately, the encounter of theory and historiography can only be staged from within and with the help of texts, that is to say, through textual interpretation. That means nothing less than re-presenting the history of early German film theory and criticism in a framework defined by its own parameters. *The Cinema's Third Machine* has hopefully made a first step in this direction.

# Notes

## Introduction

**1.** Elsaesser propounds a different reading of the cinema-film opposition that is influenced by theoretical concerns: "German theory — the writings of Béla Balázs, Rudolf Arnheim, and Siegfried Kracauer — generally seems to be film theory as opposed to cinema theory. . . . By contrast, German *cultural* theory, in the form of Frankfurt School critical sociology, has tended to marginalize the cinema. . . . However, both sides of German theory might yet prove productive, especially if . . . the perspective taken intersects with aspects of the postmodern debate" (1987b, 66).

**2.** Through the editorial work of Miriam Hansen, David Bathrick, and Eric Rentschler, *New German Critique* has played an important role in introducing these questions and debates to an American readership and in continuing them within the larger framework of film studies and cultural studies; in this context, see the special issues on Weimar film theory (vol.40, 1987) and Weimar mass culture (vol.51, 1990), and the recent issue on Siegfried Kracauer (vol.54, 1991).

**3.** As the editors of *Frauen und Film,* Heide Schlüpmann and Gertrud Koch have contributed greatly to the reassessment of Weimar film and film theory from a feminist perspective.

**4.** Comparisons to early French or American writings on film might clarify to what degree early German film criticism and theory expresses social, cultural, educational, and aesthetic concerns that were typical of early cinema in general, and to what degree it addresses specific problems, for instance in its attention to questions of national identity. The following studies offer very useful introductions. On early French film theory and criticism, see Abel 1988. For two studies on French literature that make references to the German debates, see Albersmeier 1984 and Lenk 1989. On early American film theory and criticism, see Lounsbury 1973.

## Chapter 1

**1.** Some sources list the *Erste Internationale Kinematographen-Zeitung* (1906), published in Hamburg, as the first trade journal.

**2.** Beginning in 1908, the journal had a section on phonography, called "Aus dem Reich der Töne" (From the realm of sounds). On the relationship between quality and technology, see Wolf-Czapek, "Über den Stil des Kunstfilms," *Der Kinematograph*, 10 Aug. 1910.

**3.** Film dissertations about Wilhelmine and Weimar cinema written during the Nazi period, including Sattig's, are questionable sources of information, in the presentation of empirical data as well as in the interpretation of the historical process. Dissertations that deal with issues addressed in this study include Gertraude Bub, 1938, "Der deutsche Film im Weltkrieg und sein publizistischer Einsatz, diss., Univ. of Berlin; Anneliese Giers, 1943, "Filmpresse und Organization des Filmwesens in München von den Anfängen bis 1933," diss., Univ. of Munich; Hans-Joachim Sachse, 1944, "Die politische Wertung des Films im Nachkriegsdeutschland: Filmkritiken Berliner Tageszeitungen 1919–1933," diss., Univ. of Berlin. For a complete list, see Uricchio 1987. For an early bibliography of German writings on film, see Traub and Lavies 1940.

**4.** As a rule, films will be introduced by their original titles with the English translation in parentheses.

**5.** Aware of the importance of language, pro-German language factions tried to introduce an exclusively German nomenclature for the cinema. They proposed to replace the "alien" term *Kinematographie* with *Lichtspiel* (literally "light play") and its compounds (e.g., *Lichtspieltheater, Lichtspieldrama*). The term *Lichtbild* was to refer to the photographic image, with a distinction being made between *Stehbild* (slide) and *Laufbild* (moving image). The same phenomenon can be observed in various other attempts to negotiate, through language, the relationship between film, theater, and literature; examples include standard terms like *Kinodrama* and *Filmdrama,* but also more exotic ones like *Filmbelletristik* (film literature). The emphasis on the cinema's visual qualities found expression in terms such as *Kinoballade, Filmpantomime,* and *Bildhandlung* (visual story).

**6.** A second, revised edition of this work was published by F. Podehl in 1925 with new examples, including Mayer's scenario for Murnau's *Der letzte Mann* (1924, The last laugh). A successful film scenarist and director, Dupont is best known for *Variété* (1925, Variety).

## Chapter 2

**1.** As the head of the film censorship office in Berlin, Brunner was the target of many diatribes, particularly those by the *Weltbühne* critic Kurt Tucholsky. Even the Nazi film historian Oskar Kalbus later described the period as follows: "Everybody was against the 'flickers' [*Kientopp*]. The censors, with the fanatic Dr. Brunner as their leader, the police, the firefighters, the press" (1935, 1:13).

**2.** As late as 1924, film critic Willy Haas used a similar developmental model to conclude "that the child [film] has not yet been born, that the mother — the broad masses — still feeds it from her own flesh and blood" (Beyfuß and Kossowsky 1924, 33).

**3.** Häfker coined the term *Spielfilm* (play film), which became the standard term for the feature film. Later, the less common *Lichtspiel* (light play) was introduced to emphasize film's distance from literature through the linguistic reference to photography (i.e., in the emphasis on *light* rather than *play*) and to endow film with an aura of preciousness.

**4.** Ackerknecht was instrumental in organizing the Bilderbühnenbund Deutscher Städte, an association of communal cinemas founded in 1918 in Stettin. A later publication, *Lichtspielfragen* (1928, Questions of cinema), shows his continuing interest in film pedagogy.

**5.** Another position was taken by Hermann Lemke, who, in his Kinematographische Reformvereinigung (Cinematographic Reform Association), tried to unite educational and commercial interests. Founded in 1907 in Berlin with the intention of improving communication between nonprofit organizations, public agencies, and the film industry, the association offered support at a time when public acceptance of the cinema and financial backing for film companies were still the exception. Lemke repeatedly stated that only "the collaboration of big capital, the film industry, and the cultural institutions (educators, school administrators, scientists) would improve cinematography" (1912, 56). Oscar Kalbus later accused Lemke of secretly working for the French film industry (Beyfuß 1924, 1).

**6.** The author alternately used the terms *Schundfilm*, *Filmdrama*, and *Kinodrama* when discussing the melodrama, the sentimental love story, and the adventure film. For him, questions of spectatorship were obviously more important than considerations of genre or subject matter.

**7.** For a very different assessment, see the critic Manfred Georg's comments on film and pacificsm from the year 1916: "It is a simple equation that wars can be prevented more easily when the nations are more familiar with each other. Trust comes with understanding. Understanding through looking, feeling, seeing the other. And nowhere can the indigenous subject see the customs and emotions of other nations better than in their mediation by foreign artists" (*Stationen* 1989, 43)

## Chapter 3

**1.** Arguing along similar lines but emphasizing the health risks, an anonymous critic maintained that "only a few [people] recognize the greatest and most serious danger posed by the cinema. When a youngster goes to the cinema once, twice, or three times a week, the atmosphere already destroys him psychologically, not to speak of the content" (Lange 1920, 52). As early as 1906, teachers spoke out against "the presence of children in the theaters of living photographs, for many cinematographic images . . . are still inferior in quality, and full of ugly, harmful, and morally dubious things, and they are shown in screening rooms that fail to comply with the minimum requirements of hygiene. The schools must thwart these visits to the cinema through educational measures" (quoted by Kinter 1985, 46).

**2.** For an introduction to mass culture in Wilhelmine Germany, see the special issue of *New German Critique* 29 (Spring/Summer 1983), ed. by Peter U. Hohendahl.

**3.** The distinction between proletarian culture and mass culture played a crucial part in the scholarship on early cinema in the 1970s. The goal was often to establish the tradition of a proletarian cinema or identify the desire for cheap entertainment with residues of petty-bourgeois consciousness (see Buck 1977, III).

**4.** A well-known film director and screenwriter in the twenties and one of the more successful Hollywood émigrées, Viertel is remembered best for his screenplay for Béla Balázs's cross-section film, *Die Abenteuer eines Zehnmarkscheins* (1926, The adventures of a ten-mark bill), and King Vidor's Depression epic *Our Daily Bread* (1934).

**5.** Döblin later wrote a film scenario, *Die geweihten Töchter* (1923, The holy daughters), and other film texts (see Döblin 1983).

## Chapter 4

**1.** Literary scholars like Kaes, Koebner, and Heller have pointed repeatedly to the metadiscursive quality of the debate; my understanding is indebted to their writings. Thomas Koebner compares the reception of cinema to a shocklike effect, with the experience of an antagonistic society resulting in its imaginary reunification through film (1977, 26). Anton Kaes, in "The Debate about Cinema," maintains that the "the incursion of film into the literary domain between 1909 and 1929 forced mainstream literature into a self-reflective mode, which had important social and aesthetic consequences. During these years, cinema became an object of discussion to the extent that it challenged traditionally held notions of poetry and culture. As the new medium gained power, it threatened literature's monopoly and destabilized the contemporary cultural system. The increasing tension between the old and the new medium, and the pressure to relieve that tension, found expression in a vigorous discourse about the relationship between literature and cinema — a relationship that has institutional, socioeconomic, and aesthetic dimensions" (1987, 7). Along similar lines, Heinz B. Heller speaks of film as a catalyst in the debate on literature and society; accordingly, he describes his *Literarische Intelligenz und Film* as the attempt "to document and evaluate, from the perspective of various media, the changes in aesthetic theory and practice of the cultural, and specifically, literary intelligentsia in the socio-historical context of the first third of our century." (1984, 5).

**2.** Not surprisingly, the paradigms of literature and literary history still dominate much scholarly work on silent cinema in Germany. Examples include Durzak 1966, Jahn 1962, and, for a general introduction, Paech 1988.

**3.** Famous "cinema poets" included Jacob van Hoddis, Rudolf Leonhard, Ludwig Rubiner, Alfred Lichtenstein, and Ferdinand Hardekopf. Many poems and stories refer to the cinema only in the title, thus using the new medium as a metaphor, or a model, for their poetic experiments; some have been anthologized by Strempel and Ripkens 1984.

**4.** Frank Wedekind, Peter Altenberg, and other writers answered the question "Ist das Kinematographen-Drama ein Kunstwerk?" published in *Erste Internationale Film-Zeitung* 6 (Feb.–Apr. 1912). *Der Kinematograph* of 25 Sept. 1912, presented a similar questionnaire, "Das Kino im Urteil bekannter Zeitgenossen" with responses from Frank Wedekind, Bertha von Suttner, Friedrich Freksa, and others.

**5.** Only a small number of Expressionist plays were adapted to the screen, among them Frank Wedekind's *Der Erdgeist* (1917, 1929), Georg Kaiser's *Von Morgens bis Mitternachts* (1920, From morn till midnight), and Walter Hasenclever's *Die Pest* (1920, The plague), which was, according to the publisher Paul Cassirer, "the first film text in book form." The vast majority of literary adaptations were based on the classics of world literature (Goethe, Schiller, Shakespeare, Molière) and late-nineteenth-century authors, especially the Naturalists (Hauptmann, Strindberg, Ibsen, Sudermann). On the influence of film on the modern drama, and the work of Kaiser in particular, see Kahn 1923–24. On the problems of adaptation, see Ritscher 1914.

**6.** *Circenses* refers to the Roman motto *panem et circenses* (bread and circuses).

**7.** Tom Levin argues convincingly how Lukács's critical position on film changed from these early thoughts on filmic realism — with the important distinction between the possible and the real — to the normative thrust of his later "technologico-positivistic metaphysics of indexicality" (1987–88, 56). For a feminist reading that examines Lukács's notion of presence in relation to questions of gender, see Schlüpmann 1990c, 278–86. For a general assessment of Lukács's film aesthetics (without a discussion of the 1913 essay), see Aristarco 1965.

**8.** Compare Ernst Reinhard, who offers a much bleaker analysis: "The theater has been built as a class theater; it has been dominated by the spirit of one class. But our times have seen the rise and the empowerment of a class previously ignored by the theater. Thus what is happening had to happen: the people's total alienation from the theater. . . . They turn away and satisfy their needs elsewhere" (1926, 20). For a comparative analysis about the film-theater debate in France that includes brief digressions on the German situation, see Lenk 1989, 57–60, 115–17, 149–51, 295–98, and 353–58.

**9.** The later writings of Germany's most prominent theater producers bear witness to a continuous sense of ambivalence. Max Reinhardt, the great innovator of the stage, was the first to translate the experience of mass society into his vision of a theater of the masses, "the theater of five thousand." But in spite of the dynamic mass choreography, the masterly use of dramatic lighting, and the mixture of disparate generic elements that characterized his monumental stage productions, Reinhardt's theoretical writings on film (and his own films) were surprisingly uninspired. His view on the cinema, as formulated in 1924, sounded peculiarly dated. "This art form has grown on alien soil and continues to thrive on it. It is a parasite (and, by the way, a very dangerous parasite!) of the theater, of literature, of painting" (1974, 328). Reinhardt directed, among other films, *Die Insel der Seligen* (1914, The isle of the blessed), and *Die venetianische Nacht* (1916, The Venetian night). On Reinhardt and film, see Werner 1987.

Leopold Jessner, who was known for his anti-Naturalist stage sets (e.g., the famous Jessner stairs) remained skeptical, even as he acknowledged the cinema's importance: "It has become the living newspaper of our times, a vivid communicator of foreign culture and history, the servant of science. Even if it wanted only to entertain, today's educated classes flock to it with more than a superficial interest, almost as if they would go to the theater" (1979, 242). Like Reinhardt, Jessner directed a number of films, including *Die Hintertreppe* (1921, Backstairs) and *Erdgeist* (1920, Earth spirit).

It was left to Erwin Piscator to explore the artistic potential of film, as is made evident by his multimedia stage productions and his theoretical writings on a future revolutionary theater. The seemingly effortless transcendence of distances made possible by means of montage and camera movement provided, in his view, a theoretical model for the much more difficult overcoming of distances in the political arena. Expanding the proscenium stage to a four-dimensional space (i.e., a space comprising stage and auditorium) and making the audience part of the action, Piscator argued, represented the first steps toward an actively political theater and its new protagonist, the working masses (1968, 2:93–94, 97–99).

## Chapter 5

**1.** On this point, see Miriam Hansen. "Tentatively, I would argue that the block of resistance in the cinema's path to cultural respectability (and thus acceptance into the dominant public sphere) was sexual and gender-related, rather than primarily class-related" (1983, 173).

**2.** As Hofmannsthal's own film projects reveal, the fascination with gestures and facial expressions produced some blind spots in his reflections on mime. His film pantomime, *Das fremde Mädchen* (1913, The strange girl), written for the dancer Grete Wiesenthal, received only negative reviews; later film projects, including the scenarios *Defoe* and *Lucidor* (an early sketch for the libretto of *Arabella*) were never completed.

## Chapter 6

**1.** *Kino* is an abbreviation of *der Kinematograph* (masc.); hence also *der Kino* (masc.) and, as the more neutral term, *das Kino* (neutr.). The expression *der/das Kientopp* (pl. *die Kientöppe*) was already obsolete by 1914 and, from then on, was used to evoke nostalgically the childhood of film.

**2.** The titles of books and articles published between 1913 and 1925 are very telling in this regard; for a few examples, see Güttinger 1984b, 23–27. Other neologisms like *filmaturgisch* (as opposed to the *film dramaturgisch*), proposed by Paul Beyer (1921, 89), or *Szenologie* (as opposed to *Dramaturgie*), proposed by Bernhard Diebold (1932, 403), showed a similar tendency in the film aesthetics to emphasize the emancipation of film from the other arts.

**3.** For a general introduction to Weimar culture, see Gay 1970, Bullivant 1977, Willet 1978, Schrader and Schebera 1988, Trommler and Hermand 1988. Standard introductions to the silent German cinema include Eisner 1977 and Kracauer 1947. For a historical survey, also see Plummer et al. 1982. On the film industry in particular, see Bächlin 1975 (34–54) and Spiker 1975 (33–79). For more sociological approaches, see Huaco 1965 and Monaco 1976. For a selection of classical films, see Brennicke and Hembus 1983 and Dahlke and Karl 1988.

**4.** Linda Schulte-Sasse concludes her overview of Weimar film criticism with the following remark: "Although the language of reviews from the twenties often appears maudlin and artificial today, the same aesthetic categories and reverence for autonomous 'art' still dominate journalistic critiques and literary criticism. For this reason the dangers inherent in them may be easily overlooked" (1982, 59).

**5.** This article inspired an exchange of words with Ludwig Wolff, the director of one of the reviewed films. See Wolff 1921, Siemsen 1921c, and Siemsen 1921d.

## Chapter 7

**1.** One of Hauptmann's plays, *Die Austreibung* (The expulsion), was adapted to the screen in 1923 by F. W. Murnau.

**2.** It would be interesting to study the academic discourses in greater detail, especially how the categories of law and economics change film as a discursive subject and cultural practice. A case in point is the extensive debate on authorship from a legal perspective. One of many dissertations dealing with this problem is Walter Bernstein's "Der Filmautor und seine urheberrechtlichen Befugnisse" (1923, Univ. of Breslau). It focuses on the rights of the scenarist, whereas Max Daniel's "Das Verfilmungsrecht" (1922, Univ. of Würzburg) and Werner Frehse's "Der Verfilmungsvertrag: Seine Grundlagen und seine Rechtsnatur" (1926, Univ. of Kiel) are concerned with the problem of literary adaptations and potential conflicts between writers and film studios. Emphasizing film's contribution to science and technology, some dissertations also expand its field of application to disciplines like physics, medicine, and psychology. This is evidenced by Johannes Vieweg's "Die Stadien der geistigen Entwicklung: Eine Untersuchung zur Aussagepsychologie an Erwachsenen und Kindern mit Hilfe des Kinematographen" (1918, Univ. of Leipzig) and Frieda Fuchs's "Experimentelle Studien über das Bewegungsbild" (1928, Univ. of Frankfurt am Main). The cinema's educational values are discussed in Ernst Degner's "Kinematographische Darstellungen im Dienst der sozialen Hygiene" (1918, Univ. of Berlin) and Heinrich Schüen's "Geographischer Lehrfilm und moderne Geographie: Eine methodisch-kritische Untersuchung" (1927, Univ. of Greifswald).

However, the largest number of film dissertations written in the late twenties focus on economic questions. While some deal with specific problems such as the local entertainment tax and city ordinances, others discuss the contribution of the film industry to Germany's active trade balance. Examples include Franz Hayler's "Die deutsche Filmindustrie und ihre Bedeutung für Deutschlands Handel" (1925, Univ. of Würzburg) and Kurt Andersen's "Über die deutsche Filmindustrie und ihre volkswirtschaftliche Bedeutung unter Berücksichtigung ihrer internationalen Beziehungen" (1927, Univ. of Munich). A few dissertations also take a historical perspective, with Rahel Lipschütz's "Der Ufa-Konzern: Geschichte, Aufbau und Bedeutung im Rahmen des deutschen Filmgewerbes" (1932, Univ. of Berlin), a historical study of Germany's largest film studio, being one of the first film historical dissertations.

**3.** In the published and revised version of his dissertation, *Die Seele des Lichtspiels,* Bloem continues to target the problem of mechanical reproduction. Again, he paints horror visions of cultural decline, but he also shows a greater willingness to consider practical solutions. Again, he ostracizes the film drama, this spearhead of a new barbarism, but he also identifies the steps necessary for the salvation of spiritual culture. Analyzing film's emotional appeal, Bloem insists that the lack of distance between filmic image and reality required an increased artistic effort and a radical will to form, if harmful excesses are to be prevented. Only through strong authorial control and an intense need to create could film rise from "soulless sensuality" to "sensual soulfulness" (Bloem 1922, 143) and fulfill its foremost goal, the "reconciliation of culture and civilization" (1922, 185).

**4.** The book is dedicated to Otto Gebühr, who played Frederick the Great in the immensely popular *Fridericus* films. Stindt developed further some of his ideas in an article on the close-up (Stindt 1925) which elicited a sharp response from Balázs 1982, 351–54.

**5.** In *Kulturbedeutung und Kulturgefahren des Films* (1927, The cultural significance and the cultural dangers of film), a shorter, popularized version of the first book, Harms paid more attention to the relationship between film's commercial success, its artistic potential, and the entertainment needs of mass audiences. Whereas the first book dealt with fundamental laws, the second one concentrated on the tensions within film that needed to be resolved. The author's attention to conflict suggests the growing influence of external forces that, given his formalist approach, are immediately transformed into formal oppositions. Film, Harms argues, must strike a balance between objective documentation and the claims of universalism and the forces of the imagination, with its inherent tendency toward exaggeration and stylization. The struggle between these opposing tendencies, he warns, continues in the different positions on film's role in society and gives rise to its use for propagandistic purposes. "Film's cultural significance lies in its absolute capability for objective documentation, [but] its cultural danger [lies] in the falsification of documents" (1927, 31). Kracauer criticized such "insights that identify well-known phenomena without analyzing their causes" (1928).

**6.** A source of confusion to later readers, "Expressionist influences" also refers to stylistic elements commonly associated with Futurism and New Objectivity. For a number of key texts on film and Expressionism, including an excerpt from *Expressionismus und Film*, see *Stationen der Moderne* 1989, 75–87.

**7.** An article on the 1918 film season reflects Richter's early interest in questions of film criticism, for instance, when he complains about the resistance of the daily press to publish reviews. "An objective criticism that considers the content, the technical execution, and the artistic possibilities of a film can only be welcomed by the film industry and support its endeavors" (1989b, 70).

**8.** The majority of film stills are taken from abstract films by Eggeling, Richter, Moholy-Nagy, and Fischinger or Soviet films by Eisenstein, Pudovkin, and Vertov; the few stills from American films serve primarily as bad examples. A similar use of graphic design, illustrations, and content can be found in Werner Gräff's books, *Es kommt der neue Fotograf!* (1929, Here comes the new photographer!) and *Das Buch vom Film* (1931, The book about film), which contains stills and sketches accompanied by brief notes on topics such as "the studio," "film architecture," and "sound film." Gräff's books seem to have been aimed at younger readers and were reviewed positively (see Kracauer 1929).

**9.** Calling for a socially responsible film in *The Struggle for the Film*, Richter explored in great detail the social and cultural function of mainstream cinema. He developed a concept of progressive film that combined many of his original thoughts with a broader critique of the social conditions by pointing to the monotony of industrial working conditions and a social reality that had become inaccessible to critical analysis. Richter's critique of the dominant cinema and his rejection of the narrative film was motivated, above all, by a passionate interest in film's visual potential, and not by his resistance to its foundation in mass culture. "The progressive cinema, on the contrary, ought to seek a method which will enable it so to develop the audience's capacities for thought and judgment that they can link the action on the screen with their own lives, it ought to develop methods which will achieve this goal, and at the same time completely satisfy the masses' need for spectacle and entertainment" (1986, 133). The book contains an extensive bibliography. Surprisingly, Noël Carroll's 1987–88 review essay on *The Struggle for the Film* and its significance for today's film avant-garde does not mention Richter's earlier book, *Filmgegner von heute*.

**10.** Profiting from insights he had gained as the director of the sound film syndicate Tobis, Bagier later wrote a book about problems of the sound film, *Das tönende Licht* (1943, The sounding light). He worked on the sound for Pabst's *Westfront 1918* (1930) and other films.

## Chapter 8

**1.** During the twenties and early thirties, the Russian-born Stepun taught sociology at the University of Dresden.

**2.** For the wider implications, compare Zweig's "Der Angriff der Gegenstände," *Das Tage-Buch* 4 (1923): 557–60. For a discussion of this essay, see Heller 1984, 184–86.

**3.** Schulz wrote the scenario for Sternheim's *Die Hose* (1927), directed by Hans Behrendt. For some personal remarks, see "Das Film-Manuskript. Bemerkungen eines Filmautors," *Das Tage-Buch* 10: 520–26. For a critical discussion of the problems of scenario writing, see Haas 1921–22, "Das künstlerische Film-Manuskript," *Das blaue Heft* 3: 371–76.

**4.** To mention only those scenarists who also wrote criticism, *Film-Kurier* critic Willy Haas collaborated with Thea von Harbou on the original script for Murnau's *Der brennende Acker* (1922, The burning field). Making a name for himself with skilled literary adaptations, Haas brought Hugo Bettauer's novel to the screen for Pabst's *Die freudlose Gasse* (1925, The joyless street). The poet, dramatist, and critic Rudolf Leonhard worked on several Pabst films, including *Tagebuch einer Verlorenen* (1929, Diary of a lost girl), based on the novel by Margarete Böhme, and *Die Liebe der Jeanne Ney* (1927, The love of Jeanne Ney), after Ilja Ehrenburg's novel of the same name. Starting out as a theater critic and novelist, Willy Rath had his greatest successes in the early twenties; he is best known for his work on Urban Gad's film adaptation of Gerhart Hauptmann's drama *Hanneles Himmelfahrt* (1922, Hannele's ascent to heaven).

**5.** Compare an earlier statement by Brecht on film and kitsch: "There are effective films that even have an effect on people who regard them as kitsch, but there are no effective films written by people who regard them as kitsch" (1967, 18:137). On Brecht and the poetics of film, see Kaes 1987, 29–32. On Brecht and media in general, see Gersch 1975 and Mueller 1989. On Balázs and Brecht, see Palmier 1977, 77–112.

**6.** Perceiving the mass infatuation with stars as a reaction to the economic crisis, Kracauer reviewed a number of these star biographies, including Hans Albers, Marlene Dietrich, and Charlie Chaplin (Kracauer 1931).

**7.** When Thea Lossen loses her eyesight at the end, Rosa Porten repeats a motif from *Das Liebesglück der Blinden* (1910), in which Henny Porten plays a blind girl. The blond "film princess" in the novel also has a sister, Edith, who, like Rosa Porten herself, is married to an assistant director. Theodor Heinrich Mayer's Chaplin novel *Clown der Welt* (1931) relies on the same blend of fiction and biragraphy; the Austrian novelist tells the story of a poor, unhappy Austrian clown, Josef Brüwer, who achieves world fame as the Hollywood star Joe Jackson.

**8.** Bronnen had proclaimed earlier that it "is no coincidence that there is money in film, and poverty in the theater. Every period pays for its essence. The cinemas are an extract of this epoch, the theater only its surrogate" (Güttinger 1984a, 480). Bronnen would soon abandon such sarcasm for a career in public broadcasting under the Nazis.

**9.** From 1908 to 1910, Baum was married to the journalist Max Prels, the author of *Der Kino* (1923). Many of her novels were serialized in the *Berliner Illustrirte*, and some were adapted to the screen; the most famous one, *Menschen im Hotel* (1929), was filmed twice, in 1932 by Edmund Goulding as *Grand Hotel*, and in 1959 by Gottfried Reinhardt.

**10.** For more references, see the bibliographies in Greve at al. 1976 and Traub and Lavies 1940.

**11.** Wesse also refers to himself: "in an ecstatic hymn by a contemporary lyricist, Curt Wesse, I read the following celebratory verse" (1928, 143).

## Chapter 9

**1.** On the goals of the association, see Franz Höllering, "Eroberung des Films I," *Film und Volk* 1.3–4 (June 1928): 4–5 and "Eroberung des Films II," *Film und Volk* 1.5 (Aug. 1928): 4–5; and S. Alher, "Revolution von unten," *Film und Volk* 1.5 (Aug. 1928): 6.

**2.** A political activist and journalist, Eggebrecht wrote several scenarios, including one for one of the last silent films, Max Mack's *Der Kampf der Tertia* (1928, Tertia's struggle).

**3.** From 1922 to 1924, Beyfuß headed Ufa's *Kulturfilm* department; in the late twenties, he contributed to *Film und Volk*.

**4.** Harry Liedtke had gained enormous popularity as the romantic lead in film comedies, Gerhart Hauptmann was the most famous and respected German dramatist of the time, and Gustav Stresemann had been chancellor and foreign minister in the Weimar Republic.

**5.** Kalbus wrote and directed one of the first cross-section films, *Henny Porten. Leben und Laufbahn einer Filmkünstlerin* (1928, The life and career of a film actress).

## Chapter 10

**1.** Heller uses the writings of Balázs and Arnheim to distinguish between sociological and aesthetic approaches in film criticism (1984, 24–28).

**2.** Compare Arnheim's 1935 definition of film criticism in 1977, 172–76.

**3.** Many of the formulations appear in *Der Geist des Films,* a collection of his published shorter works. As a rule, discussion of Balázs's key concepts will be based on the articles and reviews in which they first appear. Thus the emphasis will be on the historical context rather than on the three books that constitute his film theoretical oeuvre.

**4.** The book was first published in Russian as *Iskusstvo Kino* (Moscow: Goskinoizdat, 1945); the first German edition appeared two years later as *Der Film. Werden und Wesen einer neuen Kunst,* trans. Alexander Sacher-Masoch (Vienna: Globus, 1947).

**5.** On the contribution of Hungarian intellectuals to German and Austrian culture, see Congdon 1991, 100–36. On Balázs's life in German exile, see Ralmon 1977. On his contribution to early film theory, see Grignaffini 1989, 78–84. For a brief biographical sketch, see Diederichs in Balázs 1982, 11–41 and, by the same author, the biographical entry in *Cinegraph.*

**6.** On Balázs's literary and political activities in Berlin, see Gersch in Bálazs 1982, 19–32, and, for a very detailed account of Balázs's life, see Zsuffa 1987.

**7.** Notwithstanding such ostracization, Balázs's writings influenced Benjamin, Kracauer, and Adorno, as Koch argues persuasively (Koch 1987).

**8.** For two different assessments that focus on Balázs's stature as a Marxist film theoretician, see Palmier 1977, 7, and Diederichs 1982, 14. For a more balanced evaluation, see Koch 1987, 167.

**9.** On film theory and physiognomy, see Jampolski 1986.

**10.** Hartmut Bitomsky makes a similar point when he writes that "Balázs never lets us forget where his knowledge comes from: from the watching of films, not just from the reading of texts about films. In other words, his theory never leaves the stage of reception" (Bitomsky 1972, 537).

**11.** The opening chapter of *Der sichtbare Mensch* appears revised as Chapter V, "Der sichtbare Mensch," in *Theory of the Film* (1970, 39–45).

**12.** On the contradiction between Balázs's idealist terminology and his revolutionary pathos, see Heller 1984, 231–43.

**13.** Koch makes a similar point: "Thus Balázs ultimately remained within the pale of an anthropologically centered aesthetics, which assumes a basic human bent and need for expressive behavior" (1987, 176). At the same time, Koch emphasizes the progressive qualities inherent in what she calls Balázs's Romantic phenomenology—that is, an "aesthetic democratization of reality."

**14.** On Balázs and *Lebensphilosophie,* see Karádi and Vezér 1985, 7–27. On his theory of acting, and the influence of *Bild und Film* critics in particular, see Diederichs 1986b.

**15.** On Balázs and Gestalt psychology, see Schubert 1988.

**16.** Later editions of the book delete the word *white.* The entire paragraph is missing from the "Der sichtbare Mensch" section in *Theory of the Film.*

**17.** On the "beauty of nature" (*Naturschöne*) in Balázs, see Koch 1987, 169–70.

**18.** Balázs's critical style inspired the following comparison: "Like a hunter in action, he tells of living films that roam the movies in packs; at the same time, he also describes them as the first anatomist and biologist" (Musil 1978, 1138). And in a letter to Max Frisch, Musil asked: "Don't reject B. B., of whom you don't have a favorable opinion; this book of his is really good" (1817).

**19.** Balázs's essentially romantic approach to politics can also be seen in his defense of Arnod Fanck's *Der heilige Berg* (1927, The sacred mountain). Engaging in a fictitious argument with left-liberal critics such as Kracauer, Balázs defended this "greatest director of nature films" against those "who don't take so bloody seriously the social struggle that they would want to do something about it. Rather their aversion also comes out against the glorious revolutionary pathos of the Russian films . . . against pathos in general, it seems. May they continue to remain uninvolved and dry up in their comfortable objectivity that requires no surrender, no sacrifice, no fanaticism" (Balázs 1984, 290). Disapproving of such pathos in life as well as cinema, Kracauer called the film "a monstrous composition of body culture fantasies, sun worshiping, and cosmic indulgence. Even the hardened old hand, who is left untouched by the customary psychobabble, finds himself thrown off balance" (1979, 399–400).

**20.** Introducing Balázs as the author of *Das sichtbare Gesicht* (The visible face) instead of *Der sichtbare Mensch* (The visible man), Fodor seems particularly offended by what he describes as disregard for the revolutionary proletariat and its accomplishments. For a more favorable assessment, see F. B.'s review in *Der Querschnitt* 11 (1931): 66.

**21.** Under the polemical title "Béla forgets the scissors," Eisenstein commented on Balázs's theoretical blind spots in 1926 (Eisenstein 1973, 2:134–41). Gersch, however, argues that "as a theoretician, Balázs internalized the most advanced film language of the period, the sublation of mise-en-scène through montage" (Balázs 1984, 37).

## Chapter 11

**1.** For a Marxist assessment that focuses on the critique of ideology in Kracauer's early writings, see Schweinitz 1988 and Wuss 1988. On Kracauer's relationship to Critical Theory, and his contribution to modern sociology in particular, see Frisby 1986, 109–86.

**2.** Witte quotes a review of Lang's *Die Nibelungs* as Kracauer's first review (Kracauer 1974, 275). Kracauer signed his articles for the *Frankfurter Zeitung* "raca," "Kr.," or "Ginster." On the concept of feuilleton in the *Frankfurter Zeitung*, see Todorow 1988.

**3.** For a selection of Brentano's film reviews for the *Frankfurter Zeitung*, see Brentano 1981. For a chronological account of Kracauer's life, see Belke and Renz 1988. For a short biographical sketch, see Jay 1976. For an introduction to Kracauer's work, see Schröter 1980, Mülder 1985, and Kessler and Levin 1990. For further reference, see the extensive bibliography in Mülder 1985. On the influence of Jewish thought on Kracauer's early writings on film, see Hansen 1991. For a bibliography of works in translation, see Levin 1991.

**4.** For a comparison of reviews of Chaplin's *City Lights* by Kracauer, Pinthus, Arnheim, and Ihering, see Witte's afterword to Kracauer 1974, 268–74.

**5.** On Kracauer's rejection of art cinema and its elitist underpinnings, see Knops 1988, 477. On its implications for the historiography of Weimar cinema, also see Knops 1989.

**6.** For a more traditional approach to Kracauer's concept of realism, see Beyse 1977.

**7.** Drawing attention to this unique quality, Witte introduces the term "production criticism" in order to distinguish Kracauer's writings from a criticism based on taste (Kracauer 1974, 267).

**8.** On the notion of surface and its various meanings, see Mülder 1985, 86–92, and Mülder 1987. On the relationship between theories of mass culture and a "new immanence without depth or transcendence," see Elsaesser 1987b. On the notion of distraction and on Kracauer's debt to Kant, see Schlüpmann 1990a.

**9.** Frieda Grafe found an underlying conservatism in Kracauer's reading of the ornament, arguing that "the subtext of his criticism implies that he, even in the cinema, insists on the individual's old traditional place at the center. *Decorative, ornamental* for him means *empty,* without depth, a surface pretending plenitude" (1976, 37).

**10.** Note the affinities between Kracauer's notion of distraction and Benjamin's notion of shock. Benjamin introduced *shock* to describe the seemingly disparate phenomena of the worker's experience at the machine and that of the pedestrian strolling down the boulevards, visiting loud bars, and conforming to traffic rules. "Thus technology has subjected the human sensorium to a complex kind of training. There came a day when a new and urgent stimulus was met by film. In a film, perception in the form of shocks was established as a formal principle" (1969, 175). These shock effects anticipate the functioning of cinematic representation which, after all, depends on the city's nervous and exciting atmosphere in order to be truly appreciated. Moreover, the new mass media are successful precisely because they reject the kind of appreciation required vis-à-vis a traditional work of art. Benjamin elaborates on the consequences of these changes. "Reception in a state of distraction, which is increasingly noticeable in all fields of art and is symptomatic of profound changes in apperception, finds in film its true means of exercise," he argues in "The Work of Art in the Age of Mechanical Reproduction" (1969, 240), thereby also defending the project of modernity against the claims of traditional aesthetics. The dramatic changes in the means of mechanical reproduction, he concludes in this famous essay, could even lead to new relationships between art and the masses: "Thus, for contemporary man the representation of reality by the film is incomparably more significant than that of the painter, since it offers, precisely because of the thoroughgoing permeation of reality with mechanical equipment, an aspect of reality which is free of all equipment. And that is what one is entitled to ask from a work of art" (1969, 234). Like Kracauer, Benjamin believes in the possibility of overcoming the repressive aspects of mass culture by returning to its material basis. With the critical and receptive tendencies coinciding in the moment of visual pleasure, the cinema, according to Benjamin, will eventually become the locus of a new kind of collectivity, subject only to the needs of the masses.

**11.** My translation is indebted to Levin (Kracauer 1987a). Pointing to Kracauer's radical departure from earlier theories of mass diversion, Schlüpmann argues elsewhere: "Kracauer transforms the cinema from a familiar site of experiences and locus of reflection back into a strange phenomenon whose meaning remains to be established. . . . It is no longer a matter of simply being for or against the cinema as a place where the needs of the masses are satisfied. Rather, it is a question of whether the cinema will be established as a tool of social domination or whether an aesthetic opposition from below will be able to assert itself" (1987, 101–2).

**12.** Calico cotton is used in book-binding and, less frequently, set construction.

**13.** There is an interesting connection between "The Cult of Distraction" and the concept of realism in *Theory of Film;* it can be located in the latter's subtitle, *The Redemption of Physical Reality,* and the way it embodies the desires of an imaginary spectator: "He misses 'life.' And he is attracted to cinema because it gives him the illusion of vicariously partaking of life in its fullness" (1960, 167).

On the continuities in Kracauer's work and his relationship to Critical Theory, see Schlüpmann 1987.

**14.** On Kracauer's notion of gendered spectatorship in relation to Sartre and cinema, see Harvey 1991. In her feminist critique of Kracauer, Petro argues: "Following Kracauer's observations, we may draw the conclusion that women's relationship to modernity in the 1920s was entirely different from what was commonly projected onto the figure of woman during the Weimar period. Indeed, we may suspect that women's relationship to modernity and mass culture has all too frequently been confused with male desire, and with male perceptions of gender" (1987, 139–40). For a different reading that emphasizes "the collective nature and depersonalizing force of modern visual pleasure," see Elsaesser 1984, 77–82.

### Chapter 12

**1.** For a brief introduction to Arnheim, see Diederichs 1975. By the same author, see the afterword to Arnheim 1979 and the biographical entry in *Cinegraph* 1984.

**2.** Compare the introduction to *Film as Art,* where the tone is much more individualistic, with Arnheim referring to himself as "a monomaniac, who sank into his studies of the motion picture whatever he had learned about psychology and art" (1957, 2).

**3.** The references are to Thea von Harbou, Fritz Lang's wife and scenarist; Hans Poelzig, the set designer for *Der Golem* and other Expressionist films; the Lang science-fiction film *Die Frau im Mond;* Opel, a car manufacturer; Otto Gebühr, the actor playing Fredrick the Great in the *Fridericus* films; and Hans Günther's racist treatise, *Rassenkunde des deutschen Volkes* (1922).

**4.** On photography, also see "Die Seele in der Silberschicht," *Die Weltbühne* 21 (1925): 141–43.

**5.** Koch uses these oppositions to make a very similar point (1990, 170).

**6.** Compare the discussion of parallelism, counterpoint, and asynchronism in Arnheim 1974, 282–302.

**7.** Under the traumatic influence of the ban, Arnheim contributed an article about "Jews and Film" to Siegmund Kaznelson's *Juden im deutschen Kulturbereich* (1934).

**8.** This discussion is missing in the American edition of *Film as Art;* it appears in *Film als Kunst* (1974) under the title "Ästhetische Grundbegriffe," 51–57.

**9.** On photography, mechanical reproduction, and imitation theories of art, see Carroll 1988, 20–29.

**10.** For a detailed discussion, see Carroll 1988, 17–91. Reading *Film as Art* in conjunction with *Art and Visual Perception,* Carroll takes an approach that emphasizes its underlying philosophical assumptions but pays no attention to the historical field that shaped these ideas; he also follows the widespread practice of placing Arnheim, the silent-film theorist, in opposition to Kracauer, the sound-film theorist.

**11.** Compare Koch, who summarizes Arnheim's contribution as follows: "The historical merit of Arnheim consists perhaps mainly in his shaping of film criticism beyond mere antithetical dichotimization of formal description and valorizing interpretation. For Arnheim the reproduction of the *form,* the *Gestalt,* the *structure* itself is based on the performative faculty of vision; the metaphorization of interpretation is a function of this" (1990, 178).

**12.** My translation is indebted to Koch (1990, 168). Compare Carroll: "Thus, *Film as Art* is a curious book—a work essentially of the early thirties, rewritten and adapted for the fifties. Arnheim never recanted the extremism of the earlier edition. If anything, the passage of time radicalized Arnheim's position as a silent-film advocate" (1988, 18–19). Carroll neglects to mention the book's much more far-reaching political implications; what he elsewhere refers to as "the authoriative statement of Arnheim's position" (1988, 7) is also the product of a deliberate rewriting of the history of film theory on the part of Arnheim; "adapted for the fifties," then, also denotes Cold War.

**13.** The long chapter on the sound film summarizes and repeats ideas first formulated in the *Weltbühne* articles. As a matter of fact, the articles are often more concise in their assessment of the artistic and economic problems associated with the sound film.

# Bibliography

Abel, Richard. 1988. *French Film Theory and Criticism. A History/Anthology 1907–1939*. 2 vols. Princeton, N.J.: Princeton Univ. Press.

Ackerknecht, Erwin. 1918. *Das Lichtspiel im Dienste der Bildungspflege. Handbuch für den Lichtspielreformer*. Berlin: Weidmannsche Buchhandlung.

———. 1928. *Lichtspielfragen*. Berlin: Weidmannsche Buchhandlung.

Adler, Max. 1920. "Masse und Mythos." *Die Neue Schaubühne* 2: 299–33.

Adler, Wilhelm. 1917. *Wie schreibe ich einen Film? Ein Lehr- und Hilfsbuch für Filmschriftsteller*. Weimar: Hoffmann.

Adorno, Theodor W. 1984. "Der wunderliche Realist. Über Siegfried Kracauer." *Noten zur Literatur* 3: 388–408. Frankfurt am Main: Suhrkamp.

———. and Max Horckheimer. 1972. *Dialectic of Enlightenment*. New York: Herder and Herder.

Albersmeier, Franz-Josef, ed. 1979. *Texte zur Theorie des Films*. Stuttgart: Reclam.

———. 1984. *Die Herausforderung des Films an die französische Literatur*. Heidelberg: Winter.

Alex. 1922. "Kritik oder Reklame?" *Film-Kurier,* 23 Dec.

Alher, S. 1928. "Revolution von unten." *Film und Volk* 1.5: 6–7.

Allen, Richard. 1987. "The Aesthetic Experience of Modernity: Benjamin, Adorno, and Contemporary Film Theory." *New German Critique* 40: 225–40.

Altenloh, Emilie. 1912–13. "Theater und Kino." *Bild und Film* 11–12: 264–66.

———. 1914. *Zur Soziologie des Kino*. Jena: Diederichs.

Altenberg, Peter. [1912] 1984. "Das Kino." Reprinted in Güttinger 1984a, 63–64.

Amann, Markus. 1983. "Massenpsychologie und Massendarstellung im Film." Ph.D. diss., Univ. of Munich.

Andra, Fern. 1919. *Der Weg, der ins Glaushaus führte. Der Roman eines Frauenlebens*. Berlin: Boutain.

Andrew, Dudley. 1976. *The Major Film Theories. An Introduction*. London: Oxford Univ. Press.

Aristarco, Guido. 1965. "Lukács' Beiträge zu Film und Filmkritik." In *Festschrift zum achtzigsten Geburtstag von Georg Lukács,* ed. Frank Benseler, 588–604. Neuwied: Luchterhand.

Arnheim, Rudolf. 1925. "Die Seele in der Silberschicht." *Die Weltbühne* 21: 141–43.

———. 1928a. "Experimentell-psychologische Untersuchungen zum Ausdrucksproblem." Ph.D. diss., Univ. of Berlin.

———. 1928b. "Filmbücher." *Die Weltbühne* 24: 926.

———. 1928c. "Die Kunst im Volke." *Die Weltbühne* 24: 97–100.

———. 1928d. *Stimme von der Galerie. 5 kleine Aufsätze zur Kultur der Zeit*. Preface by Hans Reimann. Berlin: Benary.

———. 1929a. "Kinematographisches." *Die Weltbühne* 25: 774–77.

———. 1929b. "Psychotische Montage." *Die Weltbühne* 25: 378–81.

———. 1932a. "Die Anmaßung der Sinne." *Die Weltbühne* 28: 211–16.

———. 1932b. "Kurbeln und Knipsen." *Die Weltbühne* 28: 910.

———. 1933. *Film as Art*. Trans. from the German by L. M. Sieverking and F. D. Morrow. London: Faber & Faber.

———. 1954. *Art and Visual Perception: A Psychology of the Creative Eye*. Berkeley: Univ. of California Press.

———. 1957. *Film as Art*. Selections from 1933 British edition of *Film as Art,* with new preface by the author. Berkeley: Univ. of California Press.

———. [1934] 1959. "Juden und Film." In *Juden im deutschen Kulturbereich,* ed. Siegmund Kaznelson, 270–91. 2nd. enl. ed. Berlin: Jüdischer Verlag.

———. 1966. *Towards a Psychology of Art*. Berkeley: Univ. of California Press.

———. 1969. *Visual Thinking*. Berkeley: Univ. of California Press.

———. [1932] 1974. *Film als Kunst. Mit einem Vorwort zur Neuausgabe*. Munich: Hanser.

———, ed. 1977. *Kritiken und Aufsätze zum Film*. Ed. Helmut H. Diederichs. Munich: Hanser.

Bab, Julius. 1912. "Die Kinematographenfrage." *Rheinlande* 22: 311–14.

———. 1920. "Kinematographen-Frage." *Die Hilfe* 26: 28–30.

Bächlin, Peter. 1975. *Der Film als Ware*. Frankfurt am Main: Fischer.

Bagier, Guido. 1928. *Der kommende Film. Eine Abrechnung und eine Hoffnung. Was war? Was ist? Was wird?* Stuttgart: Deutsche Verlagsanstalt.

———. 1943. *Das tönende Licht*. Berlin: A. Gross.

Balázs, Béla. 1924. *Der sichtbare Mensch oder die Kultur des Films*. Vienna: Deutsch-österreichischer Verlag.

———. 1930. *Der Geist des Films*. Halle/Saale: Wilhelm Knapp.

———. 1932. "Die Furcht des Intellektuellen vor dem Sozialismus." *Die Welt-bühne* 28: 93–96, 131–34, 166–68, 207–10.

———. 1947. *Der Film. Werden und Wesen einer neuen Kunst*. Trans. from the Russian by Alexander Sacher-Masoch. Vienna: Globus.

———. [1955] 1970. *Theory of the Film. Character and Growth of a New Art*. Trans. from the Hungarian by Edith Bone. New York: Dover.

———. 1973. *Essay, Kritik 1922–1932*. Ed. Gertraude Kühn, Manfred Lichtenstein, and Eckhardt Jahnke. Berlin/GDR: Staatliches Filmarchiv der DDR.

———. 1982–84. *Schriften zum Film*. 2 vols. Ed. Helmut H. Diederichs, Wolfgang Gersch, and Magda Nagy. Berlin/GDR, Budapest: Hanser.

Barkhausen, Hans. 1982. *Filmpropaganda für Deutschland im Ersten und Zweiten Weltkrieg*. Hildesheim: Olms.

Barlow, John D. 1982. *German Expressionist Film*. Boston: Twayne.

Baum, Vicki. [1932] 1990. *Leben ohne Geheimnis*. Frankfurt am Main: Ullstein.

Beck, Leo. 1919. *Wie werde ich Filmschauspieler?* Munich: Lender.

Behne, Adolf. 1914. "Kinokunst." *Sozialistische Monatshefte* 20: 267–68.

Beilendorf, Wolfgang, ed. 1974. *Poetik des Films*. Munich: Hanser.

Belke, Ingrid, and Irina Renz, eds. 1988. *Siegfried Kracauer 1889–1966. Marbacher Magazin* 47.

Benjamin, Walter. 1969. *Illuminations*. Ed. Hannah Ahrendt. Trans. from the German by Harry Zohn. New York: Schocken.

———. 1980. *Gesammelte Werke*. 12 vols. Ed. Rolf Tiedemann and Hermann Schweppenhäuser. Frankfurt am Main: Suhrkamp.

Berg-Ganschow, Uta, and Wolfgang Jacobson, eds. 1987. *. . . Film . . . Stadt . . . Kino . . . Berlin . . .* . Berlin: Argon.

Berman, Russell. 1983. "Writing for the Book Industry. The Writer under Organized Capitalism." *New German Critique* 29: 39–56.

Beyer, Paul. 1921. "Film! Kunst!" *Der Kritiker* 3: 88–90.

Beyfuß, Edgar. 1929. "Tonfilm oder stummer Film?" *Film und Volk* 2.8: 4–5.

Beyfuß, Edgar, and Alexander Kossowsky, eds. 1924. *Das Kulturfilmbuch*. Berlin: Chryselius.

Beyse, Jochen. 1977. "Film und Wiederspiegelung. Interpretation und Kritik der Theorie Siegfried Kracauers." Ph.D. diss., Univ. of Cologne.

Bitomsky, Harmut. 1972. Introduction to Balázs 1972, *Der Geist des Films*. *Filmkritik* 190: 537.

Bloem, Walter. 1921. "Das Lichtspiel als Gegenstand der ästhetischen Kritik." Ph.D. diss., Univ. of Tübingen.

——. 1922. *Die Seele des Lichtspiels. Ein Bekenntnis zum Film*. Leipzig: Grethlein. Trans. 1924 by Allan W. Porterfield as *The Soul of the Moving Picture*. New York: E. P. Dutton.

Bock, Hans-Michael. 1982. ". . . ein bewußtes Schreiben mit einem Ziel." *Kirche und Film* (epd) 7: 10–12.

Brauneck, Manfred. 1973. *Die Rote Fahne. Kritik, Theorie, Feuilleton*. Munich: Wilhelm Fink.

Brecht, Bertolt. 1967. *Gesammelte Werke*. 20 vols. Frankfurt am Main: Suhrkamp.

——. 1973. *Dreigroschenbuch*. Frankfurt am Main: Suhrkamp.

Bredow, Wilfried von, and Rolf Zurek, eds. 1975. *Film und Gesellschaft in Deutschland. Dokumente und Materialien*. Hamburg: Hoffmann & Campe.

Brennicke, Ilona, and Joe Hembus, eds. 1983. *Klassiker des deutschen Stummfilms 1910–1930*. Munich: Goldmann.

Brentano, Benjamin von. 1981. *Wo in Europa ist Berlin? Bilder aus den zwanziger Jahren*. Frankfurt am Main: Insel.

Bronnen, Arnolt. [1928] 1987. *Film und Leben Barbara la Marr*. Berlin/GDR: Henschelverlag.

Brunner, Karl. 1913. *Der Kinematograph von heute—eine Volksgefahr*. Berlin: Verlag des Vaterländischen Schriften-Verbandes.

Bub, Gertraude. 1938. "Der deutsche Film im Weltkrieg und sein publizistischer Einsatz." Ph.D. diss., Univ. of Berlin.

Buchner, Hans. 1927. *Im Banne des Films. Die Weltherrschaft des Films*. Munich: Deutscher Volksverlag Dr. E. Boepple.

Buck, Elmar. 1977. "Film/Kino und Proletariat?" In *Die schöne Leiche in der Rue Bellechasse,* ed. Elmar Buck, Leo Kreuzer, and Jürgen Peters, 107–35. Reinbek: Rowohlt.

Bullivant, Keith, ed. 1977. *Culture and Society in the Weimar Republic*. Rowman and Littlefield: Manchester Univ. Press.

Burger, Hella. 1978. "Konzepte zur Filmkritik aus den Jahren 1927–1933." In *Medium und Kunst,* ed. Gerhard Charles Rump, 120–65. Hildesheim: Olms.

Carroll, Noël. 1987–88. "Hans Richter's *The Struggle for the Film*." *Millennium Film Journal* 19: 104–13.

——. 1988. *Philosophical Problems of Classical Film Theory*. Princeton, N.J.: Princeton Univ. Press.

Chytry, Josef. 1989. *The Aesthetic State: a Quest in Modern German Thought*. Berkeley: Univ. of California Press.

*Cinegraph. Lexikon zum deutschsprachigen Film.* 1984. Ed. Hans-Michael Bock. Munich: edition text + kritik.

Congdon, Lee. 1991. *Exile and Social Thought. Hungarian Intellectuals in Germany and Austria 1919–1933.* Princeton, N.J.: Princeton Univ. Press.

Conradt, Walther. 1910. *Kirche und Kinematograph.* Berlin: Hermann Walther.

Courths-Mahler, Hedwig. 1928. *Harald Landry, der Filmstar.* Leipzig: Rothbart.

Dahlke, Günther, and Günter Karl, eds. 1988. *Deutsche Spielfilme von den Anfängen bis 1933. Ein Filmführer.* Berlin/GDR: Henschelverlag.

Deak, Istvan. 1969. *Weimar Germany's Left-Wing Intellectuals: A Political History of the "Weltbühne" and Its Circle.* Berkeley: Univ. of California Press.

Delmont, Joseph. 1926. *Der Casanova von Bautzen.* Berlin: Neue Berliner Verlags-Gesellschaft.

Demeter, Karl. 1926. "Soziale Grundlagen des Kinowesens." *Deutsche Rundschau* 43: 57–62.

Diebold, Bernhard. 1932. "Film und Drama." *Die Neue Rundschau* 43: 402–10.

Diederichs, Helmut H. 1975. "'Stumme Schönheit und tönender Unfug.' Rudolf Arnheim—Theoretiker des Films als visueller Kunst." *medium* 9: 24–27.

——. 1982. "Die erste deutsche Filmzeitschrift. Vor 75 Jahren 'Der Kinematograph.'" *medium* 2: 42–43.

——. 1983. "'Kinostücke' oder 'Erzählungen im Kinostil.' Pinthus' 'Kinobuch' in seiner Zeit." *Kirche und Film* (epd) 36: 27–30.

——. 1985a. "Die Anfänge der deutschen Filmpublizistik 1895–1909. Die Filmberichterstattung der Schaustellerzeitschrift 'Der Komet' und die Gründung der Filmfachzeitschriften." *Publizistik* 30: 55–71.

——. 1985b. "Kino im Kopf." *medium* 15: 94–95.

——. 1985c. "Der Schriftsteller als Stummfilmpublikum. " *epd Film* 2: 7.

——. 1986a. *Anfänge deutscher Filmkritik.* Stuttgart: Robert Fischer & Uwe Wiedlerroither.

——. 1986b. "Béla Balázs und die Schauspielertheorie des Stummfilms: 'Der sichtbare Mensch' und seine Vorläufer." In *Wechsel-Wirkungen. Ungarische Avantgarde in der Weimarer Republik,* ed. Hubertus Gaßner, 554–59. Marburg: Jonas.

——. 1990. "Naturfilm als Gesamtkunstwerk. Hermann Häfker und sein 'Kinetographie'-Konzept." *Augenblick* 8: 37–60.

Diehl, Oskar. 1922. *Mimik im Film.* Munich: G. Müller.

Döblin, Alfred. 1910. "Anti-kritisches." *Der Sturm* 1: 280.

——. 1983. *Drama Hörspiel Film*. Ed. Erich Kleinschmidt. Olten: Walter.

Doering, August. 1913. "Dichter und Kino." *Der Merkur* 4: 299–301.

Dovifat, Emil. 1961. "Die Publizistik der Weimarer Zeit." In *Die Zeit ohne Eigenschaften. Eine Bilanz der zwanziger Jahre,* ed. Leonard Reinisch, 119–36. Stuttgart: Kohlhammer.

Drucker, S[amuel]. 1914. "Das Kinoproblem und unsere politischen Gegner." *Die Neue Zeit* 32: 868.

Dunger, Hella. 1978. "Konzepte zur Filmkritik aus den Jahren 1927–1933." In *Medium und Kunst,* ed. G. C. Rump, 120–65. Hildesheim: Olms.

Dupont, Ewald André. 1919a. *Wie ein Film geschrieben wird und wie man ihn verwertet.* Berlin: R. Kühn.

——. 1919b. "Filmkritik und Filmreklame." *Film-Kurier,* 24 Aug.

Durzak, Manfred. 1966. "Hermann Broch und der Film." *Der Monat* 18: 68–75.

Eagelton, Terry. 1990. *The Ideology of the Aesthetic.* London: Basil Blackwell.

Ebert, Jürgen. 1987. "Der 'sachliche' Kritiker. Über Herbert Ihering." In . . . *Film . . . Stadt . . . Kino . . . Berlin . . . ,* ed. Uta Berg-Ganschow and Wolfgang Jacobson, 139–44. Berlin: Argon.

Eckardt, Eva von. 1929. "Ende gut, alles gut? Psychologisches zur Ästhetik des Films." *Der Kreis* 6: 338–45.

Eger, Lydia. 1920. *Kinoreform und Gemeinden.* Dresden: von Zahn & Jaensch.

Ehrenburg, Ilja. 1931. *Die Traumfabrik. Chronik des Films.* Berlin: Malik.

Einstein, Carl. 1980. *Werke.* Ed. Rolf-Weter Baacke and Jens Kwasny. Berlin: Medusa.

Eisenstein, Sergei. 1973. *Schriften.* 2 vols. Ed. and trans. Hans-Joachim Schlegel. Munich: Hanser.

Eisner, Lotte. 1977. *The Haunted Screen.* Trans. Roger Greaves. Berkeley: Univ. of California Press.

Elsaesser, Thomas. 1984. "Film History and Visual Pleasure: Weimar History." In *Cinema Histories, Cinema Practices,* ed. Patricia Mellencamp and Phil Rosen, 47–84. Los Angeles: American Film Institute.

——. 1987a. "Dada/Cinema?" In *Dada and Surrealist Film,* ed. Rudolf Kuenzli, 13–27. New York: Willis Locker & Owens.

——. 1987b. "'The Gamble with History': Film Theory or Cinema Theory." *New German Critique* 40: 77–80.

Elsner, Alexander. 1912–13. "Zur Frage einer Kinokritik," *Bild und Film* 2: 262.

——. 1914. "Zur Kinofrage." *Die Neue Zeit* 32: 671–73.

*Erobert den Film: Proletariat und Film in der Weimarer Republik.* 1977. Ed. Neue Gesellschaft für Bildende Kunst und Freunde der deutschen Kinemathek e.V. West Berlin: NGBK.

Estermann, Alfred. 1965. *Die Verfilmung literarischer Werke*. Bonn: Bouvier.

Faber, Marion. 1979. "Hofmannsthal and the Film." *German Life and Letters* 32.3: 187–95.

Feld, Hans. 1982. "Jews in the Development of the German Film Industry. Notes from the Recollections of a German Film Critic." In *Leo Baeck Institute Year Book* 27:337–65.

Finger, Willy. 1918. *Deutschkunde und Kinodrama. Eine deutschkundliche literarische Kampfschrift*. Berlin: Richters Druckerei.

Fischer, Hans. 1915. *Filmaufnahme in Krähenwinkel*. Bonn: Anton Heidelmann.

Fischer, Samuel. 1926. "Bemerkungen zur Bücherkrise." *Die literarische Welt* 43: 1.

Fodor, T. K. 1932. Review of *Der Geist des Films*. *Die Linkskurve* 4.2: 34–35.

Förster, Franz. 1914. "Das Kinoproblem und die Arbeiter." *Die Neue Zeit* 32: 486.

Fred, W. 1911–12. "Der heilige Kientopp und das olympische Mirakel." *Pan* 2: 232–33.

Freud, Sigmund. 1953–66. *Standard Edition of the Complete Psychological Works of Sigmund Freud*. 24 vols. Trans. and ed. Alex Strachey. London: The Institute of Psycho-Analysis and the Hogarth Press.

Frey, Reiner. 1980. "Die Anfänge der Zuschauerfilmkritik, das Beispiel 'Arbeiterbühne und Film.'" *Filmfaust* 19: 8–16.

Friedell, Egon. 1923–24. "Film und Kunst." *Freie deutsche Bühne* 5: 156–59.

Friedemann, Hermann. 1919. "Schnaps-Schund-Film." *Deutsche Montags-Zeitung*, 11 Nov.

Frisby, David. 1986. *Fragments of Modernity*. Cambridge, Mass.: MIT Press.

Fritz, Walter. 1966. "Arthur Schnitzler und der Film." *Journal of the International Arthur Schnitzler Research Association* 5.4: 11–52.

Fülöp-Miller, René. 1931. *Die Phantasiemaschine. Eine Saga der Gewinnsucht*. Leipzig: Paul Zsolnay.

Furthman-Durden, Elke C. 1986. "Hugo von Hofmannsthal and Alfred Döblin: The Confluence of Film and Literature." *Monatshefte* 78.4: 442–55.

Gad, Urban. 1921. *Der Film. Seine Mittel—seine Ziele*. Trans. from the Danish by Julia Koppel. Berlin: Schuster & Loeffler.

Gaupp, Robert, and Konrad Lange. 1912. *Der Kinematograph als Volksunterhaltungsmittel*. Munich: Dürerbund.

Gay, Peter. 1970. *Weimar Culture. The Outsider as Insider*. New York: Harper & Row.

Geréb, Anna. 1988. "Notiz zu Béla Balázs." *Beiträge zur Film- und Fernsehwissenschaft* 29.34: 149–53.

Gersch, Wolfgang. 1975. *Film bei Brecht*. Munich: Hanser.

Gleichen-Rußwurm, Alexander von. 1917. "Lichtspiel und Dichtung." In *Die Bedeutung des Films und Lichtbildes*. Munich: Flugschrift des Vereins "Deutsche Wacht."

Goldschmidt, Alfons. 1928. "Filmwirtschaft." *Film und Volk* 1.1: 21–23.

Goll, Claire. [1922] 1973. *Lyrische Films. Gedichte*. Basel: Neldeln.

Goll, Yvan. 1917. "Der Kino-Direktor." *Die Aktion* 7: 688.

———. 1920. *Die Chaplinade. Eine Kinodichtung*. Dresden: Kaemmerer.

Gräff, Werner. 1929. *Es kommt der neue Fotograf!* Stuttgart: Deutsche Verlagsanstalt.

———. 1931. *Das Buch vom Film*. Stuttgart: Thiedemann.

Grafe, Frieda. 1976. *Fritz Lang*. Munich: Hanser.

Greve, Ludwig, Margot Pehle, and Heidi Westhoff, eds. 1976. *Hätte ich das Kino! Die Schriftsteller und der Stummfilm*. Ausstellungskatalog des Schiller Nationalmuseums. Stuttgart: Kösel.

Grignaffini, Givanna. 1989. *Sapere e teorie del cinema. Il periodo del muto*, 78–84. Bologna: Cooperativea Libraria Universitaria Editrice Bologna.

Gruber, Helmut. 1965. "Willi Münzenberg: Propagandist for and against the Comintern." *International Review of Social History* 10.2: 188–210.

———. 1966. "Willi Münzenberg's German Communist Propadanda Empire 1921–1933." *The Journal of Modern History* 38: 278–97.

Guerster, Eugen. 1928. "Zur Soziologie des Films." *Die Tat* 20: 210–14.

Gunning, Tom. 1986. "The Cinema of Attractions: Early Film, Its Spectator and the Avant-Garde." *Wide Angle* 8.3–4: 63–70.

Güttinger, Fritz, ed. 1984a. *Kein Tag ohne Kino. Schriftsteller über den Stummfilm*. Frankfurt am Main: Deutsches Filmmuseum.

———. 1984b. *Der Stummfilm im Zitat der Zeit*. Frankfurt am Main: Deutsches Filmmuseum.

Guttmann, Richard. 1919. *Variété. Beiträge zur Psychologie des Pöbels*. Vienna: Deutsch-österreichischer Verlag.

Haas, Willy. 1921. "Sprechbildbühne und Lichtbildbühne." *Die Neue Schaubühne* 3: 153–55.

———. 1921–22. "Das künstlerische Film-Manuskript." *Das blaue Heft* 3: 371–76.

———. 1922. "Fachkritik und litherarische Filmkritik." *Film-Kurier*, 15 Mar.

———. 1924. "Tageskritik und fachliche Kritik." *Film-Kurier*, 11 Feb.

———. 1927. "Der Sinn der Filmkritik. Offene Antwort an Hans Siemsen." *Die Literarische Welt* 3: 7.

Habermas, Jürgen. 1972. *Strukturwandel der Öffentlichkeit*. Frankfurt am Main: Suhrkamp.

Häfker, Hermann. 1913. *Kino und Kunst*. M. Gladbach: Volksvereins-Verlag.

———. 1914. *Kino und Erdkunde*. M. Gladbach: Volksvereins-Verlag.

———. 1915. *Der Kino und die Gebildeten*. M. Gladbach: Volksvereins-Verlag.

Hake, Sabine. 1987. "Girls and Crisis: The Other Side of Diversion." *New German Critique* 40: 147–64.

———. 1990a. "'Pardon, ich suche den Autor dieses Films!' – Zu Fritz von Unruh's 'Phaea.'" In *Wegbereiter der Moderne. Festschrift für Klaus Jonas,* ed. Helmut Koopmann and Clark Muenzer, 171–84. Tübingen: Max Niemeyer.

———. 1990b. "Chaplin Reception in Weimar Germany." *New German Critique* 51: 87–111.

Halter, Hermann. 1921. *Die Kino-Frage. Ein Wort zur Aufklärung über das heutige Kinounwesen*. Meiringen: Walter Loepthien-Klein.

Hansen, Miriam. 1983. "Early Silent Cinema: Whose Public Sphere?" *New German Critique* 29: 147–84.

———. 1991. "Decentric Perspectives: Kracauer's Early Writings on Film and Mass Culture." *New German Critique* 54: 47–76.

Happel, Reinhold, and Margot Michaelis. 1980. "Wem gehört die Welt? – Filme der Arbeiterbewegung in der Weimarer Republik." In *Film und Realität in der Weimarer Republik,* ed. Helmut Korte, 91–102. Frankfurt am Main: Fischer.

Harms, Rudolf. 1926. *Philosophie des Films. Seine ästhetischen und metaphysischen Grundlagen*. Zurich: Felix Meiner.

———. 1927. *Kulturbedeutung und Kulturgefahren des Films*. Karlsruhe in Baden: G. Braun.

Harvey, Robert. 1991. "Sartre/Cinema: Spectator/Art That Is Not One." *Cinema Journal* 30.3: 51–53.

Hein, Birgit, and Wulf Herzogenrath, eds. 1977. *Film als Film: 1910 bis heute*. Cologne: Kölnischer Kunstverein.

Heller, Heinz-B. 1982a. "Der destruktive Intellektuelle. Anmerkungen zu einem Sozialtypus im expressionistischen Film." In *Expressionismus – sozialer Wandel und künstlerische Erfahrung,* ed. Horst Meixner and Silvio Vietta, 73–88. Munich: Fink.

———. 1982b. "Literatur und Film." In *Zwischen den Weltkriegen,* ed. Thomas Koebner, 161–94. Wiesbaden: Athenaion.

———. 1984. *Literarische Intelligenz und Film. Zu Veränderungen der ästhetischen Theorie und Praxis under dem Eindruck des Films 1910–1930 in Deutschland*. Tübingen: Max Niemeyer.

———. 1987. "Aus-bilder. Anfänge der deutschen Filmpresse." In . . . *Film* . . .

*Stadt . . . Kino . . . Berlin . . .*, ed. Uta Berg-Ganschow and Wolfgang Jacobson, 117–26. Berlin: Argon.

———. 1990. "Massenkultur und ästhetische Urteilskraft. Zur Geschichte und Funktion der deutschen Filmkritik vor 1933." In *Die Macht der Filmkritik. Positionen und Kontroversen*, ed. Norbert Gorb and Karl Prümm, 23–44. Munich: edition text + kritik.

Hellwig, Albert. 1911. *Schundfilms. Ihr Wesen, ihre Gefahren und ihre Bekämpfung.* Halle a.d.S.: Verlag der Buchhandlung des Waisenhauses.

Hesse, Hermann. [1927] 1961. *Steppenwolf.* Trans. from the German by Basil Creighton. New York: Holt, Rinehart and Winston.

Hickethier, Knut. 1986. "Schauspieler zwischen Theater und Kino in der Stummfilmzeit." In *Grenzgänger zwischen Theater und Kino. Schauspielerporträts aus dem Berlin der Zwanziger Jahre*, 11–42. Berlin: Edition Mythos Berlin.

Hirschbach, Frank, Friedrich Achberger, Sarah Bryant-Bertail, et al., eds. 1980. *Germany in the Twenties: The Artist as Social Critic.* New York: Holmes & Meier.

Höllering, Franz. 1928. "Eroberung des Films." 2 parts. *Film und Volk* 1.3–4: 4–5; 1.5: 4–5.

Höllriegel, Arnold [pseud. Richard Bermann]. 1913. "Gedrucktes Kino." *Die Schaubühne* 9: 1028–29.

———. [c. 1928]. *Du sollst dir kein Bildnis machen. Ein Roman aus Hollywood.* Munich: Drei Masken.

Honigsheim, Paul. 1920. "Die soziologischen und soziopsychologischen Grundlagen des Kinos." *Der Bildwart*: 552–63.

Huaco, George A. 1965. *The Sociology of Film Art.* Foreword by Leo Lowenthal. London: Basic.

Hübner, Hermann. 1928. "Diese Filmkritik." *Film und Volk* 1.5: 8–10.

Hummel, Christoph. 1986. Review of Heller, *Literarische Intelligenz. epd Film* 2: 8.

Ickes, Paul. 1919. "Film-Kritik?" *Film-Kurier*, 10 Sept.

Ihering, Herbert. 1961. *Von Reinhardt bis Brecht.* 3 vols. Ed. Edith Krull. Berlin/GDR: Aufbau-Verlag.

Iros, Ernst [Julius Rosenstiel]. 1928. "Ästhetik und Dramaturgie der Filmdichtung." *Erwachen* 2: 276–82.

———. 1938. *Wesen und Dramaturgie des Films.* Zurich: Niehans.

Jacob, Heinrich Eduard. 1930. *Blut und Zelluloid.* Berlin: Rowohlt.

Jacobs, Lewis. 1934. Review of *Film As Art. Experimental Cinema* 5: 48.

Jacobsen, Wolfgang. 1989. *Erich Pommer. Ein Produzent macht Filmgeschichte.* Berlin: Stiftung Deutsche Kinemathek and Argon.

Jacobsen, Wolfgang, Karl Prümm, and Benno Wenz, eds. 1991. *Willy Haas. Der Kritiker als Mitproduzent. Texte zum Film 1920–1933.* Berlin: Edition Hentrich.

Jacobson, Eugen. 1918. *Flimmeritis. Was jeder vom Kino wissen muß.* Berlin: Verlag der Illustrierten-Film Woche.

Jahn, Wolfgang. 1962. "Kafka und die Anfänge des Kinos." *Jahrbuch der deutschen Schillergesellschaft* 9: 353–68.

Jampolski, Michail. 1986. "Die Geburt einer Filmtheorie aus dem Geiste der Physiognomik." *Beiträge zur Film- und Fernsehwissenschaft* 27.2: 79–98.

Jay, Martin. 1976. "The Extraterritorial Life of Siegfried Kracauer." *Salmagundi* 31–32: 49–106.

Jessner, Leopold. 1979. *Schriften. Theater der zwanziger Jahre.* Ed. Hugo Fetting. Berlin/GDR: Henschel.

Jossé, Harald. 1984. *Die Entstehung des Tonfilms. Beitrag zu einer faktenorientierten Mediengeschichtschreibung.* Freiburg and Munich: Karl Alber.

Kaes, Anton, ed. and intro. 1978. *Kino-Debatte. Texte zum Verhältnis von Literatur und Film 1909–1929.* Munich and Tübingen: Max Niemeyer.

———. 1979. "The Expressionist Vision in Theater and Cinema." In *Expressionism Reconsidered: Affinities and Relationships,* ed. Gertrud Bauer Pickar and Karl Eugen Francke, 89–98. Munich: Fink.

———. 1982. "Verfremdung als Verfahren: Film und Dada." In *Sinn aus Unsinn. Dada International,* ed. Wolfgang Paulsen and Helmut G. Hermann, 71–83. Munich: Francke.

———, ed. 1983. *Weimarer Republik: Manifeste und Dokumente zur deutschen Literatur 1918–1933.* Stuttgart: Metzler.

———. 1985. "Mass Culture and Modernity: Notes Toward a Social History of Early American and German Cinema." In *America and the Germans: An Assessment of a Three-Hundred Year History,* ed. Frank Trommler and Joseph McVeigh, 2: 317–31. Philadelphia: Univ. of Pennsylvania Press.

———. 1987. "The Debate about Cinema: Charting a Controversy (1909–1929)." Trans. David J. Levin. *New German Critique* 40: 7–33.

Kahn, Harry. 1923–24. "Das dynamische Drama." *Der neue Merkur* 7: 501–8.

Kalbus, Oskar. 1920a. "Lichtspieltheorien." *Film-Kurier,* 21 Jan.

———. 1920b. "Die Stummheit des Filmbildes." *Der Kinematograph* 723.

———. 1920c. "Film und Literatur." *Film-Kurier,* 7 April.

———. 1922a. *Der deutsche Lehrfilm in der Wissenschaft und im Unterricht.* Berlin: Carl Heymanns Verlag.

———. 1922b. "Politik und Film." *Der Kinematograph* 805, 810, 819. 3-part article.

———. 1935. *Vom Werden deutscher Filmkunst*. 2 vols. Altona-Bahrenfeld: Cigaretten-Bilderdienst.

Karádi, Eva, and Erzsébet Vezér, eds. 1985. *Georg Lukács, Karl Mannheim und der Sonntagskreis*. Frankfurt am Main: Sendler.

Kästner, Erich. [1928] 1949. "Ästhetik des Films." *Filmkunst* 3: 178.

Keiner, Reinhold. 1987. *Hanns Heinz Ewers und der phantastische Film*. Hildesheim: Olms.

Keply, Vance Jr. 1983. "The Workers' International Relief and the Cinema of the Left, 1921–1935." *Cinema Journal* 23.1. 7–23.

Kern, Hans. 1925. "Kinokultur oder Filmkultur?" *Eckart* 2: 111.

Kerr, Alfred. 1917. *Gesammelte Schriften in zwei Reihen*. Berlin: S. Fischer.

———. 1927. *Russische Filmkunst*. Berlin: E. Pollak.

———. 1991. *Werke in Einzelbänden*. 3 vols. Ed. Hermann Haarmann and Klaus Siebenhaar. Berlin: Argon.

Kessler, Michael, and Thomas Y. Levin, eds. 1990. *Siegfried Kracauer: Neue Interpretationen*. Tübingen: Stauffenburg Verlag.

Keun, Irmgard. [1932] 1986. *Das kunstseidene Mädchen*. Munich: Ernst Klett.

Kienzl, Hans. 1911. "Theater und Kinematograph." *Der Strom* 1: 219.

Kinter, Jürgen. 1985. *Arbeiterbewegung und Film (1895–1933). Zur Geschichte der Arbeiter- und Alltagskultur und der gewerkschaftlichen und sozialdemokratischen Kultur- und Medienarbeit*. Hamburg: Medienpädagogik-Zentrum.

Knops, Tilo-Rudolf. 1988. "Zwischen Weimar und Hollywood: Zum Widerstreit von Erfahrung und Theorie bei Kracauer." *Rundfunk und Fernsehen* 38: 465–83.

———. 1989. "Siegfried Kracauer und die Mesalliance von Film und Bildungsbürgertum in der Weimarer Republik." In *Filmgeschichte schreiben. Ansätze, Entwürfe und Methoden*, ed. Knut Hickethier, 78–92. Berlin: Edition Sigma.

———. 1990. "Melodrama und Montagekino bei S. Kracauer. Zur Komplementarität ihrer Einschätzung in der deutschen Filmkultur." In *Siegfried Kracauer: Neue Interpretationen*, ed. Martin Kessler and Thomas Y. Levin, 129–45. Tübingen: Stauffenburg Verlag.

Koch, Gertrud. 1987. "Béla Balázs: The Physiognomy of Things." Trans. Miriam Hansen. *New German Critique* 40: 167–78.

———. 1990. "Rudolf Arnheim: The Materialist of Aesthetic Illusion—Gestalt Theory and Reviewer's Practice." *New German Critique* 51: 164–78.

Koebner, Thomas. 1977. "Der Film als neue Kunst. Reaktionen der literarischen Intelligenz. Zur Theorie des Stummfilms (1911–1924)." In *Litera-turwissenschaft — Medienwissenschaft*, ed. Helmut Kreuzer, 1–31. Heidelberg: Winter.

Köhrer, Erich. 1913. "Literarische Films." *Die Gegenwart* 42: 741–43.

Kommer, Helmut. 1979. *Früher Film und späte Folgen. Zur Geschichte der Film- und Fernseherziehung*. Berlin: Basis.

Korte, Helmut, ed. 1980. *Film und Realität in der Weimarer Republik*. Frankfurt am Main: Fischer.

Kortländer, Bernd. 1982. "Vom 'Student von Prag' zu 'Horst Wessel' — Hanns Heinz Ewers und der Film." In *Düsseldorf kinematographisch*, ed. Filminstitut der Landeshauptstadt Düsseldorf, 137–45. Düsseldorf: Triltsch.

Kossowsky, A[lexander]. 1927. "Der Filmjournalist." *Deutsche Presse,* 16 Apr.

Kracauer, Siegfried. 1927. "Bücher vom Film." *Frankfurter Zeitung,* 10 July.

——. 1928. "Bücher vom Film." *Frankfurter Zeitung,* 30 Sept.

——. 1929. "Zwei Filmbücher." *Frankfurter Zeitung,* 3 Nov.

——. 1930. "Ein neues Filmbuch." *Frankfurter Zeitung,* 2 Nov.

——. 1931. "Ein paar Bücher vom Film." *Frankfurter Zeitung,* 19 July.

——. 1932. "Neue Filmliteratur." *Frankfurter Zeitung,* 10 Jan.

——. 1937. *Orpheus in Paris: Jacques Offenbach and the Paris of his Times*. Trans. G. David and E. Mosbacher. London: Constable.

——. 1947. *From Caligari to Hitler: A Psychological Study of the German Film*. Princeton, N.J.: Princeton Univ. Press.

——. 1960. *Theory of Film: The Redemption of Physical Reality*. New York: Oxford Univ. Press.

——. [1930] 1971. *Die Angestellten. Aus dem neuesten Deutschland*. Ed. Karsten Witte. Frankfurt am Main: Suhrkamp.

——. 1974. *Kino. Essays, Studien, Glossen zum Film*. Ed. Karsten Witte. Frankfurt am Main: Suhrkamp.

——. [1927] 1975. "The Mass Ornament." Trans. Barbara Correll and Jack Zipes. *New German Critique* 5: 67–76.

——. 1977. *Das Ornament der Masse. Essays 1920–31*. Ed. Karsten Witte. Frankfurt am Main: Suhrkamp.

——. [1922] 1978. *Soziologie als Wissenschaft*. Ed. Karsten Witte. Frankfurt am Main: Suhrkamp.

——. 1979. *Von Caligari bis Hitler*. Trans. Ruth Baumgarten. Ed. Karsten Witte. Frankfurt am Main: Suhrkamp.

——. 1987a. The Cult of Distraction: On Berlin's Picture Palaces." Trans. Thomas Y. Levin. *New German Critique* 40: 91–96.

———. 1987b. *Straßen in Berlin und anderswo*. Berlin: Das Arsenal.

———. 1990. *Schriften 5*. 3 vols. Ed. Inka Mülder-Bach. Frankfurt am Main: Suhrkamp.

———. In press. *The Ornament of the Masses*. Ed. and trans. Thomas Y. Levin. Cambridge, Mass.: Harvard Univ. Press.

Kraszna-Krausz, Andor. 1932. Review of *Film als Kunst*. *Die Weltbühne* 28: 447–49.

Kraus, Karl. 1908. "Apokalypse." *Die Fackel* 261–62: 1–14.

———. 1913–14. "Ein reiner Künstler." *Die Fackel* 391–92: 19.

———. [1919] 1957. *Die letzten Tage der Menschheit*. Munich: Kösel.

Krechel, Ursula. 1972. "Information und Wertung. Untersuchungen zum theater- und filmkritischen Werk von Herbert Ihering." Ph.D. diss., Univ. of Cologne.

Krull, Edith. 1964. *Herbert Ihering*. Berlin, GDR: Henschel.

Kuh, Anton. 1929. "Geräuschfilm in Berlin." *Der Querschnitt* 9: 593.

Kuhlbrodt, Dieter. 1987. "Der Fachkritiker. Über Willy Haas." In . . . *Film* . . . *Stadt* . . . *Kino* . . . *Berlin* . . . , ed. Uta Berg-Ganschow and Wolfgang Jacobson, 133–38. Berlin: Argon.

———. 1990. "Adorno. Bloch. Baudrillard. Und das Schreiben über das Kino von Dore O., Vlado Kristl und Joachim Bode." In *Die Macht der Filmkritik. Positionen und Kontroversen,* ed. Norbert Grob and Karl Prümm, 104–8. Munich: edition text + kritik.

Kühn, Gertraude, Karl Tümmler, and Walter Wimmer, eds. 1975. *Film und revolutionäre Arbeiterbewegung in Deutschland 1918–1932. Dokumente und Materialien zur Erweiterung der Filmpolitik der revolutionären Arbeiterbewegung und zu den Anfängen einer sozialistischen Filmkunst in Deutschland*. 2 vols. Berlin, GDR: Henschel.

Kullmann, Max. 1935. "Die Entwicklung des deutschen Lichtspieltheater." Ph.D. diss., Univ. of Nuremberg.

Kurtz, Rudolf. 1921. "Kampf ums Kino. Wider Hans Siemsen" *Die Weltbühne* 17: 166–168.

———. 1926. *Expressionismus und Film*. Berlin: Lichtbild-Bühne.

Kyser, Hans. 1928–29a. "Das Filmmanuskript." *Die Literatur* 31: 629–30.

———. 1928–29b. "Wie entsteht und wie schreibt man ein Filmmanuskript?" *Die Literatur* 31: 691–94.

Landsberger, Arthur. 1920. *Miss Rockefeller filmt. Ein Filmroman*. Munich: Thespis.

Lange, Brigitta. 1987. "Extrakt, Steigerung, Erregung, Komposition. Über

Kurt Pinthus." In *. . . Film . . . Stadt . . . Kino . . . Berlin . . .* , ed. Uta Berg-Ganschow and Wolfgang Jacobson, 145–48. Berlin: Argon.

Lange, Konrad. 1918. *Nationale Kinoreform*. M. Gladbach: Volksvereins-Verlag.

———. 1920. *Das Kino in Gegenwart und Zukunft*. Stuttgart: Ferdinand Enke.

Langer, Resi. 1919. *Kinotypen. Vor und hinter den Filmkulissen*. Hannover: Der Zweemann.

Lapp, Adolf. 1912. "Der epische Kintop." *März* 6: 356.

Laroche. 1919. "Die Kinokritik." *Der Kritiker* 1.25: 9–10.

Lasker-Schüler, Else. 1912–13. "Kinematographisches." *Der Sturm* 3: 18–19.

LeBon, Gustave. 1897. *The Crowd. A Study of the Popular Mind*. London: T. Fisher Unwin.

Lemke, Hermann. 1912. *Die Kinematographie der Gegenwart, Vergangenheit und Zukunft*. Leipzig: Hof-Verlagsbuchhandlung Edmund Demme.

Lenk, Sabine. 1989. *Théâtre contre Cinéma. Die Diskussion um Kino und Theater vor dem Ersten Weltkrieg in Frankreich*. Münster: MAKS.

Lensing, Leo A. 1982. " 'Kinodramatisch': Cinema in Karl Kraus' *Die Fackel* and *Die letzten Tage der Menschheit*." *German Quarterly* 55: 480–98.

Lenz-Levy, Paul. 1910. "Literatur—Film—Dramen," *Der Kinematograph*, 8 June.

Leonhard, Rudolf. 1920. "Bemerkungen zur Ästhetik und Soziologie des Films." *Die neue Schaubühne* 2: 250–53, 279–80; 3: 67–69, 196–99.

Levin, Thomas Y. 1987. "From Dialectic to Normative Specificity: Reading Lukács on Film." *New German Critique* 40: 35–64.

———. 1990. "Der enthüllte Kracauer." In *Siegfried Kracauer: Neue Interpretationen*, ed. Michael Kessler and Thomas Y. Levin, 229–47. Tübingen: Stauffenburg Verlag.

———. 1991. "The English-Language Reception of Kracauer's Work: A Bibliography." *New German Critique* 54: 183–92.

Lewin, Robert. 1912. "Kino-Kultur." *März* 6: 314–16.

Lichtenstein, Alfred. 1962. *Gesammelte Gedichte*. Ed. Klaus Kanzog. Zurich: Arche.

*Lichtträger im Chaos*. 1925. Essen: Schriftenreihe der Essener Volkszeitung.

Lichtwitz, Manuel. 1986. "Die Auseinandersetzung um den Stummfilm in der Publizistik und Literatur 1907–1914." Ph.D. diss., Univ. of Göttingen.

Lorant, Stefan. [1928] 1986. *Wir vom Film*. Munich: Lianne Kolf.

Lorenz, Thorsten. 1988. *Wissen ist Macht. Die Philosophie des Kinos*. Munich: Wilhelm Fink.

Lounsbury, Myron Osborne. 1973. *The Origins of American Film Criticism 1909–1939*. New York: Arno Press.

Lubitsch, Ernst. 1920. "Uns fehlen Kinodichtungen." *Das Tage-Buch* 1: 1145–46.

Lüdeke, Willi. 1973. *Der Film in Agitation und Propaganda der revolutionären deutschen Arbeiterbewegung (1919–1933)*. West Berlin: Oberbaumverlag.

Lukács, Georg. [1913] 1981. "Thoughts on an Aesthetic for the Cinema." Trans. Barrie Ellies-Jones. *Framework* 14: 2–6.

Mack, Max, ed. 1916. *Die zappelnde Leinwand*. Berlin: Dr. Eyster.

———. 1919. *Wie komme ich zum Film?* Berlin: Kühn.

———. 1920. "Die künstlerischen Aufgaben des Films." *Lichtbild-Bühne* 7: 12–13.

Magnus, Erwin. 1924. *Lichtspiel und Leben. Filmplaudereien*. Berlin: Dürr & Weber.

Mann, Heinrich. 1928. "Film und Volk." *Film und Volk* 1.2: 4–6.

Mann, Thomas. [1924] 1975. *The Magic Mountain*. Trans. from the German by H. T. Lowe-Porter. New York: Knopf.

Märten, Lu. 1925. "Kunst und Proletariat." *Die Aktion* 15: 663–68.

———. 1928. "Filmkategorisches." *Die Neue Bücherschau* 6: 231–35.

Mayer, Theodor Heinrich. 1921. *Film. Novellen*. Leipzig: Staackmann.

———. 1931. *Clown der Welt*. Berlin: Atlantik.

Mayr, F. 1931. "Ist der Film tot?" *Der Gegner* 5: 25–26.

Mehring, Franz. 1961. *Gesammelte Schriften*. 16 vols. Ed. Thomas Höhle. Berlin, GDR: Henschel.

Melcher, G[ustav]. 1909. "Von der lebenden Photographie und dem Kino-Drama." *Der Kinematograph*, 12 Feb.

Mellini, Arthur. 1911. Editorial, *Lichtbild-Bühne*, 4 Mar.

Metz, Christian. 1982. *The Imaginary Signifier. Psychoanalysis and the Cinema*. Trans. Celia Britton, Annwyl Williams, Ben Brewster and Alfred Guzzetti. Bloomington: Indiana Univ. Press.

Moholy-Nagy, László. 1965. "Theater, Zirkus, Variété." In *Die Bühne im Bauhaus*, 45–53. Mainz: Florian Kupferberg.

———. [1927] 1969a. *Painting Photography Film*. Trans. from the German by Janet Seligman. Cambridge, Mass.: MIT Press.

———. [1932] 1969b. "Probleme des neuen Films." In *'Die Form.' Stimme des Deutschen Werkbundes 1925–1934*, ed. Felix Schwarz and Frank Gloor, 247–55. Hamburg: Bertelsmann.

Monaco, Paul. 1976. *Cinema and Society: France and Germany during the Twenties*. New York: Elsevier.

Moreck, Curt. 1926. *Sittengeschichte des Kinos*. Dresden: Paul Aretz.

Morus [pseud. Richard Lewinsohn]. 1927. "Großfilm und Kleinauto." *Die Weltbühne* 23: 187.

Muckermann, Richard. 1925. "Der Film, sein Werden, Wachsen und Wollen." In *Lichtträger im Chaos*. Essen: Schriftenreihe der Essener Volkszeitung.

Mueller, Roswitha. 1989. *Bertolt Brecht and the Theory of Media*. Lincoln: Univ. of Nebraska Press.

Mülder, Inka. 1985. *Siegfried Kracauer — Grenzgänger zwischen Theorie und Literatur. Seine frühen Schriften 1913–1933*. Stuttgart: Metzler.

———. 1987. "Der Umschlag der Negativität. Zur Verschränkung von Phänomenologie und Filmästhetik in Siegfried Kracauers Metaphorik der 'Oberfläche.'" *Deutsche Vierteljahreszeitschrift* 61: 359–73.

Müller, Fritz. 1912. "Kinodichter." *Bild und Film* 2: 13.

Mungenast, E[rnst] M[oritz]. 1928. *Asta Nielsen*. Stuttgart: Walter Hädecke.

Münzenberg, Willi. 1925. *Erobert den Film! Winke aus der Praxis für die Praxis proletarischer Filmpropaganda*. Berlin: Neuer Deutscher Verlag.

Murray, Bruce. 1990. *Film and the German Left in the Weimar Republic. From "Caligari" to "Kuhle Wampe."* Austin: Univ. of Texas Press.

Musil, Robert. 1978. *Gesammelte Werke*. 9 vols. Ed. Adolf Frisé. Reinbek: Rowohlt.

Naumann, Friedrich. 1964. *Ästhetische Schriften*. Ed. Heinz Ladendorf. Cologne: Opladen.

Neergard, Ebbe. 1929. "Die Soziologie des Films." *Film und Volk* 3.5: 4–5.

Negt, Oskar, and Alexander Kluge. 1977. *Öffentlichkeit und Erfahrung. Zur Organisationsanalyse von bürgerlicher und proletarischer Öffentlichkeit*. Frankfurt am Main: Suhrkamp.

Nestriepke, Siegfried. 1926. *Wege zu neuer Filmkultur*. Berlin: Volksbühnen-Verlag.

———. 1929. "Die technischen und kulturellen Möglichkeiten des Films." In *Film und Funk. Sozialistischer Kulturtag in Frankfurt am Main, 28–29 Sept. 1929*, 15–29. Berlin: Sozialistischer Kulturbund.

Neumann, Robert. 1928. "Kino." *Westermanns Monatshefte* 73: 380.

Noack, Victor. 1913. *Der Kino. Etwas über sein Wesen und seine Bedeutung*. Gautzsch bei Leipzig: Felix Dietrich.

Olimsky, Fritz. 1931. *Tendenzen des Filmwirtschaft und deren Auswirkung auf die Filmpresse*. Berlin: Berliner Börsen-Zeitung.

Oswald, Richard. 1920. "Gebt uns Filmkritiker." *Das Tage-Buch* 49: 1578–79.

Ott, Richard. 1918. *Der Weg zum Film*. Berlin: Lichtbild-Bühne.

Overmans, Jakob. 1920. *Roman, Theater und Kino im neuen Deutschland*. Freiburg im Breisgau: Herdersche Buchhandlung.

Paech, Anne. 1985. *Kino zwischen Stadt und Land. Geschichte des Kinos in der Provinz: Osnabrück*. Marburg: Jonas.

Paech, Joachim. 1988. *Literatur und Film*. Stuttgart: Metzler.

Pahl, Walter. 1925. "Kino und Kultur." *Kulturwille* 2.11: 218.

———. 1926. "Die psychologischen Wirkungen des Films, unter besonderer Berücksichtigung ihrer sozialpsychologischen Bedeutung." Ph.D. diss., Univ. of Leipzig.

Palmier, Jean-Michel. 1977. "Béla Balázs, théoricien marxiste du cinéma." Intro. to *L'ésprit du cinéma*, 7–117. Trans. J. M. Chavy. Paris: Payot.

Pander, Hans. 1919. "Die Filmkritik. Eine Erwiderung an Laroche." *Der Kritiker* 1.26: 6–7.

Pankau, Johannes G. 1989. Review of Heller's *Literarische Intelligenz*. *Seminar* 25.1: 76–78.

Paul, Peter. 1914. *Das Filmbuch. Wie schreibe ich einen Film und wie mache ich ihn zu Geld?* Berlin: Borngräber.

Pauli, Hans. 1981. *Filmmusik: Stummfilm*. Stuttgart: Klett.

Perry, Laurie Loomis. 1982. "A Survey of Leftist Film Activity in the Weimar Republic." In *Film and Politics in the Weimar Republic,* ed. Thomas Plummer, Bruce Murray, Linda Schulte-Sasse, et al., 35–45. New York: Holmes & Meier.

Peterkirsten, Jo Haïri. 1918. *Volks-Filme*. Dresden: n.p.

Petro, Patrice. 1983. "From Lukács to Kracauer and Beyond: Social Film Histories and the German Cinema." *Cinema Journal* 22.3: 47–67.

———. 1987. "Discourse on Sexuality in the Early German Film Theory." *New German Critique* 40: 115–46.

———. 1989. *Joyless Streets. Women and Melodramatic Representation in Weimar Germany*. Princeton, N. J.: Princeton Univ. Press.

Pfeiffer, Heinrich, ed. 1924. *Das deutsche Lichtspielbuch. Filmprobleme von gestern und heute*. Berlin: August Scherl.

Pfenning, Gustav. 1928. *Der Filmautor*. Mühlhausen and Thüringen: G. Danner, 1928.

Piepenstock, Alfred. 1928. "Klassenkunst." *Film und Volk* 2.2: 5–6.

Pieper, Lorenz. 1912. "Kino und Drama." *Bild und Film* 1: 4.

Pinthus, Kurt. 1928. "Die Film-Krisis." *Das Tage-Buch* 9: 574–80.

———. 1930. "Zukunft des Tonfilms." *Das Tage-Buch* 11: 203–4.

———. 1931. "Die erste deutsche Filmkritik." *Der Querschnitt* 11: 139.

———, ed. [1913] 1983. *Das Kinobuch*. Frankfurt am Main: Fischer.

Piscator, Erwin. 1968. *Schriften*. 2 vols. Ed. Ludwig Hoffmann. Berlin, GDR: Henschel.

Planck, Otto. 1919. *Gegen das Kinounwesen! Materialsammlung zur Kinoreform*. Stuttgart: Ev. Volksbund für Württemberg.

Plummer, Thomas G., Bruce Murray, Linda Schulte-Sasse, et al., eds. 1982. *Film and Politics in the Weimar Republic.* New York: Holmes & Meier.

Polgar, Alfred. 1911. "Das Drama im Kinematographen." *Der Strom* 1: 45–48.

———. 1917. "Belehrender Film." *Die Schaubühne* 13: 401.

———. 1924. "Chaplin." *Die Weltbühne* 20: 28–29.

———. 1926. "Berlin, Sommer 1922." Repr. in *Hinterland,* 232. Berlin: Rowohlt.

———. 1927a. "Der Kuß." Repr. in *Orchester von oben,* 293–97. Berlin: Rowohlt.

———. 1927b. "Verkehrte Welt." Repr. in *An den Rand geschrieben,* 227–32. Berlin: Rowohlt.

Pordes, Victor. 1919. *Das Lichtspiel. Wesen, Dramaturgie, Regie.* Vienna: R. Lechner.

Porges, Friedrich. 1919. *Fünfzig Meter Kinoweisheit. Aus der Werkstatt eines Erfahrenen über Filmdichtung, Filmregie, Filmaufnahme und Filmdarstellung.* Vienna: Harbauer.

Porten, Henny. 1919. *Wie ich wurde.* Berlin: Volkskraft.

Porten, Rosa. 1919. *Die Filmprinzess. Roman aus der Kino-Welt.* Berlin: Eysler.

Prawer, Siegbert. 1979. "A New Muse Climbs Parnassus: German Debates about Literature and the Cinema 1909–1929." *German Life and Letters* 32.3: 196–205.

Prels, Max. c.1922. *Kino.* Bielefeld: Velhagen & Klasing. Trans. 1976 as *Kino: A Study of the German Film 1915–1919.* New York: Gordon Press.

Prümm, Karl. 1992. "Empfindsame Reisen in die Filmstadt." In *Babelsberg. 1912 Ein Filmstudio 1992,* ed. Wolfgang Jacobsen, 117–34. Berlin: Argon.

Ralmon, John. 1977. "Béla Balázs in Exile." *Film Quarterly* 30.3: 12–19.

Rath, Willy. 1913a. "Die Bühne in Not?" *Konservative Monatsschrift* (May-June).

———. 1913b. *Kino und Bühne.* M. Gladbach: Volksvereins-Verlag.

———. 1913c. "Zur Ästhetik des Lichtspiels." *Eckart* (Aug.).

Rauh, Sabine. 1984. "Das Feuilleton der deutschen Parteizeitungen 1924 bis 1929. Merkmale tendenziöser Kritik zu Film und Sprechtheater in der Weimarer Republik." Ph.D. diss., Univ. of Bochum.

Re, Franco Lo. 1983. *Il Kitsch el l'anima. Il "Kinobuch" di Kurt Pinthus. Litterature e cinema nel primo espressionismo tedesco.* Bari: Dedalo.

Reichenberger, F. 1913–14. "Der Kinematograf." *Der Sturm* 4: 156–57.

Reichwaldau, Franz. 1920. "Das ideale Kino." *Die Weltbühne* 16: 84–86.

Reimann, Hans. 1922. "Du sollst nicht aufs Kino schimpfen!" *Das Tage-Buch* 3: 1705–6.

Reinhard, Ernst. 1926. *Theater, Kino, Volk.* Bern: n.p.

Reinhardt, Max. 1974. *Schriften. Aufzeichnungen Briefe Reden.* Ed. Hugo Fetting. Berlin, GDR: Henschel.

Rennert, Malwine. 1913. Review of Rath's *Kino und Bühne*. *Bild und Film* 3.2: 46.

Richter, Hans. 1926. "Die eigentliche Sphäre des Films," *G* 5: 18.

———. 1967. *Köpfe und Hinterköpfe*. Zurich: Arche.

———. [1929] 1968. *Filmgegner von heute — Filmfreunde von morgen*. Intro. Walter Schobert. Frankfurt am Main: Fischer.

———. [1929] 1969. "Neue Mittel der Filmgestaltung." Repr. in *'Die Form.' Stimme des Deutschen Werkbundes 1925–1934*, ed. Felix Schwarz and Frank Gloor, 230–32. Hamburg: Bertelsmann.

———. [1921] 1971. "Principles of the Art of Motion." Repr. in *De Stijl*, ed. Hans L. C. Jaffé, 144–46. New York: Harry N. Abrams.

———. [1939] 1979. *Der Kampf um den Film. Für einen gesellschaftlich verantwortlichen Film*. Ed. Jürgen Römhild. Frankfurt am Main: Fischer.

———. 1986. *The Struggle for the Film. Towards a Socially Responsible Film*. Trans. Ben Brewster. Foreword A. L. Rees. New York: St. Martin's Press.

———. 1989a. *Malerei und Film*. Frankfurt am Main: Deutsches Filmmuseum.

———. [1919] 1989b. "Das Jahr 1918 im Film." Repr. in *Stationen der Moderne im Film II. Texte Manifeste Pamphlete*, 68–70. Berlin: Freunde der Deutschen Kinemathek.

Ritscher, Wolfgang. 1914. "Grenzen und Theater und Kino." *Bühne und Welt* 16: 333–35.

Rost, Hans. 1916–17. "Vom Guckkasten zum Kino." In *Paul Kellers Monatsblätter. Die Bergstadt* 5: 381.

Rothschild, Ernst. 1920. "Film und Erotik. Bemerkungen zu künstlerischen und pädagogischen Prinzipienfragen." *Die Neue Schaubühne* 2: 317–28.

Rudolf, Arthur. 1928. "Kritik der Filmkritik." *Die neue Bücherschau* 6: 592–93.

Rügner, Ulrich. 1988. *Filmmusik in Deutschland zwischen 1924 und 1934*. Hildesheim: Olms.

Ruttmann, Walter. [c. 1919] 1989. "Malerei mit Zeit." In *Walter Ruttmann. Eine Dokumentation*, ed. Jeanpaul Goergen, 73–74. Berlin: Freunde der Deutschen Kinemathek.

S. 1930. "Über Jutzi und den Film. " *Film und Volk* 3.1: 7.

Salmon, Heinz. 1924. *Film-Götter (Frechheiten aber Wahrheiten). Eine durchaus ernsthafte Betrachtung einer lustigen Angelegenheit*. Berlin: Alexander Grübel.

Samuleit, Paul, and Emil Born. 1914. *Der Kinematograph als Volks- und Jugendbildungsmittel*. Berlin: n.p.

Sattig, Ewald. 1937. "Die deutsche Filmpresse." Ph.D. diss., Univ. of Leipzig.

Schacht, Roland. 1927. "Grundlagen der Filmkritik." *Der Kunstwart* 40: 195.

Schäfer, Dieter. 1982. "Anmerkungen zu einer Düsseldorfer Filmgeschichte — von den Anfängen bis 1945." In *Düsseldorf kinematographisch,* ed. Filminstitut der Landeshauptstadt Düsseldorf, 11–46. Düsseldorf: Triltsch.

Schickele, René. 1913. *Schreie auf dem Boulevard.* Berlin: Paul Cassirer.

Schlaikjer, Erich. 1920. *Im Kampf mit der Schande. Gesammelte Aufsätze aus dunkler Zeit.* Berlin: Verlag der Täglichen Rundschau.

Schloemp, Felix. 1914. *Der Allotria Kientopp.* Berlin: Carl Henschel.

Schlüpmann, Heide. 1982. "Kinosucht." *Frauen und Film* 33: 45–50.

———. 1986. "Größe, die uns erhebt . . . 'Die Teilhabe der Frauen am Chauvinismus: zwei Filmkritikerinnen schreiben 1915 zu dem Cines-Film 'Cajus Julius Cäsar.'" *Frauen und Film* 40: 62–72.

———. 1987. "Phenomenology of Film: On Siegfried Kracauer's Writings of the 1920s." Trans. Thomas Y. Levin. *New German Critique* 40: 97–114.

———. 1990a. "Der Gang ins Kino — ein Ausgang aus selbstverschuldeter Unmündigkeit. Zum Begriff des Publikums in Kracauers Essayistik der Zwanziger Jahre." In *Siegfried Kracauer: Neue Interpretationen,* ed. Martin Kessler and Thomas Y. Levin, 267–84. Tübingen: Stauffenburg Verlag.

———. 1990b. "Melodrama and Social Drama in the Early German Cinema." Trans. Jamie Owen Daniel. *Camera Obscura* 22: 73–89.

———. 1990c. *Unheimlichkeit des Blicks. Das Drama des frühen deutschen Kinos.* Frankfurt am Main: Stroemfeld/Roter Stern.

Schmitt, Walter. 1932. "Das Filmwesen und seine Wechselbeziehungen zur Gesellschaft. Versuch einer Soziologie des Filmwesens." Ph.D. diss., Univ. of Freudenstadt.

Schönhuber, Franz X. 1917. "Kinokitsch und kein Ende." *März* 9: 933–38.

———. 1918. *Das Kinoproblem im Lichte von Schülerantworten.* Leipzig: A. Haase.

Schrader, Bärbel, and Jürgen Schebera. 1988. *The "Golden" Twenties. Art and Literature in the Weimar Republic.* Trans. Katherine Vanovitch. New Haven: Yale Univ. Press.

Schröter, Michael. 1980. "Weltzerfall und Rekonstruktion. Zur Physiognomik Siegfried Kracauers." *Text und Kritik* 68: 18–41.

Schubert, Renate. 1988. "Psychologische Sichten auf theoretische Arbeiten von Arnheim und Balázs." *Beiträge zur Film- und Fernsehwissenschaft* 29.34: 138–149.

Schulte-Sasse, Linda. 1982. "Film Criticism in the Weimar Press." In *Film and Politics in the Weimar Republic,* ed. Thomas Plummer, Bruce Murray, Linda Schulte-Sasse, et al., 47–59. New York: Holmes & Meier.

Schultze, Ernst. 1911. *Der Kinematograph als Bildungsmittel. Eine kulturpolitische Untersuchung.* Halle a. d. S.: Verlag der Buchhandlung des Waisenhauses.

Schulz, Franz. 1921. "Das Kino, der Bürger und der keusche Privatdozent." *Die Neue Schaubühne* 3: 80–84.

———. 1929. "Das Film-Manuskript. Bemerkungen eines Filmautors." *Das Tage-Buch* 10: 520–26.

Schulze, Volker. 1977. "Frühe kommunale Kinos und die Kinoreformbewegung in Deutschland bis zum Ende des Ersten Weltkriegs." *Publizistik* 22: 61–71.

Schumann, Wolfgang. 1924. "Kino und Film von heute." *Kinofragen der Zeit.* Munich: Callwey.

Schütte, Wolfram. 1971. "Film und Roman. Einige Notizen zur Kinotechnik in Romanen der Weimarer Republik." In *Heinrich Mann,* ed. Heinz Ludwig Arnold, 70–80. Munich: edition text + kritik.

Schütz, E. H. 1973. "Lu Märtens Versuche zur Eigengesetzlichkeit des Films." *Alternative* 16: 95–98.

Schweigert, Rudolf. 1977. "Publizistische Medien" and "Der Film in der Weimarer Republik." In *Weimarer Republik,* 368–437, 438–516. West Berlin: Elefanten Press.

Schweinitz, Jörg. 1988. "Die Grundlagen des filmtheoretischen Denkens bei Siegfried Kracauer." *Beiträge zur Film- und Fernsehwissenschaft* 29.34: 111–26.

Seeber, Guido. 1927–29. *Der praktische Kameramann.* 2 vols. Berlin: Lichtbild-Bühne.

———. 1930. *Kamera-Kurzweil: Allerlei interessante Möglichkeiten beim Knipsen und Kurbeln.* Berlin: Union deutscher Verlagsgesellschaft.

———. 1979. *Das wandernde Bild. Der Filmpionier Guido Seeber.* Ed. Stiftung Deutsche Kinemathek. West Berlin: Elefanten Press.

Sellmann, Adolf. 1912. *Der Kinematograph als Volkserzieher?* Langensalza: n.p.

———. 1914. *Kino und Schule.* M. Gladbach: Volksvereins-Verlag.

Sieburg, Friedrich. 1920. "Die Transzendenz des Filmbildes." *Die Neue Schaubühne* 2: 144–46.

Siemsen, Hans. 1921a. "Die Filmerei." *Die Weltbühne* 17: 101–5.

———. 1921b. "Deutsche Filme." *Die Weltbühne* 17: 253–57.

———. 1921c. "Erwiderung an Ludwig Wolff." *Die Weltbühne* 17: 358–60.

———. 1921d. "Noch immer Kino." *Die Weltbühne* 17: 530–34.

———. 1922a. "Chaplin." *Die Weltbühne* 18: 368.

———. 1922b. "Kino-Elend." *Die Weltbühne* 18: 168–70.

———. 1924. *Charlie Chaplin.* Leipzig: Feuer.

———. 1925. "Kino. Kritik. Und Kino-Kritik." *Die Neue Schaubühne* 5: 34–40.

———. 1927a. "Die Situation der deutschen Filmkritik." *Die Weltbühne* 23: 144–47.

———. 1927b. "Die Kritik." *Die Weltbühne* 23: 712–15.

———. 1927c. "Eine Filmkritik, wie sie sein soll." *Die Weltbühne* 23: 950.

———. 1986. *Schriften.* 2 vols. Ed. Michael Föster. Essen: Torso, 1986.

Simmel, Georg. [1901] 1957. "Die künstlerische Bedeutung des Gesichts." Repr. in *Brücke und Tor,* ed. Michael Landmann, 153–59. Stuttgart: K. F. Koehler.

———. [1903] 1971. "The Metropolis and Mental Life." In *On Individuality and Social Forms: Selected Writings,* ed. Donald Levine, 323–39. Chicago: Univ. of Chicago Press.

Skolnar, Olaf, ed. 1920. *Illustrierter Film-Almanach für das Jahr 1921.* Berlin: Deutscher Film-Verlag.

Sochaczewer, Ludwig. 1922. "Erzieher des Films." *Film-Kurier,* 2 Sept.

Spielhagen, Hans. 1929. "Tonfilm." *Film und Volk* 2.6: 7–8.

Spiker, Jürgen. 1975. *Film und Kapital. Der Weg der deutschen Filmwirtschaft zum nationalsozialistischen Einheitskonzern.* Berlin: Volker Spiess.

*Stationen der Moderne im Film II. Texte Manifeste Pamphlete.* 1989. Berlin: Freunde der Deutschen Kinemathek.

Steinbrinck, Otto. 1925. "Gesetze der Filmkunst." In *Lichtträger im Chaos.* Essen: Schriftenreihe der Essener Volkszeitung.

Stepun, Fedor. 1932. *Theater und Kino.* Berlin: Bühnenvolksbund.

Stern, Fritz. 1961. *The Politics of Cultural Despair: A Study in the Rise of German Ideology.* Berkeley: Univ. of California Press.

Sternheim, Julius. 1920. "Der Filmautor, gestern und morgen." *Das Tage-Buch* 1: 1142–44.

Stindt, Georg Otto. 1924. *Das Lichtspiel als Kunstform. Die Philosophie des Films, Regie, Dramaturgie und Schauspieltechnik.* Bremerhaven: Atlantis.

———. 1925. "Die Ästhetik der Großaufnahme." *Die Filmtechnik* 6: 114–15.

Stoessl, Otto. 1917. "Der Kinematograph." *Unterwelt. Novellen.* Munich: Georg Müller.

Stratz, Rudolph. 1926. *Filmgewitter.* Berlin: August Scherl.

Strempel, Hans, and Martin Ripkens, eds. 1984. *Das Kino im Kopf. Eine Anthologie.* Zurich: Arche.

Sudendorf, Werner. 1987. "Täglich: Der Film-Kurier." In . . . *Film . . . Stadt . . . Kino . . . Berlin . . . ,* ed. Uta Berg-Ganschow and Wolfgang Jacobson, 127–32. Berlin: Argon.

Surmann, Rolf. 1982. *Die Münzenberg-Legende. Zur Publizistik der revolutionären deutschen Arbeiterbewegung 1921–1933*. Cologne: Prometh.

Tannenbaum, Herbert. 1912. *Kino und Theater*. Munich: Max Steinbach.

——. 1987. *Der Filmtheoretiker Herbert Tannenbaum*. Ed. Helmut H. Diederichs. Frankfurt am Main: Filmmuseum.

Thal, Ottwin. 1985. *Realismus und Fiktion. Literatur- und filmtheoretische Beiträge von Adorno, Lukács, Kracauer und Benjamin*. Dortmund: Nowotny.

Thiess, Frank. 1925. *Das Gesicht des Jahrhunderts*. Stuttgart: Engelhorns.

Tobers, Hermann. 1925–26. "Kinokultur oder Filmkultur?" *Eckart* 2: 111.

Todorow, Almut. 1988. "'Wollten die Eintagsfliegen in den Rang höherer Insekten aufsteigen?' Die Feuilletonkonzeption der *Frankfurter Zeitung* während der Weimarer Republik im redaktionellen Selbstverständnis." *Deutsche Vierteljahreszeitschrift* 62: 697–740.

Toller, Ernst. 1978. *Gesammelte Werke*. 5 vols. Ed. John M. Spalek and Wolfgang Frühwald. Munich: Hanser.

Traub, Hans, and Hanns Wilhelm Lavies, eds. 1940. *Das deutsche Filmschrifttum. Bibliographie der Bücher und Zeitschriften über das Filmwesen 1896–1939*. Leipzig: Karl Hiersemann.

Treuer, Hermann. 1928. *Filmkünstler. Wir über uns selbst*. Berlin: Sibyllen-Verlag.

Troll, Georg. 1919. "Möglichkeiten des Kinos." *Die Weltbühne* 15: 176–77.

Trommler, Frank, and Jost Hermand. 1988. *Die Kultur der Weimarer Republik*. Frankfurt am Main: Fischer.

Tucholsky, Kurt [pseud. Peter Panter]. 1921. "Für Hans Siemsen." *Die Weltbühne* 17: 168–70.

——. 1987. *Gesammelte Werke*. 10 vols. Ed. Mary Gerold-Tucholsky and Fritz Raddatz. Reinbeck: Rowohlt.

Turszinsky, Walter. 1910. "Kinodramen und Kinomimen." *Die Schaubühne* 6: 989.

Ullmann, Kurt. 1913. *Wege zu einer neuen Filmkunst*. Berlin: Richard Falk.

Unruh, Fritz von. 1987. *Sämtliche Werke*. 6 vols. Ed. Hanns Martin Elster and Bodo Rollka. Berlin: Haude & Spener.

Uricchio, William. 1987. "German University Dissertations with Motion Picture Related Topics: 1910–1945." *Historical Journal of Film, Radio and Television* 7.2: 175–90.

Usai, Paolo Cherchi, and Lorenzo Codelli, eds. 1990. *Before Caligari: German Cinema 1895–1920*. Pordenone: Le Giornate del Cinema Muto.

Vietta, Silvio. 1975. "Expressionistische Literatur und Film. Einige Thesen zum wechselseitigen Einfluß ihrer Darstellung und Wirkung." *Mannheimer Beiträge aus Forschung und Lehre* 10: 294–99.

Vietta, Silvio, and Hans-Georg Kamper. 1983. *Expressionismus*. Munich: Wilhelm Fink.

Virilio, Paul. 1989. *War and Cinema: The Logistics of Perception*. Trans. Patrick Camiller. London and New York: Verso.

Walser, Robert. 1978. *Das Gesamtwerk*. 12 vols. Ed. Jochen Greven. Frankfurt am Main: Suhrkamp.

Warstat, Dieter Hellmuth. 1982. *Frühes Kino der Kleinstadt*. Berlin: Volker Spiess.

Warstat, Willi, and Franz Bergmann. 1913. *Kino und Gemeinde*. M. Gladbach: Volksvereins-Verlag.

Weber, Alfred. 1923. *Die Not der geistigen Arbeiter*. Munich: Duncker & Humblot.

Weber, Richard, ed. 1974. *Arbeiterbühne und Film. Zentralorgan des Arbeiter-Theater-Bundes Deutschlands*. Cologne: Gaehme Henke.

——, ed. 1975. *Film und Volk. Organ des Volksfilmverbandes*. Cologne: Gaehme Henke.

Wegener, Paul. [1919] 1954. "Wie ein Film geschrieben wird." In *Paul Wegener. Sein Leben und seine Rollen. Ein Buch von ihm und über ihn,* ed. Kai Möller, 102–13. Hamburg: Rowohlt.

*Weimarer Republik*. 1977. Eds. Kunstamt Kreuzberg und das Institut für Theaterwissenschaft der Universität Köln. Berlin: Kunstamt Kreuzberg.

Werner, Gösta. 1987. "'König Ödipus' als Film? Reinhardt, Hofmannsthal und der frühe deutsche Stummfilm." *Hofmannsthalblätter* 35–36: 121–28.

Wesse, Curt. 1928. *Großmacht Film. Das Geschöpf von Kunst und Technik*. Berlin: Deutsche Buch-Gemeinschaft.

Willet, John. 1978. *Art and Politics in the Weimar Period. The New Sobriety 1917–1933*. New York: Pantheon.

——. 1988. *The Theater of the Weimar Republic*. New York: Holmes & Meier.

Wippermann, Klaus W. 1972. "Die deutschen Wochenschauen im Ersten Weltkrieg." *Publizistik* 16: 268–78.

Witte, Karsten, ed. 1982. *Theorie des Kinos. Ideologiekritik der Traumfabrik*. Frankfurt am Main: Suhrkamp.

Wolf-Czapek, K. W. 1910. "Über den Stil des Kunstfilms." *Der Kinematograph,* 10 Aug.

Wolff, Ludwig. 1921. "Brief an Hans Siemsen," *Die Weltbühne* 17: 315–16.

Wolfradt, Willi. 1920. Review of Mierendorff's *Hätte ich das Kino. Freie Deutsche Bühne* 2: 214–15.

Wuss, Peter. 1988. "Zur Aneignung des filmtheoretischen Erbes aus der Weimarer Republik und danach." *Beiträge zur Film- und Fernsehwissenschaft* 29.34: 89–110.

———. 1990. *Kunstwert des Films und Massencharakter des Mediums. Konspekte zur Geschichte der Theorie des Spielfilms*. Berlin, GDR: Henschel.

Zaddach, Gerhard. 1929. "Der literarische Film. Ein Beitrag zur Geschichte der Lichtspielkunst." Ph.D. diss., Univ. of Breslau.

Zehder, Hugo, ed. 1923. *Der Film von morgen*. Dresden: Rudolf Kaemmerer.

Zetkin, Clara. [1919] 1983. "Gegen das Kinounwesen." Repr. in *Beiträge zur Film- und Fernsehwissenschaft* 24.2: 95.

Zglinicki, Friedrich von. 1956. *Der Weg des Films. Die Geschichte der Kinematographie und ihrer Vorläufer*. Berlin: Rembrandt.

———. 1986. *Die Wege der Traumfabrik*. West Berlin: Transit.

Zmegac, Victor. 1970. "Exkurs über den Film im Umkreis des Expressionismus." *Sprache im technischen Zeitalter* 53: 243–57.

Zobeltitz, Fedor von. 1911. "Film-Literatur." *Das literarische Echo* 13.15: 1102.

Zsuffa, Joseph. 1987. *Béla Balázs. The Man and the Artist*. Berkeley: Univ. of California Press.

Zweig, Arnold. 1922. "Theoretische Grundlegung des Films in Thesen." *Das Tage-Buch* 3: 371–75.

———. 1923. "Der Angriff der Gegenstände." *Das Tage-Buch* 4: 557–60.

———. 1931. "Cinéma." *Knaben und Männer*. Berlin: Gustav Kiepenheuer.

# Index

Index

Other volumes in the series Modern German Culture and Literature include:

*The Institutions of Art: Essays by Peter and Christa Bürger*
Translated by Loren A. Kruger

*A History of German Literary Criticism*
Edited by Peter Uwe Hohendahl

*Bertolt Brecht and the Theory of Media*
by Roswitha Mueller

*Art and Enlightenment: Aesthetic Theory after Adorno*
by David Roberts

Printed in the United States
147939LV00003B/69/A